The Witch-Cult in Western Europe

by

Margaret Alice Murray

IAEGCA

Portuguese Institute of Higher Studies in Geopolitics and Auxiliary Sciences

Lisbon, 2015

Title:
The Witch-Cult in Western Europe

Author:
Margaret Alice Murray

Copyright:
Public Domain
Original Edition 1921 © Oxford University Press
This Edition © IAEGCA

Cover Design:
Nelson Fonseca

Book Design:
Flávio Gonçalves

ISBN: 978-989-99294-0-1

Publishers:
IAEGCA
Flávio Gonçalves

Contact:
iaegca@gmail.com
http://www.geopol.com.pt
 /iaegca

Printed in the United States of America and in the European Union

The Witch-Cult in Western Europe

by

Margaret Alice Murray

www.geopol.com.pt

**Portuguese Institute of Higher Studies in Geopolitics
and Auxiliary Sciences**

ÍNDICE

———————————————

PREFACE

The mass of existing material on this subject is so great that I have not attempted to make a survey of the whole of European 'Witchcraft', but have confined myself to an intensive study of the cult in Great Britain. In order, however, to obtain a clearer understanding of the ritual and beliefs I have had recourse to French and Flemish sources, as the cult appears to have been the same throughout Western Europe. The New England records are unfortunately not published *in extenso*; this is the more unfortunate as the extracts already given to the public occasionally throw light on some of the English practices. It is more difficult to trace the English practices than the Scotch or French, for in England the cult was already in a decadent condition when the records were made; therefore records in a purely English colony would probably contain much of interest.

The sources from which the information is taken are the judicial records and contemporary chroniclers. In the case of the chroniclers I have studied their facts and not their opinions. I have also had access to some unpublished trials among the Edinburgh Justiciary Records and also in the Guernsey Greffe.

The following articles have already appeared in various journals, to whose editors I am indebted for kind permission to republish: 'Organization of Witch Societies' and 'Witches and the number Thirteen' in *Folk Lore*; 'The God of the Witches' in the *Journal of the Manchester Oriental Society*; 'Child Sacrifice', 'Witches' Familiars', 'The Devil's Mark', 'The Devil's Officers', 'Witches' Fertility Rites', 'Witches Transformations', in *Man*; and 'The Devil of North Berwick' in the *Scottish Historical Review*.

My thanks are due to Georgiana Aitken, W. Bonser, and Mary Slater for much kind help, also to Prof. C. G. Seligman for valuable suggestions and advice as to lines of research.

M. A. MURRAY.
UNIVERSITY COLLEGE,
LONDON.

INTRODUCTION

The subject of Witches and Witchcraft has always suffered from the biassed opinions of the commentators, both contemporary and of later date. On the one hand are the writers who, having heard the evidence at first hand, believe implicitly in the facts and place upon them the unwarranted construction that those facts were due to supernatural power; on the other hand are the writers who, taking the evidence on hearsay and disbelieving the conclusions drawn by their opponents, deny the facts *in toto*. Both parties believed with equal firmness in a personal Devil, and both supported their arguments with quotations from the Bible. But as the believers were able to bring forward more texts than the unbelievers and had in their hands an unanswerable argument in the Witch of Endor, the unbelievers, who dared not contradict the Word of God, were forced to fall back on the theory that the witches suffered from hallucination, hysteria, and, to use the modern word, 'auto-suggestion'. These two classes still persist, the sceptic predominating. Between the believer who believed everything and the unbeliever who disbelieved everything there has been no critical examination of the evidence, which presents a new and untouched field of research to the student of comparative religion.

Among the believers in witchcraft everything which could not be explained by the knowledge at their disposal was laid to the credit of supernatural powers; and as everything incomprehensible is usually supposed to emanate from evil, the witches were believed to be possessed of devilish arts. As also every non-Christian God was, in the eyes of the Christian, the opponent of the Christian God, the witches were considered to worship the Enemy of Salvation, in other words, the Devil. The greater number of these writers, however, obtained the evidence at first hand, and it must therefore be accepted although the statements do not bear the construction put upon them. It is only by a careful comparison with the evidence of anthropology that the facts fall into their proper places and an organized religion stands revealed.

The common beliefs as to the powers of the witches are largely due to the credulous contemporary commentators, who misunderstood the evidence and then exaggerated some of the facts to suit their preconceived ideas of the supernatural powers of the witches; thereby laying themselves open to the ridicule of all their opponents, past and present. Yet the ridicule is not fully deserved, for the facts are there, though the explanation is wrong; for even the two points, which are usually considered the ultimate proof of the absurdity and incredibility of the whole system—the flying on a broomstick through the window or up the chimney, and the transformation into animals—are capable of explanation. The first can be accounted for when the form of early mound-dwellings is taken into consideration, and when it is remembered that among savage tribes there are often taboos connected with the door, the two-faced god being essentially a deity of the door. Besides this the fertility rites connected with the broom should be taken into account. The second should be compared with similar accounts of transformation into animals among the cults of other nations. Mr. A. B. Cook's comment on the Greek ritual applies quite as well to Western as to Eastern Europe: 'We may venture on the general statement that within the bounds of Hellenic mythology *animal-metamorphosis commonly points to a preceding animal cult.*'[1]

It is interesting to note the class of mind among those contemporary writers who believed in the reality of the facts confessed at the trials as compared with those who disbelieved. It will be seen that the most brilliant minds, the keenest intellects, the greatest investigators, were among the believers: Bodin, Lord Bacon, Raleigh, Boyle, Cudworth, Selden, Henry More, Sir Thomas Browne, Matthew Hale, Sir George Mackenzie, and many others, most of whom had heard the evidence at first hand. The sceptics were Weyer, pupil of the occultist Cornelius Agrippa; Reginald Scot, a Kentish country squire; Filmer, whose name was a byword for political bigotry; Wagstaffe, who went mad from drink; and Webster, a fanatical preacher.[2] The sceptics, with the exception of Weyer, appear to have had little or no first-hand evidence;

---

[1] *Journal of Hellenic Studies*, 1894, p. 160. The italics are in the original.
[2] See James Crossley's Introduction to Potts's *Discoverie of Witchcraft*, Chetham Society, pp. v-xii.

their only weapon was an appeal to common sense and sentiment combined; their only method was a flat denial of every statement which appeared to point to supernatural powers. They could not disprove the statements; they could not explain them without opposing the accepted religious beliefs of their time, and so weakening their cause by exposing themselves to the serious charge of atheism; therefore they denied evidence which in the case of any other accusation would have been accepted as proof.

The evidence which I now bring forward is taken entirely from contemporary sources, i.e. the legal records of the trials, pamphlets giving accounts of individual witches, and the works of Inquisitors and other writers. I have omitted the opinions of the authors, and have examined only the recorded facts, without however including the stories of ghosts and other 'occult' phenomena with which all the commentators confuse the subject. I have also, for the reason given below, omitted all reference to charms and spells when performed by one witch alone, and have confined myself to those statements only which show the beliefs, organization, and ritual of a hitherto unrecognized cult.

In order to clear the ground I make a sharp distinction between Operative Witchcraft and Ritual Witchcraft. Under Operative Witchcraft I class all charms and spells, whether used by a professed witch or by a professed Christian, whether intended for good or for evil, for killing or for curing. Such charms and spells are common to every nation and country, and are practised by the priests and people of every religion. They are part of the common heritage of the human race and are therefore of no practical value in the study of any one particular cult.

Ritual Witchcraft—or, as I propose to call it, the Dianic cult— embraces the religious beliefs and ritual of the people known in late mediaeval times as 'Witches'. The evidence proves that underlying the Christian religion was a cult practised by many classes of the community, chiefly, however, by the more ignorant or those in the less thickly inhabited parts of the country. It can be traced back to pre-Christian times, and appears to be the ancient religion of Western

Europe. The god, anthropomorphic or theriomorphic, was worshipped in well-defined rites; the organization was highly developed; and the ritual is analogous to many other ancient rituals. The dates of the chief festivals suggest that the religion belonged to a race which had not reached the agricultural stage; and the evidence shows that various modifications were introduced, probably by invading peoples who brought in their own beliefs. I have not attempted to disentangle the various cults; I am content merely to point out that it was a definite religion with beliefs, ritual, and organization as highly developed as that of any other cult in the world.

The deity of this cult was incarnate in a man, a woman, or an animal; the animal form being apparently earlier than the human, for the god was often spoken of as wearing the skin or attributes of an animal. At the same time, however, there was another form of the god in the shape of a man with two faces. Such a god is found in Italy (where he was called Janus or Dianus), in Southern France (see pp. 62, 129), and in the English Midlands. The feminine form of the name, Diana, is found throughout Western Europe as the name of the female deity or leader of the so-called Witches, and it is for this reason that I have called this ancient religion the Dianic cult. The geographical distribution of the two-faced god suggests that the race or races, who carried the cult, either did not remain in every country which they entered, or that in many places they and their religion were overwhelmed by subsequent invaders.

The dates of the two chief festivals, May Eve and November Eve, indicate the use of a calendar which is generally acknowledged to be pre-agricultural and earlier than the solstitial division of the year. The fertility rites of the cult bear out this indication, as they were for promoting the increase of animals and only rarely for the benefit of the crops. The cross-quarter-days, February 2 and August 1, which were also kept as festivals, were probably of later date, as, though classed among the great festivals, they were not of so high an importance as the May and November Eves. To February 2, Candlemas Day, probably belongs the sun-charm of the burning wheel, formed by the whirling dancers, each carrying a blazing torch;

but no special ceremony seems to be assigned to August 1, Lammas Day, a fact suggestive of a later introduction of this festival.

The organization of the hierarchy was the same throughout Western Europe, with the slight local differences which always occur in any organization. The same organization, when carried to America, caused Cotton Mather to say, 'The witches are organized like Congregational Churches.' This gives the clue at once. In each Congregational Church there is a body of elders who manage the affairs of the Church, and the minister who conducts the religious services and is the chief person in religious matters; and there may also be a specially appointed person to conduct the services in the minister's absence; each Church is an independent entity and not necessarily connected with any other. In the same way there was among the witches a body of elders—the Coven—which managed the local affairs of the cult, and a man who, like the minister, held the chief place, though as God that place was infinitely higher in the eyes of the congregation than any held by a mere human being. In some of the larger congregations there was a person, inferior to the Chief, who took charge in the Chief's absence. In Southern France, however, there seems to have been a Grand Master who was supreme over several districts.

The position of the chief woman in the cult is still somewhat obscure. Professor Pearson sees in her the Mother-Goddess worshipped chiefly by women. This is very probable, but at the time when the cult is recorded the worship of the male deity appears to have superseded that of the female, and it is only on rare occasions that the God appears in female form to receive the homage of the worshippers. As a general rule the woman's position, when divine, is that of the familiar or substitute for the male god. There remains, however, the curious fact that the chief woman was often identified with the Queen of Faerie, or the Elfin Queen as she is sometimes called.

This connexion of the witches and fairies opens up a very wide field; at present it is little more than speculation that the two are identical, but there is promise that the theory may be proved at some later date when the subject is more fully worked out. It is now a commonplace of anthropology that the tales of fairies and elves preserve the tradition of a dwarf race which once inhabited Northern and Western Europe. Successive invasions drove them to the less fertile parts of each country which they inhabited, some betook themselves to the inhospitable north or the equally inhospitable mountains; some, however, remained in the open heaths and moors, living as mound-dwellers, venturing out chiefly at night and coming in contact with the ruling races only on rare occasions. As the conqueror always regards the religion of the conquered as superior to his own in the arts of evil magic, the dwarf race obtained the reputation of wizards and magicians, and their god was identified by the conquerors with the Principle of Evil. The identification of the witches with the dwarf or fairy race would give us a clear insight into much of the civilization of the early European peoples, especially as regards their religious ideas.

The religious rites varied according to circumstances and the requirements of the people. The greater number of the ceremonies appear to have been practised for the purpose of securing fertility. Of these the sexual ritual has been given an overwhelming and quite unwarranted importance in the trials, for it became an obsession with the Christian judges and recorders to investigate the smallest and most minute details of the rite. Though in late examples the ceremony had possibly degenerated into a Bacchanalian orgy, there is evidence to prove that, like the same rite in other countries, it was originally a ceremonial magic to ensure fertility. There is at present nothing to show how much of the Witches' Mass (in which the bread, the wine, and the candles were black) derived from the Christian ritual and how much belonged to the Dianic cult; it is, however, possible that the witches' service was the earlier form and influenced the Christian. The admission ceremonies were often elaborate, and it is here that the changes in the religion are most clearly marked; certain ceremonies must have been introduced when another cult was superimposed and became paramount, such as the specific renunciation of a previous religion which was obligatory on all new candidates, and the payment to the member who brought a new recruit into the fold. The other rites—the feasts and dances—show that it was a joyous religion; and as such it must have been quite incomprehensible to the gloomy Inquisitors and Reformers who suppressed it.

Much stress has always been laid by the sceptical writers on the undoubted fact that in many cases the witch confused dreams with reality and believed that she had visited the Sabbath when credible witnesses could prove that she had slept in her bed all the time. Yet such visions are known in other religions; Christians have met their Lord in dreams of the night and have been accounted saints for that very reason; Mahomed, though not released from the body, had interviews with Allah; Moses talked with God; the Egyptian Pharaohs record similar experiences. To the devotee of a certain temperament such visions occur, and it is only to be expected that in every case the vision should take the form required by the religion of the worshipper. Hence the Christian sees Christ and enters heaven; Mahomed was caught up to the Paradise of the true believers; the anthropomorphic Jehovah permitted only a back view to His votary; the Egyptian Pharaohs beheld their gods alive and moving on the earth. The witch also met her god at the actual Sabbath and again in her dreams, for that earthly Sabbath was to her the true Paradise, where there was more pleasure than she could express, and she believed also that the joy which she took in it was but the prelude to a much greater glory, for her god so held her heart that no other desire could enter in. Thus the witches often went to the gibbet and the stake, glorifying their god and committing their souls into his keeping, with a firm belief that death was but the entrance to an eternal life in which they would never be parted from him. Fanatics and visionaries as many of them were, they resemble those Christian martyrs whom the witch-persecutors often held in the highest honour.

Another objection is that, as the evidence of the witches at the trials is more or less uniform in character, it must be attributed to the publication by the Inquisitors of a questionary for the use of all judges concerned in such trials; in short, that the evidence is valueless, as it was given in answer to leading questions. No explanation is offered by the objectors as to how the Inquisitors arrived at the form of questionary, nor is any regard given to the injunction to all Inquisitors to acquaint themselves with all the details of any heresy which they were commissioned to root out; they were to obtain the information from those who would recant and use it against the accused; and to instruct other judges in the belief and ritual of the heresy, so that they also might recognize it and act accordingly. The objectors also overlook the fact that the believers in any given religion, when tried for their faith, exhibit a sameness in their accounts of the cult, usually with slight local differences. Had the testimony of the witches as to their beliefs varied widely, it would be *prima facie* evidence that there was no well-defined religion underlying their ritual; but the very uniformity of their confessions points to the reality of the occurrence.

Still another objection is that the evidence was always given under torture, and that the wretched victims consequently made reckless assertions and accusations. In most of the English and many of the Scotch trials legal torture was not applied; and it was only in the seventeenth century that pricking for the mark, starvation, and prevention of sleep were used. Even then there were many voluntary confessions given by those who, like the early Christian martyrs, rushed headlong on their fate, determined to die for their faith and their god.

Yet even if some of the evidence were given under torture and in answer to leading questions, there still remains a mass of details which cannot be explained away. Among others there are the close connexions of the witches with the fairies, the persistence of the number thirteen in the Covens, the narrow geographical range of the domestic familiar, the avoidance of certain forms in the animal transformations, the limited number of personal names among the women-witches, and the survival of the names of some of the early gods.

In England the legal method of executing a witch was by hanging; after death the body was burnt and the ashes scattered. In Scotland, as a rule, the witch was strangled at the stake and the body burned, but there are several records of the culprit being sentenced to burning alive. In France burning alive was the invariable punishment.

In cases where popular fury, unrestrained by the law, worked its own vengeance on individuals, horrible scenes occurred; but these were the exception, and, examining only the legal aspect of the subject, it will be found that witches had a fair trial according to the methods of the period, and that their punishment was according to the law. There was, however, one popular method of dealing with a person accused of witchcraft which is interesting as showing the survival of a legal process, obsolete as regards the law itself, but remaining in full force among the people. This is the ordeal by water. In the Laws of Athelstan the full detail of this ordeal is given: after the person who was to undergo the ordeal had been prepared by prayer and fasting, he was tied, the right thumb to the right big toe, the left thumb to the left big toe, and was then cast into the water with suitable prayers to the Almighty to declare the right; if he sank he was considered innocent, if he floated he was guilty. The witch was 'tried' in the same way, except that she was tied 'crossways', i.e. the right thumb to the left big toe, and the left thumb to the right big toe. So great was the belief in this test that many women accused of witchcraft insisted on undergoing this ordeal, which was often conducted with solemnity and decency under the auspices of the minister of the parish and other grave persons. Unless there was strong feeling against the woman for other reasons, the mere fact of her floating did not rouse the populace against her, and she merely returned home; Widow Coman, for instance, was 'ducked' on three separate occasions at her own request.

The theologians of the sixteenth and seventeenth centuries were greatly exercised by the conclusive evidence which proved that people known to be devout and professing Christians had been present at the Sabbath, joined in the ceremonies, and worshipped the witches' god. The Inquisitors recognized the fact, and devote many pages of their books to the discussion of the course to be followed in the case of Christian priests, coming finally to the conclusion that if a priest merely went to the Sabbath but was not in any way in an official position there his sacred character preserved him from evil. The theologians of the Reformed Churches, who could not accept the sanctity of the priesthood with the same ease and were also desirous of finding some means of accounting for the presence of the devout laity, boldly evolved the theory that the Devil could for his own purposes assume the shape of good Christians in order to mislead the witches. By this plea the accused often succeeded in escaping when the examiners were religious ministers, but it was of no value to them when the trial was in a court of law, and the fact of their presence at an illegal assembly was proved. Lord Coke's definition of a witch summed up the law on the subject: 'A witch is a person who hath conference with the Devil, to consult with him or to do some act', and any person proved to have had such conference was thus convicted of a capital offence and sentenced accordingly. This accounts for the fact, commented on by all students of witch-trials, that a witch was often condemned even though she had invariably used her skill for good and not for evil; for healing the sick, not for casting sickness. If it were proved that she had obtained her knowledge from the 'Devil' she had broken the law and must die.

I. CONTINUITY OF THE RELIGION

Of the ancient religion of pre-Christian Britain there are few written records, but it is contrary to all experience that a cult should die out and leave no trace immediately on the introduction of a new religion. The so-called conversion of Britain meant the conversion of the rulers only; the mass of the people continued to follow their ancient customs and beliefs with a veneer of Christian rites. The centuries brought a deepening of Christianity which, introduced from above, gradually penetrated downwards through one class after another. During this process the laws against the practice of certain heathen rites became more strict as Christianity grew in power, the Church tried her strength against 'witches' in high places and was victorious, and in the fifteenth century open war was declared against the last remains of heathenism in the famous Bull of Innocent VIII.

This heathenism was practised only in certain places and among certain classes of the community. In other places the ancient ritual was either adopted into, or tolerated by, the Church; and the Maypole dances and other rustic festivities remained as survivals of the rites of the early cult.

Whether the religion which survived as the witch cult was the same as the religion of the Druids, or whether it belonged to a still earlier stratum, is not clear. Though the descriptions of classical authors are rather too vague and scanty to settle such a point, sufficient remains to show that a fertility cult did once exist in these islands, akin to similar cults in the ancient world. Such rites would not be suppressed by the tribes who entered Great Britain after the withdrawal of the Romans; a continuance of the cult may therefore be expected among the people whom the Christian missionaries laboured to convert.

As the early historical records of these islands were made by Christian ecclesiastics, allowance must be made for the religious bias of the writers, which caused them to make Christianity appear as the only religion existing at the time. But though the historical records are silent on the subject the laws and enactments of the different communities, whether lay or ecclesiastical, retain very definite evidence of the continuance of the ancient cults.

In this connexion the dates of the conversion of England are instructive. The following table gives the principal dates:

- 597-604. Augustine's mission. London still heathen. Conversion of Æthelbert, King of Kent. After Æthelbert's death Christianity suffered a reverse.
- 604. Conversion of the King of the East Saxons, whose successor lapsed.
- 627. Conversion of the King of Northumbria.
- 628. Conversion of the King of East Anglia.
- 631-651. Aidan's missions.
- 635. Conversion of the King of Wessex.
- 653. Conversion of the King of Mercia.
- 654. Re-conversion of the King of the East Saxons.
- 681. Conversion of the King of the South Saxons.

An influx of heathenism occurred on two later occasions: in the ninth century there was an invasion by the heathen Danes under Guthrum; and in the eleventh century the heathen king Cnut led his hordes to victory. As in the case of the Saxon kings of the seventh century, Guthrum and Cnut were converted and the tribes followed their leaders' example, professed Christianity, and were baptized.

But it cannot be imagined that these wholesale conversions were more than nominal in most cases, though the king's religion was outwardly the tribe's religion. If, as happened among the East Saxons, the king forsook his old gods, returned to them again, and finally forsook them altogether, the tribe followed his lead, and, in public at least, worshipped Christ, Odin, or any other deity whom the king favoured for the moment; but there can be hardly any doubt that in private the mass of the people adhered to the old religion to which they were accustomed. This tribal conversion is clearly marked when a heathen king married a Christian queen, or vice versa; and it must also be noted that a king never changed his religion without careful consultation with his chief men.[3] An example of the two religions existing side by side is found in the account of Redwald, King of the

---

[3] Hunt, vol. i

East Saxons, who 'in the same temple had an altar to sacrifice to Christ, and another small one to offer victims to devils'.[4]

The continuity of the ancient religion is proved by the references to it in the classical authors, the ecclesiastical laws, and other legal and historical records.

1st cent. Strabo, 63 B.C.-A.D. 23.

'In an island close to Britain, Demeter and Persephone are venerated with rites similar to the orgies of Samothrace.'[5]

4th cent. Dionysius says that in islands near Jersey and Guernsey the rites of Bacchus were performed by the women, crowned with leaves; they danced and made an even greater shouting than the Thracians.[6]

7th cent. Theodore, Archbishop of Canterbury, 668-690.

The *Liber Poenitentialis*[7] of Theodore contains the earliest ecclesiastical laws of England. It consists of a list of offences and the penance due for each offence; one whole section is occupied with details of the ancient religion and of its rites. Such are:

Sacrifice to devils.

Eating and drinking in a heathen temple, (*a*) in ignorance, (*b*) after being told by the [Christian] priest that it is sacrilege and the table of devils, (*c*) as a cult of idols and in honour of idols.

'Not only celebrating feasts in the abominable places of the heathen and offering food there, but also consuming it. Serving this hidden idolatry, having relinquished Christ. If anyone at the kalends of January goes about as a stag or a bull; that is, making himself into a wild animal and dressing in the skin of a herd animal, and putting on the heads of beasts; those who in such wise transform themselves into the appearance of a wild animal, penance for three years because this is devilish.'

The Laws of Wihtraed, King of Kent,[8] 690.

---

[4] Bede, Bk. II, ch. xv.
[5] Strabo, *Geography*, Bk. IV, c. iv, 6.
[6] Dionysius, *Periegetes*, ll. 1120-5.
[7] Thorpe, ii, pp. 32-4.
[8] Thorpe, i, p. 41.

Fines inflicted on those who offer to devils.

8th cent. *The Confessionale and Poenitentiale of Ecgberht*, first Archbishop of York,[9] 734-766.

Prohibition of offerings to devils; of witchcraft; of auguries according to the methods of the heathen; of vows paid, loosed, or confirmed at wells, stones, or trees; of the gathering of herbs with any incantation except Christian prayers.

The Law of the Northumbrian priests.[10]

'If then anyone be found that shall henceforth practise any heathenship, either by sacrifice or by "fyrt", or in any way love witchcraft, or worship idols, if he be a king's thane, let him pay X half-marks; half to Christ, half to the king. We are all to love and worship one God, and strictly hold one Christianity, and totally renounce all heathenship.'

9th cent. *Decree attributed to a General Council of Ancyra.*[11]

'Certain wicked women, reverting to Satan, and seduced by the illusions and phantasms of demons, believe and profess that they ride at night with Diana on certain beasts, with an innumerable multitude of women, passing over immense distances, obeying her commands as their mistress, and evoked by her on certain nights.'

10th cent. *Laws of Edward and Guthrum.*[12] After 901.

'If anyone violate christianity, or reverence heathenism, by word or by work, let him pay as well, as *wite* or *lah-slit*, according as the deed may be.'

Laws of King Athelstan,[13] 924-940.

'We have ordained respecting witchcrafts, and *lyblacs*, and *morthdaeds*: if anyone should be thereby killed, and he could not deny it, that he be liable in his life. But if he will deny it, and at the threefold ordeal shall be guilty; that he be cxx days in prison.'

Ecclesiastical canons of King Edgar,[14] 959.

---

[9] Id., ii, p. 157 seq.
[10] Id., ii, pp. 299, 303.
[11] Scot, p. 66.—Lea, iii, p. 493.
[12] Thorpe, i, p. 169.
[13] Id., i, p. 203.
[14] Id., ii, p. 249.

'We enjoin, that every priest zealously promote Christianity, and totally extinguish every heathenism; and forbid well worshipings, and necromancies, and divinations, and enchantments, and man worshipings, and the vain practices which are carried on with various spells, and with "frithsplots",[15] and with elders, and also with various other trees, and with stones, and with many various delusions, with which men do much of what they should not.—And we enjoin, that every Christian man zealously accustom his children to Christianity, and teach them the Paternoster and the Creed. And we enjoin, that on feast days heathen songs and devil's games be abstained from.'

Laws of King Ethelred,[16] 978-1016.

'Let every Christian man do as is needful to him; let him strictly keep his Christianity.... Let us zealously venerate right Christianity, and totally despise every heathenism.'

11th cent. *Laws of King Cnut*,[17] 1017-1035.

'We earnestly forbid every heathenism: heathenism is, that men worship idols; that is, that they worship heathen gods, and the sun or the moon, fire or rivers, water-wells or stones, or forest trees of any kind; or love witchcraft, or promote *morth-work* in any wise.'

13th cent. Witchcraft made into a sect and heresy by the Church.
The priest of Inverkeithing presented before the bishop in 1282 for leading a fertility dance at Easter round the phallic figure of a god; he was allowed to retain his benefice.[18]

14th cent. In 1303 the Bishop of Coventry was accused before the Pope for doing homage to the Devil.[19]

Trial of Dame Alice Kyteler, 1324.

Tried for both operative and ritual witchcraft, and found guilty.

Nider's Formicarius, 1337.

A detailed account of witches and their proceedings in Berne, which had been infested by them for more than sixty years.

---

[15] Frith = brushwood, splot = plot of ground; sometimes used for 'splotch, splash'.
[16] Thorpe, i, pp. 311, 323, 351.
[17] Id., i, p. 379.
[18] *Chronicles of Lanercost*, p. 109, ed. Stevenson.
[19] Rymer, ii, 934.

15th cent. Joan of Arc burnt as a witch, 1431. Gilles de Rais executed as a witch, 1440.

Bernardo di Bosco, 1457.

Sent by Pope Calixtus III to suppress the witches in Brescia and its neighbourhood.

Bull of Pope Innocent VIII, 1484.

'It has come to our ears that numbers of both sexes do not avoid to have intercourse with demons, Incubi and Succubi; and that by their sorceries, and by their incantations, charms, and conjurations, they suffocate, extinguish, and cause to perish the births of women, the increase of animals, the corn of the ground, the grapes of the vineyard and the fruit of the trees, as well as men, women, flocks, herds, and other various kinds of animals, vines and apple trees, grass, corn and other fruits of the earth; making and procuring that men and women, flocks and herds and other animals shall suffer and be tormented both from within and without, so that men beget not, nor women conceive; and they impede the conjugal action of men and women.'

It will be seen by the foregoing that so far from the Bull of Pope Innocent VIII being the beginning of the 'outbreak of witchcraft', as so many modern writers consider, it is only one of many ordinances against the practices of an earlier cult. It takes no account of the effect of these practices on the morals of the people who believed in them, but lays stress only on their power over fertility; the fertility of human beings, animals, and crops. In short it is exactly the pronouncement which one would expect from a Christian against a heathen form of religion in which the worship of a god of fertility was the central idea. It shows therefore that the witches were considered to deal with fertility only.

Looked upon in the light of a fertility cult, the ritual of the witches becomes comprehensible. Originally for the promotion of fertility, it became gradually degraded into a method for blasting fertility, and thus the witches who had been once the means of bringing prosperity to the people and the land by driving out all evil influences, in process of time were looked upon as being themselves the evil influences, and were held in horror accordingly.

The actual feelings of the witches towards their religion have been recorded in very few cases, but they can be inferred from the few records which remain. The earliest example is from Lorraine in 1408, 'lequel méfait les susdites dames disoient et confessoient avoir enduré à leur contentement et saoulement de plaisir que n'avoient eu onc de leur vie en tel pourchas'.[20] De Lancre took a certain amount of trouble to obtain the opinions of the witches, whereby he was obviously scandalized.

'Vne sorciere entre autres fort insigne nous dict qu'elle auoit tousiours creu, que la sorcelerie estoit la meilleure religion.—Ieanne Dibasson aagee de vingt neuf ans nous dict que le sabbat estoit le vray Paradis, où il y a beaucoup plus de plaisir qu'on ne peut exprimer. Que ceux qui y vont trouuent le temps si court à force de plaisir & de contentemẽt, qu'ils n'en peuuent sortir sans vn merveilleux regret, de maniere qu'il leur tarde infiniment qu'ils n'y reuiennent.—Marie de la Ralde, aagee de vingt huict ans, tres belle femme, depose qu'elle auoit vn singulier plaisir d'aller au sabbat, si bien que quand on la venoit semondre d'y aller elle y alloit comme à nopces: non pas tant pour la liberté & licence qu'on a de s'accointer ensemble (ce que par modestie elle dict n'auoir iamais faict ny veu faire) mais parce que le Diable tenoit tellement liés leurs coeurs & leurs volontez qu'à peine y laissoit il entrer nul autre desir.... Au reste elle dict qu'elle ne croyoit faire aucun mal d'aller au sabbat, & qu'elle y auoit beaucoup plus de plaisir & contentement que d'aller à la Messe, parce que le Diable leur faisoit à croire qu'il estoit le vray Dieu, & que la ioye que les sorciers prenoyent au sabbat n'estoit qu'vn commencement d'vne beaucoup plus grande gloire.—Elles disoyent franchement, qu'elles y alloyent & voyoient toutes ces execrations auec vne volupté admirable, & vn desir enrager d'y aller & d'y estre, trouuãt les iours trop reculez de la nuict pour faire le voyage si desiré, & le poinct ou les heures pour y aller trop lentes, & y estant, trop courtes pour vn si agreable seiour & delicieux amusement.—En fin il a le faux martyre: & se trouue des Sorciers si acharnez à son seruice endiablé, qu'il n'y a torture ny supplice qui les estonne, & diriez qu'ils vont au vray martyre & à la

---

[20] Bournon, p. 23.

mort pour l'amour de luy, aussi gayement que s'ils alloient à vn festin de plaisir & reioüyssance publique.—Quand elles sont preuenues de la Iustice, elles ne pleurent & ne iettent vne seule larme, voire leur faux martyre soit de la torture, soit du gibet leur est si plaisant, qu'il tarde à plusieurs qu'elles nesoiẽt executées à mort, & souffrẽt fort ioyeusement qu'on leur face le procez, tant il leur tarde qu'elles ne soient auec le Diable. Et ne s'impatientent de rien tant en leur prison, que de ce qu'elles ne lui peuuent tesmoigner cõbiẽ elles souffrent & desirent souffrir pour luy.'[21]

Bodin says, 'Il y en a d'autres, ausquelles Satan promet qu'elles seront bien heureuses apres cette vie, qui empesche qu'elles ne se repentent, & meurent obstinees en leur mechanceté'.[22]

Madame de Bourignon's girls at Lille (1661) 'had not the least design of changing, to quit these abominable Pleasures, as one of them of Twenty-two Years old one day told me. *No*, said she, *I will not be other than I am; I find too much content in my Condition*.'[23] Though the English and Scotch witches' opinions are not reported, it is clear from the evidence that they were the same as those of the Basses-Pyrénées, for not only did they join of their own free will but in many cases there seems to have been no need of persuasion. In a great number of trials, when the witches acknowledged that they had been asked to become members of the society, there follows an expression of this sort, 'ye freely and willingly accepted and granted thereto'. And that they held to their god as firmly as those de Lancre put to death is equally evident in view of the North Berwick witches, of Rebecca West and Rose Hallybread, who 'dyed very Stuburn, and Refractory without any Remorss, or seeming Terror of Conscience for their abominable Witch-craft';[24] Major Weir, who perished as a witch, renouncing all hope of heaven;[25] and the Northampton witches, Agnes Browne and her daughter, who 'were never heard to pray, or to call

[21] De Lancre, *Tableau*, pp. 124, 125, 126, 135, 208, 458.
[22] Bodin, *Fléau*, p. 373.
[23] Bourignon, *Parole*, p. 87.—Hale, p. 27.
[24] *Full Tryals of Notorious Witches*, p. 8.
[25] *Records of the Justiciary Court of Edinburgh*, ii, p. 14.—Arnot, p. 359.

vppon God, never asking pardon for their offences either of God or the world in this their dangerous, and desperate Resolution, dyed'; Elinor Shaw and Mary Phillips, at their execution 'being desired to say their Prayers, they both set up a very loud Laughter, calling for the Devil to come and help them in such a Blasphemous manner, as is not fit to Mention; so that the Sherif seeing their presumptious Impenitence, caused them to be Executed with all the Expedition possible; even while they were Cursing and raving, and as they liv'd the Devils true Factors, so they resolutely Dyed in his Service': the rest of the Coven also died 'without any confession or contrition'.[26]

---

[26] *Witches of Northamptonshire*, p. 8.

II. THE GOD

1. As God

It is impossible to understand the witch-cult without first understanding the position of the chief personage of that cult. He was known to the contemporary Christian judges and recorders as the Devil, and was called by them Satan, Lucifer, Beelzebub, the Foul Fiend, the Enemy of Salvation, and similar names appropriate to the Principle of Evil, the Devil of the Scriptures, with whom they identified him.

This was far from the view of the witches themselves. To them this so-called Devil was God, manifest and incarnate; they adored him on their knees, they addressed their prayers to him, they offered thanks to him as the giver of food and the necessities of life, they dedicated their children to him, and there are indications that, like many another god, he was sacrificed for the good of his people.

The contemporary writers state in so many words that the witches believed in the divinity of their Master. Danaeus, writing in 1575, says, 'The Diuell com̃aundeth them that they shall acknowledge him for their god, cal vpõ him, pray to him, and trust in him.—Then doe they all repeate the othe which they haue geuen vnto him; in acknowledging him to be their God.'[27] Gaule, in 1646, nearly a century later, says that the witches vow 'to take him [the Devil] for their God, worship, invoke, obey him'.[28]

The witches are even more explicit, and their evidence proves the belief that their Master was to them their God. The accusation against Elisabeth Vlamyncx of Alost, 1595, was that 'vous n'avez pas eu honte de vous agenouiller devant votre Belzebuth, que vous avez adoré'.[29] The same accusation was made against Marion Grant of Aberdeen, 1596, that 'the Deuill quhome thow callis thy god ... causit

---

[27] Danaeus, E 1, ch. iv.
[28] Gaule, p. 62.
[29] Cannaert, p. 45.

the worship him on thy kneis as thy lord'.[30] De Lancre (1609) records, as did all the Inquisitors, the actual words of the witches; when they presented a young child, they fell on their knees and said, 'Grand Seigneur, lequel i'adore', and when the child was old enough to join the society she made her vow in these words: 'Ie me remets de tout poinct en ton pouuoir & entre tes mains, ne recognois autre Dieu: si bien que tu es mon Dieu'.[31] Silvain Nevillon, tried at Orleans in 1614, said, 'On dit au Diable nous vous recognoissons pour nostre maistre, nostre Dieu, nostre Createur'.[32] The Lancashire witch, Margaret Johnson, 1633, said: 'There appeared vnto her a spirit or divell in the similitude and proportion of a man. And the said divell or spirit bidd her call him by the name of Mamillion. And saith, that in all her talke and conferense shee calleth her said Divell Mamillion, my god.'[33] According to Madame Bourignon, 1661, 'Persons who were thus engaged to the Devil by a precise Contract, will allow no other God but him'.[34] Isobel Gowdie confessed that 'he maid vs beliew that ther wes no God besyd him.—We get all this power from the Divell, and when ve seik it from him, ve call him "owr Lord".—At each tyme, quhan ve wold meitt with him, we behoowit to ryse and mak our curtesie; and we wold say, "Ye ar welcom, owr Lord," and "How doe ye, my Lord."'[35] The Yorkshire witch, Alice Huson, 1664, stated that the Devil 'appeared like a *Black Man* upon a Black Horse, with Cloven Feet; and then I fell down, and did Worship him upon my Knees'.[36] Ann Armstrong in Northumberland, 1673, gave a good deal of information about her fellow witches: 'The said Ann Baites hath severall times danced with the divell att the places aforesaid, calling him, sometimes, her protector, and, other sometimes, her blessed saviour.—She saw Forster, Dryden, and Thompson, and the rest, and

---

[30] *Spalding Club Miscellany*, i, pp. 171, 172.
[31] De Lancre, *Tableau*, pp. 398, 399.
[32] Id., *L'Incredulité*, p. 801.
[33] Baines, i, p. 607 note. For the name Mamillion see Layamon's *Brut*, p. 155, Everyman Library.
[34] Bourignon, *Vie*, p. 222.—Hale, p. 37.
[35] Pitcairn, iii, pp. 605, 607, 613.
[36] Hale, p. 58.

theire protector, which they call'd their god, sitting at the head of the table.—When this informer used meanes to avoyd theire company, they threatned her, if she would not turne to theire god, the last shift should be the worst.'[37] At Crighton, 1678, the Devil himself preached to the witches, 'and most blasphemously mocked them, if they offered to trust in God who left them miserable in the world, and neither he nor his Son Jesus Christ ever appeared to them when they called on them, as he had, who would not cheat them'.[38] Even in America, 1692, Mary Osgood, the wife of Capt. Osgood, declared that 'the devil told her he was her God, and that she should serve and worship him'.[39]

Prayers were addressed to the Master by his followers, and in some instances the prayer was taught by him. Alice Gooderidge of Stapenhill in Derbyshire, 1597, herself a witch and the daughter of a witch, was charged by Sir Humphrey Ferrers 'with witchcraft about one Michael's Cow: which Cow when shee brake all thinges that they tied her in, ranne to this Alice Gooderige her house, scraping at the walls and windowes to haue come in: her olde mother Elizabeth Wright, tooke vpon her to help; vpon condition that she might haue a peny to bestow vpon her god, and so she came to the mans house kneeled downe before the Cow, crossed her with a sticke in the forehead, and prayed to her god, since which time the Cow continued wel'.[40] Antide Colas, 1598, confessed that 'Satan luy commãda de le prier soir & matin, auant qu'elle s'addonnat à faire autre oeuure'.[41] Elizabeth Sawyer, the witch of Edmonton, 1621, was taught by the Devil; 'He asked of me to whom I prayed, and I answered him to Iesus Christ, and he charged me then to pray no more to Iesus Christ, but to him the Diuell, and he the Diuell taught me this prayer, *Sanctibecetur nomen tuum*, Amen'.[42] Part of the dittay against Jonet Rendall, an Orkney witch, 1629, was that 'the devill appeirit to you, Quhom ye called Walliman.—Indyttit and accusit for y^t of your

[37] *Surtees Soc.*, xl, pp. 191, 193.
[38] Fountainhall, i. 15.
[39] Howell, vi, 660.—J. Hutchinson, ii, p. 31.
[40] *Alse Gooderidge*, pp. 9, 10.
[41] Boguet, p. 54.
[42] *Wonderfull Discouerie of Elizabeth Sawyer*, C 4, rev.

awne confessioune efter ye met your Walliman upoun the hill ye cam to Williame Rendalls hous quha haid ane seik hors and promeised to haill him if he could geve yow tua penneys for everie foot, And haveing gottin the silver ye hailled the hors be praying to your Walliman, Lykeas ye have confest that thair is nather man nor beast sick that is not tane away be the hand of God bot for almis ye ar able to cur it be praying to your Walliman, and yt thair is nane yt geves yow almis bot they will thryve ather be sea or land it ye pray to yor Walliman'.[43] The witches of East Anglia, 1645, also prayed; '*Ellen* the wife of *Nicholas Greenleife* of *Barton* in *Suffolke*, confessed, that when she prayed she prayed to the Devill and not to God.—*Rebecca West* confessed that her mother prayed constantly (and, as the world thought, very seriously), but she said it was to the devil, using these words, *Oh my God, my God*, meaning him and not the LORD.'[44]

A good example of the change of the word 'God', when used by the witch, into the word 'devil' when recorded by the Christian writer, is found at Bute in 1662: 'Jonet Stewart declares that quhen Alester McNivan was lying sick that Jonet Morisone and NcWilliam being in her house the said Jonet desyred NcWilliam to goe see the said Allester the said NcWilliam lifting up her curcheffe said "devill let him never be seene till I see him and devill let him never ryse" ... [NcWilliam was asked] if she lifted up her curcheffe quhen Jonet Morisone desyred her to goe see Alester McNivan, saying "god let him never ryse till I goe see him."'[45]

2. As a Human Being. (a) Man

The evidence of the witches makes it abundantly clear that the so-called Devil was a human being, generally a man, occasionally a woman. At the great Sabbaths, where he appeared in his grand array, he was disguised out of recognition; at the small meetings, in visiting his votaries, or when inducing a possible convert to join the ranks of the witch-society, he came in his own person, usually dressed plainly in the costume of the period. When in ordinary clothes he was

---

[43] *County Folklore*, iii, Orkney, pp. 103, 107-8.
[44] Stearne, pp. 28, 38
[45] *Highland Papers*, iii, pp. 16, 17.

indistinguishable from any other man of his own rank or age, but the evidence suggests that he made himself known by some manual gesture, by a password, or by some token carried on his person. The token seems to have been carried on the foot, and was perhaps a specially formed boot or shoe, or a foot-covering worn under the shoe.[46]

Besides the Grand Master himself there was often a second 'Devil', younger than the Chief. There is no indication whatsoever as to the method of appointing the head of the witch-community, but it seems probable that on the death of the principal 'Devil' the junior succeeded, and that the junior was appointed from among the officers (see chap. vii). This suggestion, however, does not appear to hold good where a woman was the Chief, for her second in command was always a man and often one well advanced in years. The elderly men always seem to have had grey beards.

Danaeus in 1575 summarizes the evidence and says of the Devil, 'he appeareth vnto them in likenesse of a man, insomuch that it hapneth many tymes, that among a great company of men, the Sorcerer only knoweth Satan, that is present, when other doo not know him, although they see another man, but who or what he is they know not'.[47] De Lancre says, 'On a obserué de tout temps que lors qu'il veut receuoir quelcun à faire pacte auec luy, il se presente tousiours en homme'.[48] Cooper states that 'the Wizards and Witches being met in a place and time appointed, the devil appears to them in humane shape'.[49] Even a modern writer, after studying the evidence, acknowledges that the witches 'seem to have been undoubtedly the

---

[46] It is possible that the shoe was cleft like the modern 'hygienic' shoe. Such a shoe is described in the ballad of the *Cobler of Canterbury*, date 1608, as part of a woman's costume:

> 'Her sleevës blue, her traine behind,
> With silver hookes was tucked, I find;
> Her shoës broad, and forked before.'

[47] Danaeus, ch. iv.
[48] De Lancre, *Tableau*, p. 69.
[49] Cooper, *Pleasant Treatise*, p. 2.

victims of unscrupulous and designing knaves, who personated Satan'.[50]

The witches not only described the personal appearance of the Devil, but often gave careful details as to his clothes; such details are naturally fuller when given by the women than by the men.

England.—John Walsh of Dorsetshire, 1566, described the Devil, whom he called his Familiar, as 'sometymes like a man in all proportions, sauing that he had clouen feete'.[51] The Lancashire witch, Anne Chattox, 1613, said, 'A thing like a Christian man did sundry times come to this Examinate, and requested this Examinate to giue him her Soule: And in the end, this Examinate was contented to giue him her sayd Soule, shee being then in her owne house, in the Forrest of Pendle; wherevpon the Deuill then in the shape of a Man, sayd to this Examinate: Thou shalt want nothing.' Elizabeth Southerns of the same Coven said that 'there met her this Examinate a Spirit or Deuill, in the shape of a Boy, the one halfe of his Coate blacke, and the other browne'.[52] To Margaret Johnson, one of the later Lancashire witches, 1633, there appeared 'a spirit or divell in the similitude and proportion of a man, apparelled in a suite of black, tyed about wth silke pointes'.[53] The Yarmouth witch, 1644, 'when she was in Bed, heard one knock at her Door, and rising to her Window, she saw, it being Moonlight, a tall black Man there'.[54] The Essex witches, 1645, agreed very fairly in their description of the man who came amongst them: according to Elizabeth Clarke he appeared 'in the shape of a proper gentleman, with a laced band, having the whole proportion of a man.... He had oftentimes knocked at her dore in the night time; and shee did arise open the dore and let him in'; Rebecca Weste gave evidence that 'the Devil appeared in the likeness of a proper young man'; and Rebecca Jones said that the Devil as 'a very handsome young man came to the door, who asked how she did'; on another occasion she

---

[50] Burns Begg, p. 217.
[51] *Examination of John Walsh.*
[52] Potts, D 3, B 2.
[53] Baines, i, p. 607 note.
[54] Hale, p. 46.

met the Devil, 'as shee was going to St. Osyth to sell butter', in the form of a 'man in a ragged sute'.[55] There are two accounts of the evidence given by the Huntingdonshire witch, Joan Wallis of Keiston, 1646: Stearne says that she 'confessed the Devill came to her in the likenesse of a man in blackish cloathing, but had cloven feet'. Davenport's record is slightly different: 'Blackman came first to her, about a twelve-moneth since, like a man something ancient, in blackish cloathes, but he had ugly feet uncovered.'[56] The evidence of the Suffolk witches, 1645-6, is to the same effect; Thomazine Ratcliffe of Shellie confessed that 'there came one in the likeness of a man.— One *Richmond*, a woman which lived at *Brampford*, confessed the Devill appeared to her in the likenesse of a man, called *Daniel* the Prophet.—One *Bush* of *Barton*, widdow, confessed that the Devill appeared to her in the shape of a young black man'.[57] All the Covens of Somerset, 1664, were evidently under one Chief; he came to Elizabeth Style as 'a handsome man'; to Elizabeth Style, Anne Bishop, Alice Duke, and Mary Penny as 'a Man in black Clothes, with a little Band'; to Christian Green 'in the shape of a Man in blackish Clothes'; and to Mary and Catherine Green as 'a little Man in black Clothes with a little Band'.[58] To the Yorkshire witch, Alice Huson, 1664, he appeared 'like a *Black Man* on a Horse upon the Moor', and again 'like a*Black Man* upon a Black Horse, with Cloven Feet'.[59] Abre Grinset of Dunwich, in Suffolk, 1665, said 'he did appear in the form of a Pretty handsom Young Man'.[60] In Northumberland, 1673, Ann Armstrong said that 'she see the said Ann Forster [with twelve others and] a long black man rideing on a bay galloway, as she thought, which they call'd there protector'.[61] The Devonshire witch Susanna Edwards, 1682, enters into some detail: 'She did meet with a gentleman in a field called the Parsonage Close in the town of Biddiford. And saith that his

---

[55] Howell, iv, 833, 836, 840, 854-5.
[56] Stearne, p. 13.—Davenport, p. 13.
[57] Stearne, pp. 22, 29, 30.
[58] Glanvil, pt. ii, pp. 136, 137, 147, 149, 156, 161-5.
[59] Hale, p. 58.
[60] Petto, p. 18.
[61] Denham Tracts, ii, p. 301.

apparel was all of black. Upon which she did hope to have a piece of money of him. Whereupon the gentleman drawing near unto this examinant, she did make a curchy or courtesy unto him, as she did use to do to gentlemen. Being demanded what and who the gentleman she spake of was, the said examinant answered and said, That it was the Devil'.[62] In Northamptonshire, 1705, he came to Mary Phillips and Elinor Shaw as 'a tall black Man'.[63]

Scotland.—The earliest description is in the trial of Bessie Dunlop of Lyne in Ayrshire in 1576, and is one of the most detailed. Bessie never spoke of the person, who appeared to her, as the 'Devil', she invariably called him Thom Reid; but he stood to her in the same relation that the Devil stood to the witches, and like the Devil he demanded that she should believe on him. She described him as 'ane honest wele elderlie man, gray bairdit, and had ane gray coitt with Lumbart slevis of the auld fassoun; ane pair of gray brekis, and quhyte schankis, gartanit aboue the kne; ane blak bonet on his heid, cloise behind and plane befoir, with silkin laissis drawin throw the lippis thairof; and ane quhyte wand in his hand'.[64] Alison Peirson, 1588, must have recognized the man who appeared to her, for she 'wes conuict of the vsing of Sorcerie and Wichcraft, with the Inuocatioun of the spreitis of the Dewill; speciallie, in the visioune and forme of ane Mr. William Sympsoune, hir cousing and moder-brotheris-sone, quha sche affermit wes ane grit scoller and doctor of medicin'.[65] Though the Devil of North Berwick, 1590, appeared in disguise, it is not only certain that he was a man but his identity can be determined. Barbara Napier deposed that 'the devil wess with them in likeness of ane black man ... the devil start up in the pulpit, like a mickle blak man, with ane black beard sticking out like ane goat's beard, clad in ane blak tatie [tattered] gown and ane ewill favoured scull bonnet on his heid; hauing ane black book in his hand'. Agnes Sampson's description in the official record was very brief: 'he had on

---

[62] Howell, viii, 1035.
[63] *Elinor Shaw and Mary Phillips*, p. 6.
[64] Pitcairn, i, pt. ii, pp. 51-6.
[65] Id., i, pt. ii, p. 162.

him ane gown, and ane hat, which were both black';[66] but Melville, who probably heard her evidence, puts it more dramatically: 'The deuell wes cled in ane blak gown with ane blak hat vpon his head.... His faice was terrible, his noise lyk the bek of ane egle, gret bournyng eyn; his handis and leggis wer herry, with clawes vpon his handis, and feit lyk the griffon.'[67] John Fian merely mentions that the first time the Devil came he was clothed in white raiment.[68] The evidence from Aberdeen, 1596-7, points to there being two Chiefs, one old and one young. Ellen Gray confessed that 'the Devill, thy maister, apperit to thee in the scheap of ane agit man, beirdit, with a quhyt gown and a thrummit [shaggy] hatt'. Andro Man 'confessis that Crystsunday cum to hym in liknes of ane fair angell, and clad in quhyt claythis'. Christen Mitchell stated that 'Sathan apperit to the in the lyknes of a littill crippill man'; and Marion Grant gave evidence that 'the Deuill, quhom thow callis thy god, apperit to thee in ane gryte man his licknes, in silkin abuilzeament [habiliment], withe ane quhyt candill in his hand'.[69] Isobell Haldane of Perth, 1607, was carried away into a fairy hill, 'thair scho stayit thrie dayis, viz. fra Thursday till Sonday at xii houris. Scho mett a man with ane gray beird, quha brocht hir furth agane.' This man stood to her in the same relation as Thom Reid to Bessie Dunlop, or as the Devil to the witches.[70] Jonet Rendall of Orkney, 1629, saw him 'claid in quhyt cloathis, with ane quhyt head and ane gray beard'.[71] In East Lothian, 1630, Alexander Hamilton met the Devil in the likeness of a black man.[72] At Eymouth, 1634, Bessie Bathgate was seen by two young men 'at 12 hours of even (when all people are in their beds) standing bare-legged and in her sark valicot, at the back of hir yard, conferring with the devil who was in green cloaths'.[73] Manie Haliburton of Dirlton, 1649, confessed that, when

---

[66] Id., i, pt. ii, pp. 245-6, 239. Spelling modernized.
[67] Melville, pp. 395-6.
[68] Pitcairn, i, pt. ii, p. 210.
[69] *Spalding Club Miscellany*, i, pp. 124, 127, 164, 172.
[70] Pitcairn, ii, p. 537.
[71] *County Folklore*, iii, p. 103. Orkney.
[72] From the record of the trial in the Justiciary Court, Edinburgh.
[73] *Spottiswode Miscellany*, ii, p. 65.

her daughter was ill, 'came the Devill, in licknes of a man, to hir hous, calling himselff a phisition'.[74] He came also as 'a Mediciner' to Sandie Hunter in East Lothian in 1649.[75] In the same year he appeared as a black man to Robert Grieve, 'an eminent Warlock' at Lauder.[76] In the same year also 'Janet Brown was charged with having held a meeting with the Devil appearing as a man, at the back of Broomhills'.[77] Among the Alloa witches, tried in 1658, Margret Duchall 'did freelie confes hir paction with the diwell, how he appeared first to hir in the liknes of a man in broun cloathis, and ane blak hat'; while Kathren Renny said 'that he first appeared to hir in the bodis medow in the liknes of a man with gray cloathis and ane blew cap'.[78] The years 1661 and 1662 are notable in the annals of Scotch witchcraft for the number of trials and the consequent mass of evidence, including many descriptions of the Grand-master. At Forfar, in 1661, Helen Guthrie said that at several meetings the devil was present 'in the shape of a black iron-hued man'; Katherine Porter 'saw the divill and he had ane blacke plaid about him'; when Issobell Smyth was alone gathering heather, 'hee appeared to hir alone lik ane braw gentleman'; and on another occasion 'like a light gentleman'.[79] Jonet Watson of Dalkeith, also in 1661, said 'that the Deivill apeired vnto her in the liknes of ane prettie boy, in grein clothes.... Shoe was at a Meitting in Newtoun-dein with the Deavill, who had grein clothes vpone him, and ane blak hatt vpone his head'.[80] In the same year an Edinburgh Coven was tried: Jonet Ker was accused that 'as you wer comeing from Edr to the park you mett with the devill at the bough in the liknes of a greavous black man'; Helene Casso 'met with the devill in liknes of a man with greine cloaths in the links of Dudingstone qr he wes gathering sticks amongst the whines'; Isobel Ramsay 'mett with the devill in the Liknes of a pleasant young man who said qr live you

[74] Pitcairn, iii, p. 599.
[75] Sinclair, p. 122.
[76] Id., p. 47.
[77] Arnot, p. 358.
[78] *Scottish Antiquary*, ix, pp. 50, 51.
[79] Kinloch, pp. 114, 128, 132.
[80] Pitcairn, iii, p. 601.

goodwyf and how does the minister And as you wes goeing away he gave you a sexpence saying God bud him give you that qch you wared and bought meall therwith As also you had ane uther meiting wt the devill in yor awne house in the liknes of yor awne husband as you wes lying in yor bed at qch tyme you engadged to be his servant'; Jonet Millar 'did meit wt the devill in liknes of ane young man in the hous besyd the standing stane'.[81] The trials of the Auldearne witches in 1662 are fully reported as regards matters which interested the recorder; unfortunately the appearance of the Devil was not one of these, therefore Isobel Gowdie's description is abbreviated to the following: 'He was a meikle black roch man. Sometimes he had boots and sometimes shoes on his foot; but still [always] his foot are forked and cloven.'[82] At Crook of Devon in Kinross-shire, in the same year, nine of the witches describe the men they saw, for evidently there were two 'Devils' in this district; Isobel Rutherford said that 'Sathan was in the likness of a man with gray cloathes and ane blue bannet, having ane beard'; Bessie Henderson, 'the Devil appeared to you in the likeness of ane bonnie young lad, with ane blue bonnet'; Robert Wilson, 'the Devil was riding on ane horse with fulyairt clothes and ane Spanish cape'; Bessie Neil, 'Sathan appeared to you with dun-coloured clothes'; Margaret Litster, 'Sathan having grey clothes'; Agnes Brugh, 'the Devil appeared in the twilight like unto a half long fellow with an dusti coloured coat'; Margaret Huggon, 'he was an uncouth man with black cloathes with ane hood on his head'; Janet Paton, 'Sathan had black coloured clothes and ane blue bonnet being an unkie like man'; Christian Grieve, 'Sathan did first appear to yow like ane little man with ane blue bonnet on his head with rough gray cloaths on him'.[83] Marie Lamont of Innerkip, also in 1662, said that 'the devil was in the likeness of a meikle black man, and sung to them, and they dancit'; he appeared again 'in the likeness of a black man with cloven featt'.[84] At Paisley, in 1678, the girl-witch Annabil Stuart said that 'the

---

[81] From the records in the Justiciary Court, Edinburgh.
[82] Pitcairn, iii, p. 603.
[83] Burns Begg, pp. 221-39.
[84] Sharpe, pp. 131, 134.

Devil in the shape of a Black man came to her Mother's House'; her brother John was more detailed in his description, he observed 'one of the black man's feet to be cloven: and that the black man's Apparel was black; and that he had a bluish Band and Handcuffs; and that he had Hogers[85] on his Legs without Shoes'; Margaret Jackson of the same Coven confirmed the description, 'the black man's Clothes were black, and he had white Handcuffs'.[86] The clearest evidence is from an unpublished trial of 1678 among the records in the Justiciary Court in Edinburgh:

'Margaret Lowis declaires that about Elevin years ago a man whom she thought to be ane Englishman that cured diseases in the countrey called [blank] Webb appeared to her in her own house and gave her a drink and told her that she would have children after the taking of that drink And declares that that man made her renunce her baptisme ... and declares that she thought that the man who made her doe these things wes the divill and that she has hade severall meitings with that man after she knew him to be the divill.... Margaret Smaill prisoner being examined anent the Cryme of witchcraft depones that having come into the house of Jannet Borthvick in Crightoun she saw a gentleman sitting with her, and they desyred her to sitt down and having sitten down the gentleman drank to her and she drank to him and therefter the said Jannet Borthvick told her that that gentleman was the divill and declares that at her desyre she renunced her baptisme and gave herself to the divill.'

At Borrowstowness in 1679 Annaple Thomson 'had a metting with the devill in your cwming betwixt Linlithgow and Borrowstownes, where the devil, in the lyknes of ane black man, told yow, that yow wis ane poore puddled bodie.... And yow the said Annaple had ane other metting, and he inveitted yow to go alongst, and drink with him'. The same devil met Margaret Hamilton 'and conversed with yow at the town-well of Borrowstownes, and several tymes in yowr awin howss, and drank severall choppens of ale with you'.[87] The

---

[85] *Hogers*, a coarse stocking without the foot.
[86] Glanvil, pt. ii, pp. 291-5, 297.
[87] *Scots Magazine*, 1814, p. 200.

Renfrewshire trials of 1696 show that all Mrs. Fulton's grandchildren saw the same personage; Elizabeth Anderson, at the age of seven, 'saw a black grim Man go in to her Grandmothers House'; James Lindsay, aged fourteen, 'met his Grandmother with a black grim Man'; and little Thomas Lindsay was awaked by his grandmother 'one Night out of his Bed, and caused him take a Black Grimm Gentleman (as she called him) by the Hand'.[88] At Pittenweem, in 1704, 'this young Woman Isobel Adams [acknowledged] her compact with the Devil, which she says was made up after this manner, *viz.* That being in the House of the said Beatie Laing, and a Man at the end of the Table, Beatie proposes to Isobel, that since she would not Fee and Hire with her, that she would do it, with the Man at the end of the Table; And accordingly Isobel agreed to it, and spoke with the Man at that time in General terms. Eight days after, the same Person in Appearance comes to her, and owns that he was the Devil.'[89] The latest instance is at Thurso in 1719, where the Devil met Margaret Nin-Gilbert 'in the way in the likeness of a man, and engaged her to take on with him, which she consented to; and she said she knew him to be the devil or he parted with her'.[90]

In Ireland one of the earliest known trials for ritual witchcraft occurred in 1324, the accused being the Lady Alice Kyteler. She was said to have met the Devil, who was called Robin son of Artis, 'in specie cuiusdam aethiopis cum duobus sociis ipso maioribus et longioribus'.[91]

In France also there is a considerable amount of evidence. The earliest example is in 1430, when Pierronne, a follower of Joan of Arc, was put to death by fire as a witch. She persisted to the end in her statement, which she made on oath, that God appeared to her in human form and spoke to her as friend to friend, and that the last time she had seen him he was clothed in a scarlet cap and a long white

---

[88] *Narrative of the Sufferings of a Young Girle*, pp. xxxix-xli—*Sadd. Debell.*, pp. 38-40.
[89] *A true and full Relation of the Witches of Pittenweem*, p. 10.—Sinclair, p. lxxxix.
[90] Sharpe, p. 191.
[91] *Camden Society*, Lady Alice Kyteler, p. 3.

robe.[92] Estebene de Cambrue of the parish of Amou in 1567 said that the witches danced round a great stone, 'sur laquelle est assis un grand homme noir, qu'elles appellent Monsieur'.[93] Jeanne Hervillier of Verberie near Compiègne, in 1578, daughter of a witch who had been condemned and burnt, 'confessa qu'à l'aage de douze ans sa mere la presenta au diable, en forme d'vn grand homme noir, & vestu de noir, botté, esperonné, auec vne espée au costé, & vn cheual noir à la porte'.[94] Françoise Secretain of Saint Claud in 1598 stated 'qu'elle s'estoit donnée au Diable, lequel auoit lors la semblance d'vn grand homme noir'; Thievenne Paget, from the same district, 'racontoit que le Diable s'apparut à elle la premiere fois en plein midy, en forme d'vn grand homme noir'; and Antide Colas 'disoit, que Satan s'apparut à elle en forme d'vn homme, de grande stature, ayant sa barbe & ses habillemens noirs'.[95] Jeanne d'Abadie, in the Basses-Pyrénées, 1609, 'dit qu'elle y vid le Diable en forme d'homme noir & hideux, auec six cornes en la teste, parfois huict'.[96] Silvain Nevillon, tried at Orleans in 1614, 'dit que le Sabbat se tenoit dans vne maison, où il vit à la cheminée cõme ledit Sabbat se faisoit, vn homme noir, duquel on ne voyoit point la teste. Vit aussi vn grand homme noir à l'opposite de celuy de la cheminée. Dit que les deux Diables qui estoient au Sabbat, l'vn s'appelloit l'Orthon, & l'autre Traisnesac.'[97] Two sisters were tried in 1652: one 'dict avoir trouvé ung diable en ghuise d'ung home à pied'; the other said that 'il entra dans sa chambre en forme d'ung chat par une fenestre et se changea en la posture d'un home vestu de rouge'.[98]

In Belgium, Digna Robert, 1565, met 'un beau jeune homme vètu d'une casaque noire, qui était le diable, et se nommait Barrebon.... À

---

[92] *Journal d'un bourgeois de Paris*, p. 687.
[93] De Lancre, *Tableau*, p. 123.
[94] Bodin, p. 226.
[95] Boguet, pp. 8, 96.
[96] De Lancre, *Tableau*, p. 130.
[97] Id., *L'Incredulité*, pp. 799, 800. The second Devil is called Tramesabot on p. 802.
[98] Van Elven, *La Tradition*, v (1891), p. 215. Neither the witches' names nor the place are given.

la Noël passée, un autre diable, nommé Crebas, est venu près d'elle.'
Elisabeth Vlamynx of Ninove in the Pays d'Alost, 1595, was accused
'que vous avez, avant comme après le repas, vous septième ou
huitième, dansé sous les arbres en compagnie de votre Belzebuth et
d'un autre démon, tous deux en pourpoint blanc à la mode française'.
Josine Labyns in 1664, aged about forty: 'passé dix-neuf ans le diable
s'est offert à vos yeux, derrière votre habitation, sous la figure d'un
grand seigneur, vètu en noir et portant des plumes sur son chapeau.'[99]

In the copper mines of Sweden, 1670, the Devil appeared as a
minister.[100] In the province of Elfdale in the same year his dress was
not the usual black of that period: 'He used to appear, but in different
Habits; but for the most part we saw him in a gray Coat, and red and
blue Stockings; he had a red Beard, a high-crown'd Hat, with Linnen
of divers colours wrapt about it, and long Garters upon his
Stockings.'[101] This is not unlike the costume of Thom Reid as
described, more than a century before, by Bessie Dunlop.

In America the same evidence is found. At Hartford, 1662, 'Robert
Sterne testifieth as followeth: I saw this woman goodwife Seager in
ye woods with three more women and with them I saw two black
creatures like two Indians but taller'; and Hugh Crosia 'sayd ye deuell
opned ye dore of eben booths hous made it fly open and ye gate fly
open being asked how he could tell he sayd ye deuell apeered to him
like a boye and told him hee ded make them fly open and then ye boye
went out of his sight.'[102] Elizabeth Knap at Groton, 1671, 'was with
another maid yt boarded in ye house, where both of them saw ye
appearance of a mans head and shoulders, wth a great white
neckcloath, looking in at ye window, which shee hath since confessed,
was ye Devill coming to her.—One day as shee was alone in a lower
roome she looked out of ye window, and saw ye devill in ye habit of
an old man, coming over a great meadow.'[103] At Salem, 1692, Mary

---

[99] Cannaert, pp. 44, 53-4, 60.
[100] Fountainhall, i, p. 14.
[101] Horneck, pt. ii, p. 316.
[102] Taylor, pp. 81, 118.
[103] Green, pp. 9, 14.

Osgood saw him as a black man who presented a book; and Mary Lacey described him as a black man in a high-crowned hat.[104]

The evidence suggests that an important part of the Devil's costume was the head-covering, which he appears to have worn both in and out of doors. Though the fact is not of special interest in itself, it may throw light on one of the possible origins of the cult.

In 1576 Bessie Dunlop met Thom Reid, who was clearly the Devil; he was 'ane honest wele elderlie man, gray bairdit, and had ane gray coitt with Lumbart slevis of the auld fassoun; ane pair of gray brekis and quhyte schankis, gartanit aboue the kne; ane blak bonet on his heid, cloise behind and plane befoir, with silkin laissis drawin throw the lippis thairof.'[105] At North Berwick in 1590, 'the deuell, cled in a blak gown with a blak hat vpon his head, preachit vnto a gret nomber of them.'[106] Another description of the same event shows that 'the Devil start up in the pulpit, like a mickle black man clad in a black tatie gown; and an evil-favoured scull-bonnet on his head'.[107] At Aberdeen in 1597 Ellen Gray described the Devil as 'ane agit man, beirdit, with a quhyt gown and a thrummit hat'.[108] In 1609, in the Basses-Pyrénées, when the Devil appeared as a goat, 'on luy voit aussi quelque espece de bonet ou chapeau au dessus de ses cornes.'[109] The Alloa Coven in 1658 spoke of 'a man in broun clathis and ane blak hat'; and on two occasions of 'a young man with gray cloathis and ane blew cap'.[110] In 1661 Janet Watson of Dalkeith 'was at a Meitting in Newtoun-dein with the Deavill, who had grein cloathes vpone him, and ane blak hatt vpone his head'.[111] Five members of the Coven at Crook of Devon in 1662 spoke of the Devil's head-gear: 'Sathan was in the likeness of a man with gray cloathes and ane blue bannet, having ane beard. Ane bonnie young lad with ane blue bonnet. Ane uncouth

[104] Howell, vi, 660, 664; J. Hutchinson, ii, pp. 31, 37.

[105] Pitcairn, i, pt. ii, p. 51.

[106] Melville, p. 395.

[107] Pitcairn, i, pt. ii, p. 246. Spelling modernized.

[108] *Spalding Club Misc.*, i, p. 127.

[109] De Lancre, *Tableau*, p. 68.

[110] *Scottish Antiquary*, ix, pp. 50, 51.

[111] Pitcairn, iii, p. 601.

man with black clothes with ane hood on his head. Sathan had all the said times black coloured cloathes and ane blue bonnet being an unkie like man. Ane little man with ane blue bonnet on his head with rough gray cloathes on him.'[112] In 1662 in Connecticut Robert Sterne saw 'two black creatures like two Indians, but taller';[113] as he was at a little distance it is probable that he took a plumed or horned head-dress to be the same as the Indian head-gear. In Belgium in 1664 Josine Labyns saw the Devil wearing a plumed hat.[114] In Somerset in 1665 Mary Green said that when he met the witches 'the little Man put his hand to his Hat, saying How do ye, speaking low but big'.[115] At Torryburn Lilias Adie said that the light was sufficient to 'shew the devil, who wore a cap covering his ears and neck'.[116] In Sweden in 1670 the Devil came 'in a gray Coat, and red and blue Stockings, he had a red Beard, a high-crown'd Hat, with Linnen of divers colours wrapt about, and long Garters upon his Stockings'.[117] At Pittenweem in 1670 the young lass Isobel Adams saw the Devil as 'a man in black cloaths with a hat on his head, sitting at the table' in Beatty Laing's house.[118]

(b) Woman

The Queen of Elphin, or Elfhame, is sometimes called the Devil, and it is often impossible to distinguish between her and the Devil when the latter appears as a woman. Whether she was the same as the French Reine du Sabbat is equally difficult to determine. The greater part of the evidence regarding the woman-devil is from Scotland.

In 1576 Bessie Dunlop's evidence shows that Thom Reid, who was to her what the Devil was to witches, was under the orders of the Queen of Elfhame:

[112] Burns Begg, pp. 221, 223, 234, 235, 239.
[113] Taylor, p. 81.
[114] Cannaert, p. 60.
[115] Glanvil, pt. ii, p. 164.
[116] Chambers, iii, p. 298.
[117] Glanvil, pt. ii, p. 316.
[118] Sinclair, p. lxxxix.

'Interrogat, Gif sche neuir askit the questioun at him, Quhairfoir he com to hir mair [than] ane vthir bodye? Ansuerit, Remembring hir, quhen sche was lyand in child-bed-lair, with ane of her laiddis, that ane stout woman com in to hir, and sat doun on the forme besyde hir, and askit ane drink at her, and sche gaif hir; quha alsua tauld hir, that that barne wald de, and that hir husband suld mend of his seiknes. The said Bessie ansuerit, that sche remembrit wele thairof; and Thom said, That was the Quene of Elfame his maistres, quha had commandit him to wait vpoun hir, and to do hir gude. Confessit and fylit.'[119]

In 1588 Alison Peirson 'was conuict for hanting and repairing with the gude nychtbouris and Quene of Elfame, thir diuers ʒeiris bypast, as scho had confest be hir depositiounis, declaring that scho could nocht say reddelie how lang scho wes with thame; and that scho had freindis in that court quhilk wes of hir awin blude, quha had gude acquentence of the Quene of Elphane. And that scho saw nocht the Quene thir seuin ʒeir.'[120] In 1597 at Aberdeen Andro Man was accused that

'thriescoir yeris sensyne or thairby, the Devill, thy maister, come to thy motheris hous, in the liknes and scheap of a woman, quhom thow callis the Quene of Elphen, and was delyverit of a barne, as apperit to the their, thow confessis that be the space of threttie two yeris sensyn or thairby, thow begud to have carnall deall with that devilische spreit, the Quene of Elphen, on quhom thow begat dyveris bairnis, quhom thow hes sene sensyn.... Thow confessis that the Devill, thy maister, quhom thow termes Christsonday, and supponis to be ane engell, and Goddis godsone, albeit he hes a thraw by God, and swyis [sways] to the Quene of Elphen, is rasit be the speaking of the word *Benedicite*.... Siclyk, thow affermis that the Quene of Elphen hes a grip of all the craft, bot Christsonday is the gudeman, and hes all power vnder God.... Vpon the Ruidday in harvest, in this present yeir, quhilk fell on a Wedinsday, thow confessis and affermis, thow saw Christsonday cum out of the snaw in liknes of a staig, and that the Quene of Elphen was their, and vtheris with hir, rydand on quhyt haikneyes, and that

---

[119] Pitcairn, i, pt. ii, p. 56.
[120] Id., i, pt. ii, p. 163.

thay com to the Binhill and the Binlocht, quhair thay vse commonlie to convene, and that thay quha convenis with thame kissis Christsonday and the Quene of Elphenis airss. Thow affermis that the quene is verray plesand, and wilbe auld and young quhen scho pleissis; scho mackis any kyng quhom scho pleisis, and lyis with any scho lykis'.[121]

Another Aberdeen witch, Marion Grant, was accused in the same year and confessed, 'that the Devill, thy maister, quhome thow termes Christsonday, causit the dans sindrie tymes with him and with Our Ladye, quha, as thow sayes, was a fine woman, cled in a quhyt walicot'.[122] In Ayrshire in 1605 Patrick Lowrie and Jonet Hunter were accused that they 'att Hallowevin assemblit thame selffis vpon Lowdon-hill, quhair thair appeirit to thame are devillische Spreit, in liknes of ane woman, and callit hir selff Helen Mcbrune'.[123] In the Basses-Pyrénées in 1609, one could 'en chasque village trouuer vne Royne du Sabbat, que Sathan tenoit en delices cõme vne espouse priuilegiée'.[124] At the witch-mass the worshippers 'luy baisent la main gauche, tremblans auec mille angoisses, & luy offrent du pain, des œufs, & de l'argent: & la Royne du Sabbat les reçoit, laquelle est assise à son costé gauche, & en sa main gauche elle tient vne paix ou platine, dans laquelle est grauée l'effigie de Lucifer, laquelle on ne baise qu'après l'auoir premièrement baisée à elle'.[125] In 1613 the Lancashire witch, Anne Chattox, made a confused statement as to the sex of the so-called spirits; it is however quite possible that the confusion is due to the recorder, who was accustomed to consider all demons as male: 'After their eating, the Deuill called Fancie, and the other Spirit calling himselfe Tibbe, carried the remnant away: And she sayeth that at their said Banquet, the said Spirits gaue them light to see what they did, and that they were both shee Spirites and Diuels.'[126] In 1618 at Leicester Joan Willimott 'saith, that shee hath a Spirit which shee calleth Pretty,

[121] *Spalding Club Misc.*, pp. 119-21.
[122] Id., i, p. 171.
[123] Pitcairn, ii, p. 478.
[124] De Lancre, *L'Incredulité*, p. 36.
[125] Id., *Tableau*, p. 401.
[126] Potts, B 4.

which was giuen vnto her by William Berry of Langholme in Rutlandshire, whom she serued three yeares; and that her Master when he gaue it vnto her, willed her to open her mouth, and hee would blow into her a Fairy which should doe her good; and that shee opened her mouth, and he did blow into her mouth; and that presently after his blowing, there came out of her mouth a Spirit, which stood vpon the ground in the shape and forme of a Woman, which Spirit did aske of her her Soule, which she then promised vnto it, being willed thereunto by her Master.'[127] William Barton was tried in Edinburgh about 1655:

'One day, says he, going from my own house in Kirkliston, to the Queens Ferry, I overtook in Dalmeny Muire, a young Gentlewoman, as to appearance beautiful and comely. I drew near to her, but she shunned my company, and when I insisted, she became angry and very nyce. Said I, we are both going one way, be pleased to accept of a convoy. At last after much entreaty she grew better natured, and at length came to that Familiarity, that she suffered me to embrace her, and to do that which Christian ears ought not to hear of. At this time I parted with her very joyful. The next night, she appeared to him in that same very place, and after that which should not be named, he became sensible, that it was the Devil. Here he renounced his Baptism, and gave up himself to her service, and she called him her beloved, and gave him this new name of Iohn Baptist, and received the Mark.'[128]

At Forfar in 1662 Marjorie Ritchie 'willingly and friely declared that the divill appeired to her thrie severall tymes in the similitud of a womane, the first tyme in on Jonet Barrie's house, the second tyme whyle she was putting vp lint in the companie of the said Jonet, and that the divill did take her by the hand at that tyme, and promised that she should never want money; and therafter that the divill appeired to her in the moiss of Neutoune of Airly, wher and when she did renunce her baptism'.[129] In 1670 Jean Weir, sister of the notorious Major Weir, gave an account of how she entered the service of the Devil; the ceremony began as follows: 'When she keeped a school at Dalkeith,

---

[127] *Wonderful Discovery of Margaret and Phillip Flower*, p. 117.
[128] Sinclair, p. 160.
[129] Kinloch, p. 144.

and teached childering, ane tall woman came to the declarants hous when the childering were there; and that she had, as appeared to her, ane chyld upon her back, and on or two at her foot; and that the said woman desyred that the declarant should imploy her to spick for her to the Queen of Farie, and strik and battle in her behalf with the said Queen (which was her own words).'[130] Among the Salem witches in 1692, 'this Rampant Hag, Martha Carrier, was the person, of whom the Confessions of the Witches, and of her own Children among the rest, agreed, That the Devil had promised her, she should be Queen of Hell.[131]

3. Identification

As it is certain that the so-called 'Devil' was a human being, sometimes disguised and sometimes not, the instances in which these persons can be identified are worth investigating. In most cases these are usually men, and the names are often given, but it is only in the case of the Devil of North Berwick that the man in question is of any historic importance; the others are simply private individuals of little or no note.

Elizabeth Stile of Windsor, in 1579, gives a description of Father Rosimond's changes of form, which points to his being the Chief of the Windsor witches: 'She confesseth, her self often tymes to haue gon to Father Rosimond house where she founde hym sittyng in a Wood, not farre from thence, vnder the bodie of a Tree, sometymes in the shape of an Ape, and otherwhiles like an Horse.'[132] In the reign of Elizabeth, 1584, there is a list of eighty-seven suspected persons, among whom occur the names of 'Ould Birtles the great devil, Roger Birtles and his wife and Anne Birtles, Darnally the sorcerer, the oulde witche of Ramsbury, Maud Twogood Enchantress, Mother Gillian witch' and several other 'oulde witches'.[133] The account by

---

[130] Law, p. 27 note.
[131] Cotton Mather, p. 159.
[132] *Rehearsall both straung and true*, par. 24.
[133] *Calendar of State Papers. Domestic*, 1584, p. 220.

John Stearne the pricker, in 1645, indicates that one of the magistrates of Fenny Drayton was the local Devil: 'Some will say, It is strange they should know when they should be searched, if it be kept private. I answer, Let it be kept never so private, it hath been common, and as common as any other thing, as they themselves have confessed: for so did they of Fenny-Drayton in Cambridge-shire, who made very large Confessions, as, that the devil told them of our coming to town.'[134] One of the clearest cases, however, is that of Marsh of Dunstable in 1649, 'whom Palmer confessed to be head of the whole Colledge of Witches, that hee knows in the world: This Palmer hath been a witch these sixty years (by his own confession) long enough to know and give in the totall summe of all the conjuring conclave, and the Society of Witches in England.'[135]

In Scotland a certain number of identifications are also possible. Alison Peirson, tried in 1588, learnt all her charms and obtained all her knowledge from the Devil, who came to her in the form of Mr. William Sympson, her mother's brother's son, who was a great scholar and doctor of medicine in Edinburgh.[136]Jonet Stewart in 1597 'learnt her charms from umquhill Michaell Clark, smyth in Laswaid, and fra ane Italean strangear callit Mr. John Damiet, ane notorious knawin Enchanter and Sorcerer'.[137] In the trial of Marion Pardon of Hillswick in 1644 'it was given in evidence that a man spoke of the devil as Marion Pardon's pobe, i.e. nurse's husband or foster father'.[138] In a case tried at Lauder in 1649 there is an indication that one of the magistrates was the Chief of the witches; Robert Grieve accused a certain woman at a secret session of the court, 'but the Devil came that same night unto her, and told her that Hob Grieve had fyled her for a witch'.[139] Isobel Ramsay in 1661 was accused that 'you had ane uther meiting wt the devill in yor awne hous in the liknes of yor awne husband as you wes lying in yor bed at qch tyme you engadged to be

---

[134] Stearne, p. 45.

[135] Gerish, *The Divel's Delusions* p. 11.

[136] Pitcairn, i, pt. ii, pp. 161-4.

[137] Id., ii, pp. 26-7.

[138] Hibbert, p. 578.

[139] Sinclair, p. 48.

his servant and receaved a dollar from him'.[140] When a man had special knowledge as to which women were witches, it is suggestive that he might be himself the Devil; as in the case of the Rev. Allan Logan, who 'was particularly knowing in the detection of witches. At the administration of the communion, he would cast his eye along, and say: "You witch wife, get up from the table of the Lord", when some poor creature would rise and depart.'[141]

It seems probable that the infamous Abbé Guibourg was the head of the Paris witches, for it was he who celebrated the 'black mass' and performed the sacrifice of a child, both of which were the duties of the 'Devil'.[142]

At Salem also the account given by the witches of the Rev. George Burroughs points to his filling the office of 'Devil', for he was 'Head Actor at some of their Hellish Randezvouses, and one who had the promise of being a King in Satan's kingdom.—He was the person who had Seduc'd and Compell'd them into the snares of Witchcraft'.[143] That Burroughs was a religious person is no argument against his being also the 'Devil' of Salem. Apart from the well-known psychological fact that a certain form of religious feeling can exist at the same time as the propensity to and practice of sexual indulgence, there is proof that many of the witches were outwardly religious according to the tenets of Christianity. So many Christian priests were also followers of the witch-religion that the Inquisitors of the sixteenth century were greatly exercised in their minds as to how to deal with the offenders. Antide Colas confessed that she attended the midnight mass on Christmas Eve, then went to a witch meeting, and returned to the church in time for the mass at dawn on Christmas morning.[144] At Ipswich in 1645 'Mother Lakeland hath been a professour of Religion, a constant hearer of the Word for these many years, and yet a witch (as she confessed) for the space of near twenty years'.[145] The best-

---

[140] From the record in the Justiciary Office, Edinburgh.
[141] Chambers, iii, p. 299.
[142] Ravaisson, 1679, pp. 334-6.
[143] Mather, pp. 120, 125; J. Hutchinson, *History*, ii, pp. 37 seq.
[144] Boguet, p. 125.
[145] *Lawes against Witches and Conivration*, p. 7.

known case of the kind is that of Major Weir in Edinburgh in 1670, whose outward appearance tallies with the usual descriptions of the Devil, and whose conduct is only explainable on the supposition that he actually was the Chief of the witches: 'His garb was still a cloak, and somewhat dark, and he never went without his staff. He was a tall black man, and ordinarily looked down to the ground; a grim countenance, and a big nose.'[146] His reputation for piety was so great that a woman, who had actually seen him commit an offence against the criminal law, was flogged for mentioning the fact and thus defaming a man of such extreme and well-established piety. He was tried as a witch on his own unsolicited confession, and was burnt together with his staff, dying 'impenitent' and renouncing all hope of a Christian heaven. The most interesting case historically, however, is that of the Devil of the North Berwick witches (1590). The number of people involved was thirty-nine, i.e. three Covens; but though the names of all were known, only four were tried. The records are given in considerable detail, and the identification of the Chief is therefore possible.

The character of the accused in this case is of great importance when considering the evidence. Nothing more unlike the conventional idea of witches can well be imagined than the man and women who were arraigned on that occasion. Agnes Sampson, the wise wife of Keith, was 'a woman not of the base and ignorant sort of Witches, but matron-like, grave and settled in her answers, which were all to some purpose'. John Fian, or Cunynghame, was a schoolmaster, therefore a man of education; Effie McCalyan, the daughter of Lord Cliftonhall, was a woman of family and position; Barbara Napier was also of good family. These were clearly the moving spirits of the band, and they were all persons capable of understanding the meaning and result of their actions.[147]

The accusation against the witches was that they had met together to plot the murder of the King and Queen by witchcraft. The trial therefore was on a double charge, witchcraft and high treason, and

---

[146] Wilson, ii, p. 158.
[147] The trials are published by Pitcairn, i, pt. ii.

both charges had to be substantiated. Keeping in mind Lord Coke's definition of a witch as 'a person who has conference with the Devil to take counsel or to do some act', it is clear that the fact of the Devil's bodily presence at the meetings had to be proved first, then the fact of the 'conference', and finally the attempts at murder. The reports of the trial do not, however, differentiate these points in any way, and the religious prepossession of the recorders colours every account. It is therefore necessary to take the facts without the construction put upon them by the natural bias of the Christian judges and writers. The records give in some detail the account of several meetings where the deaths of the King and Queen were discussed, and instructions given and carried out to effect that purpose. At each meeting certain ceremonies proper to the presence of the Grand Master were performed, but the real object of the meeting was never forgotten or even obscured.

The actual evidence of the affair was given by Agnes Sampson (also called Anny Simpson or Tompson), John Fian, Euphemia or Effie McCalyan, and Barbara Napier. As it was a case of high treason, the two leaders, Sampson and Fian, were tortured to force them to divulge the name of the prime mover. Both these two and Effie McCalyan were condemned and executed; Barbara Napier, equally guilty according to the evidence but more fortunate in her jurors, was released; for which action the jurors themselves were subsequently tried.

Though the means used by the witches may seem ridiculous, the murderous intention is very clear. First they performed incantations to raise a storm to wreck the Queen's ship on her way to Scotland, and the storm which actually arose very nearly effected their purpose. As it failed, however, they betook themselves to the accredited method of melting a waxen image, but they were also ready to use poisons, which were to their minds the most virulent that could be prepared.

I have arranged the evidence so as to make as far as possible a consecutive narrative of the occurrences.

John Fian, tried December 26, 1590. The first items relate to his consulting with the Devil and working witchcraft. 7. Item, Fylit, for the rasing of wyndis att the Kingis passing to Denmark, and for the sending of ane letter to Marioun Linkup in Leyth, to that effect, bidding hir to meit him and the rest, on the see, within fyve dayes; quhair Satan delyuerit ane catt out of his hand to Robert Griersoune, gevand the word to 'Cast the same in the see hola!': And thaireftir, being mountit in a schip, and drank ilk ane to otheris, quhair Satane said, 'ye shall sink the schip', lyke as thay thocht thay did. 8. Item, Fylit, for assembling him selff with Sathane, att the Kingis returning to Denmark; quhair Satan promeist to raise ane mist, and cast the Kingis Majestie in Ingland.

Agnes Sampson, tried January 27, 1591. The first part of the dittay is entirely occupied with her conferences with the devil and her healing the sick by his advice. 40. Item, fylit and convict, of the delyuerie of ane letter, quhilk John Fiene, clerk, maid in George Mutis bak[e] hous in the Pannis, accumpaneit with the gudwyff of the hous, Gelie Duncan [and eight others], quha convenit thair for rasing of storme, to stay the Quene's hame cuming to Scotland; eftir consultatioun, quhether Gelie Duncan or Bessie Thomsoun wes meitest to send the letter with; and concludit to send the said Gelie, quhilk letter wes send to Marioun Lenchop in Leyth. The effect quhairoff is this: Marioun Lenchop, ye sall warne the rest of the sisteris, to raise the wind this day, att eleavin houris, to stay the Quenis cuming in Scotland. Lyke as they that wer convenit at the Pannis sould do their part be-eist; and to meit thame that wer in the Pannis; and att thair meting, thay sould mak the storme vniversall thro the see. [Then follows the method of doing this by casting in a cat.]

[From *Newes from Scotland*.] The said Agnis Tompson (Sampson) confessed, that the Divell, being then at North Barrick Kirke attending their comming, in the habit or likenesse of a man ... and having made his ungodly exhortations, wherein he did greatly inveigh against the King of Scotland, he received their oathes for their good and true service towards him, and departed; which done, they returned to sea, and so home again. At which time, the witches demaunded of the Divell, 'why he did beare such hatred to the Kinge?' who aunswered,

'By reason the King is the greatest enemie hee hath in the world.' All which their confessions and depositions are still extant upon record.

Barbara Napier, tried May 8, 1591. Released. Assisors tried June 7, and acquitted. The said Barbara was accusit, that scho gaif hir presens, in the maist develisch and tressonabill Conventioune, haldin be hir and hir complices in the Divellis name, vpoune Lambmes-ewin last, att the New-heavincallit Aitchesounes-heavin, betuix Musselburcht and Prestonpannis, sin his Majestie come furth of Denmark; quhair war assemblit nyne principallis, to witt, Agnes Sampsoune, Jonett Straittoun, Ewfame McCalyeane, hir selff, Johne Fiene, Robert Griersoun, George Moitis wyffe in Prestoune, Margrett Thomsoune, and Donald Robesoune; quhilk is nyne persounes, the Devill, quha wes with thame in liknes of ane blak man, thocht maist meit to do the turne for the quhilk thay wer convenit; and thairfore, he sett thame nyne nerrest to him selff, in ane cumpany; and thay, togidder with the wyffe of Saltoune myle and the rest of the inferiouris, to the nowmer of threttie persounes, standand skairse the lenth of ane buird frae the foirsaid nyne persounes in ane vthir cumpany;[148] Agnes Sampsoune proponit the distructioune of his hienes persoune, saying to the Dewill, 'We haif ane turne ado, and we would fain be att itt gif we could, and thairfore help ws to itt'. The Dewill ansuerit, he sould do quhat he could, bott it wald be lang to, because it wald be thoirterit [thwarted], and he promeist to hir and thame ane pictour of walx, and ordenit hir and thame to hing, roist, and drop ane taid, and to lay the droppis of the taid [mixed with other supposedly virulent poisons], in his hienes way, quhair his Maiestie wald gang inowre or outowre, or in ony passage quhair itt mycht drop vpoun his hienes heid or body, for his hienes distructioune, that ane vther mycht haif rewlit in his Maiesties place, and the ward [government] mycht haif gane to the Dewill. Att the quhilk conventioune, his hienes name wes pronunceit in Latine; and Agnes Sampsoune wes appointit to mak the pictour and to gif it to the Devill to be inchantit, quhilk scho maid in deid, and gaif itt to him; and he

---

[148] There were present on this occasion thirty-nine persons, or three Covens. See chap. vii on the Organization.

promiseit to giff it to the said Barbara and to Effie McCalyan, att the nixt meting to be roistit. Margarett Thomsoun was appointit to dropp the taid. There wes ane appointit to seik sum of his hienes linning claithes, to do the turne with.

Agnes Sampson, continued. Anny Sampsoun affirmed that sche, in company with nyn vthers witches, being convenit in the nycht besyd Prestounpannes, the deuell ther maister being present standing in the midis of thame; ther a body of wax, schaipen and maid be the said Anny Sampsoun, wrappit within a lynnyng claith, was fyrst delyuerit to the deuell; quhilk efter he had pronuncit his verde, delyuerit the said pictour to Anny Sampsoun, and sche to hir nyxt marrow, and sa euery ane round about, saying, 'This is King James the sext, ordonit to be consumed at the instance of a noble man Francis Erle Bodowell!' Efterwart again, at ther meting be nycht at the kirk of Northberick, wher the deuell, cled in a blak gown with a blak hat vpon his head, preachit vnto a gret nomber of them out of the pulpit, having lyk leicht candles rond about him. The effect of his language was till knaw, what skaith they had done, whow many they had won to ther oppinion sen their last meting, what succes the melting of the pictour had tane, and sic vain toyes. And because ane auld sely pure plowman, callit Grey Meill, chancit to say that 'nathing ailit the King yet, God be thankit' the deuell gaif him a gret blaw. Then dyuers amang them enterit in a raisonyng, maruelling that all ther deuellerie culd do na harm to the King, as it did till others dyuers. The deuell answerit, 'Il est vn home de Dieu'.[149]

Euphemia McCalyan, tried June 9, 1591, executed (burnt alive) June 25, 1591. Evidence was first given as to her practising witchcraft and consorting with well-known witches. Item, indyttit and accusit, of the conventicle had att North Berwick Kirk, tuentie dayes before Michelmas, 1590; and thair inquyring for the Kings pictour, gewin by Annie Sampsoun to the Dewill, to be inchantit, for the tressonabill

---

[149] *Bannatyne Club*, Melville, *Memoirs*, p. 395. The sycophantic Melville adds; 'And certanly he is a man of God, and dois na wrang wittingly, bot is inclynit to all godlynes, justice and virtu; therfore God hes preserued him in the midis of many dangers.'

distructioun of the King. Item, indyttit and accusit, for being att ane Conventioun haldin at the New Heaven callit the Fayrie-hoillis, att Lambmes last wes, to the effect immediatlie aboue writtin. Item, Indytit and accusit, for an Conventioun halden by yow and utheris notorious Wichis, youre associattis, att the Brwme-hoillis, quhair yow and thay tuik the sea, Robert Griersoun being your admerell and Maister-manne. [Then comes the recital of the magical means used to raise a tempest], quhairby the Quene wes putt back be storme. Item, Indytit, for consulting with the said Annie Sampsoun, Robert Griersoun, and diuers vtheris Wichis, for the tressonabill staying of the Quene's hame-cuming, be storme and wind; and rasing of storme, to that effect; or ellis to haif drownit hir Majestie and hir cumpany, be coniuring of cattis and casting of thame in the sea, at Leith, at the bak of Robert Griersounis hous.

Barbara Napier, continued. And siclyke, the said Barbara was accusit, that sche gaif hir bodelie presens vpoun Alhallowewin last was, 1590 yeiris, to the frequent conuentioune haldin att the Kirk of North-Berwick, quhair sche dancit endlang the Kirk-yaird, and Gelie Duncan playit on ane trump, Johnne Fiene missellit [muffled] led the ring; Agnes Sampsoun and hir dochteris and all the rest following the said Barbara, to the nowmer of sevin scoir of persounes.... And the Devill start vp in the pulpett, lyke ane mekill blak man, haifand ane blak buik in his hand, callit on ewerie ane of thame, desyring thame all to be guid serwandis to him, and he sould be ane guid maister to thame. Robert Griersoun and Johne Fian stuid on his left hand; and the said Robert ffand grit fault with the Dewill, and cryit out, that all quhilkis wer besyd mycht heir, becaus his hienes pictour was nocht gewin thame, as wes promesit; the said Effie McCalyan remembrand and bid[d]and the said Robert Griersoun to speir for the pictour, meaning his Maiesties pictour, quhilk sould have been roistit. Robert Griersoun said thir wordis, 'Quhair is the thing ye promiseit?' meaning the pictour of walx, dewysit for roisting and vndoing his hienes persoune, quhilk Agnes Sampsoune gaif to him; and Robert cryit to 'haif the turne done'; yit his hienes name was nocht nameit, quhill thay that wer wemen nameit him; craifand in playne termes his hienes pictour. Bot he ansuerit, 'It sould be gottin the nixt meitting; and he wald hald the nixt assemblie for that caus the soner: It was nocht reddie at that tyme.' Robert Griersoune ansuerit, 'Ye promiseit twyis and begylit ws.' And four honest-like wemene wer very ernist and instant to haif itt. And the said Barbara and Effie McCalyane gatt than ane promeis of the Dewill, that his hienes pictour sould be gottin to thame twa, and that rycht sone: And this mater of his hienes pictour was the caus of that assemblie.

This ends the evidence of the witches; the point to be proved now is the identity of the man whom they believed in and obeyed as God incarnate.

In all cases of murder or attempted murder it is necessary to find the person who would benefit, for murder is differentiated from manslaughter by the fact that it is deliberately planned and that it is done for a motive. In the case of the witches of North Berwick, the man who instigated the meetings, and to whom consequently suspicion points, was Francis Stewart Earl of Bothwell. His position as regards both the King and the witches must therefore be investigated.

Francis, afterwards Earl of Bothwell, was the eldest son of John Stewart and Jane Hepburn, sister of that Earl of Bothwell whom Mary Queen of Scots married. Francis succeeded his maternal uncle in title and estates. His father, Lord John Stewart, was an illegitimate son of James V. The Pope, however, legitimized all the natural children of James V; and Mary, after her accession, granted letters of legitimation[150] to her two half-brothers, John Stewart, and James, afterwards the Regent Moray. John was slightly the elder of the two, and had he been legitimate would have been the heir to the exclusion of Mary. The Regent Moray left only daughters, whereas John Stewart had several sons, of whom Francis was the eldest. Francis might therefore claim to be the next heir male to the throne of Scotland, and possibly of England, had James VI died without children. James's own opinion of the matter is shown in his speech to his Parliament in 1592, when he denounced Bothwell as an aspirant to the throne, although he

---

[150] *Reg. Mag. Sig. Scot.*, No. 565, Feb. 7, 1550/1.

was 'but a bastard, and could claim no title to the crown'. Bothwell, however, was himself no bastard, though his father was. But the significance of the witches' attempt, as well as the identity of the chief personage at their meeting, is given in Barbara Napier's evidence as to the reason for the attempted murder of the King, 'that another might have ruled in his Majesty's place, and the government might have gone to the Devil'. By changing the title 'the Devil' by which he was known to the witches, to the title 'Earl of Bothwell' by which he was known outside the community, the man and the motive are manifest. This hypothesis is borne out by the contemporary accounts.

The trial of the witches created a great stir, and Bothwell's name was freely coupled with the witches'. He denied all complicity; this was only natural, as confession would have meant an acknowledgement of high treason. But his followers might have betrayed him. The two leaders, Agnes Sampson and John Fian, were tortured. Sampson admitted that the wax image was made at the instance of Francis, Earl of Bothwell; an admission sufficiently damning, but beyond that she would say nothing. The real danger to Bothwell lay in Fian. Under torture he made admissions and signed a confession in the presence of the King. He was then

'by the maister of the prison committed to ward, and appointed to a chamber by himselfe; where, foresaking his wicked wayes, acknowledging his most ungodly lyfe, shewing that he had too much folowed the allurements and enticements of Sathan, and fondly practised his conclusions, by conjuring, witchcraft, inchantment, sorcerie, and such like, hee renounced the Devill and all his wicked workes, vowed to lead the lyfe of a Christian, and seemed newly converted to God. The morrow after, upon conference had with him, he granted that the Devill had appeared unto him in the night before, appareled all in blacke, with a white wande in his hande; and that the Devill demaunded of him, "If hee woulde continue his faithfull service, according to his first oath and promise made to that effect": Whome (as hee then saide) he utterly renounced to his face, and said unto him in this manner, "Avoide! Sathan, avoide! for I have listned too much unto thee, and by the same thou hast undone me; in respect whereof I utterly forsake thee". To whome the Devill answered, that "once ere thou die thou shalt bee mine". And with that (as he sayd) the Devill brake the white wand, and immediately vanished foorth of his sight. Thus, all the daie, this Doctor Fian continued verie solitarie, and seemed to have a care of his owne soule, and would call uppon God, showing himselfe penitent for his wicked life; nevertheless, the same night, hee found such meanes that he stole the key of the prison doore and chamber in which he was, which in the night hee opened and fled awaie to the Saltpans, where hee was alwayes resident, and first apprehended. Of whose sodaine departure, when the Kings Majestie had intelligence, hee presently commanded diligent inquirie to bee made for his apprehension; and for the better effecting thereof hee sent publike proclamations into all partes of his lande to the same effect. By means of whose hot and harde pursuite he was agayn taken, and brought to prison; and then, being called before the Kings Highnes, hee was reexamined, as well touching his departure, as also touching all that had before happened. But this Doctor, notwithstanding that his owne confession appeareth, remaining in recorde under his owne hande writting, and the same thereunto fixed in the presence of the Kings Majestie and sundrie of his Councell, yet did hee utterly denie the same. Whereupon the Kings Majestie, perceiving his stubborne wilfulnesse, conceived and imagined, that in the time of his absence, hee had entered into newe conference and league with the Devill his maister'. [Fian was then subjected to the most horrible tortures that could be devised.] 'And notwithstanding all these grievous paines and cruel torments, hee would not confess anie thinges; so deeply had the Devill entered into his heart, that hee utterly denied all that which he before avouched; and would saie nothing thereunto, but this, that what hee had done and sayde before, was onely done and sayde, for fear of paynes which he had endured'.[151]

He continued steadfast and was executed at the Castle Hill.

The character of Fian is perfectly consistent. Under torture he signed a confession, which confession might have implicated Bothwell. That night Bothwell himself, or one of his emissaries,

---

[151] *Newes from Scotland.* Quoted in Pitcairn, i, pt. ii, pp. 213-23.

obtained access to the prisoner and arranged for his escape. The wretched Fian was faced with death either way; if he retracted his confession, he would die as a criminal by the hands of the law; if he held to it, he would die as a traitor by the hands of his comrades. There was no alternative. All that day he 'continued verie solitarie', calling upon God, but by night he had made his choice and fled. He apparently escaped without difficulty. The story of his stealing the keys of his own cell and of the prison door is absurd; the escape was obviously effected by connivance just as later on Bothwell's own escape was effected. Fian went back to his own home, where, according to James's surmise, he had an interview with the Devil (i.e. Bothwell), and there he tamely waited till the officers of the law came and recaptured him. This tameness is not in keeping with the rest of his character. A man with sufficient courage and resource to get out of a strongly guarded prison would have made good his escape; an easy enough matter in those turbulent times. Fian then must have been retaken because he wished to be retaken. For fear of torture and in hope of pardon he signed the first confession, implicating Bothwell,[152] yet later he endured agonies of torture with the certainty of death rather than acknowledge one word which might lead to the discovery that James was bent upon. James's surmise was perhaps more than a mere guess; it was prompted by his knowledge of the facts. Fian had had an interview with his Master, whom he believed to be God Incarnate, and like many a Christian martyr he atoned for the first betrayal by steadfast courage through cruel torment even to death.

Reading the accounts in the light of this supposition, it is seen that every one, including James, suspected Bothwell. Even if they did not acknowledge his divinity, they feared the magical powers which, as Chief of the Witches, he was supposed to wield. It is impossible to study the details of this period without realizing the extraordinary fear which James had of his cousin; it was fear with an underlying horror, totally different from his feeling towards his other turbulent subjects.

---

[152] It is perhaps significant that the confession of John Fian, and the trials of both Barbara Napier and of Bothwell himself for witchcraft, have disappeared from the Justiciary Records.

When Bothwell, seeking pardon, was introduced into Holyrood Palace by Lady Athol in the early morning of July 24, 1593, he entered the King's chamber. James, always undignified, was caught in the middle of his morning toilet; he tried to run into the Queen's room, but the way was barred by Bothwell's friends and the door was locked. 'The king, seeing no other refuge, asked what they meant. Came they to seek his life? let them take it—they would not get his soul.'[153] This remark, made in the urgency and excitement of the moment, is highly significant. Had Bothwell been, like many of James's other enemies, merely an assassin, James would not have spoken of his soul. But Bothwell as the Devil of the witches had the right to demand the yielding of the soul, and James was aware of the fact.

The birth of James's children removed Bothwell's hopes of succession; the power of the witch organization, of which he was the Chief, was broken by the death of its leaders. He had made a strong bid for power, he failed, fled the country, and finally died in poverty at Naples. There George Sandys the traveller heard of him: 'Here a certaine *Calabrian* hearing that I was an *English* man, came to me, and would needs perswade me that I had insight in magicke: for that Earle *Bothel* was my countryman, who liues at *Naples*, and is in those parts famous for suspected negromancie.'[154]

The Devil being actually a human being, the letter of introduction to him, given by a man-witch to a would-be proselyte, becomes quite credible. It is worth quoting verbatim:

'Monseigneur, d'autant qu'il me faut retirer de la Religion des Chrestiens, afin que ie multiplie vostre party, duquel estant, il est raisonnable que ie vous glorifie et assemble tant de gens que ie pourray, ie vous enuoye ce porteur pour estre du nombre: c'est pourquoy ie vous prie de l'aider en ses amours.'

Satan's reply to the novice shows a distinctly human trace of temper:

'Vous autres Chrestiens vous estes perfides et obstinez: Quand vous auez quelque violent desir, vous vous departez de vostre maistre, et

---

[153] Burton, v, p. 283.
[154] Sandys, p. 250.

auez recours à moy: mais quand vostre desir est accompli, vous me tournez le dos comme à vn ennemi, et vous en retournez à vostre Dieu, lequel estant benin et clement, vous pardonne et reçoit volontiers. Mais fay moy vne promesse escrite et signee de ta main, par laquelle tu renonces volontairement ton Christ et ton Baptesme, et me promets que tu adhereras et seras auec moy iusqu'au iour du iugement; et apres iceluy tu te delecteras encore auec moy de souffrir les peines eternelles, et i'accompliray ton desir.'[155]

4. As an Animal

In many religions the disguising of the principal personage—whether god or priest—as an animal is well known. The custom is very ancient—such disguised human beings are found even among the palaeolithic drawings in France; and on a slate palette belonging to the late pre-dynastic period of Egypt there is a representation of a man disguised as a jackal and playing on a pipe.[156] The ritual disguise as an animal is condemned, with great particularity, as devilish, in the *Liber Poenitentialis* of Theodore of the seventh century (see *supra*, p. 21), showing that it continued in force after the conversion of England to an outward appearance of Christianity. From the analogy of other religions in which the custom occurs, it would appear that it is a ritual for the promotion of fertility; the animal represented being either the sacred animal of the tribe or the creature most used for food.

The suggestion that the Devil was a man, wearing either an animal's skin or a mask in the form of an animal's head as a ritual disguise, accounts as nothing else can for the witches' evidence as to his appearance and his changes of form. A confusion, however, exists from the fact that the witches, and therefore the recorders, usually spoke of the familiars as the Devil; but in almost every case the disguised man can, on examination of the evidence, be distinguished from the animal familiar.

---

[155] De Lancre, *Tableau*, pp. 176, 177.
[156] Quibell, pl. xxviii. The palette itself is now in the Ashmolean Museum, Oxford.

The animal forms in which the Devil most commonly appeared were bull, cat, dog, goat, horse, and sheep. A few curious facts come to light on tabulating these forms; i.e. the Devil appears as a goat or a sheep in France only; he is never found in any country as a hare, though this was the traditional form for a witch to assume; nor is he found as a toad, though this was a common form for the familiar; the fox and the ass also are unknown forms; and in Western Europe the pig is an animal almost entirely absent from all the rites and ceremonies as well as from the disguises of the Devil.

The witches never admitted in so many words that the Devil was a man disguised, but their evidence points strongly to the fact. In some cases the whole body was disguised, in others a mask was worn, usually over the face. The wearing of the mask is indicated partly by descriptions of its appearance, and partly by the description of the Devil's voice. The Lorraine witches in 1589 said that the Devils 'können nimmermehr die Menschliche Stimme so aussdrücklich nachreden, dass man nicht leicht daran mercke, dass es eine gemachte falsche Stimme sey. Nicolaea Ganatia, und fast alle andere sagen, dass sie eine Stimme von sich geben, gleich denen, so den Kopff in ein Fass oder zerbrochenen Hafen stecken und daraus reden. Auch geben sie etwann eine kleine leise Stimme von sich.'[157] The North Berwick Devil in 1590 was purposely disguised out of all recognition: 'The Devil start up in the pulpit, like a mickle black man, with a black beard sticking out like a goat's beard; and a high ribbed nose, falling down sharp like the beak of a hawk; with a long rumpill' [tail].[158] This was Barbara Napier's account; Agnes Sampson describes the same personage, 'The deuell caused all the company to com and kiss his ers, quhilk they said was cauld like yce; his body was hard lyk yrn, as they thocht that handled him; his faice was terrible, his noise lyk the bek of an egle, gret bournyng eyn: his handis and legis wer herry, with clawis vpon his handis and feit lyk the griffon, and spak with a how voice.'[159] Boguet states that 'on demanda à George Gandillon, si lors

[157] Remigius, pt. i, p. 38.
[158] Pitcairn, i, pt. ii, p. 246. Spelling modernized.
[159] Melville, p. 395.

qu'il fut sollicité par Satã de se bailler à luy, Satan parloit distinctement. Il respondit que non, & qu'à peine pouuoit il comprendre ce qu'il disoit.'[160] The evidence of the witches in the Basses-Pyrénées makes it clear that a disguise was worn, and that a mask was placed on the back either of the head or of the person; this also explains part of Agnes Sampson's evidence given above. The effect of the mask at the back of the head was to make the man appear two-faced, 'comme le dieu Janus'. In the other case 'le diable estoit en forme de bouc, ayant vne queue, & au-dessoubs vn visage d'homme noir ... & n'a parole par ce visage de derriere.—Vne grande queüe au derriere, & vne forme de visage au dessoubs: duquel visage il ne profere aucune parole, ains luy sert pour donner à baiser à ceux qui bon luy semble.—Marie d'Aspilecute dit qu'elle le baisa à ce visage de derriere au dessoubs d'vne grande queuë; qu'elle l'y a baisé par trois fois, & qu'il auoit ce visage faict comme le museau d'vn bouc.— Bertrand de Handuch, aagee de dix ans, confessa que le cul du grãd maistre auoit vn visage derriere, & c'estoit le visage de derriere qu'on baisoit, & non le cul.'[161] The Devil of the Basses-Pyrénées evidently wore a mask over the face, for he had 'la voix effroyable & sans ton, quand il parle on diroit que cest vn mullet qui se met à braire, il a la voix casse, la parole malarticulee, & peu intelligible, parcequ'il a tousiours la voix triste & enroüee'. On occasions also 'il quitoit la forme de Bouc, & prenoit celle d'homme'.[162] In 1614 at Orleans Silvain Nevillon said 'qu'il vit à la cheminée vn homme noir duquel on ne voyoit pas la teste. Vit aussi vn grand homme noir à l'opposite de celuy de la cheminée, & que ledit hoᵐe noir parloit comme si la voix fut sortie d'vn poinson. Dit: Que le Diable dit le Sermõ au Sabbat, mais qu'on n'entend ce qu'il dit, parce qu'il parle coᵐe en grõdant.'[163] The devil who appeared to Joan Wallis, the Huntingdonshire witch, in 1649, was in the shape of a man dressed in black, but he 'was not as her husband, which speaks to her like a man,

---

[160] Boguet, p. 56.
[161] De Lancre, *Tableau*, pp. 68, 73, 126.
[162] De Lancre, *Tableau*, pp. 225, 398.
[163] Id., *L'Incredulité*, pp. 799-801.

but he as he had been some distance from her when he was with her'.[164] Thomazine Ratcliffe, a Suffolk witch, said that the Devil 'spoke with a hollow, shrill voyce'.[165] According to Mary Green (1665) the Somerset Devil, who was a little man, 'put his hand to his Hat, saying, How do ye? speaking low but big'.[166] In the same year Abre Grinset, another Suffolk witch, confessed that she met the Devil, who was in the form of 'a Pretty handsom Young Man, and spake to her with a hollow Solemn Voice'.[167] John Stuart at Paisley (1678) said the Devil came to him as a black man, 'and that the black man's Apparel was black; and that the black man's Voice was hough and goustie'.[168]

The coldness of the devil's entire person, which is vouched for by several witches, suggests that the ritual disguise was not merely a mask over the face, but included a covering, possibly of leather or some other hard and cold substance, over the whole body and even the hands. Such a disguise was apparently not always worn, for in the great majority of cases there is no record of the Devil's temperature except in the sexual rites, and even then the witch could not always say whether the touch of the Devil was warm or not. In 1565 the Belgian witch, Digna Robert, said the devil 'était froid dans tous ses membres'.[169] In 1590, at North Berwick, 'he caused all the company to com and kiss his ers, quhilk they said was cauld lyk yce; his body was hard lyk yrn, as they thocht that handled him'.[170] In 1598 Pierre Burgot, whose statement is quoted by several authors, 'a confessé, que le Diable luy donna à baiser sa main senestre, qui estoit noire, comme morte, & toute froide'.[171] In 1609, in the Basses-Pyrénées, Isaac de Queyran, aged 25, said that he and others 'le baiserent à vne fesse qui estoit blanche & rouge, & auoit la forme d'vne grande cuisse d'vn

---

[164] Stearne, p. 13.
[165] Id., p. 22.
[166] Glanvil, pt. ii, p. 164.
[167] Petto, p. 18.
[168] Glanvil, pt. ii, pp. 294-5.
[169] Cannaert, p. 54.
[170] Melville, *Memoirs*, p. 395.
[171] Boguet, pp. 53-4.

homme, & estoit velue'.[172] This shows the ritual disguise of the person and suggests the use of an animal's hide with the hair still attached. In 1645 the Essex witch Rebecca West said 'he kissed her, but was as cold as clay'.[173] At Salisbury in 1653, when the witch Anne Bodenham persuaded Anne Styles to join the community, 'then appeared two Spirits in the likenesse of great Boyes, with long shagged black hair, and stood by her looking over her shoulder, and the Witch took the Maids forefinger of her right hand, and pricked it with a pin, and squeezed out the blood and put it into a Pen, and put the Pen in the Maids hand, and held her hand to write in a great book, and one of the Spirits laid his hand or Claw upon the Witches whilest the Maid wrote; and the Spirits hand did feel cold to the Maid as it touched her hand, when the witches hand and hers were together writing'.[174] At Forfar in 1661 three of the witches agreed as to the coldness of the Devil; 'Elspet Alexander confesses that the divill kissed hir selfe that night and that it was ane cold kisse; Katheren Porter confesseth that the divill tooke hir by the hand, that his hand was cold; Isobell Smith confessed that he kissed hir and his mouth and breath were cold.'[175] In 1662 the Crook of Devon witches were also in accord. Isabel Rutherford 'confesst that ye was at ane meeting at Turfhills, where Sathan took you by the hand and said "welcome, Isabel", and said that his hand was cold.—Margaret Litster confessed that Sathan took you be the hand and stayed the space of half an hour, Sathan having grey clothes and his hand cold.—Janet Paton confessed that Sathan asked you gif ye would be his servant, whilk ye did, and Sathan took you be the hand, and ye said that his hand was cold.' On the other hand Agnes Murie 'knew not whether his body was hot or cold'.[176] According to Isobel Gowdie at Auldearne in 1662, 'he was a meikle blak roch man, werie cold';[177] at Torryburn, Lilias Adie found his skin was

---

[172] De Lancre, *Tableau*, p. 148.

[173] Howell, iv, 842.

[174] More, pp. 196-7.

[175] Kinloch, pp. 115, 129, 132.

[176] Burns Begg, pp. 219, 221, 228, 230.

[177] Pitcairn, iii, p. 603.

cold;[178] and the Crighton witches in 1678 said, 'he was cold, and his breath was like a damp air'.[179] In 1697 little Thomas Lindsay declared that 'Jean Fulton his Grand-mother awaked him one Night out of his Bed, and caused him take a Black Grimm Gentleman (as she called him) by the Hand; which he felt to be cold'.[180]

The evidence as to the forms assumed by the Devil is tabulated here under each animal, each section being arranged in chronological order.

1. *Bull.*—In 1593 at Angers 'Michel des Rousseaux, agé de 50 ans, dict que ledict homme noir appellé Iupin se transforma aussitost en Bouc ... et apres leur auoir baillé des boüetes de poudre, il se trãsforma en Bouuard'.[181] At Aberdeen in 1597 Marion Grant confessed that 'the Devill apperit to the, sumtyme in the scheap of a beist, and sumtyme in the scheap of a man'. Jonet Lucas of the same Coven said that the Devil was with them, 'beand in likenes of ane beist'. Agnes Wobster, also of the same Coven, acknowledged that 'thaireftir Satan apperit to the in the likenes of a calff, and spak to the in manner forsaid, and baid the be a gude servand to him'.[182] In 1608 Gabriel Pellé confessed that he went with a friend to the Sabbath, where 'le Diable estoit en vache noire, & que cette vache noire luy fit renoncer Dieu'.[183] De Lancre says that at Tournelle the Devil appeared 'parfois comme vn grand Bœuf d'airain couché à terre, comme vn Bœuf naturel qui se repose'.[184] At Lille in 1661 the witches 'adored a beast with which they committed infamous things'.[185] According to Isobel Gowdie in 1662, the Devil of Auldearne changed his form, or disguise, continually, 'somtym he vold be lyk a stirk, a bull, a deir, a rae, or a dowg'.[186] [In the above, I have taken the word 'beast' in its usual meaning as an animal of the cattle tribe, but it is quite possible that the Lille

---

[178] Chambers, iii, 298.
[179] Fountainhall, i, p. 14.
[180] *Narrative of the Sufferings of a Young Girle*, p. xli; *Sadd. Debell.*, p. 40.
[181] De Lancre, *L'Incredulité*, p. 769.
[182] *Spalding Club Misc.*, i, p. 129.
[183] De Lancre, *L'Incredulité*, p. 794.
[184] Id., *Tableau*, p. 68.
[185] Bourignon, *Parole*, p. 87; Hale, p. 26.
[186] Pitcairn, iii, p. 613.

beast, *beste* in the original, may have been a goat and not a bull. This seems likely from the fact that the sacrifice was by fire as in the other places where the Devil used the goat-disguise.]

2. *Cat.*—The earliest example of the cat-disguise is in the trial of the Guernsey witches in 1563, when Martin Tulouff confessed:

'q̄ il y a viron ung quartier d'an passez q̄ il soy trouva auvecq̄s la Vieillesse aultremẽt dit Collenette Gascoing, en la rue de la fosse au Coully, là ou l y avoet chinq ou vi chatz, d'ou il y en avoet ung qui estoet noir, qui menoit la dance, et danssoient et luy dyst lad^te Collenette, q̄ il besait led^t Chat et d^t q̄ il estoet sur ses pieds plat, et que ladite Collenette le besa p de derriere, et luy p la crysse, et q̄ frãcoize Lenouff sa mère y estoet et Collette Salmon fae de Collas du port, laqlle alloet devãt et s'agenouillerent to^s devãt le Chat et l'adorerẽt en luy baillãt le^r foy, et luy dist ladite Vieillesse q̄ ledit Chat estoet le diable.'[187]

Françoise Secretain, in 1598, saw the Devil 'tantost en forme de chat'. Rolande de Vernois said, 'Le Diable se presenta pour lors au Sabbat en forme d'vn groz chat noir.'[188] In 1652 another French witch confessed that 'il entra dans sa chambre en forme d'ung chat et se changea en la posture d'un home vestu de rouge', who took her to the Sabbath.[189] Both the Devonshire witches, Mary Trembles and Susanna Edwards, in 1682, stated that they saw him as a lion, by which they possibly meant a large cat.[190] In this connexion it is worth noting that in Lapland as late as 1767 the devil appeared 'in the likeness of a cat, handling them from their feet to their mouth, and counting their teeth'.[191]

3. *Dog.*—At Chelmsford in 1556 Joan Waterhouse 'dydde as she had seene her mother doe, callynge Sathan, whiche came to her (as she sayd) in the lykenes of a great dogge'.[192] In 1616 Barthélemy Minguet of Brécy was tried for witchcraft. 'Enquis, comme il a aduis

---

[187] From a trial in the Guernsey Greffe.
[188] Boguet, pp. 8, 70, 411.
[189] *La Tradition*, v (1891), p. 215.
[190] Howell, viii, 1034, 1036.
[191] Pinkerton, i, p. 473.
[192] *Witches of Chelmsford*, p. 34; Philobiblon Soc., viii.

quand le Sabbat se doit tenir. Respond, que c'est le Diable qui luy vient dire estant en forme de chien noir, faict comme vn barbet, parle à luy en ceste forme. Enquis, en quelle forme se met le Diable estant au Sabbat. Respond, qu'il ne l'a iamais veu autrement qu'en forme de barbet noir. Enquis, quelles ceremonies ils obseruent estant au Sabbat. Respond, que le Diable estant en forme de barbet noir (comme dessus est dit) se met tout droit sur les pattes de derriere, les preche'.[193] etc. In Guernsey in 1617 Isabel Becquet went to Rocquaine Castle, 'the usual place where the Devil kept his Sabbath; no sooner had she arrived there than the Devil came to her in the form of a dog, with two great horns sticking up: and with one of his paws (which seemed to her like hands) took her by the hand: and calling her by her name told her that she was welcome: then immediately the Devil made her kneel down: while he himself stood up on his hind legs; he then made her express detestation of the Eternal in these words: *I renounce God the Father, God the Son, and God the Holy Ghost*; and then caused her to worship and invoke himself.'[194] Barton's wife, about 1655, stated that 'one Night going to a dancing upon Pentland-hills, he went before us in the likeness of a rough tanny-Dog, playing on a pair of Pipes, and his tail played ey wig wag wig wag'.[195] In 1658 an Alloa witch named Jonet Blak declared that he appeared to her first as 'a dog with a sowis head'.[196] In 1661 Jonet Watson of Dalkeith said that 'the Deivill apeired vnto her, in the liknes of ane prettie boy, in grein clothes, and went away from her in the likns of ane blak doug'.[197] According to Marie Lamont of Innerkip in 1662, 'the devill in the likeness of a brown dog' helped to raise a storm.[198] Margaret Hamilton, widow of James Pullwart of Borrowstowness in 1679, was accused that she met 'the devil in the likeness of a man, but he removed from you in the likeness of an black dog'.[199] The Highland witches in the eighteenth

---

[193] De Lancre, *L'Incredulité*, p. 805.
[194] Goldsmid, p. 12.
[195] Sinclair, p. 163.
[196] *Scottish Antiquary*, ix, 51.
[197] Pitcairn, iii, p. 601.
[198] Sharpe, p. 132.
[199] *Scots Magazine*, 1814, p. 201. Spelling modernized.

century saw the devil as a dog; he was 'a large black ugly tyke', to whom the witches made obeisance; the dog acknowledged the homage 'by bowing, grinning, and clapping his paws'.[200] In the case of the dog-disguise, there is again a similarity with Lapp beliefs and customs, the appearance of the Devil as a dog being not uncommon in Lapland.[201]

4. *Goat.*—An interesting point as regards this form of disguise is that it does not occur in Great Britain, nor have I found it so far in Belgium. It prevailed chiefly in France, from which all my examples are taken. At Poictiers in 1574 'trois Sorciers & vne Sorciere declarent qu'ils estoyent trois fois l'an, à l'assemblée generale, où plusieurs Sorciers se trouuoyent prés d'vne croix d'vn carrefour, qui seruoit d'enseigne. Et là se trouuoit vn grand bouc noir, qui parloit comme vne personne aux assistans, & dansoyent à l'entour du bouc.'[202] At Avignon in 1581 'when hee comes to be adored, he appeareth not in a humane forme, but as the Witches themselues haue deposed, as soone as they are agreed of the time that he is to mount vpon the altar (which is some rock or great stone in the fields) there to bee worshipped by them, hee instantly turneth himselfe into the forme of a great black Goate, although in all other occasions hee vseth to appeare in the shape of a man.[203] In Lorraine in 1589 the Devil 'sich in einen zottelichten Bock verwandelt hat, und viel stärker reucht und übeler stinckt als immer ein Bock im Anfang des Frühlings thun mag'.[204] In Puy de Dôme in 1594 Jane Bosdeau's lover took her to a meeting, and 'there appeared a great Black Goat with a Candle between his Horns'.[205] In 1598 'Satan apres auoir prins la figure d'vn Bouc, se consume en feu'.[206] In the Basses-Pyrénées in 1609:

---

[200] Stewart, p. 175. The whole account is marred by the would-be comic style adopted by the author.

[201] Pinkerton, i, p. 473.

[202] Bodin, p. 187.

[203] Michaelis, *Discourse*, p. 148.

[204] Remigius, pt. i, p. 90.

[205] F. Hutchinson, *Historical Essay*, p. 42.

[206] Boguet, p. 141.

'le Diable estoit en forme de bouc, ayant vne queue, & au-dessoubs vn visage d'homme noir, & n'a parole par ce visage de derriere.—Marie d'Aguerre dit qu'il y a vne grande cruche au milieu du Sabbat, d'où sort le Diable en forme de bouc.—D'autres disent qu'il est comme vn grand bouc, ayant deux cornes devant & deux en derriere; que celles de devant se rebrassent en haut comme la perruque d'vne femme. Mais le commun est qu'il a seulement trois cornes, & qu'il a quelque espece de lumiere en celle du milieu. On luy voit aussi quelque espece de bonet ou chapeau au dessus de ces cornes. On a obserué de tout temps que lorsqu'il veut receuoir quelcun à faire pacte auec luy, il se presente tousiours en homme, pour ne l'effaroucher ou effraier: car faire pacte auec vn Bouc ouuertement, tiendroit plus de la beste que de la creature raisonnable. Mais le pacte faict, lors qu'il veut receuoir quelqu'vn à l'adoration, communemẽt il se represente en Bouc.'[207]

Silvain Nevillon confessed at Orleans in 1614 'qu'il a veu le Diable en plusieurs façons, tantost comme vn bouc, ayant vn visage deuant & vn autre derriere'.[208]

5. *Horse.*—I give here only the references to the Devil when actually disguised as a horse, but there are a very great number of cases where he appeared riding on a horse. These cases are so numerous as to suggest that the horse was part of the ritual, especially as the riding Devil usually occurs in places where an animal disguise was not used, e.g. in 1598, in Aberdeen, where Andro Man 'confessis that Crystsunday rydis all the tyme that he is in thair cumpanie'.[209] The actual disguise as a horse is not common. Elizabeth Stile of Windsor in 1579 'confesseth, her self often tymes to haue gon to Father Rosimond house where she found hym sittyng in a Wood, not farre from thence, vnder the bodie of a Tree, sometymes in the shape of an Ape, and otherwhiles like an Horse'.[210] Helen Guthrie in 1661 stated that when the Forfar witches were trying to sink a ship, 'the divell wes

---

[207] De Lancre, *Tableau*, pp. 67, 68, 69, 126.

[208] Id., *L'Incredulité*, p. 800.

[209] *Spalding Club Misc.*, i, p. 125. Cp. Elworthy on the Hobby-horse as the Devil, *Horns of Honour*, p. 140.

[210] *Rehearsall both Straung and True*, par. 24.

there present with them all, in the shape of ane great horse. They returned all in the same liknes as of befor, except that the divell wes in the shape of a man.'[211] Mary Lacey of Salem in 1692 said that he appeared in the shape of a horse. 'I was in bed and the devil came to me and bid me obey him.'[212]

6. *Sheep.*—The sheep-disguise, which is perhaps a form of the goat, is usually found in France only. In 1453 'Guillaume Edeline, docteur en théologie, prieur de S. Germain en Laye, et auparavant Augustin, et religieux de certaines aultres ordres ... confessa, de sa bonne et franche voulonté, avoir fait hommage audit ennemy en l'espèce et semblance d'ung mouton'.[213] Iaquema Paget and Antoine Gandillon in 1598 said that 'il prenoit la figure d'vn mouton noir, portant des cornes'.[214] In 1614 at Orleans Silvain Nevillon was induced to reveal all he knew; 'dit qu'il a veu le Diable en plusieurs façons, tantost comme vn bouc, ores comme vn gros mouton'.[215]

The rarer animal disguises are the deer and the bear. Of these the deer is found at Aberdeen in 1597, Andro Man 'confessis and affermis, thow saw Christsonday cum owt of the snaw in liknes of a staig';[216] at Auldearne in 1662, 'somtym he vold be lyk a stirk, a bull, a deir, a rae, or a dowg';[217] at Hartford, Connecticut, 1662, Rebecca Greensmith said that 'the devil first appeared to her in the form of a deer or fawn'.[218] The bear is still rarer, as I have found it only twice—once in Lorraine, and once in Lancashire. In 1589 'es haben die Geister auch etwann Lust sich in Gestalt eines Bären zu erzeigen'.[219] In 1613 Anne Chattox declared that the Devil 'came vpon this Examinate in the night time: and at diuerse and sundry times in the likenesse of a Beare, gaping as though he would haue wearied [worried] this Examinate.

---

[211] Kinloch, pp. 122-3.
[212] Howell, vi, 663-4; J. Hutchinson, ii, pp. 36-7.
[213] Chartier, iii, 44-5.
[214] Boguet, p. 70.
[215] De Lancre, *L'Incredulité*, p. 800.
[216] *Spalding Club Misc.*, i, p. 121.
[217] Pitcairn, iii, p. 613.
[218] Taylor, p. 98.
[219] Remigius, p. 98.

And the last time of all shee, this Examinate, saw him, was vpon Thursday last yeare but one, next before Midsummer day, in the euening, like a Beare, and this Examinate would not then speake vnto him, for the which the said Deuill pulled this Examinate downe.'[220]

---

[220] Potts, E 3.

III. ADMISSION CEREMONIES

1. General

In the ceremonies for admission, as in all the other ceremonies of the cult, the essentials are the same in every community and country, though the details differ. The two points which are the essence of the ceremony are invariable: the first, that the candidates must join of their own free will and without compulsion; the second, that they devote themselves, body and soul, to the Master and his service.

The ceremonies of admission differed also according to whether the candidate were a child or an adult. The most complete record of the admission of children comes from the Basses-Pyrénées in 1609:

'Les Sorcieres luy offrêt des petits enfans le genoüil en terre, lui disant auec vne soubmission, *Grand seigneur, lequel i'adore, ie vous ameine ce nouueau seruiteur, lequel veut estre perpetuellement vostre esclaue*: Et le Diable en signe de remerciement & gratification leur respond, *Approchez vous de moy*: à quoy obeissant, elles en se trainant à genouil, le luy presentent, & luy receuant l'enfant entre ses bras, le rend à la Sorciere, la remercie, & puis luy recommande d'en auoir soing, leur disant par ce moyen sa troupe s'augmentera. Que si les enfans ayans attainct l'aage de neuf ans, par malheur se voüent au Diable sans estre forcez ny violentez d'aucun Sorcier, ils se prosternent par terre deuant Satan: lequel iettant du feu par les yeux, leur dit, Que demandez vous, voulez vous estre à moy? ils respondent qu'ouy, il leur dict, Venez vous de vostre bonne volonté? ils respondent qu'ouy, Faictes donc ce que ie veux, & ce que ie fay. Et alors la grande maistresse & Royne du Sabbat qui leur sert de pedagogue, dict à ce nouueau qui se presente, qu'il die à haute voix, *Ie renie Dieu premierement, puis Iesus Christ son Fils, le S. Esprit, la vierge, les Saincts, la Saincte Croix, le Chresme, le Baptesme, & la Foy que ie tiens, mes Parrain & Marraine, & me remets de tout poinct en ton pouuoir & entre tes mains, ne recognois autre Dieu: si bien que tu es mon Dieu & ie suis ton esclaue*. Aprés on luy baille vn crapaud habillé auec son capot ou manteau, puis il commande qu'on l'adore; si bien qu'obeyssans & estants mis à genouil, ils baisent le Diable auprés de l'œil gauche, à la poitrine, à la fesse, à la cuisse, & aux parties honteuses, puis leuant la queue ils luy baisent le derriere.'[221]

The novice was then marked by a scratch from a sharp instrument, but was not admitted to the 'high mysteries' till about the age of twenty.[222] As no further ceremonies are mentioned, it may be concluded that the initiation into these mysteries was performed by degrees and without any special rites.

At Lille, about the middle of the seventeenth century, Madame Bourignon founded a home for girls of the lowest classes, 'pauvres et mal-originées, la plus part si ignorantes au fait de leur salut qu'elles vivoient comme des bêtes'.[223] After a few years, in 1661, she discovered that thirty-two of these girls were worshippers of the Devil, and in the habit of going to the Witches' Sabbaths. They 'had all contracted this Mischief before they came into the House'.[224] One of these girls named Bellot, aged fifteen, said 'that her Mother had taken her with her when she was very Young, and had even carried her in her Arms to the Witches Sabbaths'.[225] Another girl of twelve had been in the habit of going to the Sabbath since she also was 'very Young'. As the girls seem to have been genuinely fond of Madame Bourignon, she obtained a considerable amount of information from them. They told her that all worshippers of the Devil 'are constrained to offer him their Children. When a child thus offered to the Devil by its Parents, comes to the use of Reason, the Devil then demands its Soul, and makes it deny God and renounce Baptism, and all relating to the Faith, promising Homage and Fealty to the Devil in manner of a Marriage, and instead of a Ring, the Devil gives them a Mark with an iron awl [aleine de fer] in some part of the Body.'[226]

---

[221] De Lancre, *Tableau*, p. 398.

[222] Id. ib., p. 145.

[223] Bourignon, *Vie*, p. 201.

[224] Id., *Parole*, p. 85; Hale, p. 26.

[225] Id., *Vie*, p. 211; Hale, p. 29.

[226] Id. ib., p. 223; Hale, p. 37.

It is also clear that Marguerite Montvoisin[227] in Paris had been instructed in witchcraft from an early age; but as the trial in which she figures was for the attempted poisoning of the king and not for witchcraft, no ceremonies of initiation or admission are recorded.

In Great Britain the ceremonies for the reception of children are not given in any detail, though it was generally acknowledged that the witches dedicated their children to the Devil as soon as born; and from the evidence it appears that in many cases the witches had belonged to that religion all their lives. It was sometimes sufficient evidence against a woman that her mother had been a witch,[228] as it presupposed that she had been brought up as a worshipper of the Devil.

The Anderson children in Renfrewshire were all admitted to the society at an early age.[229] Elizabeth Anderson was only seven when she was first asked to swear fealty to the 'black grim Man.' James Lindsay was under fourteen, and his little brother Thomas was still 'below pupillarity' at the time of the trial, where he declared that he had been bribed, by the promise of a red coat, to serve 'the Gentleman, whom he knew thereafter to be the Devil'.[230] At Forfar in 1661, Jonet Howat was so young that when Isabel Syrie 'presented hir to the divell, the divell said, What shall I do with such a little bairn as she?' He accepted her, however, and she was evidently the pet of the community, the Devil calling her 'his bonny bird'.[231] At Paisley, Annabil Stuart was fourteen when, at her mother's persuasion, she took the vows of fidelity to the Devil.[232]

Elizabeth Frances at Chelmsford (tried in 1556) was about twelve years old when her grandmother first taught her the art of witchcraft.[233] Elizabeth Demdike, the famous Lancashire witch, 'brought vp her owne Children, instructed her Graund-children, and

---

[227] Ravaisson (the years 1679-81).
[228] Reg. Scot., Bk. II, p. 36 (quoting from *C. Agrippa*).
[229] *Narrative of the Sufferings of a Young Girle*, p. xxxix.
[230] Ib., pp. xl, xli.
[231] Kinloch, pp. 124, 125.
[232] Glanvil, ii, p. 291.
[233] Philobiblon Society, viii, p. 24.

tooke great care and paines to bring them to be Witches'.[234] One of her granddaughters, Jennet Device, was aged nine at the time of the trial.

In Sweden the children were taken regularly to the assemblies,[235] and in America[236] also a child-witch is recorded in the person of Sarah Carrier, aged eight, who had made her vows two years before at her mother's instigation.

The ceremony for the admission of adults who were converts to the witch religion from Christianity follow certain main lines. These are (1) the free consent of the candidate, (2) the explicit denial and rejection of a previous religion, (3) the absolute and entire dedication of body and soul to the service and commands of the new Master and God.

The ceremonies being more startling and dramatic for adults than for children, they are recorded in Great Britain with the same careful detail as in France, and it is possible to trace the local variations; although in England, as is usual, the ceremonies had lost their significance to a far greater extent than in Scotland, and are described more shortly, probably because they were more curtailed.

The legal aspect of the admission ceremonies is well expressed by Sir George Mackenzie, writing in 1699 on the Scotch laws relating to witchcraft in the seventeenth century:

'As to the relevancy of this Crime, the first Article useth to be *paction* to serve the Devil, which is certainly relevant, *per se*, without any addition.... Paction with the Devil is divided by Lawyers, in *expressum, & tacitum*, an express and tacit Paction. Express Paction is performed either by a formal Promise given to the Devil then present, or by presenting a Supplication to him, or by giving the promise to a Proxie or Commissioner impowered by the Devil for that effect, which is used by some who dare not see himself. The *Formula* set down by *Delrio*, is, *I deny God Creator of Heaven and Earth, and I adhere to thee, and believe in thee.* But by the Journal Books it appears, that the ordinary Form of express Paction confest by

---

[234] Potts, B 2.
[235] Horneck, pt. ii., pp. 317-20.
[236] Howell, vi, 669; J. Hutchinson, *Hist. of Massachusetts*, ii, p. 44.

our Witness, is a simple Promise to serve him. Tacit Paction is either when a person who hath made no express Paction, useth the Words or Signs which Sorcerers use, knowing them to be such.... Renouncing of Baptism is by *Delrio* made an effect of Paction, yet with us it is relevant, *per se* ... and the Solemnity confest by our Witches, is the putting one hand to the crown of the Head, and another to the sole of the Foot, renouncing their Baptism in that posture. *Delrio* tells us, that the Devil useth to Baptize them of new, and to wipe off their Brow the old Baptism: And our Witches confess always the giving them new Names.... The Devil's Mark useth to be a great Article with us, but it is not *per se* found relevant, except it be confest by them, that they got that Mark with their own consent; *quo casu*, it is equivalent to a Paction. This Mark is given them, as is alledg'd, by a Nip in any part of the body, and it is blew.'[237]

Reginald Scot,[238] writing considerably earlier, gives a somewhat similar account of the English witches, though couched in less legal phraseology:

'The order of their bargaine or profession is double; the one solemne and publike; the other secret and priuate. That which is called solemne or publike, is where witches come togither at certeine assemblies, at the times prefixed, and doo not onelie see the diuell in visible forme; but confer and talke familiarlie with him. In which conference the diuell exhorteth them to obserue their fidelitie vnto him, promising them long life and prosperitie. Then the witches assembled, commend a new disciple (whom they call a nouice) vnto him: and if the diuell find that yoong witch apt and forward in renunciation of christian faith, in despising anie of the seuen sacraments, in treading upon crosses, in spetting at the time of eleuation, in breaking their fast on fasting daies, and fasting on sundaies; then the diuell giueth foorth his hand, and the nouice joining hand in hand with him, promiseth to obserue and keepe all the diuell's commandements. This done, the diuell beginneth to be more bold with hir, telling hir plainlie that all this will not serue his turne; and therefore requireth homage at hir

---

[237] Mackenzie, Title x, pp. 47, 48.
[238] Reginald Scot, Bk. III, pp. 40-2.

hands: yea, he also telleth hir, that she must grant him both hir bodie and soule to be tormented in euerlasting fire: which she yeeldeth vnto. Then he chargeth hir, to procure as manie men, women, and children also, as she can, to enter into this societie.... Sometimes their homage with their oth and bargaine is receiued for a certeine terme of yeares; sometimes for euer. Sometimes it consisteth in the deniall of the whole faith, sometimes in part. The first is, when the soule is absolutelie yeelded to the diuell and hell-fier: the other is, when they haue but bargained not to obserue certeine ceremonies and statutes of the church; as to conceale faults at shrift, to fast on sundaies, etc. And this is doone either by oth, protestation of words, or by obligation in writing, sometimes sealed with wax, sometimes signed with bloud.'

Forbes says that

'an express Covenant is entred into betwixt a Witch, and the Devil appearing in some visible Shape. Whereby the former renounceth God and his Baptism, engages to serve the Devil, and do all the Mischief he can as Occasion offers, and leaves Soul and Body to his Disposal after Death. The Devil on his part articles with such Proselytes, concerning the Shape he is to appear to them in, the Services they are to expect from him, upon the Performance of certain Charms or ceremonious Rites. This League is made verbally, if the Party cannot write. And such as can write, sign a written Covenant with their Blood.'[239]

The general order of the ceremony of admission can be gathered from the evidence given at the trials, though no one trial gives the order in its entirety. The ceremony might take place privately, at a local meeting, or in full Sabbath; it was the same for either sex, except that the men were not usually introduced, the women were sometimes introduced, sometimes not. If there were any sort of introduction, it was by some one who was acquainted with the candidate; usually the person who had induced her to join. She was brought before the Devil, who asked her if she would be his faithful servant, and if she would renounce her previous religion, and dedicate herself to his service, taking him as her God. After the renunciation and vows, the Devil

---

[239] W. Forbes, ii, 33, ed. 1730.

baptized her in his own great name, and among the Scotch witches gave her a new name by which she was known afterwards at the Sabbaths and other meetings. The ceremony concluded by giving the witch a mark or 'flesh-brand' on some part of the body.

2. The Introduction

It is not clear whether the introduction of a candidate by a member of the society was an early or a late detail. It is quite possible that it was early, the introducer standing in the same relation to the candidate as the Christian sponsors stand to a candidate for baptism. On the other hand, it is quite comprehensible that, when the witch religion became an object of persecution, no new member could be admitted unless vouched for by some trustworthy person. In the cases where the first meetings with the Devil are recorded, both systems are apparently in vogue. Occasionally, however, the accounts show a confusion on the part of the recorder. Thus Anne Chattox said that Mother Demdike introduced her to the Devil in Mother Demdike's own house, and that she there yielded her soul to him; and in another place she is reported as saying that 'a thing like a Christian man, for foure yeares togeather, did sundry times come to this Examinate, and requested this Examinate to giue him her Soule: And in the end, this Examinate was contented to giue him her sayd Soule, shee being then in her owne house, in the Forrest of Pendle.'[240] The two statements are not inconsistent if we conclude that in her own house she consented to join the society, and in Mother Demdike's presence she took the vows. As a rule the men seem to have joined at the direct invitation of the Devil himself, especially when they came of witch families.

3. The Renunciation and Vows

The renunciation of previous errors of faith and the vows of fidelity to the new belief are part of the ceremony of admission of any convert to a new religion. The renunciation by the witches was explicit, but

---

[240] Potts, B 4, D 3.

the records are apt to pass it over in a few words, e.g. 'I denied my baptism,' 'I forsook God and Christ,' 'Ils renient Dieu, la Vierge, et le reste,' 'Vne renonciation expresse à Iesu-Christ & à la foy'; but occasionally the words are given in full. Mackenzie, quoting from Del Rio, gives the formula thus: 'I deny God Creator of Heaven and Earth, and I adhere to thee, and believe in thee.'[241] The actual formula is still extant in the case of the priest Louis Gaufredy, tried before the Parliament of Aix in 1611:

'Ie Louys Gaufredy renonce à tous les biens tant spirituels que corporels qui me pourroyent estre conferez de la part de Dieu, de la vierge Marie & de tous les Saincts de Paradis, pareillement de mon patron S. Iean Baptiste, S. Pierre, S. Paul, & S. François, & de me donner de corps & d'ame à Lucifericy present auec tous les biens que ie feray à iamais: excepté la valeur du Sacrement pour le regard de ceux qui le recevront: Et ainsi le signe et atteste.'[242]

Jeannette d'Abadie, aged sixteen, said that she was made to 'renoncer & renier son Createur, la saincte Vierge, les Saincts, le Baptesme, pere, mere, parens, le ciel, la terre & tout ce qui est au monde'.[243] The irrevocability of this renunciation was impressed upon the Swedish witches in a very dramatic manner: 'The Devil gave them a Purse, wherein there were shavings of Clocks with a Stone tied to it, which they threw into the water, and then were forced to speak these words: *As these Shavings of the Clock do never return to the Clock from which they are taken, so may my Soul never return to Heaven.*'[244]

The vows to the new God were as explicit as the renunciation of the old. Danaeus says, 'He commaundeth them to forswere God theyr creator and all his power, promising perpetually to obey and worship him, who there standeth in their presence.'[245] The English witches merely took the vow of fealty and obedience, devoting themselves body and soul to him; sometimes only the soul, however, is

---

[241] Mackenzie, p. 47, ed. 1699.
[242] De Lancre, *Tableau*, p. 182.
[243] Id. ib., p. 131.
[244] Horneck, pt. ii, p. 322.
[245] Danaeus, ch. ii, E 1.

mentioned: but the Scotch witches of both sexes laid one hand on the crown of the head, the other on the sole of the foot, and dedicated all that was between the two hands to the service of the Master.[246] There is a slight variation of this ceremony at Dalkeith in 1661, where the Devil laid his hand upon Jonet Watson's head, 'and bad her "give all ower to him that was vnder his hand", and shoe did so'.[247]

In Southern France the candidates, after renouncing their old faith, 'prennent Satan pour leur pere et protecteur, & la Diablesse pour leur mere'.[248] At Lille the children called the ceremony the Dedication,[249] showing that the same rite obtained there.

4. The Covenant

The signing of a covenant does not occur in every case and was probably a late introduction. Forbes, as quoted above, gives the contract between the Devil and his follower, with the part which each engages to perform. In Somerset the witches signed whether they could write or not, those who could not write putting a cross or circle as their mark.[250]

The free consent of the candidate is a point always insisted on, and by the confessions of the witches themselves the consent was often not merely freely but actually willingly given. Isobel Crawford of the Irvine Coven in 1618 was accused that the devil 'come to hir awin dur in similitud of ane blak man, and prommeist, gif sche wold be his servand, sche sould have geir aneuch, and sould not want. Quhairunto sche was ever reddy to accord.'[251] Little Jonet Howat said that the Devil 'bade her renounce her God, and she answered, Marry, shall I'.[252] In the dittay against Christian Grieve, it is stated that 'Sathan

---

[246] Lord Fountainhall mentions a case where a pregnant woman excepted the unborn child, at which the devil was very angry. *Decisions*, i, p. 14.
[247] Pitcairn, iii, p. 601.
[248] De Lancre, *Tableau*, p. 123.
[249] Bourignon, *Vie*, p. 214; Hale, p. 31.
[250] Glanvil, ii, pp. 136, 148.
[251] *Isobel Inch*, p. 16.
[252] Kinloch, p. 125. Spelling modernized.

desired you to be his servant whilk ye willingly granted to be.... And sicklike the minister posing you upon the foresaid particulars especially anent the renunciation of your Baptism, ye answered that Sathan speired at you if ye would do it and ye answered "I warrand did I."'[253] Bessie Henderson and Janet Brugh, of the same Coven, acknowledged the same. To the former 'the Devil appeared and asked you gif you would be his servant whilk ye freely and instantly accepted and granted thereto'.[254] Janet Brugh was rather more emphatic: 'Sathan desired you to be his servant whilk ye willingly promised to be and likeways desired you to renounce your baptism whilk ye willingly did.'[255]

The written contract appealed very strongly to the legal minds of the judges and magistrates, and it is therefore often mentioned, but in Great Britain there is no record of the actual wording of any individual covenant; the Devil seems to have kept the parchment, paper, or book in his own custody. In France, however, such contracts occasionally fell into the hands of the authorities; the earliest case being in 1453, when Guillaume Edeline, Prior of St. Germain-en-Laye, signed a compact with the Devil, which compact was afterwards found upon his person.[256] The witch Stevenote de Audebert, who was burnt in January 1619, showed de Lancre 'le pacte & conuention qu'elle auoit faict auec le Diable, escrite en sang de menstruës, & si horrible qu'on auoit horreur de la regarder'.[257]

The contract was said to be signed always in the blood of the witch, and here we come to a confusion between the mark made *on* the person and the mark made *by* the person. It seems clear that part of the ceremony of initiation was the cutting of the skin of the candidate to the effusion of blood. This is the early rite, and it seems probable that when the written contract came into vogue the blood was found to be a convenient writing-fluid, or was offered to the Devil in the form of

---

253 Burns Begg, p. 239.
254 Id., pp. 223-4.
255 Id., p. 237.
256 Lea, iii, p. 536.
257 De Lancre, *L'Incredulité*, p. 38.

a signature. This signing of a book plays a great part in the New England trials.

The contract was usually for the term of the witch's life, but sometimes it was for a term of years, the number of which varies considerably. As Scot says, 'Sometimes their homage with their oth and bargaine is receiued for a certeine terme of yeares; sometimes for ever.'[258] Popular belief assigns seven years as the length of time, at the end of which period the Devil was supposed to kill his votary. The tradition seems to be founded on fact, but there is also a certain amount of evidence that the witch was at liberty to discontinue or renew the contract at the end of the allotted term. Such a renewal seems also to have been made on the appointment of a new Chief. In France, England, and New England the term of years is mentioned; in Scotland it is mentioned by the legal authorities, but from the fact that it occurs seldom, if ever, in the trials it would seem that the contract of the Scotch witches was for life.

Magdalene de la Croix, Abbess of a religious house in Cordova in 1545, made a contract 'for the space of thirty years', she being then a girl of twelve.[259] In Paris in 1571 'il y eut vn aduocat lequel confessa qu'il auoit passé l'obligation au Diable renonceant à Dieu, & icelle signee de son propre sang. Encores s'est il verifié par plusieurs procez, que l'obligation reciproque entre le diable, & le sorcier, contient quelquesfois le terme d'vn an, deux ans, ou autre temps.'[260] At Faversham in 1645 Joan Williford said 'that the Devil promised to be her servant about twenty yeeres, and that the time is now almost expired'.[261] In Huntingdonshire in 1646 Elizabeth Weed of Great Catworth confessed that 'the Devill then offer'd her, that hee would doe what mischiefe she should require him; and said she must covenant with him that he must have her soule at the end of one and twenty years, which she granted'.[262] In 1652 Giles Fenderlin of Leaven

---

[258] Reg. Scot, Bk. III, p. 41.
[259] *Pleasant Treatise*, p. 88.
[260] Bodin, *Fléau*, p. 172.
[261] *Examination of Joan Williford*, p. 4.
[262] Davenport, p. 1.

Heath was tried for that when he was a soldier at Bell in Flanders he made a five-years' covenant with a Jesuit; 'after the said five years was expired, in 1643 he renew'd the said Covenant with the Jesuit for 14 years longer: whereupon he drew a Covenant for him with the Devil, pricking the two fore-fingers of his right hand with an needle, and drew bloud, wherewith he writ his name with his own bloud, and then covenanted with the Devil, That if he should be safely protected during the space of 14 years aforesaid, while such time as it expired, that then he was to take away both body and soul as his own right and interest.'[263] At Lille in 1661 Madame Bourignon's girls indicate the renewal of the contract: 'The Devil gives them a Mark, which Marks they renew as often as those Persons have any desire to quit him. The Devil reproves them then more severely and obligeth them to new Promises, making them also new Marks for assurance or pledge, that those Persons should continue faithful to him.'[264] In Somerset in 1664 Elizabeth Style said that the Devil 'promised her Mony, and that she should live gallantly, and have the pleasure of the World for Twelve years, if she would with her Blood sign his Paper, which was to give her Soul to him'.[265] At Groton in New England in 1671, according to Elizabeth Knap, 'the terme of time agreed upon with him was for 7 yeers; one yeere shee was to be faithfull in his service, and then ye other six hee would serve her, and make her a witch'.[266] At Newcastle-on-Tyne in 1673 Ann Armstrong 'deposeth that Ann Drydon had a lease for fifty yeares of the divill, whereof ten ar expired. Ann Forster had a lease of her life for 47 yeares, whereof seaven are yet to come. Lucy Thompson had a lease of two and forty, whereof two are yet to come, and, her lease being near out, they would have perswaded this informer to have taken a lease of three score yeares or upwards.'[267] In New England some of the 'afflicted' said of Goodwife C. that 'she had Covenanted with the *Devil* for ten Years, six of them were gone, and

---

[263] *Mrs. Joan Peterson*, p. 4.
[264] Bourignon, *Vie*, p. 223; Hale, p. 37.
[265] Glanvil, pt. ii, p. 136.
[266] Green, p. 14.
[267] *Surtees Soc.*, xl, p. 196.

four more to come'.[268] In modern France the belief in the contract for a term of years is recorded, but nothing is said of the renewal of the contract or of the fate of the witch who refuses such a contract. In the department of Entre-Sambre-et-Meuse the full method of entering on such a contract is known: 'Si vous voulez venir au bois avec moi, vous verrez un homme venir à vous. C'est le chef. Il vous demandera si vous voulez vous engager dans la société. Si vous acceptez, le terme d'engagement est de *sept* ans et vous gagnerez une *plaquette* par jour.'[269] Among the Walloons the neophyte takes with him a black hen, which the Devil buys, and then ratifies the contract, 'le pacte est fait pour une durée de sept ans.'[270]

5. The Baptism

Records of the baptism of candidates are rare, the rite being possibly copied from the Christian ceremony and therefore of later date. It does not seem to occur in England and hardly at all in Scotland. The earliest mention is in the Basses-Pyrénées (1609), where Jeannette d'Abadie stated 'qu'elle a veu souuent baptiser des enfans au sabbat, qu'elle nous expliqua estre des enfans des sorcieres & non autres, lesquelles ont accoutume faire plustost baptiser leurs enfans au sabbat qu'en l'Eglise'.[271] The rite, however, was practised in Bute in 1662: Margret NcLevine confessed—
'that being in a litle chamber in Balichtarach the devill came to her in the lyknes of a man and deseired hir to goe with him, and that she refusing he said I will not [blank] and she gave him [blank] she never saw afterward and that she knew it was the devill and after he went that he came bak and asked hir to give him hir hand quhich she refusing to doe he took hir by the midle finger of the rycht hand quhich he had almost cutt off hir and therwith left hir. Her finger was so sorely pained for the space of a moneth ther after that ther was no pain

---

[268] Increase Mather, p. 205.
[269] Lemoine, *La Tradition*, vi (1892), p. 106.
[270] Monseur, p. 84.
[271] De Lancre, *Tableau*, p. 131.

comparable to it, as also took her by the right leg quhich was sorly pained likewayes as also be the devill. Item he came to her againe as she was shaking straw in the barne of Ardroscidell in a very ugly shape and that there he desired hir to goe with him and she refusing he said to her I will either have thy self or then thy heart. Item that he healed her sore foot and finger quhich finger is yet be nummed. Item that before he haled her that she made a covenant with him and promised to doe him any service that he wold imploy hir in. Item that he asked quhat was her name. She answered him Margret the name that God gave me, and he said to her I baptise the Jonet.'[272]

Isobell NcNicoll 'confessed that as she was in her owne house her alone drawing acquavittie the devill came to her in the lyknes of a young man and desyred her to goe with him and confesses that she made a covenant with him quhairin he promised that she should not want meanes enough and she promised to be his servand. Item that he baptised her and gave her a new name and called her Caterine. Item that about a moneth therafter in the night as she went out of her own back dore she met with the devill and spok with him.'[273]—Jonet McNicoll 'confesses with remorse that about hallowday as she was in Mary Moore's house that there appeared to her two men the on a gross copperfaced man and the other a wele favored young man and that the copperfaced man quhom she knew to be ane evil spirit bade her goe with him. Item confesses that she made a covenant with him, and he promised that she wold not want meines eneugh and she promised to serve him and that he gave her a new name saying I baptise the Mary.'[274]—Jonet Morisoune 'traysted with the divill at the Knockanrioch, being the second tyme of her meeting with him, that shee made covenant with the devill ... quairin she promised to be his servant etc. that shee asked quhat was his name his answer was my name is Klareanough and he asked quhat was her name and she answered Jonet Morisoun, the name that God gave me, and he said

---

[272] *Highland Papers*, vol. iii, p. 6.
[273] Ib., vol. iii, p. 12.
[274] Ib., vol. iii, p. 13.

belive not in Christ bot belive in me. I baptise the Margarat.'[275] The Swedish witches (1669) were also baptized; 'they added, that he caused them to be baptized too by such Priests as he had there, and made them confirm their Baptism with dreadful Oaths and Imprecations.'[276] Curiously enough the most detailed account comes from New England (1692). Mary Osgood, wife of Captain Osgood, went 'to five mile pond, where she was baptized by the devil, who dipped her face in the water, and made her renounce her former baptism, and told her she must be his, soul and body for ever, and that she must serve him, which she promised to do. She says, the renouncing her first baptism was after her dipping.'[277] The account of Goody Lacey's experience is given in the form of question and answer:

'*Q.* Goody Lacey! how many years since they were baptized? *A.* Three or four years ago, I suppose. *Q.* Who baptized them? *A.* The old serpent. *Q.*How did he do it? *A.* He dipped their heads in the water, saying, that they were his and that he had power over them. *Q.* Where was this? *A.* At Fall's River. *Q.* How many were baptized that day? *A.* Some of the chief; I think they were six baptized. *Q.* Name them. *A.* I think they were of the higher powers.'[278]

A near approach to the ceremony of baptism is the blood-rite at Auldearne, described by Isobel Gowdie and Janet Breadheid. The Devil marked Isobel on the shoulder, 'and suked owt my blood at that mark, and spowted it in his hand, and, sprinkling it on my head, said, "I baptise the, Janet, in my awin name."' The Devil marked Janet Breadheid in the same way on the shoulder, 'and suked out my blood with his mowth, at that place; he spowted it in his hand, and sprinkled it on my head. He baptised me thairvith in his awin nam, "Christian."'[279]

---

[275] *Highland Papers*, vol. iii, p. 22.
[276] Horneck, pt. ii, p. 321.
[277] Howell, vi, 660; J. Hutchinson, ii, p. 31.
[278] J. Hutchinson, ii, p. 36.
[279] Pitcairn, iii, pp. 603, 617.

Though baptism is rare, the giving of a new name on admission is peculiar to Scotland. The names seem to have been usually nicknames derived from various sources; personal peculiarities such as 'Weill dancing Janet', or 'Able and stout'; contractions of the proper name, as 'Naip' for Barbara Napier; or a title such as 'Rob the Rowar', for Robert Grierson, who kept the rows or rolls. Most of the other names appear to have been ordinary Christian names arbitrarily bestowed. There is nothing to throw any light on the reason for the change. In 1590 at North Berwick the witch-name was considered of the highest importance.

'Robert Griersoune being namit, thay ran all hirdie-girdie and wer angrie; for it wes promesit, that he sould be callit "Ro^t the Comptroller alias Rob the Rowar" for expreming of his name.—Effie McCalzane, Robert Griersoune, and the said Barbara, hapnit to be nameit thair; quhilk offendit all the cumpany: And that they sould nocht haif bene nameit with thair awin names; Robert Griersoun, to haif bene callit *Rob the rowar*; Effie to be callit*Cane*; and the said Barbara, to be callit *Naip*.'[280]

Later, the change of name was of so little value that at Crook of Devon several of the witches could not remember what they had been called; Bessie Henderson appears to have recollected the name after a time, for it is inserted towards the end of the confession; Robert Wilson could remember the Devil's name but not his own: Agnes Brugh and Christian Grieve could remember neither the Devil's nor their own.[281]

The so-called 'christening', i.e. naming, of animals, comes rather under the head of 'sacrifice' than of baptism, for the ceremony appears to have been purificatory.

6. The Mark

The Witches' Mark, or Devil's Mark, as it is indifferently called, is one of the most important points in the identification of a witch, as the

---

[280] Id., i, pt. ii, pp. 239, 246.
[281] Burns Begg, x, pp. 224, 227, 232, 239.

infliction of it was often the final rite in the admission ceremonies. The fact that any person bore such a mark was taken as incontrovertible proof that the bearer was a witch.

There were two kinds of marks, which should be carefully differentiated, one of which was clearly natural, the other probably artificial. Both were said to be insensible to pain and not to bleed when pricked or pierced. Local anaesthesia is vouched for in much of the evidence, which suggests that there is a substratum of truth in the statements, but I can at present offer no solution of this problem.

The writers on witchcraft, particularly the legal authorities, recognize the value of the Mark as proof of witchcraft, and some differentiate between the two forms; the witches themselves made a distinction between the two, the natural being considered inferior to the artificial.

Reginald Scot in 1584 summarizes the evidence in a few words: 'The Diuell giveth to euerie nouice a marke, either with his teeth or with his clawes.'[282]The *Lawes against Witches and Conivration*, published 'by authority' in 1645, state that 'their said Familiar hath some big or little Teat upon their body, wher he sucketh them: and besides their sucking, the Devil leaveth other markes upon their bodies, sometimes like a Blew-spot, or Red-spot like a flea-biting'. Sir George Mackenzie, the famous Scotch lawyer, describing in 1699 what did and did not legally constitute a witch, says:

'The Devils Mark useth to be a great Article with us, but it is not *per se* found relevant, except it be confest by them, that they got that Mark with their own consent; *quo casu*, it is equivalent to a Paction. This Mark is given to them, as is alledg'd, by a Nip in any part of the Body, and it is blew. Delrio calls it *Stigma*, or Character, and alledges that it is sometimes like the impression of a Hare's foot, or the Foot of a Rat or Spider.'[283]

Forbes, writing in 1730, says:

'On the meaner Proselytes the Devil fixes in some secret Part of their Bodies a Mark, as his Seal to know his own by; which is like a

---

[282] Scot, Bk. III, p. 43; see also Danaeus, ch. iii.
[283] Mackenzie, title x, p. 48.

Flea Bite or blew Spot, or sometimes resembles a little Teat, and the Part so stamped doth ever after remain insensible, and doth not bleed, tho' never so much nipped or pricked by thrusting a Pin, Awl or Bodkin into it; but if the Covenanter be of better Rank, the Devil only draws Blood of the Party, or touches him or her in some Part of the Body without any visible Mark remaining.'[284]

The Mark proper appears to have been the coloured spot or design which followed the infliction of a prick or nip by the claws or teeth of the Devil on the person of the neophyte. The red mark is described as being like a flea-bite, i.e. small and circular; the blue mark seems to have been larger and more elaborate, apparently in some kind of design. From the evidence five facts are clear: (1) that the mark was coloured, (2) that it was permanent, (3) that it was caused by the pricking or tearing of the skin, (4) that the operator passed his hand or fingers over the place, (5) that the pain could be severe and might last a considerable time. Put together in this way, the facts suggest tattooing.

Among the Aberdeen witches in 1597 Andro Man was accused that 'Christsunday [the Devil] bit a mark in the third finger of thy right hand, whilk thou has yet to show'; and Christen Mitchell also was accused that 'the Devil gave thee a nip on the back of thy right hand, for a mark that thou was one of his number'.[285] According to Boguet, writing in 1598, the witches of Eastern France were usually marked on the left shoulder, and the mark was in the shape of the foot or footprint of a hare, but he also gives some exceptional cases:

'L'epaule gauche est l'endroit, où plus ordinairement il marque les Sorciers. La marque des Sorciers est tantost come vne piste ou pied de lieure, & tantost d'autre façon. On en a veu vne, qui auoit vne figure rapportant en grandeur à vn petit denier, du centre de laquelle s'estendoient plusieurs filamens vers la circonference. La marque de la Belcuenotte, qui a esté brulée à Besançon, estoit au dessus de sa nature, vn peu plus bas que le nombril. Celle, dont Guillauma Proby d'Anchay se trouua marquée au col du costé droit, estoit de mesme de

---

[284] Forbes, ii, p. 33.
[285] *Spalding Club Misc.*, i, pp. 120, 165. Spelling modernized.

---

la grandeur d'vn petit denier, tirant sur le brun. Iean de Vaux auoit la sieñe au doz, & ressembloit à vn petit chien noir.'[286]

De Lancre in 1609 says that in the Basses-Pyrénées 'comme le Diable faict sa marque, on sent vn peu de chaleur, qui penetre plus ou moins profondement la chair, que plus ou moins il pince le lieu qu'il touche'. As regards the position of the mark he says:

'Il les egratigne tous auec le bras gauche, & les ongles de la main senestre. Et tout aussi tost prenant vne espingle d'or faux, il les marque le plus souuent dans le blãc de l'œil gauche, & leur imprime vne marque qui semble vn petit crapaud' [elsewhere he says 'vne patte de crapaud']; 'par fois dans l'epaule & costé gauche, ou dans la cuisse, leur rompant & dechirant la peau & la chair iusques à effusiõ de sang; si bien que pendant trois mois ils ont de tres grandes douleurs.'[287]

Isobel Crawford of Irvine in 1618 had 'the devill's mark, quhilk was lyk ane braid dyn spott, in the inner syd of hir left thie, about ane handbraid under her lisk'.[288] The Lancashire witch, Margaret Johnson, in 1633, 'saith, that such Witches as have sharpe bones given them by the devill to pricke them, have no papps nor duggs, but their devil receiveth blood from the place, pricked with the bone, which witches are more grand witches than any that have marks'.[289] The Yarmouth witch, tried in 1644, saw a tall black man standing in the moonlight at her door: 'he told her, he must first see her Hand; and then taking out something like a Pen-knife, he gave it *a little Scratch*, so that Blood followed, and the *Mark* remained to that time.'[290] Rebecca Jones, an Essex witch tried in 1645, confessed that 'there came one morning one to the doore and knocked, and that this examinant going to the dore, shee saw there a very handsome young man, as shee then thought but now shee thinkes it was the devill; who asked this examinant how shee did, and desired to see her left wrist, which shee shewed unto him: and he then tooke a pin from this examinant's owne sleeve, and

---

[286] Boguet, pp. 315, 316, 317.
[287] De Lancre, *Tableau*, pp. 195, 399.
[288] *Isobel Inch*, p. 16.
[289] Whitaker, p. 216.
[290] Hale, p. 46.

pricked her wrist twice, and there came out a drop of bloud, which he took off with the top of his finger, and so departed'.[291] The child-witch, Jonet Howat of Forfar, tried in 1661, said that 'the devil kist hir and niped hir vpon one of hir shoulders, so as shoe hade great paine for some tyme therafter'; later he came to her, and 'calling hir his bony bird did kisse hir, and straiked her shoulder (quhich was niped) with his hand, and that presently after that shoe was eased of hir former paine'. Elspet Alexander, of the same Coven, was also marked on the shoulder; four weeks later 'the divill straiked hir shoulder with his fingers, and after that shoe hade ease in the place formerly niped by the devill'.[292] The witch girls at Lille in 1661 stated that 'le Diable leur fait quelque marque comme avec une aleine de fer en quelque partie du corps'.[293] Marie Lamont of Innerkip in 1662 confessed voluntarily that 'the devill nipit her upon the right syd, qlk was very painful for a tym, but yairefter he straikit it with his hand, and healed it; this she confesses to be his mark'.[294] In Bute in 1662 'Margaret NcWilliam was tryed for the merk there was 3 merks fund, one up her left leg, next hard be the shine bone, another betwixt her shoulders a 3° ane uthyr up her hensh, blew.... Kat Moore was tried, and it was found undernethe her richt shoulder a little whyt unsensible spott'.[295] The Somerset witches, in 1664, were marked on the fingers; it was stated of Elizabeth Style that the Devil 'prickt the fourth Finger of hir right hand, between the middle and upper joynt (where the sign at the Examination remained)'; of Alice Duke, that 'the Devil prickt the fourth finger of her right hand between the middle and upper joynt (where the mark is yet to be seen)'; and of Christian Green, that 'the Man in black prickt the fourth finger of her Right-hand between the middle and upper joints, where the sign yet remains'.[296] At Paisley in 1678 Annabil Stuart confessed 'that the Devil took her by the Hand

---

291 Howell, iv, 854-5.
292 Kinloch, pp. 124-6.
293 Bourignon, *Vie*, p. 223.
294 Sharpe, p. 132.
295 *Highland Papers*, iii, p. 17.
296 Glanvil, pt. ii, pp. 136, 148, 156.

and nipped her Arm, which continued to be sore for half an hour'.[297] At Borrowstowness the Devil took Margaret Pringle 'by the right hand, whereby it was for eight days grievowslie pained; bot having it twitched of new againe, it imediatelie becam haill'.[298] Of the Renfrewshire Coven in 1696 little Thomas Lindsay received 'a Nip on the Neck which continued sore for Ten days'; and John Reid had 'a Bite or Nipp in his Loyn, which he found painfull for a Fortnight'.[299] At Pittenweem in 1704 the 'young lass', Isobel Adams, confessed that the Devil 'put his mark in her flesh which was very painful'.[300]

The other form of the Devil's Mark was the 'little Teat'. It occurred on various parts of the body; was said to secrete milk and to give suck to the familiars, both human and animal; and was sometimes cut off by the witch before being searched. The descriptions of the 'teat' point to its being that natural phenomenon, the supernumerary nipple. Cases of polymastia or supernumerary breasts, and of polythelia or supernumerary nipples, are constantly recorded by modern medical observers. 'These accessory structures are usually situated on the chest wall, the upper part of the abdominal wall, or in the axillae, but they have been met with on the shoulder, the buttock, the thigh, and other extraordinary positions. As a rule they are functionless.'[301] Polythelia occurs in both sexes; according to Bruce, 'of 315 individuals taken indiscriminately and in succession, 7.619 per cent. presented supernumerary nipple; 9.11 per cent. of 207 men examined in succession presented supernumerary nipple; and 4.807 per cent. of 104 women.' He concludes that, 'according to present observations at least, supernumerary nipples occur much more frequently in the male than in the female.'[302] Cameron tabulates the positions of the supernumerary nipple in 105 cases: '96 were situated in thorax, 5 in

---

[297] Glanvil, pt. ii, p. 291.
[298] *Scots Magazine*, 1814, p. 200.
[299] *Narrative of the Sufferings*, pp. xli, xliv.
[300] Sinclair, p. 259.
[301] Thompson and Miles, ii, p. 341.
[302] *Journal of Anatomy*, xiii, pp. 438, 447.

axilla, 2 in back, 1 on shoulder, 1 outside of thigh.'[303] All writers on the subject agree that the phenomenon is of more common occurrence than is usually supposed, but that many cases pass unnoticed unless well marked when in men or causing discomfort by functioning when in women. This view is supported by the fact that, during the recent unparalleled opportunity for the physical examination of large numbers of men, many cases have been published in the *British Medical Journal* for 1917 as occurring among recruits for the army. The supernumerary nipple is usually very much smaller than the normal; like the normal, it is a modification of cutaneous tissue and is not attached to muscular tissue; its removal is a simple operation, in fact it would be quite possible for an unskilled operator to cut it off with a sharp knife. In women the supernumerary nipple is observed to increase at the time of the periods; in some cases during lactation so much milk is secreted as to make it a matter of indifference whether the child is suckled at the normal nipples or at the supernumerary one. In cases of polymastia the nipple is not always formed; the milk, when secreted, issuing from a small opening. Though the nipple is congenital, the supernumerary breast may develop, or at any rate become noticeable, later; the theory being that the ducts carrying the secretion from the supernumerary to the normal breast become blocked in some way, and that the milk is thus exuded through the pore in the supernumerary breast. The change in the case quoted by Cameron, as well as in the case of the witch Rose Cullender, seems to have been caused by a strain.

Making allowance for the unscientific language of the recorders of the witch trials, it will be seen that the descriptions of the 'witch-pap' or 'little Teat' exactly coincide with these anatomical facts. I give the evidence below, the trials being in chronological order. It will be observed that the cases are from England and New England only; if the phenomena of polymastia and polythelia occurred in France and Scotland, there are no records of the fact in the witch-trials of those countries.

---

[303] Id., xiii, p. 153.

. Alice Gooderidge and her mother, Elizabeth Wright, of Stapenhill near Burton-on-Trent, were tried in 1597:

'The old woman they stript, and found behind her right sholder a thing much like the vdder of an ewe that giueth sucke with two teates, like vnto two great wartes, the one behinde vnder her armehole, the other a hand off towardes the top of her shoulder. Being demanded how long she had those teates, she aunswered she was borne so. Then did they search Alice Gooderige, and found vpon her belly, a hole of the bignesse of two pence, fresh and bloudy, as though some great wart had beene cut off the place.'[304]

The witch of Edmonton, tried in 1621:

'The Bench commanded three women to search the body of Elizabeth Sawyer. They all three said, that they a little aboue the Fundiment of Elizabeth Sawyer found a thing like a Teate the bignesse of the little finger, and the length of half a finger, which was branched at the top like a teate, and seemed as though one had suckt it, and that the bottome thereof was blew, and the top of it was redde.'[305]

The greatest number of cases recorded in one place is in Essex during the trials before Sir Matthew Hale in 1645:

Anne Leech said 'that her imps did usually suck those teats which were found about the privie parts of her body. [Two women searched Mary Greenleife], and found that the said Mary had bigges or teates in her secret parts, not like emerods, nor in those places where women use to be troubled with them. The examinant, being asked how she came by those teats which were discovered in her secret parts, she saith she knows not unlesse she was born with them: but she never knew she had any such untill this time. [A woman searched Margaret Moone], she found three long teates or bigges in her secret parts, which seemed to have been lately sucked; and that they were not like pyles, for this informant knows well what they are, having been troubled with them herself. Upon the searching of her daughters, this informant found that two of them had biggs in their privy parts as the said Margaret their mother had. [Several women] were required to

---

[304] *Alse Gooderidge*, pp. 8, 9.
[305] *Elisabeth Sawyer*, B 3, obv. and rev.

search Sarah Hating, the wife of William Hating; Elizabeth Harvy widow, and Marian Hocket widow, and upon her said search (being a midwife) found such marks or bigges, that she never saw in other women: for Sarah Hating had foure teats or bigges in those parts, almost an inch long, and as bigge as this informant's little finger: That the said Elizabeth Harvy had three such biggs, and about the same scantling: And that the said Marian Hocket had no such bigges; but was found in the same parts not like other honest women. Sarah Barton, the sister of the said Marian Hocket (also suspected of being a witch) said the said Marian had cut off her bigs, whereby she might have been suspected to have been a witch, and laid plaisters to those places.'[306] 'Another Evidence deposed that she once heard the said Margaret [Landish] say, that her Imps did usually suck two Teats near the privy parts.'[307]

In Huntingdonshire in 1646 John Clarke junior, a labourer, was tried for witchcraft; John Browne, a tailor, deposed that he met Clarke on the road, Clarke 'said he was in haste; for his Father and Mother were accused for Witches, and that hee himselfe had beene searched: and this Informant answered, and so have I. Then Clarke asked this Informant, whether any thing were found about him, or not? he (this Informant) answered, that they said there were marks: Clarke said againe, had you no more wit but to have your marks found? I cut off mine three dayes before I was searched.'[308] John Palmer of St. Albans (1649) confessed that 'upon his compact with the Divel, hee received a flesh brand, or mark, upon his side, which gave suck to two familiars'.[309] There were several cases in Yorkshire: In 1649 'they searched the body of the saide Mary Sikes, and founde upon the side of her seate a redd lumpe about the biggnes of a nutt, being wett, and that, when they wrung it with theire fingers, moisture came out of it like lee. And they founde upon her left side neare her arme a litle

---

[306] Howell, iv, 838, 843, 848, 849, 850, 851.
[307] *Four Notorious Witches at Worcester*, p. 4. The place is wrongly given: it should be Essex, not Worcester.
[308] Davenport, p. 15.
[309] Gerish, *The Divel's Delusions*, p. 12.

lumpe like a wart, and being puld out it stretcht about halfe an inch. And they further say that they never sawe the like upon anie other weomen.'[310] In 1650 Frances Ward 'saith that she was one of the fower that searched Margaret Morton, and found upon her two black spotts between her thigh and her body; they were like a wart, but it was none. And the other was black on both sides, an inch bread, and blew in the middest.'[311] At Scarborough in 1651

'Margery Ffish, widdow, beinge commanded to searche the bodye of Anne Hunnam otherwise Marchant, who was accused for witchcraft; she, this informante, and Elizabeth Jackson, and Eliz. Dale, did accordingly searche the body of the saide Anne Hunnam, otherwise Marchant, and did finde a little blue spott upon her left side, into which spott this informant did thrust a pinne att which the sd. Ann Hunnam never moved or seemed to feel it, which spott grows, out of her ffleshe or skin at her waste of a great bignesse. Elizabeth Dale informeth upon oath, that she did, together with Margery Ffish, searche Ann Hunnam, otherwise Marchant, her bodye and saith that their was found on her left buttock a blue spott growing out of her fleshe or skin like a greate warte.[312]

The Kentish witch, Mary Read of Lenham, in 1652, 'had a visible Teat, under her tongue, and did show it to many, and it was likewise seen by this Observator.'[313] In the case of the Salisbury witch, Anne Bodenham, in 1652, 'Women searched the Witch in the Gaol, and they delivered on their oaths at the Assises, that they found on her shoulder a certain mark or Teat, about the length and bignesse of the Niple of a Womans breast, and hollow and soft as a Niple, with a hole on the top of it: And searching further, they likewise found in her secret place another Teat, soft, and like the former on her shoulder.'[314] In Yorkshire again, in 1654, Katherine Earle was accused, 'and the said Katherine hathe beene searched, and a marke founde upon her in the likenesse

---

[310] *Surtees Soc.*, xl, p. 30.
[311] Id., xl, p. 38.
[312] *County Folklore*, ii, p. 139.
[313] *Prod. and Trag. Hist.*, p. 6.
[314] Bower, p. 28.

of a papp'.[315] At St. Albans, about 1660, there was a man-witch, who 'had like a Breast on his side'.[316] In the same year at Kidderminster a widow, her two daughters, and a man were brought to trial; 'the man had five teats, the mother three, and the eldest daughter one. When they went to search the woman, none were visible; one advised to lay them on their backs, and keep open their mouths, and they would appear; and so they presently appeared in sight.'[317] Alice Huson, of Burton Agnes, Yorks, in 1664, stated that 'I have, I confess, a Witch-pap, which is sucked by the Unclean Spirit'.[318] Abre Grinset, of Dunwich, Suffolk, in 1665, said, 'The Devil did appear in the form of a Pretty handsom Young Man first, and since Appeareth to her in the form of a blackish Gray Cat or Kitling, that it sucketh of a Tett (which Searchers since saw in the place She mentioned).'[319] In the same year, also in Suffolk, Rose Cullender was tried for witchcraft:

'The searchers [six women] began at her head, and so stript her naked, and in the lower part of her belly they found a thing like a teat of an inch long, they questioned her about it, and she said, that she had got a strain by carrying of water which caused that excrescence. But upon narrower search, they found in her privy parts three more excrescencies or teats, but smaller than the former: this deponent farther saith, that in the long teat at the end thereof there was a little hole, and it appeared unto them as if it had been lately sucked, and upon the straining of it there issued out white milky matter.'[320]

Temperance Lloyd, a Devon witch, was tried in 1682: 'Upon search of her body this informant did find in her secret parts, two teats hanging nigh together like unto a piece of flesh that a child had suckt. And each of the said teats was about an inch in length.'[321] Bridget Bishop, one of the New England witches, was tried in 1692: 'A Jury of Women found a preternatural Teat upon her Body; But upon a

[315] *Surtees Soc.*, xl, p. 69.
[316] Gerish, *Relation of Mary Hall*, p. 24.
[317] Howell, iv, 827 note.
[318] Hale, p. 58.
[319] Petto, p. 18.
[320] Howell, vi, 696.
[321] Id., viii, 1022.

second search, within 3 or 4 hours, there was no such thing to be seen.'[322] Elizabeth Horner, another Devon witch, tried in 1696, 'had something like a Nipple on her Shoulder, which the Children [who gave evidence] said was sucked by a Toad'.[323] Widow Coman, an Essex witch, died a natural death in 1699: 'Upon her death I requested Becke the midwife to search her body in the presence of some sober women, which she did and assured me she never saw the like in her life that her fundament was open like a mouse-hole and that in it were two long bigges out of which being pressed issued blood that they were neither piles nor emrods for she knew both but excrescencies like to biggs with nipples which seemed as if they had been frequently sucked.'[324] Elinor Shaw and Mary Phillips were executed in Northampton in 1704 for witchcraft: 'The Infernal Imps did Nightly Suck each of them a large Teat, or pieces of red Flesh in their Privy Parts.'[325]

The positions of the marks are worth noting. Of the coloured mark it will be seen from the evidence given above that there were certain well-defined positions, which is in itself a strong suggestion of the artificial character of this mark. In France the usual position was the left shoulder; in the Basses-Pyrénées the left eye, the left side, and the thigh were also commonly marked; the variations given by Boguet are the abdomen, the back, and the right side of the neck. In England it seems that only the hand and wrist were marked; in Somerset the exact position was between the upper and middle joints of the fourth finger of the right hand, probably the 'ring-finger', but whether on the outer or inner surface is not recorded. In Scotland the position is very varied, the right hand, the right side, the shoulder, the back, the neck, and the loin; at Aberdeen the position on the right hand is still further defined as being on the back and on the third finger, i.e. the 'ring-finger'.

Reginald Scot does not distinguish between the two kinds of marks, when he says that if the witch 'have anie privie marke under hir arme

---

[322] Mather, p. 137.
[323] F. Hutchinson, *Historical Essay*, p. 62.
[324] Gilbert, p. 6.
[325] *Witches of Northamptonshire*, p. 6.

pokes, under hir haire, under hir lip, or in her buttocke, or in her privities; it is a presumption sufficient for the judge to proceed to give sentence of death upon her'.[326] But from the positions in which supernumerary nipples are known to occur, it would seem that he is speaking of the 'little Teat' and not of the coloured mark. In six out of the thirty-two cases of supernumerary nipple cited above, the number of nipples is not given; though from the context it would appear that more than one was often found on each of the accused. If, therefore, we allow two apiece for those cases not definitely specified, there were sixty-three such nipples, an average roughly of two to each person; the number varying, however, from one to five (this last being a man). The position of the nipple on the body is given in forty-five out of the sixty-three cases: abdomen 2, axilla 1, buttock 1, fundament 3, groin 2, pudenda 30, shoulder 3, side 3, under tongue 1. In writing of supernumerary nipples and *mammae erraticae* Williams quotes cases recorded by modern observers, in which the accessory organ occurred on the abdomen, axilla, inguinal region, outer side of thigh, shoulder, and face.[327]

---

[326] R. Scot, Bk. II, ch. 5.
[327] *Journal of Anatomy*, xxv, 225 seq.

IV. THE ASSEMBLIES

There were two kinds of assemblies; the one, known as the Sabbath, was the General Meeting of all the members of the religion; the other, to which I give—on the authority of Estebène de Cambrue—the name of Esbat, was only for the special and limited number who carried out the rites and practices of the cult, and was not for the general public.

The derivation of the word Sabbath in this connexion is quite unknown. It has clearly nothing to do with the number seven, and equally clearly it is not connected with the Jewish ceremonial. It is possibly a derivative of *s'esbattre*, 'to frolic'; a very suitable description of the joyous gaiety of the meetings.

1. Sabbath

Locomotion.—The method of going to the meetings varied according to the distance to be traversed. In an immense majority of cases the means of locomotion are not even mentioned, presumably therefore the witches went on foot, as would naturally be the case in going to the local meeting or Esbat, which was attended only by those who lived near. There are, however, a few instances where it was thought worth while to mention that the worshippers walked to the meeting. Boguet (1598), who yields to none in his accounts of magical means of going to the Sabbath, says, 'les Sorciers neãtmoins vont quelquefois de pied au Sabbat, ce qui leur aduient principalement, lors que le lieu, où ils font leur assemblée, n'est pas guieres eslongné de leur habitation', and cites in confirmation the evidence of George and Antoinette Gandillon and their father Pierre, Clauda Ianprost, Clauda Ianguillaume, Iaquema Paget, Gros Iaques, the two brothers Claude and Claude Charloz, Pierre Willermoz, l'Aranthon, Pernette Molard, Ianne Platet, and Clauda Paget.[328] Iaquema Paget's account of how she and Antoine Tornier went to a meeting on their way home from the harvest field (see p. 121), proves that they were on foot. The Lang-Niddry witches (1608) clearly walked, they 'convenit thame selffis at

---

[328] Boguet, pp. 106-7.

Deane-fute of Lang-Niddry ... thaireftir thay past altogidder to the said Beigis hous in Lang-Nydry [where they drank]; and thaireftir come with all thair speid to Seaton-thorne be-north the zet; quhair the Devill callit for the said Christiane Tod, and past to Robert Smartis house, and brocht hir out.... And thay thaireftir past altogidder, with the Devill, to the irne zet of Seatoun.... And thaireftir come all bak agane to the Deane-fute, quhair first thai convenit.'[329] The distance from Lang Niddry to Seaton Castle is under a mile. Isaac de Queyran (1609), a young fellow of twenty-five, told de Lancre that those living at a distance flew home through the air, the near ones returned on foot.[330] Barthélemy Minguet of Brécy was tried in 1616: 'Enquis, de quelle façon sa femme fut au Sabbat la premiere fois. Respond, qu'elle y fut transportée par le Diable, lequel la rapporta apres le Sabbat, & que la seconde fois qu'elle y a esté, elle y fut de son pied avec luy, & s'en retourna de son pied, & qu'elle n'y a iamais esté que ces deux fois.'[331] Helen Guthrie of Forfar (1661) said that 'herselfe, Isobell Shyrie, and Elspet Alexander, did meit togither at ane aile house near to Barrie, a litle befor sunsett, efter they hade stayed in the said house about the spaice of ane houre drinking of thrie pintis of ale togidder, they went foorth to the sandis, and ther thrie other women met them, and the divell wes there present with them all ... and they parted so late that night that she could get no lodging, but wes forced to lye at ane dyk syde all night.'[332] Christian Grieve, of Crook of Devon (1662), acknowledged 'that ye came to the foresaid meeting immediately after your goodman and the rest went to bed, and that ye locked the door and put the key under the same, and that ye and the said Margaret Young your neighbor came foot for foot to the foresaid meeting and that ye stayed at the foresaid meeting about the space of two hours and came back again on your foot, and the foresaid Margaret Young with you, and found the key of the door in that same place where you left it, and declared that neither your husband nor any other in the house

---

[329] Pitcairn, ii, pp. 542-3.
[330] De Lancre, *Tableau*, p. 148.
[331] Id., *L'Incredulité*, p. 808.
[332] Kinloch, pp. 122-3.

was waking at your return'.[333] At Lille (1661) the girl Bellot, then aged fifteen, said that 'her Mother had taken her with her when she was very Young, and had even carried her in her Arms to the Witches Sabbaths or Assemblies'.[334] At Strathdown (eighteenth century) the witches went along the side of the river Avon to Craic-pol-nain, fording the river on foot.[335]

In the cases cited above there is nothing in the least bizarre or extraordinary, but there are other methods recorded of reaching the distant meetings. Sometimes the obvious means was by riding on a horse; sometimes the witches were accused, or claimed the power, of flying through the air, of riding in the air on a stick, of riding on animals or human beings, which latter were sometimes in their own natural form and sometimes enchanted into the form of animals.

The following instances are of those who rode to or from the meetings on horseback. Agnes Sampson of North Berwick (1590) said that 'the Devil in mans likeness met her going out in the fields from her own house at *Keith*, betwixt five and six at even, being her alone and commanded her to be at North-Berwick Kirk the next night: And she passed there on horse-back, conveyed by her Good-son, called Iohn Couper'.[336] Boguet (1608) mentions, in passing, the fact that the witches sometimes rode on horses.[337] The Lancashire witches (1613), after the meeting at Malking Tower, 'went out of the said House in their owne shapes and likenesses. And they all, by that they were forth of the dores, gotten on Horseback, like vnto foals, some of one colour, some of another.'[338] This was the usual mode of locomotion among the Lancashire witches, for Margaret Johnson (1633) said that at the meeting at Hoarstones 'there was, at y^t tyme, between 30 and 40 witches, who did all ride to the said meetinge'.[339] Isobell Gowdie (1662) said, 'I haid a little horse, and wold say, "Horse and Hattock,

[333] Burns Begg, p. 239.
[334] Bourignon, *Vie*, p. 211; Hale, p. 29.
[335] Stewart, p. 174.
[336] Pitcairn, i, pt. ii, p. 239. Spelling modernized.
[337] Boguet, p. 104.
[338] Potts, G 4.
[339] Whitaker, p. 216.

in the Divellis name!'"[340] The most detailed account is from Sweden (1669):

'Another Boy confessed too, that one day he was carried away by his Mistriss, and to perform the Journey he took his own Father's Horse out of the Meadow where it was, and upon his return she let the Horse go in her own ground. The next morning the Boys Father sought for his Horse, and not finding it, gave it over for lost; but the Boy told him the whole story, and so his Father fetcht the Horse back again.'[341]

We now come to the marvellous and magical means of locomotion. The belief in the power of witches to ride in the air is very ancient and universal in Europe. They flew either unsupported, being carried by the Devil, or were supported on a stick; sometimes, however, an animal which they rode passed through the air. The flying was usually preceded by an anointing of the whole or part of the body with a magical ointment.

The earliest example of unsupported flying is from Paul Grilland (1537), who gives an account of an Italian witch in 1526, who flew in the air with the help of a magic ointment.[342]

Reginald Scot (1584) says that the ointment 'whereby they ride in the aire' was made of the flesh of unbaptized children, and gives two recipes:

[1] 'The fat of yoong children, and seeth it with water in a brasen vessell, reseruing the thickest of that which remaineth boiled in the bottome, which they laie up and keepe, untill occasion serueth to use it. They put hereunto Eleoselinum, Aconitum, Frondes populeas, and Soote.' [2] 'Sium, acarum vulgare, pentaphyllon, the blood of a flitter mouse, solanum somniferum, and oleum. They stampe all these togither, and then they rubbe all parts of their bodys exceedinglie, till they looke red, and be verie hot, so as the pores may be opened, and their flesh soluble and loose. They ioine herewithall either fat, or oil in steed thereof, that the force of the ointment maie the rather pearse

---

[340] Pitcairn, iii, p. 604.
[341] Horneck, pt. ii, p. 320.
[342] Bodin, *Fléau*, p. 178.

inwardly, and so be more effectuall. By this means in a moonlight night they seeme to be carried in the aire.'[343]

So far this is only hearsay evidence, but there is also a certain amount of first-hand testimony, the witches declaring that they actually passed through the air above ground, or had seen others do so.

In 1598 'Thieuenne Paget racontoit, que le Diable s'apparut à elle la premiere fois en plein midy, en forme d'vn grand homme noir, & que comme elle se fut baillée à luy, il l'embrassa & l'esleva en l'air, & la transporta en la maison du prel de Longchamois ... & puis la rapporta au lieu mesme, où il l'auoit prise. Antide Colas disoit, que le soir, que Satan s'apparut à elle en forme d'vn homme de grande stature, ayant sa barbe & ses habillemens noirs, il la transporta au Sabbat, & qu'aux autres fois, il la venoit prendre dans son lict, & l'emportoit comme si c'eust esté vn vent froid, l'empoignant par la teste.'[344]

Isaac de Queyran (1609), whose evidence has already been quoted, said that the witches living at a distance flew home through the air.[345] In France (1652) 'lors qu'elle vouloit aller aux danses, elle se oindoit d'ung onguen qui lui estoit donné par vn sorcier envoyé par le diable. Que lors elle s'en alloit comme ung vent aux dictes danses avecque les aultres.'[346] At Crook of Devon (1661) Bessie Henderson confessed 'that ye was taken out of your bed to that meeting in an flight'.[347] The most detail comes from an English source: the Somerset witches (1664) claimed that they habitually flew through the air by means of a magical oil and magical words. Elizabeth Style said:

'Before they are carried to their meetings, they anoint their Foreheads, and Hand-wrists with an Oyl the Spirit brings them (which smells raw) and then they are carried in a very short time, using these

---

[343] Scot, pp. 41, 184. Scot is as usual, extraordinarily inaccurate in his statements. The correct formulae, as given by Wierus, will be found in Appendix V, with notes on the ingredients by Prof. A. J. Clark.

[344] Boguet, p. 96.

[345] De Lancre, *Tableau*, p. 148.

[346] H. G. van Elven, *La Tradition*, 1891, p. 215. Unfortunately neither name nor place are given in the transcription.

[347] Burns Begg, p. 223.

words as they pass, *Thout, tout a tout, tout, throughout and about*. And when they go off from their Meetings, they say, *Rentum, Tormentum ...* all are carried to their several homes in a short space.' Alice Duke gave the same testimony, noting besides that the oil was greenish in colour. Anne Bishop, the Officer of the Somerset covens, confessed that 'her Forehead being first anointed with a Feather dipt in Oyl, she hath been suddenly carried to the place of their meeting.... After all was ended, the Man in black vanished. The rest were on a sudden conveighed to their homes.'[348]

The belief that the witches actually rode in the air seated on some concrete object, such as an animal, a human being, or a stick, is both ancient and universal, and is reflected in the ecclesiastical and civil laws, of which the earliest is the decree of the ninth century, attributed to the Council of Ancyra. 'Certeine wicked women following sathans prouocations, being seduced by the illusion of diuels, beleeve and professe, that in the night times they ride abroad with *Diana*, the goddesse of the *Pagans*, or else with *Herodias*, with an innumerable multitude, vpon certeine beasts ... and doo whatsoeuer those fairies or ladies command.'[349] The laws of Lorraine (1329-46) decree that 'celui qui fera magie, sortilège, billets de sort, pronostic d'oiseau ou se vanteroit d'avoir chevauché la nuit avec Diane ou telle autre vielle qui se dit magicienne, sera banni et payera dix livres tournois'.[350]

The witches themselves confirmed the statements about riding on animals to the Sabbath. Rolande du Vernier (1598) confessed 'que lors qu'elle y fut, elle y alla sur vn gros mouton noir, qui la portoit si viste en l'air, qu'elle ne se pouuoit recognoistre'.[351] De Lancre says that the witches 'se font porter iusqu'audit lieu, sur vne beste, qui semble parfois vn cheual, & parfoys vn homme'.[352] Margaret Johnson (1633) 'saith, if they desyre to be in any place upon a sodaine, theire devill or spirit will, upon a rodde, dogge, or any thinge els, presently convey

---

[348] Glanvil, pt. ii, pp. 139, 141, 148-9, 151.
[349] Scot, Bk. iii, p. 66; Lea, iii, p. 493. I give Scot's translation as being more racily expressed.
[350] J. Bournon, p. 19.
[351] Boguet, p. 96.
[352] De Lancre, *Tableau*, p. 123.

them thither'.[353] One of Madame Bourignon's girls, then aged twelve (1661), declared that 'her said Lover came upon a little Horse, and took her by the Hand, asking her if she would be his Mistress, and she saying Ay, she was catched up into the Air with him and the other Girls, and they flew all together to a great Castle'.[354] The Swedish witches (1669) said:

'He set us on a Beast which he had there ready, and carried us over Churches and high walls ... he gives us a horn with a Salve in it, wherewith we do anoint our selves; and then he gives us a Saddle, with a Hammer and a wooden nail, thereby to fix the Saddle; whereupon we call upon the Devil, and away we go.... For their journey they said they made use of all sorts of Instruments, of Beasts, of Men, of Spits and Posts. What the manner of their Journey is, God alone knows.... Blockula is scituated in a delicate large Meadow whereof you can see no end. They went into a little Meadow distinct from the other, where the Beasts went that they used to ride on: But the Men whom they made use of in their Journey, stood in the House by the Gate in a slumbering posture, sleeping against the wall.'[355]

Human beings were also said to be ridden upon in other places besides Sweden. Agnes Spark of Forfar (1661) said she 'hard people ther present did speake of Isabell Shirie, and say that shoe was the devill's horse, and that the divill did allwayes ryde upon hir, and that shoe was shoad lyke ane mare, or ane horse'.[356] Ann Armstrong, of a Northumbrian Coven (1673)—

'saith, that since she gave information against severall persons who ridd her to severall places where they had conversation with the divell, she hath beene severall times lately ridden by Anne Driden and Anne Forster, and was last night ridden by them to the rideing house in the close on the common.... Whilst she was lying in that condition [i.e. "a fitt"], which happened one night a little before Christmas, about the change of the moone, the informant see the said Anne Forster come

---

[353] Whitaker, p. 216.
[354] Bourignon, *Vie*, p. 214; Hale, p. 31.
[355] Horneck, pt. ii, pp. 316, 317, 318, 319, 321.
[356] Kinloch, p. 129.

with a bridle, and bridled her and ridd upon her crosse-leggd, till they come to (the) rest of her companions at Rideing millne bridg-end, where they usually mett. And when she light of her back, pulld the bridle of this informer's head, now in the likenesse of a horse; but, when the bridle was taken of, she stood up in her own shape.... And when they had done, bridled this informer, and the rest of the horses, and rid home.... Upon Collupp Munday last, being the tenth of February, the said persons met at Allensford, where this informant was ridden upon by an inchanted bridle by Michael Aynsley and Margaret his wife. Which inchanted bridle, when they tooke it from her head, she stood upp in her owne proper person.... On Monday last at night, she, being in her father's house, see one Jane Baites, of Corbridge, come in the forme of a gray catt with a bridle hanging on her foote, and breath'd upon her and struck her dead, and bridled her, and rid upon her in the name of the devill southward, but the name of the place she does not now remember. And the said Jane allighted and pulld the bridle of her head.'[357]

The method of locomotion which has most impressed the popular imagination and has become proverbial was riding on a stick, generally said to be a broomstick. It must, however, be remembered that one of the earliest cases on record of stick-riding does not definitely state that the witch flew through the air. This was the case of the Lady Alice Kyteler in 1324, when 'in rifleing the closet of the ladie, they found a Pipe of oyntment, wherewith she greased a staffe, upon the which she ambled and galloped through thick and thin, when and in what maner she listed'.[358] Though Holinshed is not always a reliable authority, it is worth while to compare this account with the stick-riding of the Arab witches and the tree-riding of the Aberdeen Covens (see pp. 110, 134).

The number of cases vouched for by the persons who actually performed or saw the feat of riding on a stick through the air are disappointingly few. Guillaume Edeline, prior of St. Germain-en-Laye

---

[357] Surtees Society, xl, pp. 191-2, 194, 197; Denham Tracts, ii, pp. 299-301, 304, 307.
[358] Holinshed, *Ireland*, p. 58.

(1453), 'se mit en telle servitude de l'ennemy, qu'il luy convenoit estre en certain lieu toutes fois qu'il estoit par ledit ennemy évocqué: ouquel lieu ilz avoient accoustumé faire leur consistoire, et ne luy falloit que monter sur ung balay, qu'aussi-tost il estoit prestement transporté là où ledit consistoire se faisoit'.[359] The Guernsey witch, Martin Tulouff (1563), confessed 'q̄ il soy est trouvé avecq la dite viellesse ou elle chevaucha ung genest et luy ung aultre, et q̄ lad^te viellesse monta a mont la chemynee et q̄ il en perdyt la veue et q̄ elle disoet devãt q̄ monter "Va au nom du diable et luciffer dessq̄ roches et espyñes" et q̄ po^r luy il ne pouvoet ainsy faire, et d^t q̄ sa mere a chevauche le genest p IV ou V foys et q̄ il l'a veue monter a mont la cheminee'.[360] Danaeus (1575) sums up the evidence of the witches themselves: 'He promiseth that himself will conuay them thither, that are so weak that they cannot trauaile of themselues: which many tymes he doth by meanes of a staffe or rod, which he deliuereth vnto thẽ, or promiseth to doo it by force of a certen oyntment, which he will geue them: and sometimes he offreth them an horse to ride vpon.'[361] Boguet's experience (1598) is more dramatic than that of Danaeus: 'Les autres y vont, tantost sur vn Bouc, tantost sur vn cheual, & tantost sur vn ballet, ou ramasse, sortans ces derniers de leurs maisons le plus souuent par la cheminee.... Les vns encor se frottent auparauant de certaine graisse, & oignement: les autres ne se frottent en aucune façon.'[362] He also records the actual evidence of individual witches: Françoise Secretain said 'qu'elle avoit esté vne infinité de fois au Sabbat & assemblee des Sorciers ... & qu'elle y alloit sur vn baston blanc, qu'elle mettoit entre ses iambes.[363]—Claudine Boban, ieune fille confessa, qu'elle, & sa mere montoient sur vne ramasse,[364] & que sortans le contremont de la cheminée elles alloient par l'air en ceste façon au Sabbat.'[365] In

---

[359] Chartier, iii, p. 45; Lea, iii, p. 536.

[360] From a trial in the Greffe, Guernsey.

[361] Danaeus, ch. iv.

[362] Boguet, p. 104.

[363] Id., pp. 9, 104.

[364] A marginal note against the word *ramasse* gives 'autrement balait, & en Lyonnois coiue'.

[365] Boguet, pp. 9, 97, 104.

Belgium Claire Goessen (1603) confessed 'qu'elle s'est trouvée à diverses assemblées nocturnes tenues par lui, dans lesquelles elle s'est laissée transporter au moyen d'un bâton enduit d'onguent'.[366] Isobell Gowdie (1662) was fully reported as regards the methods of locomotion used by the witches, though in other places her evidence is unfortunately cut short:

'I haid a little horse, and wold say, "Horse and Hattock, in the Divellis name!" And than ve void flie away, quhair ve vold, be ewin as strawes wold flie wpon an hie-way. We will flie lyk strawes quhan we pleas; wild-strawes and corne-strawes wilbe horses to ws, an ve put thaim betwixt our foot, and say, "Horse and Hattok, in the Divellis name!" ... Quhan we wold ryd, we tak windle-strawes, or been-stakes [bean-stalks], and put them betwixt owr foot, and say thryse,
Horse and Hattok, horse and goe,Horse and pellattis, ho! ho!
and immediatlie we flie away whair euir we wold.... All the Coeven did fflie lyk cattis, bot Barbara Ronald, in Brightmanney, and I, still [always] read on an horse, quhich ve vold mak of a straw or beein-stalk.'[367]

Julian Cox (1664) said that 'one evening she walkt out about a Mile from her own House, and there came riding towards her three persons upon three Broom-staves, born up about a yard and an half from the ground. Two of them she formerly knew, which was a Witch and a Wizzard.... The third person she knew not. He came in the shape of a black Man.'[368] Two of the New England witches (1692) confessed to riding on a pole; Mary Osgood, wife of Capt. Osgood of Andover, 'was carried through the air to five-mile pond ... she was transported back again through the air, in company with the forenamed persons, in the same manner as she went, and believes they were carried upon a pole'.[369] Goody Foster's evidence was reported by two authors: 'One Foster confessed that the Devil carry'd them on a pole, to a Witch-meeting; but the pole broke, and she hanging about [Martha] Carrier's

[366] Cannaert, p. 49.
[367] Pitcairn, iii, pp. 604, 608, 613.
[368] Glanvil, pt. ii, p. 194.
[369] Howell, vi, 660; J. Hutchinson, *Hist. of Massachusetts Bay*, p. 31.

neck, they both fell down, and she then received an hurt by the Fall, whereof she was not at this very time recovered.'[370] The second account is substantially the same: 'In particular Goody F. said (*Inter alia*) that she with two others (one of whom acknowledged the same) Rode from Andover to the same Village Witch meeting upon a stick above ground, and that in the way the stick brake, and gave the said F. a fall: whereupon, said she, I got a fall and hurt of which I am still sore.'[371]

Site.—The Sabbath seems to have been originally held on a fixed site. So much so was this the case that de Lancre is able to say, 'communement ils l'appellent Aquelarre, qui signifie Lane de Bouc, comme qui diroit la lane ou lãde, où le Bouc conuoque ses assemblees. Et de faict les Sorciers qui confessent, nommẽt le lieu pour la chose, & la chose ou Assemblee pour le lieu: tellement qu'encore que proprement Lane de Bouc, soit le Sabbat qui se tient és landes, si est-ce qu'ils appellent aussi bien Lane de Bouc, le Sabbat qui se tient és Eglises, & és places des villages, paroisses, maisons, & autres lieux.'[372] The confusion of the original *Lane de Bouc*, i.e. the Sabbath or Great Assembly, with local meetings is thus shown to be due to the inaccuracy of the witches themselves; and therefore it is not surprising that de Lancre and other authors should also fail to distinguish between the two. Still, in many of the records there are certain indications by which it is possible to recognize the localities where the real Sabbath, the true *Lane de Bouc*, was held.

De Lancre himself notes that the Sabbath must be held near a lake, stream, or water of some kind.[373] Bodin, however, gives a better clue, 'Les lieux des assemblees des Sorciers sont notables, & signalez de quelques arbres, ou croix.'[374] The *croix* is clearly the Christian form of the standing stone which is a marked feature in many descriptions of the Sabbath; and Bodin's statement recalls one of the laws of Cnut in

---

[370] Cotton Mather, p. 158; Burr, p. 244. *See also* J. Hutchinson, ii, pp. 35-6.
[371] Burr, p. 418.
[372] De Lancre, *Tableau*, p. 65.
[373] Id. ib., p. 72.
[374] Bodin, *Fléau*, p. 181.

the eleventh century, 'We earnestly forbid every heathenism: heathenism is, that men worship idols; that is that they worship heathen gods, or stones, or forest trees of any kind.'

Estebène de Cambrue (1567) said, 'Le lieu de ceste grande conuocation s'appelle generalement par tout le pays la Lanne de Bouc. Où ils se mettent à dancer à l'entour d'vne pierre, qui est plantée audit lieu, sur laquelle est assis vn grand homme noir.'[375] At Poictiers in 1574 four witches, one woman and three men, said that they went 'trois fois l'an, à l'assemblee generale, où plusieurs Sorciers se trouuoyẽt prés d'vne croix d'vn carrefour, qui seruoit d'enseigne'.[376] At Aberdeen in 1596 the witches acknowledged that they danced round the market cross and the 'fische croce' on All-Hallow-eve; and also round 'ane gray stane' at the foot of the hill at Craigleauch.[377] Margaret Johnson (1633) said 'shee was not at the greate meetinge at Hoarestones at the Forest of Pendle upon All Saints day'.[378] Though no stone is actually mentioned the name suggests that there had been, or still were, one or more stones standing in that place. The Swedish witches (1669) seem to have used the same site for both kinds of meetings; *Blockula* seems to have been a building of some kind, set in a meadow which was entered by a painted gate; within the building were rooms and some kind of chapel for the religious service.[379] The New England recorders (1692) did not enter into much detail, but even among them the fact is mentioned that there was 'a General Meeting of the Witches, in a Field at *Salem*-Village'.[380]

---

[375] De Lancre, *Tableau*, p. 123.
[376] Bodin, p. 187.
[377] *Spalding Club Misc.*, i, pp. 97-8, 114, 149, 153, 165, 167.
[378] Whitaker, p. 216; Baines, i, p. 607 note, where the name is given as *Hartford*. The importance of the stone in the Sabbath ceremonies is very marked in the account of a meeting in Northumberland (1673). Ann Armstrong declared that 'she and the rest had drawne their compasse nigh to a bridg end, and the devil placed a stone in the middle of the compasse, they sett themselves downe, and bending towards the stone, repeated the Lord's prayer backwards'. Denham Tracts, ii, p. 307; Surtees Soc., xl, p. 197.
[379] Horneck, pt. ii, pp. 321, 324.
[380] Mather, p. 131.

In modern times the identification of stones or of certain places with the Devil or with witch meetings is very noticeable. Out of innumerable instances I will mention only a few. In Guernsey the Catioroc is always identified as the site of the Sabbath. In Belgium 'à Godarville (Hainaut) se trouve un *tunnel* hanté par les sorcières; elles y tiennent leur sabbat'.[381]

'Un bloc de pierre isolé et d'aspect extraordinaire est généralement appelé *pierre du diable*. Exemples: A) le dolmen détruit près de Namur; B) la grande pierre en forme de table à demi encastrée dans la route qui conduit du village de Sény à celui d'Ellemelle (Candroz); C) *le fais du diable*, bloc de grès d'environ 800 mètres cubes, isolé dans la bruyère entre Wanne et Grand-Halleux près de Stavelot; D) les *murs du diable* à Pepinster, &c.—Dans plusieurs cantons, il y a un terrain que l'on appèle *tchan dè makral*, "champ des sorciers". C'est le cas près de Remouchamps, près de Tongres, près de la Gileppe et près de Grand-Halleux.'[382]

It is also noticeable how many of our own stone circles, such as the Nine Maidens, the Dancing Maidens, and so on, are connected by tradition with women who danced there on the Sabbath.

Date.—It appears from the evidence that certain changes took place in course of time in the religion; and, as might be expected, this is shown very markedly in the festivals. The ancient festivals remained all through, and to them were added the festivals of the succeeding religions. The original celebrations belonged to the May-November year, a division of time which follows neither the solstices nor the agricultural seasons; I have shown below (pp. 130, 178) that there is reason to believe these festivals were connected with the breeding seasons of the flocks and herds. The chief festivals were: in the spring, May Eve (April 30), called Roodmas or Rood Day in Britain and Walpurgis-Nacht in Germany; in the autumn, November Eve (October 31), called in Britain Allhallow Eve. Between these two came: in the winter, Candlemas (February 2); and in the summer, the Gule of August (August 1), called Lammas in Britain. To these were added the

---

[381] Harou, *La Tradition*, vi (1892), p. 367.
[382] Monseur, pp. 2, 88.

festivals of the solstitial invaders, Beltane at midsummer and Yule at midwinter; the movable festival of Easter was also added, but the equinoxes were never observed in Britain. On the advent of Christianity the names of the festivals were changed, and the date of one—Roodmas—was slightly altered so as to fall on May 3; otherwise the dates were observed as before, but with ceremonies of the new religion. Therefore Boguet is justified in saying that the witches kept all the Christian festivals. But the Great Assemblies were always held on the four original days, and it is this fact which makes it possible to distinguish with certainty between the Sabbath and the Esbat whenever dates are mentioned.

De Lancre, generalizing from the evidence before him, says, 'Quelquefois il y a des Sabbats & assemblees generales qui se font ordinairement les quatre festes annuelles';[383] and he also gives the words of a witch, tried in 1567: 'Estebène de Cambrue dit que les Sorcieres n'alloient en la grande assemblee & au grand Sabbat que quatre fois l'année.'[384] The four actual days are given in only one trial, that of Issobell Smyth at Forfar in 1661, 'By these meitings shee mett with him every quarter at Candlemas, Rud-day, Lambemas, and Hallomas',[385] but it is very clear that these were the regular days, from the mention of them individually in both England and Scotland. At North Berwick 'Barbara Napier was accused of being present at the convention on Lammas Eve at the New haven' [three Covens, i.e. thirty-nine persons, were assembled]. 'And the said Barbara was accused that she gave her bodily presence upon All Hallow even last was, 1590 years, to the frequent convention holden at the Kirk of North-Berwick, where she danced endlong the Kirk-yard, and Gelie Duncan played on a trump, John Fian, missellit, led the ring; Agnes Sampson and her daughters and all the rest following the said Barbara, to the number of seven score persons.'[386] The dittays against the witches of Aberdeen in 1596 show that 'wpoun Hallowewin last

---

[383] De Lancre, *Tableau*, p. 64.
[384] Id. ib., p. 123.
[385] Kinloch, p. 133.
[386] Pitcairn, i, pt. ii, p. 245. Spelling modernized.

bypast, att tuelff houris at ewin or thairby, thow the said Thomas Leyis ... withe ane gryit number of vtheris witchis, come to the mercatt and fische croce of Aberdene, wnder the conduct and gyding of the Dewill present withe you, all in company, playing befoir yow on his kynd of instrumentis. Ye all dansit about baythe the saidis croces, and the meill mercatt, ane lang space of tyme.'[387] Christen Michell and Bessie Thom had been not only at the Allhallow Eve meeting with Thomas Leyis but also at another before that. 'Thow confessis that, thrie yeris sensyn, vpon the Ruidday, airlie in the morning,' [Bessie Thom: 'befoir sone rysing'] 'thow, accumpaniet with ... certan vtheris witchis, thy devilische adherentis, convenit vpon Sainct Katherines Hill ... and thair, vnder the conduct of Sathan, present with yow, playing befoir yow, efter his forme, ye all dansit a devilische danse, rydand on treis, be a lang space.'[388] In 1597 Issobell Richie, Margrat Og, Helene Rogie, Jonet Lucas, Jonet Dauidsone, Issobell Oige, and Beatrice Robbie were accused of a meeting at Craigleauche, near Aberdeen: 'Thow art indyttit for the being at the twa devylische dances betuixt Lumfannand and Cragleauche, with vmquhile Margerat Bane, vpon Alhalowewin last, quhair thow conferrit with the Dewill.'[389] In Ayrshire in 1604 Patrik Lowrie and his companion-witches were accused that they 'att Hallowevin in the yeir of God foirsaid, assemblit thame selffis vpon Lowdon-hill, quhair thair appeirit to thame ane devillische Spreit'.[390] Margaret Johnson, of the second generation of Lancashire witches, in 1633 said 'shee was not at the greate meetinge at Hartford in the Forrest of Pendle on All Saintes day'.[391] Isobel Gowdie (Auldearne, 1662) does not enter into her usual detail, but merely states that 'a Grand Meitting vold be about the end of ilk Quarter'.[392]

---

[387] *Spalding Club Misc.*, i, pp. 97-8.

[388] Ib., i, Christen Michell, p. 165; Bessie Thom, p. 167.

[389] Ib., i, Issobell Richie, p. 142; Margrat Og, p. 144; Helene Rogie, p. 147; Jonet Lucas, p. 149; Jonet Dauidsone, p. 150; Issobell Oige, p. 152; Beatrice Robbie, p. 153.

[390] Pitcairn, ii, p. 478.

[391] Baines, i, p. 607 note.

[392] Pitcairn, iii, p. 606.

Of the festivals belonging to later religions several mentions are made. De Lancre, when giving a general account of the ceremonies, says that the witches of the Basses-Pyrénées went to their assemblies at Easter and other solemn festivals, and that their chief night was that of St. John the Baptist.[393] Jane Bosdeau, from the Puy-de-Dôme district (1594), bears this out, for she went to a meeting with the Devil 'at Midnight on the Eve of St. John'.[394] Antide Colas (1598) 'auoit esté au Sabbat à vn chacun bon iour de l'an, comme à Noel, à Pasques, à la feste de Dieu'.[395] Both generations of Lancashire witches (1613 and 1633) kept Good Friday.[396] Jonet Watson of Dalkeith (1661) was at a meeting 'about the tyme of the last Baille-ffyre night'.[397] The Crook of Devon witches (1662) met on St. Andrew's Day, at Yule.[398] In Connecticut (1662) the 'high frolic' was to be held at Christmas.[399]

Hour.—The actual hour at which the Sabbath was held is specified in very few cases; it appears to have been a nocturnal assembly, beginning about midnight and lasting till early dawn or cockcrow. 'Le coq s'oyt par fois és sabbats sonnãt la retraicte aux Sorciers.'[400]

In the Vosges in 1408 the meeting was held 'en la minuit et la deuxieme heure'.[401] In Lorraine in 1589 'Johannes a Villa und Agathina des Schneiders Francisci Weib, sagt, eine oder zwey Stunde vor Mitternacht were die bequemste Zeit darzu'.[402] At North Berwick, in 1590, Agnes Sampson arrived at the appointed place 'about eleven hours at even'.[403] The Aberdeen witches in 1597 held their dance 'wpon Hallowewin last bypast, at tuelff houris at ewin or thairby' (or

---

[393] De Lancre, *Tableau*, p. 398.
[394] F. Hutchinson, *Historical Essay*, p. 42.
[395] Boguet, p. 125.
[396] Chetham Society, vi, p. lxxiii; Whitaker, p. 216.
[397] Pitcairn, iii, p. 601.
[398] Burns Begg, pp. 219, 226, 237.
[399] J. Hutchinson, *History of Massachusetts Bay*, ii, p. 17; Taylor, p. 98.
[400] De Lancre, *Tableau*, p. 154.
[401] Bournon, p. 23.
[402] Remigius, pt. i, p. 72.
[403] Pitcairn, i, pt. ii, p. 239.

more particularly) 'betuixt tuell & ane houris at nycht'.[404] In 1598 the Lyons witch Françoise Secretain 'adioustoit qu'elle alloit tousiours au Sabbat enuiron la minuit, & beaucoup d'autres sorciers, que i'ay eu en main, ont dit le mesme'. Antide Colas, another Lyonnaise, went to the meeting on Christmas Eve between the midnight mass and the mass at dawn.[405]

The only daylight meeting which can be identified as a Sabbath occurred at Aberdeen, and may have been peculiar either to the locality or to the May-Day festival; or it may have been simply the continuation of the festival till the sun rose. Christen Mitchell and Bessie Thom were each accused that 'vpon the Ruidday, thrie yeris sensyn bygane, airlie in the morning, befoir sone rysing, thow convenit vpon Sanct Katherines Hill, accumpaniet with a numer of thy devilische factioun and band, the Devill your maister in cumpanie with yow'.[406]

2. The Esbat

Business.—The Esbat differed from the Sabbath by being primarily for business, whereas the Sabbath was purely religious. In both, feasting and dancing brought the proceedings to a close. The business carried on at the Esbat was usually the practice of magic for the benefit of a client or for the harming of an enemy. Sometimes the Devil appears to have ordered his followers to perform some action by which to impress the imagination of those who believed in his power though they did not worship him. Very often also the Esbat was for sheer enjoyment only, without any ulterior object, as the following quotations show:

Estebène de Cambrue (1567), who is the authority for the name Esbat as applied to local meetings, says that 'les petites assemblées qui se font pres des villes ou parroisses, où il n'y va que ceux du lieu, ils les appellent les esbats: & se font ores en vn lieu de ladicte paroisse,

---

[404] *Spalding Club Misc.*, i, pp. 97, 114, 165, 167.
[405] Boguet, pp. 119, 125.
[406] *Spalding Club Misc.*, i, pp. 165, 167.

ores en vn autre, où on ne faict que sauter & folastrer, le Diable n'y estant auec tout son grand arroy comme aux grandes assemblees'.[407] Alesoun Peirsoun (1588) was taken by a party of men and women, under the leadership of a man in green, 'fordir nor scho could tell; and saw with thame pypeing and mirrynes and gude scheir, and wes careit to Lowtheane, and saw wyne punchounis with tassis with them'.[408] Jonet Barker (1643) said that 'scho and ye said Margaret Lauder being w'hin ye said Jonet Cranstones house tua pyntis of beir war drukkin be thame thre togidder in ye said house at quhilk ye devill appeirit to thame in ye liknes of ane tryme gentill man and drank w' thame all thre and that he Imbracet the said margaret lauder in his armes at ye drinking of ye beir and put his arme about hir waist'.[409]Isobel Bairdie (1649) was accused of meeting the Devil and drinking with him, 'the devil drank to her, and she pledging him, drank back again to him, and he pledged her, saying, *Grammercie, you are very welcome.*'[410] Janet Brown (1649) 'was charged with having held a meeting with the Devil appearing as a man, at the back of Broomhills, who was *at a wanton play* with Isobel Gairdner the elder, and Janet Thomson'.[411] In Forfar Helen Guthrie (1661) confessed that she went to several meetings; at one in the churchyard 'they daunced togither, and the ground under them wes all fyre flauchter, and Andrew Watson hade his vsuale staff in his hand, altho he be a blind man yet he daunced alse nimblie as any of the companye, and made also great miriement by singing his old ballads, and that Isobell Shyrrie did sing her song called Tinkletum Tankletum; and that the divill kist every one of the women'. At another meeting 'they all daunced togither a whyle, and then went to Mary Rynd's house and sat doune together at the table ... and made them selfes mirrie; and the divell made much of them all, but especiallie of Mary Rynd, and he kist them all'.[412] Elspet Bruce of the same Coven, 'by turning the sive and sheires, reased the divell,

---

[407] De Lancre, *Tableau*, p. 123.
[408] Pitcairn, i, pt. ii, p. 163.
[409] From the record in the Justiciary Court of Edinburgh.
[410] Arnot, p. 358.
[411] Id., p. 358.
[412] Kinloch, pp. 120, 121.

who being werry hard to be laid againe, ther wes a meiting of witches for laying of him ... and at this meiting they had pipe-music and dauncing'.[413] Isobell Gowdie (1662) gives an account of one of these joyous assemblies: 'We killed an ox, in Burgie, abowt the dawing of the day, and we browght the ox with ws hom to Aulderne, and did eat all amongst ws, in an hows in Aulderne, and feasted on it.'[414] Marie Lamont (1662) also enjoyed her meetings; the first at which she was present was held in Kettie Scott's house, where the devil 'sung to them, and they dancit; he gave them wyn to drink, and wheat bread to eat, and they warr all very mirrie. She confesses, at that meiting the said Kettie Scott made her first acquaintance with the devill, and caused her to drink to him, and shak hands with him.—Shee was with Katie Scot and others at a meitting at Kempoch, wher they danced, and the devil kissed them when they went away.'[415] Annaple Thomson and the other witches of Borrowstowness (1679)—

'wis at several mettings with the devill in the linkes of Borrowstonenes, and in the howsse of you Bessie Vickar, and ye did eatt and drink with the devill, and with on another, and with witches in hir howss in the night tyme; and the devill and the said Wm Craw browght the ale which ye drank, extending to about sevin gallons, from the howss of Elizabeth Hamilton; and yow the said Annaple had ane other metting abowt fyve wekes ago, when yow wis goeing to the coalhill of Grange, and he inveitted you to go alongst, and drink with him.... And yow the said Margret Hamilton has bein the devill's servant these eight or nyne yeeres bygane; and he appered and conversed with yow at the town-well at Borrowstownes, and several tymes in yowr awin howss, and drank severall choppens of ale with you.'[416]

The magical ceremonies performed by the witches with the help of the Devil were usually for the destruction of, or for doing harm to, an enemy. Sometimes, however, the spells were originally for the

---

[413] Id., p. 122.
[414] Pitcairn, iii, p. 613.
[415] Sharpe, pp. 131, 134.
[416] *Scots Magazine*, 1814, p. 200.

promotion of fertility, but were misunderstood by the recorders and probably by the witches themselves. Alexia Violaea (1589) said that 'nachdem sie were mit ihren Gespielen umb und umb gelauffen eine ziemliche gut Weile, habe sie pflegen in die Höhe über sich zu werffen ein reines subtiles Pulverlein, welches ihr der Teuffel darzu gegeben habe, darvon Raupen, Käffern, Heuschrecken, und dergleichen andere Beschädigung mehr, so Hauffenweise wüchsen, dass die Acker darmit in einem Augenblick überall beschmeist würden'.[417] Isobel Gowdie's magical charm (1662) seems to come under this category:

'We went be-east Kinlosse, and ther we yoaked an plewghe of paddokis. The Devill held the plewgh, and Johne Yownge in Mebestowne, our Officer, did drywe the plewghe. Paddokis did draw the plewgh, as oxen; qwickens wer sowmes, a riglen's horne wes a cowter, and an piece of an riglen's horne wes an sok. We went two seuerall tymes abowt; and all we of the Coven went still wp and downe with the plewghe, prayeing to the Divell for the fruit of that land.'[418]

The greater number of meetings were occupied with business of a magical character with the intention of harming certain specified persons; though any other kind of business was also transacted. The North Berwick witches opened the graves which the Devil indicated in order to obtain the means of making charms with dead men's bones; on another occasion they attempted to wreck a ship by magic.[419] The Lang Niddry witches (1608) went to the house of Beigis Tod, where they drank, and there christened a cat.[420] The Lancashire witches (1613) met at Malking Tower for two purposes; the first was to give a name to the familiar of Alison Device, which could not be done as she was not present, being then in prison; the second was to arrange a scheme or plot for the release of Mother Demdike, the principal witch of the community, then a prisoner in Lancaster Castle; the plot

---

[417] Remigius, pt. i, p. 91.
[418] Pitcairn, iii, p. 603; see below, p. 171.
[419] Id., i, pt. ii, pp. 210-11, 217, 239.
[420] Id., ii, pp. 542-3.

involved the killing of the gaoler and governor, and the blowing up of the castle.[421] In 1630 Alexander Hamilton was tried in Edinburgh, 'the said Alexr Hamiltoun haifing concaivet ane deidlie haitrent agains umqle Elizabeth Lausone Lady Ormestoun younger becaus the said Alexr being at her zet asking for almous she choisit him therfra saying to him "away custroun carle ye will get nothing heir". The said Alexr therupon in revenge therof accompaneit wt tua wemen mentionet in his depostiones come to Saltoun woid quhair he raisit the devill and quha appeirit to him and his associattis in the likenes of ane man cled in gray and the said Alexr and his associattis haifing schawin to him the caus of thair coming desyring him to schaw to thame be quhat meanes thay micht be revendget upon the said Lady.'[422]

Margaret Johnson (1633) deposed that she was not at the great witch-meeting on All Saints' Day, but was at a smaller meeting the Sunday after, 'where there was, at yt tyme, between 30 and 40 witches, who did all ride to the said meetinge, and the end of theire said meeting was to consult for the killinge and hurtinge of men and beasts.'[423] The Forfar witches (1661) claimed to have wrecked a ship.[424] Isobel Gowdie (1662) is as usual very dramatic in her account; on one occasion the witches met to make a charm against the minister of Auldearne, Mr. Harie Forbes: 'Satan wes with ws and learned ws the wordis to say thryse ower. Quhan we haid learned all thes wordis from the Divell, we fell all down wpon owr kneis, with owr hear down ower owr showlderis and eyes, and owr handis lifted wp, and owr eyes stedfastlie fixed wpon the Divell; and said the forsaidis wordis thryse ower to the Divell, striktlie, against Maister Harie Forbes his recowering from the said seiknes.' When making an image only a few of the witches were present with the Devil.[425] Marie Lamont (1662) claimed that her Coven raised storms on two occasions; and on a third, they in the likeness of 'kats', and the Devil as a man with cloven feet,

---

[421] Potts, C 3, G 3, I 2, I 3.
[422] From the trial of 'Alexr Hamiltoun, warlok', in the Justiciary Court, Edinburgh.
[423] Whitaker, p. 216.
[424] Kinloch, p. 122.
[425] Pitcairn, iii, pp. 609, 613.

made a charm with 'wytsand' against Blackhall younger and Mr. John Hamilton.[426] Amongst the most detailed accounts of the wax or clay images, and of the ritual for killing the person whom the image represented, are those of the Somerset witches[427] (1664). The baptism of the figure is an interesting point. The Paisley witches (1678) had a meeting to make a clay figure in order to kill an enemy of the witch in whose house the meeting was held.[428] At Borrowstowness part of the accusation was that 'ye and ilk ane of yow was at ane metting with the devill and other witches at the croce of Murestane, upon the threttein of October last, where you all danced and the devill acted the pyiper, and where yow indewored to have destroyed Andrew Mitchell.'[429] In New England the witches accused George Burroughs 'that he brought Poppets to them, and Thorns to stick into those Poppets'.[430]

At the Esbats it is also evident that the Devil wished to maintain an appearance of miraculous power not only before the world at large, but in the eyes of the witches as well. This will account for the meetings on the sea-shore in raging storms when vessels were liable to be wrecked, and there are also many indications that the destruction of an enemy was effected by means more certain than the making and pricking of a wax or clay figure, means which were used after the figure had been made. Some of the methods of maintaining this prestige are of the simplest, others are noted without any explanation: 'Satan faict en ce lieu [le Sabbat] tant de choses estrãges & nouuelles que leur simplicité & abus prend cela pour quelques miracles.'[431] At Forfar (1661) the means of obtaining the result are apparent; during a great storm the Devil and the witches destroyed the bridge of Cortaquhie, and the destruction was so arranged as to appear to have been effected by magical power; but Helen Guthrie confessed that 'they went to the bridge of Cortaquhie with intentione to pull it doune, and that for this end shee her selfe, Jonnet Stout, and others of them,

---

[426] Sharpe, pp. 132-4.
[427] Glanvil, pt. ii, pp. 137-8, 164.
[428] Id., pt. ii, p. 294.
[429] *Scots Magazine*, 1814, p. 201.
[430] Mather, p. 125.
[431] De Lancre, *Tableau*, p. 135.

did thrust ther shoulderis againest the bridge, and that the divell wes bussie among them acting his pairt'. Issobell Smyth, who also assisted on the occasion, said, 'Wee all rewed that meitting, for wee hurt our selves lifting.'[432] Still more simple was the method of destroying the harvest of a field at Crook of Devon, where Bessie Henderson 'confessed and declared that Janet Paton was with you at ane meeting when they trampit down Thos. White's rie in the beginning of harvest, 1661, and that she had broad soales and trampit down more nor any of the rest'.[433] The Devil of Mohra in Sweden cared only to impress his followers; when the wall which they were building fell down 'some of the Witches are commonly hurt, which makes him laugh, but presently he cures them again'.[434]

Site.—In some places the Esbat was held at a fixed site, in others the site varied from week to week. In both cases, the locality was always in the near neighbourhood of the village whose inhabitants attended the meeting.

'Pour le lieu ordinaire c'est és carrefours, cõme disoit Isaac de Queyran, qui deposoit y auoir esté au carrefour du Palays Galienne, près la ville de Bourdeaux; ou aux places des paroisses au deuant des Eglises, & le plus souuent au droict de la grand' porte, si l'Eglise est plantée au milieu de la place comme elle est souuent, afin que le Diable plante sa chaire tout vis à vis du grand autel où on met le Sainct sacrement: comme il est en la place d'Ascain, où tous les tesmoins du lieu, nous ont dict que le Sabbat se faisoit. Il a aussi accoustumé les tenir en quelque lieu desert, & sauuage, comme au milieu d'vne lande; & encore en lieu du tout hors de passage, de voisinage, d'habitation, & de rencontre: Et communement ils s'appellent Aquelarre[435] qui signifie Lane de Bouc, comme qui diroit la lane ou lãde, où le Bouc conuoque ses assemblées.'[436]

---

[432] Kinloch, pp. 122, 133.
[433] Burns Begg, p. 224.
[434] Horneck, pt. ii, p. 323.
[435] The full name is Aquelarre de verros, prado del Cabron.
[436] De Lancre, Tableau, pp. 64-5.

Danaeus emphasizes the variation of both site and date: 'They meete togither in certen apointed places, not al of them togither, nor at once, but certen of them whom he pleaseth to call, so that he apointeth where they shall meete, and at what houre of the day, or of the nighte.'[437] The Windsor witches, however, 'did accustome to meete within the backeside of Maister Dodges in the Pittes there'.[438] Boguet's evidence also points to there being a settled site for the Esbat in each village:

'Les Sorciers du costé de Longchamois s'assembloient en vn pré, qui est sur le grand chemin tirant à S. Claude, où l'on voit les ruines d'vne maison. Ceux du costé de Coirieres tenoient leur Sabbat, sous le village de Coirieres proche l'eau, en vn lieu appellé és Combes, qui est du tout sans chemin. [Autres] se retrouuoient en vn lieu dict és Fontenelles, sous le village de Nezan, qui est vn lieu assez descouuert ... le Sabbat des Sorciers de la Moüille se tenoit en la Cour du Prioré du mesme lieu.'[439]

Jane Bosdeau (1594) went twice a week regularly to 'a Rendezvous of above Sixty Witches at Puy de dome'.[440] And the Swedish witches went so uniformly to one place that there was a special building for their rites:

'They unanimously confessed that *Blockula* is scituated in a delicate large Meadow whereof you can see no end. The place or house they met at, had before it a Gate painted with divers colours; through this Gate they went into a little Meadow distinct from the other.... In a huge large Room of this House, they said, there stood a very long Table, at which the Witches did sit down: And that hard by this Room was another Chamber where there were very lovely and delicate Beds.'[441]

On the whole, the weight of evidence in England and Scotland is in favour of Danaeus's statement that there was no fixed site, though this should be taken as referring to the local meetings only, not to the Great

---

[437] Danaeus, ch. iv.
[438] *Rehearsall*, p. 7.
[439] *Boguet*, pp. 126-7.
[440] F. Hutchinson, *Historical Essay*, p. 43.
[441] Horneck, pt. ii, p. 321.

Assemblies. The Forfar witch-trials give much information: Helen Guthrie

'wes at a meitting in the church yeard of Forfar in the Holfe therof.... Betwixt the oatseid and the bearseid [barleysowing], she wes at ane other meitting at the Pavilione hollis.... This same year, betwixt the oatseid and bearseid, she was at a thrid meiting in the church yeard of Forfar in the holfe thereof, about the same tyme of the night as at the [former] meitings, viz. at midnight.—About the beginning of the last oat seid tyme, Isabell Syrie did cary hir [Jonet Howat] to the Insch within the loch of Forfar, shoe saw at this tyme, about threteen witches with the divill, and they daunced togither.... About four wiekes after the forsaid meiting in the Insch, the said Isabell Syrie caried hir to ane other meiting at Muryknowes.—About three and a halfe yeares since, she [Elspet Alexander] was at a meiting with the divill at Peterden, midway betwixt Forfar and Dondie.... About four wiekes after this mieting at Petterden, shoe was at ane second mieting at the Muryknowes ... shoe was present at ane thrid mieting near Kerymure.'[442]

Isobel Gowdie's evidence is detailed as usual: 'The last tyme that owr Coven met, we, and an vther Coven, wer dauncing at the Hill of Earlseat; and befor that, betwixt Moynes and Bowgholl; and befor that we ves beyond the Meikleburne; and the vther Coven being at the Downie-hillis we went from beyond the Meikle-burne, and went besyd them, to the howssis at the Wood-end of Inshoch.... Befor Candlemas, we went be-east Kinlosse.'[443] The same facts were elicited from the Kinross-shire witches; Robert Wilson 'confessed ye had ane meeting with the Devill at the Stanriegate, bewest the Cruick of Devon ... the Devil appointed them to meet at the Bents of Balruddrie'.— Margaret Huggon confessed 'that ye was at another meeting with Sathan at the Stanriegate, bewest the Cruik of Devon ... lykeways ye confessed ye was at another meeting with Satan at the Heathrie Knowe be-east the Cruik of Devon, where the Gallows stands ... a meeting at the back of Knocktinnie at the Gaitside ... and another at the bents of

---

[442] Kinloch, pp. 120 seq.
[443] Pitcairn, iii, p. 603.

Newbiggin'.—Janet Brugh 'confessed that ye was at ane meeting at Stanriegate ... ye confessed that about Yule last bypast ye was at ane meeting with Sathan at Turfhills ... lykeways ye confessed that ye was at the Bents of Balruddrie and Gibson's Craig, where Sathan was present at them both'.—Christian Grieve 'freely confessed that ye was at ane meeting with Sathan at the back of Andrew Dowie his house'.[444] The Somerset witches (1664) varied in this respect. Those of Wincanton met in different places: Elizabeth Style 'hath been at several general meetings in the night at High Common, and a Common near *Motcombe*, at a place near *Marnhull*, and at other places'.—Alice Duke 'hath been at several meetings in Lie Common, and other places in the night'. But the Brewham Coven appear to have met commonly at Hussey's Knap in Brewham Forest.[445]

Occasionally a reason is given for the change of site. 'Parfois vn Sabbat finy à vn coin de paroisse, on s'en va le tenir à vne autre, où le Diable mene les mesmes personnes: mais là, on y en rencontre d'autres'.[446] Sometimes also a sidelight is thrown upon these gatherings, which explains the fact that in many cases the witches said that they did not know all the people present at a given meeting:

'Antoine Tornier, Et Iaquema Paget ont confessé, que comme elles retournoient à certain iour par ensemble de glanner, passans au long du p̄ré de Longchamois, elles apperçeurent que l'on y tenoit le Sabbat; Surquoy elles poserent bas leurs fardeaux, & allerent au lieu predict, où elles firent comme les autres, & puis se retirerent chacune en leurs maisons, apres auoir reprins leurs fardeaux.'[447]

The Salem Witches (1692) met 'upon a plain grassy place, by which was a Cart path and sandy ground in the path, in which were the tracks of Horses feet'.[448]

Date and Hour.—There was no fixed day or hour for the Esbat, and in this it differed from the Sabbath, which was always at night. The

[444] Burns Begg, pp. 226 seq.
[445] Glanvil, pt. ii, pp. 140, 148, 156, 161.
[446] De Lancre, *Tableau*, p. 64.
[447] Boguet, p. 102.
[448] Burr, p. 418.

Devil let his followers know the time, either by going to them himself or by sending a message by the officer. The message might be by word of mouth, or by some signal understood by the initiated.

Though there was no fixed day for the Esbat, it seems probable that one day in the week was observed in each locality.

Danaeus, in his general survey of the cult in 1575, says: 'He apointeth where they shall meete, and at what houre of the day, or of the night: wherein they haue no surenes, nor certentie. For these meetinges are not weekely, nor monthly, nor yeerely, but when and how often it shall seeme good to this their maister. And many times himself warneth them to meete, sometimes hee apoynteth others to warne them in his staede. But when he doth it himself, he appeareth vnto them in likenesse of a man.'[449] De Lancre says that in the Basses-Pyrénées 'le lieu où on le trouue ordinairement s'appelle Lanne de bouc, & en Basque *Aquelarre de verros, prado del Cabron*, & là les Sorciers le vont adorer trois nuicts durant, celle du Lundy, du Mercredy, & du Vendredy.—Les iours ordinaires de la conuocation du Sabbat, ou pour mieux dire les nuicts, sont celles du Mercredy venant au Ieudy, & du Vendredy venant au Samedy.—Catherine de Naguille de la paroisse d'Vstarits, aagee de onze ans, & sa compagne, nous out asseuré qu'elles auoiẽt esté au Sabbat en plein midy.'[450] Jane Bosdeau (1594) 'every Wednesday and Friday met a Rendezvous of aboue Sixty Witches at Puy de dome'.[451] Boguet says that the day of the Sabbath was variable, usually Thursday night;[452] while, according to Bodin, the most frequent was 'entre la nuict du Lundi & Mardi'.[453] Boguet also goes on to say, 'Le Sabbat ne se tient pas tousiours de nuict, ains que les Sorciers y vont aussi quelquefois de iour, selon que firent Antoine Tornier, & Iaquema Paget, & plusieurs autres de leur secte le confessent.'[454] The Lorraine witches also had the same custom:

---

[449] Danaeus, ch. iv.
[450] De Lancre, *Tableau*, pp. 62, 398.
[451] F. Hutchinson, p. 43.
[452] Boguet, p. 124.
[453] Bodin, *Fléau*, p. 182.
[454] Boguet, p. 123.

'Alle zugleich, so viel ihrer bisher in Lotharingen peinlich sind verhöret worden, bekandten, dass solche Versammlung in keiner andern Nacht, als welche zu nechst vor dem Donnerstag oder Sambstag hergehet, gehalten werden.—Johannes a Villa und Agathina des Schneiders Francisci weib, sagt, eine oder zwey Stunde vor Mitternacht, were die bequemste Zeit darzu, und zwar nicht allein zu diesen Gespensten, sondern auch sonsten zu allerhand Gespensten, Bollergeisten, Irrgeisten, &c. Aber die Stunde nach Mitternacht diene nicht darzu.'[455]

The English and Scotch evidence is to the same effect. The witches 'are likewise reported to have each of them a Spirit or Imp attending on, or assigned to them.... These give the Witches notice to be ready on all Solemn appointments, and meetings, which are ordinarily on Tuesday or Wednesday night'.[456] Janet Breadheid of the Auldearne Coven emphasizes the irregularity of the dates: 'Efter that, we vold still meit euerie ten, twelve, or twantie dayes continwally.'[457]Marie Lamont merely notes that the meetings were at night: 'The devil came to Kattrein Scott's house in the midst of the night.... When she had been at a mietting sine Zowle last, with other witches, in the night, the devill convoyed her home in the dawing.'[458] The Somerset witches had no special night: 'At every meeting before the Spirit vanisheth away, he appoints the next meeting place and time,'[459] and Mary Green went to a meeting 'on Thursday Night before Whitsunday last.'[460] At Paisley the meeting was on Thursday, the 4th of January, 1678, in the night, in John Stuart's house.[461] The Swedish witches were much harder worked: 'whereas formerly one journey a week would serve his turn, from their own Town to the place aforesaid, now they were forced to

---

[455] Remigius, pp. 71, 72.
[456] *Pleasant Treatise*, p. 4.
[457] Pitcairn, iii, p. 617.
[458] Sharpe, pp. 131, 133.
[459] Glanvil, pt. ii, p. 139.
[460] Id., pt. ii, p. 164.
[461] Id., pt. ii, pp. 293, 297.

run to other Towns and places for Children, and that some of them did bring with them some fifteen, some sixteen Children every night.'[462]

The more modern examples suggest that the date became more fixed: 'On croit que c'est toujours un vendredi soir que les sorciers et sorcières se réunissent.'[463] 'Sorciers et sorcières vont au *sabbat* le vendredi, à travers les airs.'[464]

---

[462] Horneck, pt. ii, p. 318.
[463] Monseur, p. 87.
[464] Lemoine, *La Tradition*, 1892, vi, p. 106.

V. THE RITES

1. General

The exact order of the ceremonies is never given and probably varied in different localities, but the general rule of the ritual at the Sabbath seems to have been that proceedings began by the worshippers paying homage to the Devil, who sat or stood in a convenient place. The homage consisted in renewing the vows of fidelity and obedience, in kissing the Devil on any part of his person that he chose to indicate, and sometimes in turning a certain number of times widdershins. Then followed the reports of all magic worked since the previous Sabbath, either by individuals or at the Esbats, and at the same time the witches consulted the Master as to their cases and received instructions from him how to proceed; after which came admissions to the society or marriages of the members. This ended the business part of the meeting. Immediately after all the business was transacted, the religious service was celebrated, the ceremonial of which varied according to the season of the year; and it was followed by the 'obscene' fertility rites. The whole ceremony ended with feasting and dancing, and the assembly broke up at dawn.

This was apparently the usual course of the ritual of the Sabbath; the Esbat had less ceremonial, and the religious service was not performed. The Devil himself often went round and collected the congregation; and, not being in his 'grand arroy', he appeared as a man in ordinary dress. Instead of the religious service with the adoration of the god, the witches worked the spells and charms with which they bewitched or unbewitched their enemies and friends, or they exercised new methods which they learnt from their Master, or received instructions how to practise the arts of healing and secret poisoning, of causing and blasting fertility.

There are a few general accounts of the usual course of the Sabbath ritual. Danaeus (1575) does not distinguish clearly between the two classes of meetings, but at the same time he seems to have realized that a certain order was followed:

'Satan calleth them togither into a Diuelish Sinagoge, and that he may also vnderstand of them howe well and diligently they haue fulfilled their office of intoxicating committed vnto them, and whõ they haue slaine: wherefore they meete togither in certen apointed places.... Whẽ they meete together he appeareth visibly vnto them in sundrie fourmes, as the head and chiefe of that congregation.... Then doe they all repeate the othe which they haue geuen vnto him, in acknowledging him to be their God, thẽ fal they to dauncing.... Whiche beeing all finished, then he demaundeth agayne of them what they woulde require of him.... Vnto some he geueth poysons ready made, and others he teacheth howe to make and mingle new.... Finally, if in any thing they neede his presence and helpe, by couenant he promiseth to be present with them.'[465]

Boguet (1589) is more exact, as he obtained his knowledge at first hand:

'Les Sorciers estans assemblez en leur Synagogue adorent premierement Satan ... ils luy offrent des chandelles, & le baisent aux parties honteuses de derriere. Quelquefois encor il tient vne image noire, qu'il faut baiser aux Sorciers.... Les Sorciers en second lieu dansent.... Les danses finies, les Sorciers viennent à s'accoupler.... Les Sorciers, apres s'estre veautrez parmy les plaisirs immondes de la chair, banquettent & se festoient.... Les Sorciers rendent conte à Satan de ce qu'ils ont fait dés la derniere assemblée.... Il fait renoncer de nouueau à ces miserables, Dieu, Chresme, & Baptesme. Il leur fait rafraischir le serment solennel qu'ils ont fait.'[466]

The English account is put together from foreign sources to a great extent:

'They are carried out of the house, either by the Window, Door, or Chimney, mounted on their Imps.... Thus brought to the designed place, they find a great number of others arrived there by the same means: who, before Lucifer takes his place in his throne as King, do make their accustomed homage, Adoring, and Proclaiming him their Lord, and rendring him all Honour. This Solemnity being finished,

---

[465] Danaeus, ch. iv.
[466] Boguet, pp. 131-9.

they sit to Table where no delicate meats are wanting.... At the sound of many pleasant Instruments the table is taken away, and the pleasant consort invites them to a Ball.... At the last, the lights are put out. The Incubus's in the shapes of proper men satisfy the desires of the Witches, and the Succubus's serve for whores to the Wizards. At last before Aurora brings back the day, each one mounts on his spirit, and so returns to his respective dwelling place.... Sometimes at their solemn assemblies, the Devil commands, that each tell what wickedness he hath committed.... When the assembly is ready to break up, and the Devil to dispatch them, he publisheth this law with a loud voice, *Revenge your selves or else you shall dye*, then each one kissing the Posteriors of the Devil returns upon their aiery Vehicles to their habitations.'[467]

2. Homage

In some places the witches saluted their Chief by falling on their knees, and also by certain manual gestures; in other places by curtsies and obeisances. In Scotland, France, and Belgium, another rite was also in vogue, that of kissing the Devil on any part of his person that he might direct. At Como and Brescia the witches, 'when they paid reverence to the presiding demon, bent themselves backwards, lifting a foot in the air forwards.'[468]

Remigius, writing of the Lorraine witches in 1589, says:

'Es erzehlte die Beatrix Bayona dass einer unter ihnen allen der Oberster wer, welcher in einer Zell auff einem hohen Stuhl sässe, sehr ernsthafftig und prächtig heraus, zu demselbigen trete je einer nach dem andern, mit Furcht und Zittern, falle ihm zum Zeichen seiner Ehrerbietung für die Füsse, und umbfange ihn mit aller Demuth und Reverentz.—Erstlich fallen sie nieder auff ihre Knie; darnach legen sie die Hände auswendig zusammen, als diejenigen pflegen zu thun, welche obtestiren, jedoch auff dem Rücken und verkehrter Weise, sie

---

[467] *Pleasant Treatise*, pp. 5-7.
[468] Lea, iii, p. 501.

haben den Rücken zu ihm gewandt, bleiben so lang kniend, biss er selbsten zu ihnen sagt, dass es genugsam sey.'[469]

In Somerset (1664) the witches always mention the salutation:

'At their first meeting the Man in black bids them welcome, and they all make low obeysance to him.—[Elizabeth Style, Alice Duke, Anne Bishop, Mary Penny] met about nine of the Clock in the Night, in the Common near *Trister* Gate, where they met a Man in black Clothes with a little Band, to whom they did Courtesie and due observance.—Mary Green [went with others to] Hussey's Knap in the Forrest in the Night time, where met them the Fiend in the shape of a little Man in black Clothes with a little band, to him all made obeysances.... On Thursday Night before Whitsunday last [she met several others] and being met they called out *Robin*. Upon which instantly appeared a little Man in black Clothes to whom all made obeysance, and the little Man put his hand to his Hat, saying, How do ye? speaking *low* but *big*. Then all made low obeysances to him again.'[470]

As late as the eighteenth century there is a similar account.[471]

Danaeus (1575) and Cooper (1617) are the only writers who mention the kiss in their general accounts of the ceremonies. The former says: 'Then biddeth he thẽ that they fall down & worship him, after what maner and gesture of body he pleaseth, and best liketh of. Thus some of them falle downe at his knees, some offre vnto him black burning cãdles, other kisse him in some part of his body where he appeareth visibly.'[472] Cooper mentions it as part of the admission ceremony: 'Secondly, when this acknowledgement is made, in testimoniall of this subiection, Satan offers his back-parts to be kissed of his vassall.'[473]

The ceremony is one of the earliest of which there is any record. In 1303 a Bishop of Coventry was accused at Rome of a number of

---

[469] Remigius, pt. i, pp. 89, 91.
[470] Glanvil, pt. ii, pp. 137, 139, 163, 164.
[471] W. G. Stewart, p. 175.
[472] Danaeus, ch. ii.
[473] Cooper, p. 90.

crimes, amongst others 'quod diabolo homagium fecerat, et eum fuerit osculatus in tergo'.[474] Guillaume Edeline was tried in 1453; he was 'docteur en théologie, prieur de S. Germain en Laye, et auparavant Augustin, et religieux de certaines aultres ordres. Confessa ledit sire Guillaume, de sa bonne et franche voulenté, avoir fait hommage audit ennemy en l'espèce et semblance d'ung mouton, en le baisant par le fondement en signe de révérence et d'hommage.'[475] Martin Tulouff, tried in Guernsey in 1563, went to a meeting, 'ou ly avoet chinq ou vi chatz, d'ou il y en avoet ung qui estoit noir, qui menoit la dance, et d^t q̄ il estoit sur ses pieds plat, et que ladite Collennette le besa p̱ de derriere, et luy p̱ la crysse. Et luy dist ladite vieillesse q̄ ledit chat e̱stoit le diable.'[476] Estebène de Cambrue, in 1567, described the ceremonies at the Sabbath: 'Ils se mettent à dancer à l'entour d'une pierre, sur laquelle est assis vn grand homme noir, qu'elles appellent Mõsieur, & chacun de l'assemblee luy va baiser le derriere.'[477] The witches of Poictiers in 1574 'dansoyent à l'entour du bouc: puis vn chacun luy baisoit le derriere'.[478] The same ceremony took place at North Berwick in 1590: 'Now efter that the deuell had endit his admonitions, he cam down out of the pulpit, and caused all the company to com and kiss his ers, quhilk they said was cauld lyk yce.'[479] Jane Bosdeau confessed that at meetings at Puy-de-Dôme in 1594 'all the Witches had Candles which they lighted at his, and danced in a Circle Back to Back. They kiss'd his Backside, and pray'd that he would help them.'[480] Andro Man of Aberdeen in 1597 confessed 'that all thay quha convenis with thame kissis Christsonday and the Quene of Elphenis airss'.[481] Rolande de Vernois in 1598 'confessa que le Diable se presenta pour lors au Sabbat en forme d'vn gros chat noir. Que tous ceux, qui estoient au Sabbat,

---

[474] Rymer, i, p. 956.
[475] Chartier, iii, p. 45.
[476] From a trial in the Guernsey Greffe.
[477] De Lancre, *Tableau*, p. 123.
[478] Bodin, p. 187.
[479] Melville, p. 396; *see also* Pitcairn, i, pt. ii, pp. 210-12, 239, 246.
[480] F. Hutchinson, p. 43.
[481] *Spalding Club Misc.*, i, pp. 121, 125.

alloient baiser ce gros chat noir au derriere.'[482] Cornélie van Beverwyck, aged 75, at Ghent in 1598, was accused that 'vous n'avez pas craint de vous agenouiller devant lui, de lui rendre hommage et de baiser son derriere en signe de soumission'.[483] Claire Goessen in 1603 went to 'l'assemblée nocturne de Lembeke, où, après la danse, elle a, comme tous les assistans, baisé un bouc à l'endroit de sa queue'.[484] Jeannette d'Abadie in 1609 in the Basses-Pyrénées said, regarding the renunciation which she made on admission, 'il luy faisoit renouueller toutes les fois qu'elle alloit au sabbat, puis elle l'alloit baiser au derriere.'[485] At the celebrated trial of Louis Gaufredy at Aix in 1610, Magdalene de Demandouls gave a detailed account of the homage rendered by the witches:

'First the hagges and witches, who are people of a sordid and base condition, are the first that come to adore the Prince of the Synagogue, who is Lucifers lieftenant, and he that now holdeth that place is Lewes Gaufridy: then they adore the Princesse of the Synagogue who is a woman placed at his right hand. Next they goe and worship the Diuell who is seated in a Throne like a Prince. In the second place come the Sorcerers and Sorceresses, who are people of a middle condition, and these performe the same kind of adoration with the former, kneeling vpon the ground, but not prostrating themselves as doe the other; although they kisse the hands and feet of the Diuell as the first likewise doe. In the third place come the Magicians who are Gentlemen and people of a higher ranke.'[486]

Isobel Gowdie of Auldearne in 1662 said, 'Somtym he vold be lyk a stirk, a bull, a deir, a rae, or a dowg, and he vold hold wp his taill wntill we wold kiss his arce.'[487] The explanation of this rite is given in the French authorities:

'Le Diable estoit en forme de bouc, ayant vne queue, & au dessoubs vn visage d'homme noir, où elle fut contrainte le baiser.—[Elle]

---

[482] Boguet, p. 411.

[483] Cannaert, p. 46.

[484] Id., p. 50.

[485] De Lancre, *Tableau*, p. 131.

[486] Michaelis, *Historie*, pp. 334-5.

[487] Pitcairn, iii, p. 613.

depose, Que la premiere fois qu'elle luy fut presentee elle le baisa à ce visage de derriere au dessoubs d'vne grande queuë: qu'elle l'y a baisé par trois fois, & qu'il auoit aussi ce visage faict comme le museau d'vn bouc.—Il a vne grande queuë au derriere, & vne forme de visage au dessoubs: duquel visage il ne profere aucune parole, ains luy sert pour le donner à baiser à ceux qui bon luy semble.—Es festes solemnelles on baisoit le Diable au derriere, mais les notables sorcieres le baisoient au visage.'[488] The two faces are thus distinctly vouched for, and the use of them seems to have been to distinguish the position of the witch in the society. The mask or disguise is clearly indicated in the evidence of Isaac de Queyron, who with others 'le baiserent á vne fesse qui estoit blanche & rouge, & auoit la forme d'vne grande cuisse d'vn homme, & estoit velue'.[489]

The Devil was also kissed on other parts of his person. Marion Grant of the Aberdeen witches (1597) confessed that he 'causit the kis him in dyvers pairtis, and worship him on thy kneis as thy lord'.[490] Some of the Lyons witches 'le baiserent aux parties honteuses de derriere: les autres le baisent sur l'espaule.'[491] Jeannette d'Abadie in the Basses-Pyrénées (1609) confessed 'que le Diable luy faisoit baiser son visage, puis le nombril, puis le membre viril, puis son derriere'.[492] In connexion with this last statement, it is worth comparing Doughty's account of an Arab custom: 'There is a strange custom, (not only of nomad women, but in the Arabic countries even among Christians, which may seem to remain of the old idolatry among them,) of mothers, their gossips, and even young maidens, visiting married women to kiss with a kind of devotion the *hammam* of the male children.'[493]

---

[488] De Lancre, *Tableau*, pp. 68, 126, 128.
[489] Id. ib., p. 148.
[490] *Spalding Club Misc.*, i, p. 171.
[491] Boguet, p. 131.
[492] De Lancre, *Tableau*, pp. 72, 131.
[493] Doughty, *Travels in Arabia Deserta*, i, 89.

3. The Dances

Dances as an important part of fertility rites are too well known to need description. The witches' dances, taken in conjunction with the dates of the four great Sabbaths of the year, point to the fact that they also were intended to promote fertility. There were several forms of ritual dances, varying apparently according to the form of fertility required, whether of crops, animals, or human beings. The jumping dance seems to have had for its object the growth of the crops; the higher the performers jumped the higher the crops would grow. The so-called 'obscene' or 'indecent' dance was for the promotion of fertility among animals and women. When the dancers were disguised as animals, the dance was for the increase of the animals represented; when undisguised, for the fertility of human beings.

Although the dances took place at English witch meetings, they are merely mentioned and not described. The Scotch trials give rather fuller accounts, but the chief details are from France.

The two principal forms of the dance were the ring-dance and the follow-my-leader dance, but there was also a very complicated form which was not understood by the Inquisitors, who therefore dismiss it with the words 'tout est en confusion'. It still survives, however, in the Basses-Pyrénées, in some of the very villages which were inhabited by witches in the sixteenth century—those witches whose proceedings de Lancre describes so vividly.[494]

The ring dances were usually round some object; sometimes a stone, sometimes the Devil stood or was enthroned in the middle. Thomas Leyis, with a great number of other witches, 'came to the Market and Fish Cross of Aberdeen, under the conduct and guiding of the Devil present with you, all in company, playing before you on his kind of instruments: Ye all danced about both the said crosses, and the meal market, a long space of time; in the which Devil's dance, thou the said Thomas was foremost and led the ring, and dang the said Kathren Mitchell, because she spoiled your dance, and ran not so fast about as the rest. Testified by the said Kathren Mitchell, who was

---

[494] Moret, *Mystères Égyptiens*, pp. 247 seq.

present with thee at the time forsaid dancing with the Devil.'[495] Margaret Og was indicted for going to Craigleauch 'on Hallow even last, and there, accompanied by thy own two daughters, and certain others, your devilish adherents and companions, ye danced all together, about a great stone, under the conduct of Satan, your master, a long space'.[496] Jonet Lucas was accused of 'danceing in ane ring' on the same occasion.[497] Beatrice Robbie was 'indited as a notorious witch, in coming, under the conduct of the Devil thy master, with certain others, thy devilish adherents, to Craigleauche, and there dancing altogether about a great stone, a long space, and the Devil your master playing before you'.[498] In the Basses-Pyrénées, 'Ils se mettent à dancer à l'entour d'une pierre, qui est plantée audit lieu, sur laquelle est assis un grand homme noir.'[499] Jane Bosdeau, who 'confessed freely and without Torture and continued constant in it in the midst of the Flames in which she was burnt', said that she had been to a witch-meeting, 'and danced in a circle back to back'.[500]

'Les Sorciers dansent, & font leurs danses en rond, doz contre doz. Les boiteux y vont plus dispostement que les autres [et] incitoient les autres à sauter & danser.[501] ... Quelquefois, mais rarement, ils dansent deux à deux, & par fois l'vn çà & l'autre là, & tousiours en confusion: estans telles danses semblables à celles des Fées, vrais Diables incorporez, qui regnoient il n'y a pas lõg temps.'[502] 'On y dance tousiours le dos tourné au centre de la dance, qui faict que les filles sont si accoutumées à porter les mains en arriere en cette dãce ronde, qu'elles y trainent tout le corps, & luy donnent vn ply courbé en arriere, ayant les bras à demy tournez: si bien que la plupart ont le ventre communement grand, enflé & avancé, & vn peu penchant sur le deuant. On y dance fort peu souuent vn à vn, c'est à dire vn homme

---

[495] *Spalding Club Misc.*, i, pp. 97-8. Spelling modernized.
[496] Ib., i, p. 144. Spelling modernized.
[497] Ib., p. 149.
[498] Ib., p. 153. Spelling modernized.
[499] De Lancre, *Tableau*, p. 123.
[500] F. Hutchinson, *Historical Essay*, p. 43.
[501] Compare the account of the Forfar witch-dance. Kinloch, p. 120.
[502] Boguet, pp. 131-2.

seul auec vne femme ou fille.... On n'y dançoit que trois sortes de bransles, communement se tournant les espaules l'vn à l'autre, & le dos d'vn chascun visant dans le rond de la dance, & le visage en dehors. La premiere c'est à la Bohemienne.... La seconde c'est à sauts; ces deux sont en rond.'[503] 'Ils apperceurent à l'entrée [d'vn bois], vn rond, ou cerne, dans lequel il y auoit plusieurs vestiges de pieds d'hoῦes, d'èfans, & d'Ours, ou bien d'autres bestes semblables,[504] lesquels estoient seulement enfoncez d'vn demy doigt dans la neige, quoy que pour eux ils y entrassent iusques à la ceinture.'[505]

The Swedish witches danced in the same manner. 'We used to go to a gravel pit which lay hard by a cross-way, and there we put on a garment over our heads, and then danced round.'[506] The round dance was so essentially a witch dance that More says, 'It might be here very seasonable to enquire into the nature of those large *dark Rings* in the grass, which they call *Fairy Circles*, whether they be the *Rendezvouz* of Witches, or the dancing places of those little Puppet Spirits which they call *Elves* or *Fairies*.'[507]

It will be seen from the above quotations that there were many varieties in the ring dance; this was the case also in the follow-my-leader dance. There seems to have been also a combination of the two dances; or perhaps it would be more correct to say that sometimes the ring and follow-my-leader figures were used together so as to form one complete dance, as in the modern Lancers. In both forms of the dance one of the chief members of the society was the 'ring-leader', or leader of the dance. In the follow-my-leader dance this was often the Devil, but in the ring dances this place was usually taken by the second in command. When, however, the Devil was the leader, the second-in-command was in the rear to keep up those who could not move so

---

[503] De Lancre, *Tableau*, p. 210.
[504] Compare the dittay against Bessie Thom, who danced round the Fish Cross of Aberdeen with other witches 'in the lyknes of kattis and haris'. *Spalding Club Misc.*, i, 167.
[505] Boguet, p. 127.
[506] Horneck, pt. ii, p. 316.
[507] More, p. 232.

quickly as the others. As pace was apparently of importance, and as it seems to have been a punishable offence to lag behind in the dance, this is possibly the origin of the expression 'The Devil take the hindmost'.

At North Berwick Barbara Napier met her comrades at the church, 'where she danced endlong the Kirk yard, and Gelie Duncan played on a trump, John Fian, missellit, led the ring; Agnes Sampson and her daughters and all the rest following the said Barbara, to the number of seven score of persons.'[508] Isobel Gowdie was unfortunately not encouraged to describe the dances in which she had taken part, so that our information, instead of being full and precise, is very meagre. 'Jean Martein is Maiden to the Coven that I am of; and her nickname is "Over the dyke with it", because the Devil always takes the Maiden in his hand next him, when we dance Gillatrypes; and when he would loup from [words broken here] he and she will say, "Over the dyke with it."'[509] Another Scotch example is Mr. Gideon Penman, who had been minister at Crighton. He usually 'was in the rear in all their dances, and beat up all those that were slow'.[510] Barton's wife 'one night going to a dancing upon Pentland Hills, he [the Devil] went before us in the likeness of a rough tanny Dog, playing on a pair of Pipes'.[511] De Lancre concludes his description of the dances (see above, p. 131) by an account of an 'endlong' dance. 'La troisieme est aussi le dos tourné, mais se tenant tous en long, & sans se deprendre des mains, ils s'approchent de si près qu'ils se touchent, & se rencontrent dos à dos, vn homme auec vne femme; & à certaine cadance ils se choquent & frapent impudemment cul contre cul.'[512] It was perhaps this dance which the Devil led: 'Le Diable voit parfois dancer simplement comme spectateur; parfois il mene la dance, changeant souuent de main & se mettant à la main de celles qui luy plaisent le plus.'[513] In Northumberland in 1673 'their particular divell

---

[508] Pitcairn, i, pt. ii, pp. 245-6. Spelling modernized.
[509] Id., iii, p. 606. Spelling modernized.
[510] Fountainhall, i, p. 14.
[511] Sinclair, p. 163.
[512] De Lancre, *Tableau*, p. 210.
[513] De Lancre, *Tableau*, p. 212.

tooke them that did most evill, and danced with them first.—The devill, in the forme of a little black man and black cloaths, called of one Isabell Thompson, of Slealy, widdow, by name, and required of her what service she had done him. She replyd she had gott power of the body of one Margarett Teasdale. And after he had danced with her he dismissed her, and call'd of one Thomasine, wife of Edward Watson, of Slealy.'[514]Danaeus also notes that the Devil was the leader: 'Thẽ fal they to dauncing, wherin he leadeth the daunce, or els they hoppe and daunce merely about him.'[515]This is perhaps what de Lancre means when he says that 'apres la dance ils se mettent par fois à sauter'.[516] A curious variation of the follow-my-leader dance was practised at Aberdeen on Rood Day, a date which as I have shown elsewhere corresponds with the Walpurgis-Nacht of the German witches. The meeting took place upon St. Katherine's Hill, 'and there under the conduct of Satan, present with you, playing before you, after his form, ye all danced a devilish dance, riding on trees, by a long space.'[517]

Other variations are also given. 'The dance is strange, and wonderful, as well as diabolical, for turning themselves back to back, they take one another by the arms and raise each other from the ground, then shake their heads to and fro like Anticks, and turn themselves as if they were mad.'[518] Reginald Scot, quoting Bodin, says: 'At these magicall assemblies, the witches neuer faile to danse; and in their danse they sing these words, Har har, divell divell, danse here danse here, plaie here plaie here, Sabbath sabbath. And whiles they sing and danse, euerie one hath a broome in hir hand, and holdeth it vp aloft. Item he saith, that these night-walking or rather night-dansing witches, brought out of *Italie* into *France*, that danse which

---

[514] *Surtees Soc.*, xl, pp. 195, 197.
[515] Danaeus, ch. iv.
[516] De Lancre, op. cit., p. 211.
[517] *Spalding Club Misc.*, i, pp. 165, 167. Spelling modernized. The account of the Arab witches should be compared with this. 'In the time of Ibn Munkidh the witches rode about naked on a stick between the graves of the cemetery of Shaizar.' Wellhausen, p. 159.
[518] *Pleasant Treatise of Witches*, p. 6.

is called *La Volta*.'[519] There is also a description of one of the dances of the Italian witches: 'At Como and Brescia a number of children from eight to twelve years of age, who had frequented the Sabbat, and had been re-converted by the inquisitors, gave exhibitions in which their skill showed that they had not been taught by human art. The woman was held behind her partner and they danced backward, and when they paid reverence to the presiding demon they bent themselves backwards, lifting a foot in the air forwards.'[520]

In Lorraine the round dance always moved to the left. As the dancers faced outwards, this would mean that they moved 'widdershins', i.e. against the sun. 'Ferner, dass sie ihre Täntze in einem ronden Kreiss rings umbher führen, und die Rücke zusammen gekehret haben, wie eine unter den dreyen Gratiis pfleget fürgerissen zu werden, und also zusammen tanzen. Sybilla Morelia sagt, dass der Reyhen allezeit auff der lincken Hand umbher gehe.'[521]

One form of the witches' dance seems to survive among the children in the Walloon districts of Belgium. It appears to be a mixture of the ordinary round dance and the third of de Lancre's dances; for it has no central personage, and the striking of back against back is a marked feature. 'Les enfants font une ronde et répètent un couplet. Chaque fois, un joueur désigné fait demi-tour sur place et se remet à tourner avec les autres en faisant face à l'extérieur du cercle. Quand tous les joueurs sont retournés, ils se rapprochent et se heurtent le dos en cadence.'[522]

4. The Music

The music at the assemblies was of all kinds, both instrumental and vocal. The English trials hardly mention music, possibly because the Sabbath had fallen into a decadent condition; but the Scotch and French trials prove that it was an integral part of the celebration. The Devil himself was the usual performer, but other members of the

[519] Reg. Scot, Bk. iii, p. 42. La volta is said to be the origin of the waltz.
[520] Lea, iii, p. 501.
[521] Remigius, p. 82.
[522] E. Monseur, p. 102.

society could also supply the music, and occasionally one person held the position of piper to the Devil. The music was always as an accompaniment of the dance; the instrument in general use was a pipe, varied in England by a cittern, in Scotland by 'the trump' or Jew's harp, also an instrument played with the mouth.

The Somerset witches said that 'the Man in black sometimes playes on a Pipe or Cittern, and the company dance'.[523]

The North Berwick witches (1590), when at the special meeting called to compass the death of the king, 'danced along the Kirk-yeard, Geilis Duncan playing on a Trump.'[524] The instrument of the Aberdeen Devil (1597), though not specified, was probably a pipe; it is usually called 'his forme of instrument' in the dittays. Isobel Cockie of Aberdeen was accused of being at a Sabbath on Allhallow Eve: 'Thou wast the ring-leader, next Thomas Leyis; and because the Devil played not so melodiously and well as thou crewit, thou took his instrument out of his mouth, then took him on the chaps therewith, and played thyself thereon to the whole company.'[525] At another meeting, Jonet Lucas was present: 'Thou and they was under the conduct of thy master, the Devil, dancing in ane ring, and he playing melodiously upon ane instrument, albeit invisibly to you.'[526] At Tranent (1659) eight women and a man named John Douglas confessed to 'having merry meetings with Satan, enlivened with music and dancing. Douglas was the pyper, and the two favourite airs of his majesty were "Kilt thy coat, Maggie, and come thy way with me", and "Hulie the bed will fa'."'[527] Agnes Spark at Forfar (1661) 'did see about a dozen of people dancing, and they had sweet music amongst them, and, as she thought, it was the music of a pipe'.[528] Barton's wife was at a meeting in the Pentland Hills, where the Devil 'went before us in the likeness of a rough tanny Dog, playing on a pair of Pipes. The Spring he played (says she) was, The silly bit Chiken, gar cast it a pickle and

---

[523] Glanvil, pt. ii, p. 141.

[524] Pitcairn, i, pt. ii, pp. 239, 246.

[525] *Spalding Club Misc.*, i, pp. 114-15. Spelling modernized.

[526] Id., i, p. 149. Spelling modernized.

[527] *Spottiswoode Miscellany*, ii, p. 68.

[528] Kinloch, p. 129. Spelling modernized.

it will grow meikle.'[529] At Crook of Devon (1662) the two old witches, Margaret Huggon and Janet Paton, confessed to being at a meeting, and 'the foresaids hail women was there likeways and did all dance and ane piper play'.[530]

In France the instruments were more varied. Marie d'Aspilcouette, aged nineteen, 'voyoit dancer auec violons, trompettes, ou tabourins, qui rendoyent vne tres grande harmonie'.[531] Isaac de Queyran, aged twenty-five, said that a minor devil (*diabloton*) played on a tambourine, while the witches danced.[532] But as usual de Lancre is at his best when making a general summary:

'Elles dancent au son du petit tabourin & de la fluste, & par fois auec ce long instrument qu'ils posent sur le col, puis s'allongeant iusqu'auprés de la ceinture; ils le battent auec vn petit baston: par fois auec vn violon. Mais ce ne sont les seuls instrumès du sabbat, car nous auõs apprins de plusieurs, qu'on y oyt toute sorte d'instrumens, auec vne telle harmonie, qu'il n'y a concert au monde qui le puisse esgaler.'[533]

Vocal music was also heard at the meetings, sometimes as an accompaniment of the dance, sometimes as an entertainment in itself. When it was sung as a part of the dance, the words were usually addressed to the Master, and took the form of a hymn of praise. Such a hymn addressed to the god of fertility would be full of allusions and words to shock the sensibilities of the Christian priests and ministers who sat in judgement on the witches. Danaeus gives a general account of these scenes: 'Then fal they to dauncing, wherin he leadeth the daunce, or els they hoppe and daunce merely about him, singing most filthy songes made in his prayse.'[534] Sinclair had his account from a clergyman: 'a reverend Minister told me, that one who was the Devils Piper, a wizzard confest to him, that at a Ball of dancing, the Foul Spirit taught him a Baudy song to sing and play, as it were this night,

---

[529] Sinclair, p. 163.
[530] Burns Begg, pp. 234, 235.
[531] De Lancre, *Tableau*, p. 127.
[532] Id. ib., p. 150.
[533] Id. ib., p. 211.
[534] Danaeus, ch. iv.

and ere two days past all the Lads and Lasses of the town were lilting it throw the street. It were abomination to rehearse it.'[535] At Forfar Helen Guthrie told the court that Andrew Watson 'made great merriment by singing his old ballads, and Isobell Shirrie did sing her song called Tinkletum Tankletum'.[536] Occasionally the Devil himself was the performer, as at Innerkip, where according to Marie Lamont 'he sung to us and we all dancit'.[537] Boguet notes that the music was sometimes vocal and sometimes instrumental: 'Les haubois ne manquent pas à ces esbats: car il y en a qui sont commis à faire le devoir de menestrier; Satan y iouë mesme de la flutte le plus souuent; & à d'autrefois les Sorciers se contentent de chanter à la voix, disant toutefois leurs chansons pesle-mesle, & auec vne confusion telle, qu'ils ne s'entendent pas les vns les autres.'[538] At Aix in 1610 'the Magicians and those that can reade, sing certaine Psalmes as they doe in the Church, especially*Laudate Dominum de Coelis: Confitemini domino quoniam bonus*, and the Canticle *Benedicite*, transferring all to the praise of Lucifer and the Diuels: And the Hagges and Sorcerers doe houle and vary their hellish cries high and low counterfeiting a kinde of villanous musicke. They also daunce at the sound of Viols and other instruments, which are brought thither by those that were skild to play vpon them.'[539] At another French trial in 1652 the evidence showed that 'on dansait sans musique, aux chansons'.[540]

5. The Feast

The feast, like the rest of the ritual, varied in detail in different places. It took place either indoors or out according to the climate and the season; in Southern France almost invariably in the open air, in Scotland and Sweden almost always under cover; in England sometimes one, sometimes the other. Where it was usual to have it in

---

[535] Sinclair, p. 219.
[536] Kinloch, p. 120.
[537] Sharpe, p. 131.
[538] Boguet, p. 132.
[539] Michaelis, *Hist.*, p. 336.
[540] Van Elven, v (1891), p. 215.

the open, tables were carried out and the food laid upon them; indoor feasts were always spread on tables; but in the English accounts of the open-air meal the cloth was spread, picnic-fashion, on the ground. The food was supplied in different ways; sometimes entirely by the devil, sometimes entirely by one member of the community, and sometimes—picnic-fashion again—all the company brought their own provisions. Consequently the quality of the food varied considerably; on some occasions it was very good, on others very homely. But no matter who provided it, the thanks of the feasters were solemnly and reverently given to the Master, to whose power the production of all food was due.

In a certain number of cases it is said that the food eaten at the feasts was of an unsatisfying nature. This statement is usually made in the general descriptions given by contemporary writers; it is rarely found in the personal confessions. When it does so occur, it is worth noting that the witch is generally a young girl. If this were always the case, it would be quite possible that then, as now, dancing and excitement had a great effect on the appetite, and that the ordinary amount of food would appear insufficient.

The taboo on salt is interesting, but it does not appear to have been by any means universal. It does not seem to occur at all in Great Britain, where the food at the feasts was quite normal.

Some authorities appear to think that the witches ate the best of everything. 'They sit to Table where no delicate meats are wanting to gratifie their Appetites, all dainties being brought in the twinckling of an Eye, by those spirits that attend the Assembly'.[541] Though this is dramatically expressed it is confirmed by the statements of the witches themselves. The Lancashire witches had a great feast when they met in Malking Tower to consult as to the rescue of Mother Demdike.

'The persons aforesaid had to their dinners Beefe, Bacon, and roasted Mutton; which Mutton (as this Examinates said brother said) was of a Wether of Christopher Swyers of Barley: which Wether was brought in the night before into this Examinates mothers house by the said Iames Deuice, this Examinates said brother: and in this

---

[541] *Pleasant Treatise of Witches*, p. 5.

Examinates sight killed and eaten.... And before their said parting away, they all appointed to meete at the said Prestons wiues house that day twelue-moneths; at which time the said Prestons wife promised to make them a great Feast.'[542]

The feast of the Faversham witches was also indoors. 'Joan Cariden confessed that Goodwife Hott told her within these two daies that there was a great meeting at Goodwife Panterys house, and that Goodwife Dodson was there, and that Goodwife Gardner should have been there, but did not come, and the Divell sat at the upper end of the Table.'[543] This was always the Devil's place at the feast, and beside him sat the chief of the women witches. The Somerset trials give more detail than any of the other English cases. Elizabeth Style said that 'at their meeting they have usually Wine or good Beer, Cakes, Meat or the like. They eat and drink really when they meet in their bodies, dance also and have Musick. The Man in black sits at the higher end, and *Anne Bishop* usually next him. He useth some words before meat, and none after, his voice is audible, but very low.'[544] She enters into a little more detail in another place: 'They had Wine, Cakes, and Roastmeat (all brought by the Man in black) which they did eat and drink. They danced and were merry, and were bodily there, and in their Clothes.'[545] Alice Duke gave a similar account: 'All sate down, a white Cloth being spread on the ground, and did drink Wine, and eat Cakes and Meat.'[546] The Scotch trials show that it was usually the witches who entertained the Master and the rest of the band. Alison Peirson, whose adventures among the fairies are very interesting, stated that a man in green 'apperit to hir, ane lustie mane, with mony mene and wemen with him: And that scho sanit her and prayit, and past with thame fordir nor scho could tell; and saw with thame pypeing and mirrynes and gude scheir, and wes careit to Lowtheane, and saw wyne punchounis with tassis with thame'.[547] On another occasion a very

[542] Potts, G 3, I 3, P 3.
[543] *Examination of Joan Williford*, p. 6.
[544] Glanvil, pt. ii, pp. 139-40.
[545] Id., p. 138.
[546] Id., p. 149.
[547] Pitcairn, i, pt. ii, p. 163.

considerable meeting took place 'in an old house near Castle Semple, where a splendid feast was prepared, which pleased the royal visitor so much, that he complimented his entertainers for their hospitality, and endearingly addressed them as "his bairns"'.[548] The Forfar witches had many feasts; Helen Guthrie says of one occasion:

'They went to Mary Rynd's house and sat doune together at the table, the divell being present at the head of it; and some of them went to Johne Benny's house, he being a brewer, and brought ale from hence ... and others of them went to Alexander Hieche's and brought aqua vitae from thence, and thus made themselfes mirrie; and the divill made much of them all, but especiallie of Mary Rynd, and he kist them all except the said Helen herselfe, whose hand onlie he kist; and shee and Jonet Stout satt opposite one to another at the table.'[549]

Of the meeting at Muryknowes there are several accounts. The first is by little Jonet Howat, Helen Guthrie's young daughter: 'At this meiting ther wer about twenty persones present with the divill, and they daunced togither and eat togither, having bieff, bread, and ale, and shoe did eat and drink with them hir self, bot hir bellie was not filled, and shoe filled the drink to the rest of the company.'[550] Elspet Alexander confirms this statement, 'The divill and the witches did drinke together having flesh, bread, and aile';[551] and so also does the Jonet Stout who sat opposite to Helen Guthrie at the table, 'The divill and the said witches did eat and drinke, having flesh, bread, and aile upon ane table, and Joanet Huit was caper and filled the drinke'.[552] On one occasion they tried to wreck the Bridge of Cortaquhie; 'when we had done, Elspet [Bruce] gaive the divell ane goose in hir own house, and he dated hir mor than them all, because shee was ane prettie woman.'[553] The Kinross-shire witches obtained their food from the Devil, and this is one of the few instances of complaints as to the quality of it. 'Sathan gave you [Robert Wilson] both meat and drink

---

[548] *Spottiswoode Misc.*, ii, p. 67.
[549] Kinloch, p. 121.
[550] Id., p. 124.
[551] Id., p. 126.
[552] Id., p. 127.
[553] Id., p. 133. Dated = caressed.

sundry times, but it never did you any good';[554] and Janet Brugh 'confessed that ye got rough bread and sour drink from Sathan at the Bents of Balruddrie'.[555] According to Marie Lamont, 'the devill came to Kattrein Scott's house, in the midst of the night. He gave them wyn to drink, and wheat bread to eat, and they warr all very mirrie.'[556] Isobel Gowdie's confession gives a wealth of detail as usual:

'We would go to several houses in the night time. We were at Candlemas last in Grangehill, where we got meat and drink enough. The Devil sat at the head of the table, and all the Coven about. That night he desired Alexander Elder in Earlseat to say the grace before meat, which he did; and is this:[557] "We eat this meat in the Devil's name" [etc.]. And then we began to eat. And when we had ended eating, we looked steadfastly to the Devil, and bowing ourselves to him, we said to the Devil, We thank thee, our Lord, for this.—We killed an ox, in Burgie, about the dawing of the day, and we brought the ox with us home to Aulderne, and did eat all amongst us in an house in Aulderne, and feasted on it.'[558]

At Borrowstowness the witches went to different houses for their feasts, which seem to have been supplied partly by the hostess, partly by the Devil and the guests.

'Ye and each person of you was at several meetings with the devil in the links of Borrowstowness, and in the house of you Bessie Vickar, and ye did eat and drink with the devil, and with one another, and with witches in her house in the night time; and the devil and the said William Craw brought the ale which ye drank, extending to about seven gallons, from the house of Elizabeth Hamilton.'[559]

In 1692 Goodwife Foster of Salem gave a rather charming description of the picnic feast with the Coven from Andover:

---

[554] Burns Begg, p. 227.

[555] Id., p. 238.

[556] Sharpe, p. 131.

[557] The complete grace is given on p. 167. It will be seen that it is a corrupt version of some ancient form of words.

[558] Pitcairn, iii, pp. 612, 613. Spelling modernized.

[559] *Scots Magazine*, 1814, p. 200. Spelling modernized.

'I enquired what she did for Victuals' [at the meeting]; 'She answered that she carried Bread and Cheese in her pocket, and that she and the Andover Company came to the Village before the Meeting began, and sat down together under a tree, and eat their food, and that she drank water out of a Brook to quench her thirst.'[560]

The Continental evidence varies very little from the British. Except in a few details, the main facts are practically the same. De Lancre summarizes the evidence which he himself collected, and contrasts it with what other authorities said on the subject:

'Les liures disent que les sorciers mangent au Sabbat de ce que le Diable leur a appresté: mais bien souuĕt il ne s'y trouue que des viandes qu'ils ont porté eux mesmes. Parfois il y a plusieurs tables seruies de bons viures, & d'autres fois de tres meschans: & à table on se sied selon sa qualité, ayant chacun son Demon assis auprés, & parfois vis à vis. Ils benissent leur table inuoquant Beelzebub, & le tenant pour celui qui leur faict ce bien.'[561]

The young man-witch, Isaac de Queyran, told de Lancre that the witches sat at a table with the Black Man at the end, and had bread and meat which was spread on a cloth.[562] The evidence at the trial of Louis Gaufredy at Aix in 1610 gives other details, though the eating of children's flesh is probably an exaggeration:

'They prouide a banquet, setting three tables according to the three diuersities of the people above named. They that haue the charge of bread, doe bring in bread made of corne. The drink which they haue is Malmsey. The meate they ordinarily eate is the flesh of young children, which they cooke and make ready in the Synagogue, sometimes bringing them thither aliue by stealing them from those houses where they haue opportunity to come. They haue no vse of kniues at table for feare least they should be laid a crosse. They haue also no salt.'[563]

---

560 Burr, p. 418.
561 De Lancre, *Tableau*, p. 197.
562 Id. ib., p. 148.
563 Michaelis, *Historie*, pp. 335-6.

Boguet also collected a considerable amount of information from the witches who fell into his hands:

'Les Sorciers, apres s'estre veautrez parmi les plaisirs immondes de la chair, banquettent & se festoient: leurs banquets estans composez de plusieurs sortes de viandes, selon les lieux, & qualitez des personnes. Par deçà la table estoit couuerte de beurre, de fromage, & de chair. Clauda Ianguillaume, Iaquema Paget, & quelques autres adioustoient qu'il y auoit vne grande chaudiere sur le feu, dans laquelle chacun alloit prendre de la chair. On y boit aussi du vin, & le plus souuent de l'eau.... Antoine Tornier a confessé qu'elle en auoit beu [le vin] dans vn goubelet de bois; les autres parloient seulement d'eau. Mais il n'y a iamais sel en ces repas.... Les Sorciers auant que de prendre leur repas benissent la table, mais auec des parolles remplies de blasphemes, faisans Beelzebub autheur & conseruateur de toutes choses.... Ils accordent tous, qu'il n'y a point de gout aux viandes qu'ils mangent au Sabbat, & que la chair n'est autre chair que de cheual. Et adioustent en outre, que lors qu'ils sortent de table, ils sont aussi affamez que quand ils entrent. Antide Colas racontoit particulierement que les viandes estoient froides.... Toutesfois il faut croire que bien souuent l'on mange au Sabbat à bon escient, & non par fantaisie & imagination.'[564]

The cold food occurs also in the accusation against a Belgian witch, Elizabeth Vlamynx, in 1595: 'Vous-même vous avez apporté aux convives un hochepot [hutsepot] froid, que vous aviez préparé d'avance.'[565]

In Sweden the witches collected the food and sent it to the Devil, who gave them as much of it as he thought fit. The feast was always held indoors in the house known as Blockula.

'In a huge large Room of this House, they said, there stood a very long Table, at which the Witches did sit down.... They sate down to Table, and those that the Devil esteemed most, were placed nearest to him, but the Children must stand at the door, where he himself gives them meat and drink. The diet they did use to have there, was, they

---

[564] Boguet, pp. 135-9.
[565] Cannaert, p. 45.

said, Broth with Colworts and Bacon in it, Oatmeal, Bread spread with Butter, Milk and Cheese. And they added that sometimes it tasted very well, and sometimes very ill.'[566]

6. Candles

At first sight it would seem that the candles were naturally used only to illuminate the midnight festivities, but the evidence points to the burning lights being part of the ritual. This is also suggested by the importance, in the cult, of the early-spring festival of Candlemas; a festival which has long been recognized as of pre-Christian origin.

The light is particularly mentioned in many instances as being carried by the Devil, usually on his head; the witches often lit their torches and candles at this flame, though sometimes it seems that the Devil lit the torch and then presented it to the witch. To call the chief of the cult *Lucifer* was therefore peculiarly appropriate, especially at the Candlemas Sabbath.

In 1574 the witches of Poictiers went to a cross-roads: 'là se trouuoit vn grand bouc noir, qui parloit comme vne personne aux assistans, & dansoyent a l'entour du bouc: puis vn chacun luy baisoit le derriere, auec vne chandelle ardente.'[567] The witches of North Berwick in 1590 mention candles as part of the ritual:

'At ther meting be nycht in the kirk of Northberick, the deuell, cled in a blak gown with a blak hat upon his head, preachit vnto a gret nomber of them out of the pulpit, having lyk leicht candles rond about him.[568]—John Fian blew up the Kirk doors, and blew in the lights, which were like mickle black candles, holden in an old man's hand, round about the pulpit.[569]—[John Fian] was taken to North Berwick church where Satan commanded him to make him homage with the rest of his servants; where he thought he saw the light of a candle,

---

[566] Horneck, pp. 321-2, 327.
[567] Bodin, *Fléau*, p. 187.
[568] Melville, p. 395.
[569] Pitcairn, i, pt. ii, p. 246. The ploughman, Gray Meal, who took a large part in the ceremonies, was an old man.

standing in the midst of his servants, which appeared blue lowe [flame].'[570]

In 1594 at Puy-de-Dôme Jane Bosdeau went 'at Midnight on the Eve of St John into a Field, where there appeared a great Black Goat with a Candle between his Horns'.[571] At Aberdeen in 1597 Marion Grant confessed that 'the Deuill apperit to the, within this auchteine dayis or thairby, quhome thow callis thy god, about ane hour in the nicht, and apperit to the in ane gryte man his lickness, in silkin abuilzeament [habiliment], withe ane quhyt candill in his hand'.[572] In 1598 the witches whom Boguet tried said that—

'les Sorciers estans assemblez en leur Synagogue adorent premierement Satan, qui apparoit là, tantost en forme d'vn grand homme noir, tantost en forme de bouc, & pour plus grand hommage, ils luy offrent des chandelles, qui rendent vne flamme de couleur bleüe. Quelquefois encor il tient vne image noire, qu'il fait baiser aux Sorciers. Antide Colas & ses compagnes, en baisant ceste image, offroient vne chandelle ou buche d'estrain ardente. Ces chandelles leur sont baillées par le Diable, & se perdent & esuanouissent dés lors qu'elles luy out esté offertes. Il s'en est trouué qui ont confessé qu'ils alloient allumer le plus souuent leurs chandelles à vne autre chandelle, que le Demon, estant en forme de bouc, portoit au dessus de la teste entre les deux cornes.'[573]

Some of the witches of the Basses-Pyrénées, tried in 1609, said that the Devil was—

'comme vn grand bouc, ayãt deux cornes deuant & deux en derriere. Mais le commun est qu'il a seulement trois cornes, & qu'il a quelque espece de lumiere en celle du milieu, de laquelle il a accoustumé au sabbat d'esclairer, & donner du feu & de la lumiere, mesmes à ces Sorcieres qui tiennent quelques chandelles alumees aux ceremonies de la Messe qu'ils veulent contrefaire. On luy voit aussi quelque espece de bonet ou chapeau au dessus de ses cornes.—Toute

---

[570] Id., i, pt. ii, p. 210.
[571] F. Hutchinson, *Hist. Essay*, p. 42.
[572] *Spalding Club Misc.*, i, p. 172.
[573] Boguet, p. 131.

l'assemblee le vient adorer le baisant sous la queuë, & allumant des chandelles noires.'[574]

Barthélemy Minguet of Brécy, a man of twenty-five, tried in 1616, described the ceremonies of the Sabbath; after the sermon the worshippers 'vont à l'offerte, tenant en leurs mains des chandelles de poix noire qui leur sont données par le Diable'.[575] In 1646 Elizabeth Weed of Great Catworth, Hunts, confessed that the Devil came to her at night, 'and being demanded what light was there, she answered, none but the light of the Spirit.'[576] In 1652 a French witch stated that at the Sabbath 'on dansait sans musique, aux chansons. Toutes les femmes y étoient tenues par les diables par lors il y avoit de la lumière une chandelle tenue au millieu par une femme que ne connoit.... Au milieux il y auoit une feme masquée tenant une chandelle.'[577] Barton's wife was at a witch meeting in the Pentland Hills, 'and coming down the hill when we had done, which was the best sport, he [the Devil] carried the candle in his bottom under his tail, which played ey wig wag wig wag.'[578] Helen Guthrie in 1661 does not expressly mention candles or torches, but her description of the flickering light on the ground suggests their use. She 'was at a meiting in the churchyeard of Forfar in the Holfe therof, and they daunced togither, and the ground under them wes all fyre flauchter'.[579] The Somerset witches stated that, when they met, 'the Man in Black bids them welcome, and they all make low obeysance to him, and he delivers some Wax Candles like little Torches, which they give back again at parting.'[580] The light seems to have been sometimes so arranged, probably in a lantern, as to be diffused. This was the case at Torryburn, where the assembly was lit by a light 'which came from darkness', it was sufficiently strong

---

[574] De Lancre, *Tableau*, pp. 68, 401.

[575] Id., *L'Incredulité*, p. 805.

[576] Davenport, p. 2.

[577] Van Elven, *La Tradition*, v (1891), p. 215.

[578] Sinclair, p. 163. The account given by Barton's wife of the position of the candle on the Devil's person is paralleled by the peculiarly coarse description of the Light-bearers at the witch-sabbaths at Münster. Humborg, p. 120.

[579] Kinloch, p. 120.

[580] Glanvil, pt. ii, p. 139.

for the dancers to see one another's faces, and to show the Devil wearing a cap or hood which covered his neck and ears.[581] The latest account of a witch-meeting in the eighteenth century describes how the witches of Strathdown went to Pol-nain and there were 'steering themselves to and fro in their riddles, by means of their oars the brooms, hallooing and skirling worse than the bogles, and each holding in her left hand a torch of fir'.[582]

There is one account where the candle was for use and not for ritual. John Stuart of Paisley, in 1678, admitted the Devil and some witches into his room one night in order to make a clay image of an enemy. 'Declares, that the black man did make the figure of the Head and Face and two Arms to the said Effigies. Declares, that the Devil set three Pins in the same, one in each side, and one in the Breast: And that the Declarant did hold the Candle to them all the time the Picture was making.'[583] John Stuart was the principal person on this occasion, and therefore had the honour of holding the light. The description of the event suggests that the saying 'To hold a candle to the Devil' took its rise in actual fact.

The material of which the candles or torches were made was pitch, according to de Lancre, and at North Berwick the lights were 'like lighted candles' burning with a blue flame. The white candle seems to have been essentially the attribute of the devil, the black candles or torches being distinctive of the witches. That the lights burned blue is due to the material of which the torches were made. The evanescent character of the light, when a wisp of straw was used, is noted in the evidence of Antide Colas.

7. The Sacrament

The earliest example of the religious services occurs in 1324 in the trial of Lady Alice Kyteler: 'In rifeling the closet of the ladie, they found a Wafer of sacramentall bread, hauing the diuels name stamped

---

[581] Chambers, iii, p. 298.
[582] Stewart, p. 175.
[583] Glanvil, pt. ii, p. 294.

thereon in stead of Jesus Christ.'[584] According to Boguet (1589) the Devil did not always perform the religious service himself, but mass was celebrated by a priest among his followers; this custom is found in all countries and seems to have been as common as that the Devil himself should perform the service.

'Celuy, qui est commis à faire l'office, est reuestu d'vne chappe noire sans croix, & apres auoir mis de l'eau dans le calice, il tourne le doz à l'autel, & puis esleue vn rond de raue teinte en noir, au lieu de l'hostie, & lors tous les Sorciers crient à haute voix, *Maistre, aide nous*. Le Diable en mesme temps pisse dans vn trou à terre, & fait de l'eau beniste de son vrine, de laquelle celuy, qui dit la messe, arrouse tous les assistans auec vn asperges noir.'[585]

The Devil of the Basses Pyrénées (1609) performed the religious ceremony himself:

'Il s'habille en Prestre pour dire Messe, laquelle il fait semblant de celebrer auec mille fourbes & souplesses, auprés d'vn arbre, ou parfois auprés d'vn rocher, dressant quelque forme d'autel sur des coloñes infernales, & sur iceluy sans dire le *Confiteor*, ny l'*Alleluya*, tournant les feuillets d'vn certain liure qu'il a en main, il commence à marmoter quelques mots de la Messe, & arriuant à l'offertoire il s'assiet, & toute l'assemblee le vient adorer le baisant sous la queuë, & allumant des chandelles noires: Puis luy baisent la main gauche, tremblans auec mille angoisses, & luy offrent du pain, des œufs, & de l'argent: & la Royne du Sabbat les reçoit, laquelle est assise à son costé gauche, & en sa main gauche elle tient vne paix ou platine, dans laquelle est grauee l'effigie de Lucifer, laquelle on ne baise qu'aprés l'auoir premierement baisée à elle. Puis il se met à prescher, son subiect est communément de la vaine gloire.... Il finit son sermon, & continue ses autres ceremonies, leuant vne certaine Hostie laquelle est noire & ronde, auec sa figure imprimée au dessus: & disant ces paroles, *Cecy est mon corps*, il leue l'Hostie sur ses cornes: & à cette esleuatiõ tous ceux de l'assemblee l'adorẽt en disant ces mots, *Aquerra Goity, Aquerra Beyty, Aquerra Goity, Aquerra Beyty*, qui veut dire, *Cabron*

---

[584] Holinshed, *Ireland*, p. 58.
[585] Boguet, p. 141.

arriba, Cabron abaro, de mesme en font ils au Calice repetant ces mots, iusqu'à ce qu'il a vuidé tout ce qui est dans iceluy. Puis toute l'assemblee enuironnant l'autel en forme de croissant ou demy-lune, prosternez par terre, il leur fait vn autre sermon, puis leur baille à communier par ordre, donnant à chacun vn petit morceau de l'hostie, & pour leur donner moyen de l'aualer aisément, il leur donne deux gorgees de quelque medicine infernale, & certain breuuage de si mauuais goust & odeur, que l'aualant ils suent, & neantmoins il est si froid, qu'il leur gele le corps, les nerfs, & les moüelles. Puis il s'accouple auec elles, & leur commande d'en faire de mesme, si bien qu'ils commettent mille incestes & autres pechez contre nature. Puis il les inuite à se mettre à table.'[586]

At Aix in 1610 Magdalene de Demandouls 'said that that accursed Magician Lewes [Gaufredy] did first inuent the saying of Masse at the Sabbaths, and did really consecrate and present the sacrifice to Lucifer.... She also related, that the said Magician did sprinkle the consecrated wine vpon all the company, at which time euery one cryeth, *Sanguis eius super nos & filios nostros.*'[587]

Lord Fountainhall remarks, 'In 1670 we heard that the Devil appeared in the shape of a Minister, in the copper mines of Sweden, and attempted the same villainous apery.'[588] The Scotch witches, like the Swedish, performed the rite after the manner of the Reformed Churches. In 1678—
'the devill had a great meeting of witches in Loudian, where, among others, was a warlock who formerly had been admitted to the ministrie in the presbyterian tymes, and when the bishops came in, conformed with them. But being found flagitious and wicked, was deposed by them, and now he turnes a preacher under the devill of hellish doctrine; for the devill at this tyme preaches to his witches really (if I may so term it) the doctrine of the infernall pitt, viz. blasphemies against God and his son Christ. Among other things, he told them that

---

[586] De Lancre, *Tableau*, pp. 401-2.
[587] Michaelis, *Hist.*, p. 337. The use of this phrase suggests that the sprinkling was a fertility rite.
[588] Fountainhall, i, pp. 14, 15.

they were more happy in him than they could be in God; him they saw, but God they could not see; and in mockrie of Christ and his holy ordinance of the sacrament of his supper, he gives the sacrament to them, bidding them eat it and to drink it in remembrance of himself. This villan was assisting to Sathan in this action, and in preaching.'[589]

Fountainhall in writing of the same convention of witches says that the Devil 'adventured to give them the communion or holy sacrament, the bread was like wafers, the drink was sometimes blood sometimes black moss-water. He preached and most blasphemously mocked them, if they offered to trust in God who left them miserable in the world, and neither he nor his Son Jesus Christ ever appeared to them when they called on them, as he had, who would not cheat them.'[590]

The Abbé Guibourg (1679), head of the Paris witches, 'a fait chez la Voisin, revêtu d'aube, d'étole et de manipule, une conjuration.'[591] The same Abbé celebrated mass more than once over the body of a woman and with the blood of a child, sacrificed for the occasion, in the chalice (see section on Sacrifice). The woman, who served as the altar for these masses, was always nude, and was the person for whose benefit the ceremony was performed. Marguerite Montvoisin makes this clear:

'Il est vrai aussi qu'une sage-femme qui demeurait au coin de la rue des Deux-Portes, distilla aussi les entrailles d'un enfant dont la mère y avait accouché.... Avant la distillation, les entrailles de l'enfant et l'arrière-faix de la mère avaient été portés à Saint-Denis, à Guibourg, par sa mère, la sage-femme et la mère de l'enfant, sur le ventre de laquelle sa mère, à son retour, lui dit que Guibourg avait dit la messe.'[592]

Guibourg acknowledged that, besides the one just quoted, he celebrated three masses in this way. At the first he used a conjuration. 'Il dit la deuxième messe dans une masure sur les remparts de Saint-Denis, sur la même femme, avec les mêmes cérémonies.... Dit la

---

[589] Law, p. 145.
[590] Fountainhall, i, p. 14.
[591] Ravaisson, 1679-81, p. 336.
[592] Id., p. 333.

troisième à Paris chez la Voisin sur la même femme.'[593] The woman mentioned in Guibourg's confession was Madame de Montespan herself. The following conjuration was used at the first mass: 'sur le ventre d'une femme': 'Astaroth, Asmodée, princes d'amitié, je vous conjure d'accepter le sacrifice que je vous présente de cet enfant pour les choses que je vous demande, qui sont l'amitié du Roi, de Mgr le Dauphin me soit continuée et être honorée des princes et princesses de la cour, que rien ne me soit dénié de tout ce que je demanderai au Roi, tant pour mes parents que serviteurs.'[594]

A very interesting case is that of the Rev. George Burroughs in New England (1692):

'He was Accused by Eight of the Confessing Witches, as being an Head Actor at some of their Hellish Randezvouses, and one who had the promise of being a King in Satan's kingdom, now going to be Erected.... One *Lacy* testify'd that she and the prisoner [Martha Carrier] were once Bodily present at a *Witch-meeting* in *Salem Village*; and that she knew the prisoner to be a Witch, and to have been at a Diabolical sacrament.... Another *Lacy* testify'd that the prisoner was at the *Witch-meeting*, in *Salem Village*, where they had Bread and Wine Administred unto them.... Deliverance Hobbs affirmed that this [Bridget] *Bishop* was at a General Meeting of the Witches, in a Field at *Salem*-Village, and there partook of a Diabolical Sacrament in Bread and Wine then administred.'[595]

Hutchinson had access to the same records and gives the same evidence, though even more strongly: 'Richard Carrier affirmed to the jury that he saw Mr. George Burroughs at the witch meeting at the village and saw him administer the sacrament. Mary Lacy, sen[r]. and her daughter Mary affirmed that Mr. George Burroughs was at the witch meetings with witch sacrements, and that she knows Mr. Burroughs to be of the company of witches.'[596] John Hale has a similar record: 'This D. H. [Deliverance Hobbs] confessed she was at a Witch

---

[593] Id., p. 335.
[594] Ravaisson, p. 335.
[595] Cotton Mather, pp. 120, 131, 158.
[596] J. Hutchinson, *Hist. of Massachusetts Bay*, ii, p. 55.

Meeting at Salem Village.... And the said G. B. preached to them, and such a Woman was their Deacon, and there they had a Sacrament.'[597] Abigail Williams said 'that the Witches had a *Sacrament* that day at an house in the Village, and that they had *Red Bread* and *Red Drink*'.[598] With the evidence before him Mather seems justified in saying that the witches had 'their Diabolical Sacraments, imitating the *Baptism* and the *Supper* of our Lord'.[599]

8. Sacrifices

There are four forms of sacrifice: (1) the blood sacrifice, which was performed by making an offering of the witch's own blood; (2) the sacrifice of an animal; (3) the sacrifice of a human being, usually a child; (4) the sacrifice of the god.

1. The *blood-sacrifice* took place first at the admission of the neophyte. Originally a sacrifice, it was afterwards joined to the other ceremony of signing the contract, the blood serving as the writing fluid; it also seems to be confused in the seventeenth century with the pricking for the Mark, but the earlier evidence is clear. A writer who generalizes on the witchcraft religion and who recognizes the sacrificial nature of the act is Cooper; as he wrote in 1617 his evidence belongs practically to the sixteenth century. He says:

'In further *token* of their subiection vnto Satan in yeelding vp themselues wholy vnto his deuotion, behold yet *another ceremony* heere vsually is performed: namely, *to let themselues bloud* in some apparant place of the body, yeelding the same to be *sucked by Satan,* as a *sacrifice* vnto him, and testifying thereby the full *subiection* of their *liues* and *soules* to his deuotion.'[600]

The earliest account of the ceremony is at Chelmsford in 1556. Elizabeth Francis 'learned this arte of witchcraft from her grandmother. When shee taughte it her, she counseiled her to geue of her bloudde to Sathan (as she termed it) whyche she delyuered to her

---

[597] Burr, p. 417.
[598] Increase Mather, p. 210.
[599] Cotton Mather, p. 81.
[600] Cooper, p. 91.

in the lykenesse of a whyte spotted Catte. Euery time that he [the cat] did any thynge for her, she sayde that he required a drop of bloude, which she gaue him by prycking herselfe.' Some time after, Elizabeth Francis presented the Satan-cat to Mother Waterhouse, passing on to her the instructions received from Elizabeth's grandmother. Mother Waterhouse 'gaue him for his labour a chicken, which he fyrste required of her and a drop of her blod. And thys she gaue him at all times when he dyd any thynge for her, by pricking her hand or face and puttinge the bloud to hys mouth whyche he sucked.'[601] In 1566 John Walsh, a Dorset witch, confessed that 'at the first time when he had the Spirite, hys sayd maister did cause him to deliuer one drop of his blud, whych bloud the Spirite did take away vpon hys paw'.[602] In Belgium in 1603 Claire Goessen, 'après avoir donné à boire de son sang à Satan, et avoir bu du sien, a fait avec lui un pacte.[603]

In the case of the Lancashire witch, Margaret Johnson, in 1633, it is difficult to say whether the pricking was for the purpose of marking or for a blood sacrifice; the slight verbal alterations in the two MS. accounts of her confession suggest a confusion between the two ideas; the one appears to refer to the mark, the other (quoted here) to the sacrifice: 'Such witches as have sharp bones given them by the devill to pricke them, have no pappes or dugges whereon theire devil may sucke; but theire devill receiveth bloud from the place, pricked with the bone; and they are more grand witches than any y^t have marks.'[604]In Suffolk in 1645 'one Bush of Barton widdow confessed that the Deuill appeared to her in the shape of a young black man ... and asked her for bloud, which he drew out of her mouth, and it dropped on a paper'.[605] At Auldearne, in 1662, the blood was drawn for baptizing the witch; Isobel Gowdie said, 'The Divell marked me in the showlder, and suked owt my blood at that mark, and spowted it in his hand, and, sprinkling it on my head, said, "I baptise the, Janet, in

---

[601] *Chelmsford Witches*, pp. 24, 26, 29, 30. Philobiblon Society, viii.
[602] *Examination of John Walsh.*
[603] Cannaert, p. 48.
[604] Whitaker, p. 216.
[605] Stearne, p. 29.

my awin name.'" Janet Breadheid's evidence is practically the same: 'The Divell marked me in the shoulder, and suked out my blood with his mowth at that place; he spowted it in his hand, and sprinkled it on my head. He baptised me thairvith, in his awin nam, Christian.'[606]

2. The *sacrifice of animals* was general, and the accounts give a certain amount of detail, but the ceremony was not as a rule sufficiently dramatic to be considered worth recording. The actual method of killing the animal is hardly ever given. The rite was usually performed privately by an individual; on rare occasions it was celebrated by a whole Coven, but it does not occur at the Great Assembly, for there the sacrifice was of the God himself. The animals offered were generally a dog, a cat, or a fowl, and it is noteworthy that these were forms in which the Devil often appeared to his worshippers.

The chief authorities all agree as to the fact of animal sacrifices. Cotta compares it with the sacrifices offered by the heathen:

'Some bring their cursed Sorcery vnto their wished end, by sacrificing vnto the Diuell some liuing creatures, as *Serres* likewise witnesseth, from the confession of Witches in *Henry* the fourth of *France* deprehended, among whom, one confessed to haue offered vnto his Deuill or Spirit a Beetle. This seemeth not improbable, by the Diabolicall litations (*sic*) and bloudy sacrifices, not onely of other creatures, but euen of men, wherewith in ancient time the heathen pleased their gods, which were no other then Diuels.'[607]

The number of sacrifices in the year is exaggerated by the writers on the subject, but the witches themselves are often quite definite in their information when it happens to be recorded. It appears from their statements that the rite was performed only on certain occasions, either to obtain help or as a thank-offering. Danaeus, speaking of the newly admitted witch, says, 'Then this vngracious and new servant of satan, euery day afterward offreth something of his goods to his patrone, some his dogge, some his hen, and some his cat.'[608] Scot, who

---

[606] Pitcairn, iii, pp. 603, 617.
[607] Cotta, p. 114.
[608] Danaeus, ch. iv.

always improves on his original, states that the witches depart after the Sabbath, 'not forgetting euery daie afterwards to offer to him, dogs, cats, hens, or bloud of their owne.'[609]

The earliest witch-trial in the British Isles shows animal sacrifice. In 1324 in Ireland Lady Alice Kyteler 'was charged to haue nightlie conference with a spirit called Robin Artisson, to whom she sacrificed in the high waie .ix. red cocks'.[610] In 1566 at Chelmsford Mother Waterhouse 'gaue him [i.e. the Satan-cat] for his labour a chicken, which he fyrste required of her, and a drop of her blod.... Another tyme she rewarded hym as before, wyth a chicken and a droppe of her bloud, which chicken he eate vp cleane as he didde al the rest, and she cold fynde remaining neyther bones nor fethers.'[611] Joan Waterhouse, daughter of Mother Waterhouse, a girl of eighteen, said that the Deuil came in the likeness of a great dog, 'then asked hee her what she wolde geue hym, and she saide a red kocke.'[612] John Walsh of Dorset, in 1566, confessed that 'when he would call him [the Spirit], hee sayth hee must geue hym some lyuing thing, as a Chicken, a Cat, or a Dog. And further he sayth he must geue hym twoo lyuing thynges once a yeare.'[613] In Lorraine in 1589 Beatrix Baonensis said, 'Etliche geben junge Hüner, oder wohl alte Hüner, wie Desideria Pari iensis, und Cathelonia Vincentia gethan hatten: Etliche schneiden ihre Haar ab und lieffern dieselbe dahin, etliche geben Späher, etliche Vögel oder sonst nicht viel besonders, als da sein möchte gemüntzt Geld aus Rindern Ledder, und wenn sie dergleichen nichts haben, so verschafft es ihnen ihr Geist, auff dass sie staffirt seyn.'[614] In Aberdeen in 1597 Andro Man gave evidence that 'the Devill thy maister, whom thow termis Christsunday ... is rasit be the speking of the word *Benedicite*, and is laid agane be tacking of a dog vnder thy left oxster in thi richt hand, and casting the same in his mouth, and speking the

---

[609] R. Scot, Bk. III, p. 44.
[610] Holinshed, *Ireland*, p. 58.
[611] Philobiblon Society, viii, *Chelmsford Witches*, pp. 29, 30.
[612] Id. ib., viii, p. 34.
[613] *Examination of John Walsh.*
[614] Remigius, pt. i, p. 54.

word *Maikpeblis*.'[615] At Lang Niddry in 1608 the whole Coven performed a rite, beginning at the 'irne zet of Seatoun', where they christened a cat by the name of Margaret, 'and thaireftir come all bak agane to the Deane-fute, quhair first thai convenit, and cuist the kat to the Devill.'[616] In 1630 Alexander Hamilton had consultations with the Devil near Edinburgh, 'and afoir the devill his away passing the said Alexr was in use to cast to him ather ane kat or ane laif or ane dog or any uther sic beast he come be.'[617] In Bute in 1622 Margaret NcWilliam 'renounced her baptisme and he baptised her and she gave him as a gift a hen or cock'.[618] In modern France the sacrifice of a fowl to the Devil still holds good: 'Celui qui veut devenir sorcier doit aller à un *quatre chemins* avec une *poule noire*, ou bien encore au *cimetière*, sur une *tombe* et toujours à *minuit*. Il vient alors quelqu'un qui demande: "Que venez vous faire ici?" "J'ai une poule à vendre," répond-on. Ce quelqu'un [est] le Méchant.'[619]

It is possible that the custom of burying a live animal to cure disease among farm animals, as well as the charm of casting a live cat into the sea to raise a storm, are forms of the animal sacrifice.

3. *Child Sacrifice.*—The child-victim was usually a young infant, either a witch's child or unbaptized; in other words, it did not belong to the Christian community. This last is an important point, and was the reason why unbaptized children were considered to be in greater danger from witches than the baptized. 'If there be anie children vnbaptised, or not garded with the signe of the crosse, or orizons; then the witches may or doo catch them from their mothers sides in the night, or out of their cradles, or otherwise kill them with their ceremonies.'[620] The same author quotes from the French authorities

---

[615] *Spalding Club Misc.*, i, p. 120; Burton, i, p. 252.

[616] Pitcairn, ii, pp. 542-3.

[617] From an unpublished trial in the Justiciary Court at Edinburgh. The meaning of the word *laif* is not clear. The Oxford dictionary gives *lop-eared*, the Scotch dictionary gives *loaf*. By analogy with the other accounts one would expect here a word meaning a hen.

[618] *Highland Papers*, iii, p. 18.

[619] Lemoine, vi, p. 109.

[620] Reg. Scot, Bk. III, p. 41.

the crimes laid to the charge of witches, among which are the following: 'They sacrifice their owne children to the diuell before baptisme, holding them vp in the aire vnto him, and then thrust a needle into their braines'; and 'they burne their children when they haue sacrificed them'.[621] Boguet says, 'Les Matrones, & sages femmes sont accoustumé d'offrir à Satan les petits enfans qu'elles reçoiuent, & puis les faire mourir auant qu'ils soient baptizez, par le moyẽ d'vne grosse espingle qu'elles leur enfoncent dans le cerueau.'[622] Boguet's words imply that this was done at every birth at which a witch officiated; but it is impossible that this should be the case; the sacrifice was probably made for some special purpose, for which a new-born child was the appropriate victim.

The most detailed account of such sacrifices is given in the trial of the Paris witches (1679-81), whom Madame de Montespan consulted. The whole ceremony was performed to the end that the love of Louis XIV should return to Madame de Montespan, at that time his discarded mistress; it seems to be a kind of fertility rite, hence its use on this occasion. The Abbé Guibourg was the sacrificing priest, and from this and other indications he appears to have been the Chief or Grand-master who, before a less educated tribunal, would have been called the Devil. Both he and the girl Montvoisin were practically agreed as to the rite; though from the girl's words it would appear that the child was already dead, while Guibourg's evidence implies that it was alive. Both witnesses gave their evidence soberly and gravely and without torture. Montvoisin, who was eighteen years old, stated that she had presented 'à la messe de Madame de Montespan, par l'ordre de sa mère, un enfant paraissant né avant terme, le mit dans un bassin, Guibourg l'égorgea, versa dans le calice, et consacra le sang avec hostie'. Guibourg's evidence shows that the sacrifice was so far from being uncommon that the assistants were well used to the work, and did all that was required with the utmost celerity:

'Il avait acheté un écu l'enfant qui fut sacrifié à cette messe qui lui fut présenté par une grande fille et ayant tiré du sang de l'enfant qu'il

---

[621] Id., Bk. II, p. 32.
[622] Boguet, p. 205.

piqua à la gorge avec un canif, il en versa dans le calice, après quoi l'enfant fut retiré et emporté dans un autre lieu, dont ensuite on lui rapporta le cœur et les entrailles pour en faire une deuxieme [oblation].'[623]

In Scotland it was firmly believed that sacrifices of children took place in all classes of society: 'The justices of the peace were seen familiarly conversing with the foul fiend, to whom one in Dumfries-shire actually offered up his firstborn child immediately after birth, stepping out with it in his arms to the staircase, where the devil stood ready, as it was suspected, to receive the innocent victim.'[624] In the later witch-trials the sacrifice of the child seems to have been made after its burying, as in the case of the Witch of Calder in 1720, who confessed that she had given the Devil 'the body of a dead child of her own to make a roast of'.[625]

It is possible that the killing of children by poison was one method of sacrifice when the cult was decadent and victims difficult to obtain. Reginald Scot's words, written in 1584, suggest that this was the case: 'This must be an infallible rule, that euerie fortnight, or at the least euerie moneth, each witch must kill one child at the least for hir part.'[626] Sinistrari d'Ameno, writing about a century later, says the same: 'They promise the Devil sacrifices and offerings at stated times: once a fortnight or at least each month, the murder of some child, or an homicidal act of sorcery.'[627] It is impossible to believe in any great frequency of this sacrifice, but there is considerable foundation in fact for the statement that children were killed, and it accounts as nothing else can for the cold-blooded murders of children of which the witches were sometimes accused. The accusations seem to have been substantiated on several occasions, the method of sacrifice being by poison.[628]

---

[623] Ravaisson, p. 334, 335.
[624] Sharpe, p. 147.
[625] Chambers, iii, p. 450.
[626] Scot, Bk. III, p. 42.
[627] Sinistrari de Ameno, p. 27.
[628] See, amongst others, the account of Mary Johnson (Essex, 1645), who was accused of poisoning two children; the symptoms suggest belladonna. Howell, iv, 844, 846.

The sacrifice of a child was often performed as a means of procuring certain magical materials or powers, which were obtained by preparing the sacrificed bodies in several ways. Scot says that the flesh of the child was boiled and consumed by the witches for two purposes. Of the thicker part of the concoction 'they make ointments, whereby they ride in the aire; but the thinner potion they put into flaggons, whereof whosoeuer drinketh, obseruing certeine ceremonies, immediatelie becommeth a maister or rather a mistresse in that practise and facultie.'[629] The Paris Coven confessed that they 'distilled' the entrails of the sacrificed child after Guibourg had celebrated the mass for Madame de Montespan, the method being probably the same as that described by Scot. A variant occurs in both France and Scotland, and is interesting as throwing light on the reasons for some of the savage rites of the witches: 'Pour ne confesser iamais le secret de l'escole, on faict au sabbat vne paste de millet noir, auec de la poudre du foye de quelque enfant non baptisé qu'on faict secher, puis meslant cette poudre avec ladicte paste, elle a cette vertu de taciturnité: si bien que qui en mange ne confesse iamais.'[630] At Forfar, in 1661, Helen Guthrie and four others exhumed the body of an unbaptized infant, which was buried in the churchyard near the south-east door of the church, 'and took severall peices therof, as the feet, hands, a pairt of the head, and a pairt of the buttock, and they made a py therof, that they might eat of it, that by this meanes they might never make a confession (as they thought) of their witchcraftis.'[631] Here the idea of sympathetic magic is very clear; by eating the flesh of a child who had never spoken articulate words, the witches' own tongues would be unable to articulate.

4. *Sacrifice of the God.*—The sacrifice of the witch-god was a decadent custom when the records were made in the sixteenth and seventeenth centuries. The accounts of the actual rite come from France and Belgium, where a goat was substituted for the human victim. The sacrifice was by fire in both those countries, and there are

---

[629] Scot, Bk. III, p. 41.
[630] De Lancre, *Tableau*, p. 128.
[631] Kinloch, p. 121.

indications that it was the same in Great Britain. It is uncertain whether the interval of time between the sacrifices was one, seven, or nine years.

Bodin and Boguet, each writing from his own knowledge of the subject, give very similar accounts, Bodin's being the more detailed. In describing a trial which took place in Poictiers in 1574, he says: 'Là se trouuoit vn grand bouc noir, qui parloit comme vne personne aux assistans, & dansoyent à l'entour du bouc: puis vn chacun luy baisoit le derriere, auec vne chandelle ardente: & celà faict, le bouc se consommoit en feu, & de la cëdre chacun en prenoit pour faire mourir le bœuf [etc.]. Et en fin le Diable leur disoit d'vne voix terrible des mots, Vengez vous ou vous mourrez.'[632] Boguet says that in the Lyons district in 1598 the Devil celebrated mass, and 'apres auoir prins la figure d'vn Bouc, se consume en feu, & reduit en cendre, laquelle les Sorciers recueillent, & cachent pour s'en seruir à l'execution de leurs desseins pernicieux & abominables'.[633] In 1603, a Belgian witch, Claire Goessen, was present at such a sacrifice, and her account is therefore that of an eyewitness. 'Elle s'est laissée transporter à l'assemblée nocturne de Lembeke, où, après la danse, elle a, comme tous les assistans, baisé un bouc à l'endroit de sa queue, lequel bouc fut ensuite brûlé et ses cendres distribuées et emportées par les convives.'[634] Jeanne de Belloc in 1609 'a veu le Grand maistre de l'assemblee se ietter dans les flammes au sabbat, se faire brusler iusques à ce qu'il estoit reduit en poudre, & les grandes & insignes sorcieres prendre les dictes poudres pour ensorceler les petits enfants & les mener au sabbat, & en prenoient aussi dans la bouche pour ne reueler iamais'.[635] A French witch in 1652 declared that at the Sabbath 'le diable s'y at mis en feu et en donné des cendres lesquelles tous faisaient voller en l'air pour faire mancquer les fruits de la terre'.[636] At Lille in 1661 the girls in Madame Bourignon's orphanage stated that

---

[632] Bodin, *Fléau*, pp. 187-8.
[633] Boguet, p. 141.
[634] Cannaert, p. 50.
[635] De Lancre, *Tableau*, p. 133.
[636] *La Tradition*, 1891, v, p. 215. Neither name nor place are given.

'on y adoroit une bête; & qu'on faisoit avec elle des infamies; & puis sur la fin on la brûloit, & chacun en prenoit des cendres, avec lesquelles on faisoit languir ou mourir des personnes, ou autres animaus'.[637]

The collection and use of the ashes by the worshippers point to the fact that we have here a sacrifice of the god of fertility. Originally the sprinkling of the ashes on fields or animals or in running water was a fertility charm; but when Christianity became sufficiently powerful to attempt the suppression of the ancient religion, such practices were represented as evil, and were therefore said to be 'pour faire mancquer les fruits de la terre'.

The animal-substitute for the divine victim is usually the latest form of the sacrifice; the intervening stages were first the volunteer, then the criminal, both of whom were accorded the power and rank of the divine being whom they personated. The period of time during which the substitute acted as the god varied in different places; so also did the interval between the sacrifices. Frazer has pointed out that the human victim, whether the god himself or his human substitute, did not content himself by merely not attempting to escape his destiny, but in many cases actually rushed on his fate, and died by his own hand or by voluntary submission to the sacrificer.

The witch-cult being a survival of an ancient religion, many of the beliefs and rites of these early religions are to be found in it. Of these the principal are: the voluntary substitute, the temporary transference of power to the substitute, and the self-devotion to death. As times changed and the ceremonies could no longer be performed openly, the sacrifices took on other forms. I have already suggested that the child-murders, of which the witches were often convicted, were in many cases probably offerings made to the God. In the same way, when the time came for the God or his substitute to be sacrificed, recourse was had to methods which hid the real meaning of the ceremony; and the sacrifice of the incarnate deity, though taking place in public, was consummated at the hands of the public executioner. This explanation accounts for the fact that the bodies of witches, male or female, were

---

[637] Bourignon, *Parole*, p. 87.

always burnt and the ashes scattered; for the strong prejudice which existed, as late as the eighteenth century, against any other mode of disposing of their bodies; and for some of the otherwise inexplicable occurrences in connexion with the deaths of certain of the victims.

Read in the light of this theory much of the mystery which surrounds the fate of Joan of Arc is explained. She was put to death as a witch, and the conduct of her associates during her military career, as well as the evidence at her trial, bear out the fact that she belonged to the ancient religion, not to the Christian. Nine years after her death in the flames her commander, Gilles de Rais, was tried on the same charge and condemned to the same fate. The sentence was not carried out completely in his case; he was executed by hanging, and the body was snatched from the fire and buried in Christian ground. Like Joan herself, Gilles received a semi-canonization after death, and his shrine was visited by nursing mothers. Two centuries later Major Weir offered himself up and was executed as a witch in Edinburgh, refusing to the end all attempts to convert him to the Christian point of view.

The belief that the witch must be burnt and the ashes scattered was so ingrained in the popular mind that, when the severity of the laws began to relax, remonstrances were made by or to the authorities. In 1649 the Scotch General Assembly has a record: 'Concerning the matter of the buriall of the Lady Pittadro, who, being vnder a great scandall of witchcraft, and being incarcerat in the Tolbuith of this burgh during her triall before the Justice, died in prison, The Comission of the Generall Assembly, having considered the report of the Comittee appointed for that purpose, Doe give their advyse to the Presbyterie of Dumfermling to show their dislike of that fact of the buriall of the Lady Pittadro, in respect of the maner and place, and that the said Presbyterie may labour to make the persons who hes buried her sensible of their offence in so doeing; and some of the persons who buried hir, being personallie present, are desired by the Comission to shew themselvis to the Presbyterie sensible of their miscarriage therein.'[638]

---

[638] *Scot. Hist. Soc.*, xxv, p. 348. *See also* Ross, *Aberdour and Inchcolme*, p. 339.

At Maidstone in 1652 'Anne Ashby, alias Cobler, Anne Martyn, Mary Browne, Anne Wilson, and Mildred Wright of Cranbrook, and Mary Read, of Lenham, being legally convicted, were according to the Laws of this Nation, adjudged to be hanged, at the common place of Execution. Some there were that wished rather they might be burnt to Ashes; alledging that it was a received opinion among many, that the body of a witch being burnt, her bloud is prevented thereby from becomming hereditary to her Progeny in the same evill.'[639] The witches themselves also held the belief that they ought to die by fire. Anne Foster was tried for witchcraft at Northampton in 1674: 'after Sentence of Death was past upon her, she mightily desired to be Burned; but the Court would give no Ear to that, but that she should be hanged at the Common place of Execution.'[640]

9. Magic Words

The magic words known to the witches were used only for certain definite purposes, the most important use being to raise the Devil. I have omitted the charms which are founded on Christian prayers and formulas, and quote only those which appear to belong to the witch-cult.

In the section on *Familiars* it will be seen how the witches divined by means of animals, which animals were allotted to them by the Chief. In auguries and divinations of this kind in every part of the world a form of words is always used, and the augury is taken by the first animal of the desired species which is seen after the charm is spoken.

Agnes Sampson, the leading witch of the North Berwick Coven, 1590, summoned her familiar by calling 'Elva', and then divined by a dog, whom she dismissed by telling him to 'depart by the law he lives on'. She also used the formula, 'Haill, hola!', and 'Hola!' was also the cry when a cat was cast into the sea to raise a storm.[641] A man-witch

---

[639] *Prod. and Trag. History*, p. 7.
[640] *Tryall of Ann Foster*, p. 8.
[641] Pitcairn, i, pt. ii, pp. 211, 235, 238.

of Alest, 1593, gave the devil's name as Abiron: 'quand il le vouloit voir il disoit: vien Abiron, sinon ie te quitteray.'[642]Andro Man at Aberdeen, 1597, 'confessis that the Devill, thy maister, is rasit be the speking of the word *Benedicite*, and is laid agane be tacking of a dog vnder thy left oxster in thi richt hand, and casting the same in his mouth, and speking the word *Maikpeblis*.—He grantit that this word *Benedicite* rasit the Dewill, and*Maikpeblis* laid him againe, strikin him on the faice with ane deice with the left hand.'[643] Alexander Hamilton of East Lothian, 1630, when covenanting with the devil, had 'ane battoun of fir in his hand the devill than gave the said Alexr command to tak that battoun quhan evir he had ado with him and therewt to strek thruse upone the ground and to chairge him to ruse up foule theiff'; the divining animals in this case were crows, cats, and dogs.[644] Marie Lamont of Innerkip, 1662, was instructed to call the Devil *Serpent* when she desired to speak with him.[645]

The Somerset witches, 1664, cried out *Robin* at an appointed place, and the Master then appeared in his proper form as a man: Elizabeth Style and Alice Duke also called him *Robin* when summoning him privately, and Elizabeth Style added, 'O Sathan give me my purpose', before saying what she wished done.[646] The Swedish witches, 1669, called their Chief with the cry, 'Antecessor, come and carry us to Blockula'; this they did at an appointed place, and the Devil then appeared as a man.[647]

The words used before starting to a meeting are rarely recorded; only a few remain. The earliest example is from Guernsey in 1563, when Martin Tulouff heard an old witch cry as she bestrode a broomstick, 'Va au nom du diable et luciffer p dessq roches et espyñes.' He then lost sight of her, with the inference that she flew through the air, though he acknowledged that he himself was not so

---

[642] De Lancre, *L'Incredulité*, p. 772.
[643] *Spalding Club Misc.*, i, pp. 120, 124.
[644] From the record of the trial in the Justiciary Court of Edinburgh.
[645] Sharpe, p. 132.
[646] Glanvil, pt. ii, pp. 137, 164.
[647] Horneck, pt. ii, p. 316.

successful.[648] The witches of the Basses-Pyrénées, 1609, anointed themselves before starting, and repeated the words 'Emen hetan, emen hetan', which de Lancre translates 'Ici et là, ici et là'. 'Quelquefois plus furieuses elles se batent entre elles mesmes, en disant, Ie suis le Diable, ie n'ay rien qui ne soit à toy, en ton nom Seigneur cette tienne seruante s'oingt, & dois estre quelque iour Diable & maling Esprit comme toy.' When, crossing water they cried, 'Haut la coude, Quillet,' upon which they could cross without getting wet; and when going a long distance they said, 'Pic suber hoeilhe, en ta la lane de bouc bien m'arrecoueille.'[649] Isobel Gowdie, 1662, gives two variants of the magic words used on these occasions: the first, 'Horse and hattock, in the Divellis name' is not unlike the form given by Martin Tulouff; the second is longer, 'Horse and hattock, horse and goe, Horse and pellattis, ho! ho!'[650] The Somerset witches, 1664, when starting to the meeting, said, 'Thout, tout a tout, tout, throughout and about'; and when returning, 'Rentum tormentum'. At parting they cried, 'A Boy! merry meet, merry part.'[651] They also had a long form of words which were used when applying the flying ointment, but these are not recorded.

Other magical words were used at the religious services of the witches in the Basses-Pyrénées (1609). At the elevation of the host the congregation cried, '"Aquerra goity, Aquerra beyty, Aquerra goity, Aquerra beyty," qui veut dire *Cabron arriba, Cabron abaro (sic)*'; at the elevation of the chalice at a Christian service they said, 'Corbeau noir, corbeau noir.' There were two forms of words to be used when making the sign of the cross; the first was, 'In nomine Patrica, Aragueaco Petrica, Agora, Agora Valentia, Iouanda, goure gaitz goustia,' translated as 'Au nom de Patrique, Petrique, d'Arragon, à cette heure à cette heure Valence, tout nostre mal est passé'. The second roused de Lancre's horror as peculiarly blasphemous: 'In

---

[648] From the record of the trial in the Guernsey Greffe.

[649] De Lancre, *Tableau*, pp. 123, 400.

[650] Pitcairn, iii, pp. 604, 608.

[651] Glanvil, pt. ii, pp. 139, 141. I have pointed out that the cry of 'A Boy' is possibly the Christian recorder's method of expressing the Bacchic shout 'Evoe'. See *Jour. Man. Or. Soc.*, 1916-17, p. 65.

nomine patrica, Aragueaco Petrica, Gastellaco Ianicot, Equidae iordian pot,' 'au nom de Patrique, petrique d'Arragon. Iannicot de Castille faictes moy vn baiser au derriere.'[652] The mention of the ancient Basque god Janicot makes this spell unusually interesting. As the dances were also a religious rite the words used then must be recorded here. Bodin gives the formula, 'Har, har, diable, diable, saute icy, saute là, iouë icy, iouë là: Et les autres disoyent sabath sabath.'[653] The word *diable* is clearly Bodin's own interpellation for the name of the God, for the Guernsey version, which is currently reported to be used at the present day, runs 'Har, har, Hou, Hou, danse ici', etc.; Hou being the name of an ancient Breton god.[654] Jean Weir (1670) stated that at the instigation of some woman unnamed she put her foot on a cloth on the floor with her hand upon the crown of her head, and repeated thrice, 'All my cross and troubles go to the door with thee.'[655] This seems to have been an admission ceremony, but the words are of the same sentiment as the one recorded by de Lancre, 'tout notre mal est passé.'

There were also certain magical effects supposed to be brought about by the use of certain words. Martin Tulouff (1563) claimed that he could bewitch cows so that they gave blood instead of milk, by saying 'Butyrum de armento', but he admitted that he also used powders to accomplish his purpose.[656]Isobel Gowdie (1662) described how the witches laid a broom or a stool in their beds to represent themselves during their absence at a meeting. By the time that this record was made the witches evidently believed that the object took on the exact appearance of the woman, having forgotten its original meaning as a signal to show where she had gone. The words used on these occasions show no belief in the change of appearance of the object:

'I lay down this besom [or stool] in the Devil's name,Let it not stir till

---

[652] De Lancre, *Tableau*, pp. 401, 461, 462, 464.
[653] Bodin, p. 190.
[654] The names of the smaller islands are often compounded with the name of this deity, e.g. Li-hou, Brecq-hou, &c.
[655] Law, p. 27 note.
[656] From a trial in the Guernsey Greffe.

I come again.'

Her statements regarding the change of witches into animals I have examined in the section on Familiars (p. 234). The words used to effect these changes are given in full. When a witch wished to take on the form of a hare she said:

'I sall goe intill ane haire,With sorrow, and sych, and meikle caire;And I sall goe in the Divellis nam,Ay quhill I com hom againe.'

To change into a cat or a crow the last two lines were retained unaltered, but the first two were respectively,

'I sall goe intill ane catt,With sorrow, and sych, and a blak shot'

or'I sall goe intill a craw,With sorrow, and sych, and a blak thraw.'

To return into human form the witch said:

'Haire, haire, God send thee caire.I am in an haire's liknes just now,Bot I sal be in a womanis liknes ewin now.'

From a cat or a crow, the words were 'Cat, cat, God send thee a blak shott' or 'Craw, craw, God send thee a blak thraw', with the last two lines as before. When the witch in animal form entered the house of another witch, she would say, 'I conjure thee, Goe with me'; on which the second witch would turn into the same kind of animal as the first. If, however, they met in the open, the formula was slightly different, 'Divell speid the, Goe thow with me,' the result being the same.[657]

The Somerset trials record the words used for cursing anything. These were simply 'A Pox take it', the curse being supposed to take effect at once. If the curse were pronounced over an image of a person the words were 'A Pox on thee, I'le spite thee'.[658]

Alexander Elder's grace over meat is probably a corrupt form of some ancient rite:

'We eat this meat in the Divellis nam,With sorrow, and sych, and meikle shame;We sall destroy hows and hald;Both sheip and noat in till the fald.Litle good sall come to the foreOf all the rest of the litle store.'[659]

---

[657] Pitcairn, iii, pp. 607-8, 611.

[658] Glanvil, pt. ii, pp. 137, 139, 148, 149.

[659] Pitcairn, iii, p. 612. Sych = sighing, lamentation.

The 'conjuring of cats' was a distinct feature, and is clearly derived from an early form of sacrifice. The details are recorded only in Scotland, and it is possible that Scotland is the only country in which it occurred, though the sanctity of the cat in other places suggests that the omission in the records is accidental.

In the dittay against John Fian, 1590, he was 'fylit, for the chaissing of ane catt in Tranent; in the quhilk chaise, he was careit heich aboue the ground, with gryt swyftnes, and as lychtlie as the catt hir selff, ower ane heicher dyke, nor he was able to lay his hand to the heid off:—And being inquyrit, to quhat effect he chaissit the samin? Ansuerit, that in ane conversatioune haldin at Brumhoillis, Sathan commandit all that were present, to tak cattis; lyke as he, for obedience to Sathan, chaissit the said catt, purpoiselie to be cassin in the sea, to raise windis for distructioune of schippis and boitis.'[660] Agnes Sampson of the same Coven as Fian confessed 'that at the time when his Majestie was in Denmark, shee being accompanied by the parties before speciallie named, tooke a cat and christened it, and afterwards bounde to each part of that cat, the cheefest parte of a dead man, and severall joyntis of his bodie: And that in the night following, the saide cat was convayed into the middest of the sea by all the witches, sayling in their riddles or cives, as is aforesaid, and so left the said cat right before the towne of Leith in Scotland. This doone, there did arise such a tempest in the sea, as a greater hath not bene seene.'[661] The legal record of this event is more detailed and less dramatic; the sieves are never mentioned, the witches merely walking to the Pier-head in an ordinary and commonplace manner. The Coven at Prestonpans sent a letter to the Leith Coven that—

'they sould mak the storm vniuersall thro the sea. And within aucht dayes eftir the said Bill [letter] wes delyuerit, the said Agnes Sampsoune, Jonett Campbell, Johnne Fean, Gelie Duncan, and Meg Dyn baptesit ane catt in the wobstaris hous, in maner following: Fyrst, twa of thame held ane fingar, in the ane syd of the chimnay cruik, and ane vther held ane vther fingar in the vther syd, the twa nebbis of the

---

[660] Id., i, pt. ii, p. 212.
[661] *Newes from Scotland*, see Pitcairn, i, pt. ii, p. 218.

fingars meting togidder; than thay patt the catt thryis throw the linkis of the cruik, and passit itt thryis vnder the chimnay. Thaireftir, att Begie Toddis hous, thay knitt to the foure feit of the catt, foure jountis of men; quhilk being done, the sayd Jonet fechit it to Leith; and about mydnycht, sche and the twa Linkhop, and twa wyfeis callit Stobbeis, came to the Pier-heid, and saying thir words, 'See that thair be na desait amangis ws'; and thay caist the catt in the see, sa far as thay mycht, quhilk swam owre and cam agane; and thay that wer in the Panis, caist in ane vthir catt in the see att xj houris. Eftir quhilk, be thair sorcerie and inchantment, the boit perischit betuix Leith and Kinghorne; quhilk thing the Deuill did, and went befoir, with ane stalf in his hand.'[662]

Beigis Todd was concerned in another 'conjuring of cats', this time at Seaton.

'Eftir thay had drukkin togidder a certane space, thay, in thair devillische maner, tuik ane katt, and drew the samyn nyne tymes throw the said Beigis cruik; and thaireftir come with all thair speed to Seaton-thorne, be-north the ʒet.... And thay thaireftir past altogidder, with the Devill, to the irne ʒet [iron gate] of Seatoun, quhair of new thay tuik ane cat, and drew the samyn nyne tymes throw the said Irne-ʒett: And immediatlie thaireftir, came to the barne, foiranent George Feudaris dur, quhair thai christened the said catt, and callit hir *Margaret*: And thaireftir come all bak agane to the Deane-fute, quhair first thai convenit, and cuist the kat to the Devill.'[663]

[662] Pitcairn, i, pt. ii, p. 237.
[663] Id., ii, p. 542.

VI. THE RITES (*continued*)

WITCHES' RAIN-MAKING AND FERTILITY RITES

1. General

In common with many other religions of the Lower Culture, the witch-cult of Western Europe observed certain rites for rain-making and for causing or blasting fertility. This fact was recognized in the papal Bulls formulated against the witches who were denounced, not for moral offences, but for the destruction of fertility. The celebrated Decree of Innocent VIII, which in 1488 let loose the full force of the Church against the witches, says that 'they blight the marriage bed, destroy the births of women and the increase of cattle; they blast the corn on the ground, the grapes of the vineyard, the fruits of the trees, the grass and herbs of the field'. Adrian VI followed this up in 1521 with a Decretal Epistle, denouncing the witches 'as a Sect deviating from the Catholic Faith, denying their Baptism, and showing Contempt of the Ecclesiastical Sacraments, treading Crosses under their Feet, and, taking the Devil for their Lord, destroyed the Fruits of the Earth by their Enchantments, Sorceries, and Superstitions'.

The charms used by the witches, the dances, the burning of the god and the broadcast scattering of his ashes, all point to the fact that this was a fertility cult; and this is the view taken also by those contemporary writers who give a more or less comprehensive account of the religion and ritual. Though most of the fertility or anti-fertility charms remaining to us were used by the witches either for their own benefit or to injure their enemies, enough remains to show that originally all these charms were to promote fertility in general and in particular. When the charm was for fertility in general, it was performed by the whole congregation together; but for the fertility of any particular woman, animal, or field, the ceremony was performed by one witch alone or by two at most.

The power which the witches claimed to possess over human fertility is shown in many of the trials. Jonet Clark was tried in

Edinburgh in 1590 'for giving and taking away power from sundry men's Genital-members';[664] and in the same year and place Bessie Roy was accused of causing women's milk to dry up.[665] The number of midwives who practised witchcraft points also to this fact; they claimed to be able to cause and to prevent pregnancy, to cause and to prevent an easy delivery, to cast the labour-pains, on an animal or a human being (husbands who were the victims are peculiarly incensed against these witches), and in every way to have power over the generative organs of both sexes. In short, it is possible to say that, in the sixteenth and seventeenth centuries, the better the midwife the better the witch.

The Red Book of Appin,[666] which was obtained from the Devil by a trick, is of great interest in this connexion. It was said to contain charms for the curing of diseases of cattle; among them must certainly have been some for promoting the fertility of the herds in general, and individual animals in particular. It is not unlikely that the charms as noted in the book were the result of many experiments, for we know that the witches were bound to give account to the Devil of all the magic they performed in the intervals between the Sabbaths, and he or his clerk recorded their doings. From this record the Devil instructed the witches. It is evident from the confessions and the evidence at the trials that the help of the witches was often required to promote fertility among human beings as well as among animals. The number of midwives who were also witches was very great, and the fact can hardly be accidental.

Witches were called in to perform incantations during the various events of a farm-yard. Margrat Og of Aberdeen, 1597, was 'indyttit as a manifest witche, in that, be the space of a yeirsyn or theirby, thy kow being in bulling, and James Farquhar, thy awin gude son haulding the kow, thow stuid on the ane syd of the kow, and thy dochter, Batrix Robbie, on the vther syd, and quhen the bull was lowping the kow,

---

[664] Pitcairn, i, pt. ii, p. 206; Glanvil, pt. ii, p. 301.
[665] Pitcairn, i, pt. ii, p. 207.
[666] J. G. Campbell, pp. 293-4. The book was in manuscript, and when last heard of was in the possession of the now-extinct Stewarts of Invernahyle.

thow tuik a knyff and keist ower the kow, and thy dochter keapit the sam, and keist it over to the agane, and this ye did thryiss, quhilk thou can nocht deny.'[667] At Auldearne the Coven, to which Isobel Gowdie belonged, performed a ceremony to obtain for themselves the benefit of a neighbour's crop. 'Befor Candlemas, we went be-east Kinlosse, and ther we yoaked an plewghe of paddokis. The Divell held the plewgh, and Johne Yownge in Mebestowne, our Officer, did drywe the plewghe. Paddokis did draw the plewgh as oxen; quickens wer sowmes, a riglen's horne was a cowter, and an piece of an riglen's horne was an sok. We went two seueral tymes abowt; and all we of the Coeven went still wp and downe with the plewghe, prayeing to the Divell for the fruit of that land, and that thistles and brieris might grow ther'.[668] Here the ploughing-ceremony was to induce fertility for the benefit of the witches, while the draught animals and all the parts of the plough connoted barrenness for the owner of the soil.

The most detailed account of a charm for human fertility is given in the confession of the Abbé Guibourg, who appears to have been the Devil of the Paris witches. The ceremony took place at the house of a witch-midwife named Voisin or Montvoisin, and according to the editor was for the benefit of Louis XIV or Charles II, two of the most notorious libertines of their age.

'Il a fait chez la Voisin, revêtu d'aube, d'étole et de manipule, une conjuration en présence de la Des Oeillets [attendant of Madame de Montespan], qui prétendait faire un charme pour le (Roi) et qui était accompagnée d'un homme qui lui donna la conjuration, et comme il était nécessaire d'avoir du sperme des deux sexes, Des Oeillets ayant ses mois n'en put donner mais versa dans le calice de ses menstrues et l'homme qui l'accompagnait, ayant passé dans la ruelle du lit avec lui Guibourg, versa de son sperme dans le calice. Sur le tout, la Des Oeillets et l'homme mirent chacun d'une poudre de sang de chauve-souris et de la farine pour donner un corps plus ferme à toute la

---

[667] *Spalding Club Misc.*, i, p. 143.
[668] Pitcairn, iii, p. 603. 'Toads did draw the plough as oxen, couch-grass was the harness and trace-chains, a gelded animal's horn was the coulter, and a piece of a gelded animal's horn was the sock.'

composition et après qu'il eut récité la conjuration il tira le tout du calice qui fut mis dans un petit vaisseau que la Des Oeillets ou l'homme emporta.'[669]

The ecclesiastical robes and the use of the chalice point to this being a ceremony of a religious character, and should be compared with the child-sacrifices performed by the same priest or Devil (see pp. 150, 157).

An anti-fertility rite, which in its simplicity hardly deserves the name of a ceremony, took place at Crook of Devon in Kinross-shire. Bessie Henderson 'lykeways confessed and declared that Janet Paton was with you at ane meeting when they trampit down Thos. White's rie in the beginning of harvest, 1661, and that she had broad soals and trampit down more nor any of the rest'.[670]

2. Rain-making

The rain-making powers of the witches have hardly been noted by writers on the subject, for by the time the records were made the witches were credited with the blasting of fertility rather than its increase. Yet from what remains it is evident that the original meaning of much of the ritual was for the production of fertilizing rain, though both judges and witnesses believed that it was for storms and hail.

One of the earliest accounts of such powers is given in the story quoted by Reginald Scot from the *Malleus Maleficarum*, written in 1487, a century before Scot's own book:

'A little girle walking abroad with hir father in his land, heard him complaine of drought, wishing for raine, etc. Whie father (quoth the child) I can make it raine or haile, when and where I list: He asked where she learned it. She said, of hir mother, who forbad hir to tell anie bodie thereof. He asked hir how hir mother taught hir? She answered, that hir mother committed hir to a maister, who would at anie time doo anie thing for hir. Whie then (said he) make it raine but onlie in my field. And so she went to the streame, and threw vp water

---

[669] Ravaisson, 1679-81, p. 336.
[670] Burns Begg, p. 224.

in hir maisters name, and made it raine presentlie. And proceeding further with hir father, she made it haile in another field, at hir father's request. Herevpon he accused his wife, and caused hir to be burned; and then he new christened his child againe.'[671]

Scot also gives 'certaine impossible actions' of witches when he ridicules the belief

'that the elements are obedient to witches, and at their commandement; or that they may at their pleasure send raine, haile, tempests, thunder, lightening; when she being but an old doting woman, casteth a flint stone ouer hir left shoulder, towards the west, or hurleth a little sea sand vp into the element, or wetteth a broome sprig in water, and sprinkleth the same in the aire; or diggeth a pit in the earth, and putting water therein, stirreth it about with hir finger; or boileth hogs bristles; or laieth sticks acrosse vpon a banke, where neuer a drop of water is; or burieth sage till it be rotten; all which things are confessed by witches, and affirmed by writers to be the meanes that witches vse to mooue extraordinarie tempests and raine'.[672]

More quotes Wierus to the same effect: 'Casting of Flint-Stones behind their backs towards the West, or flinging a little Sand in the Air, or striking a River with a Broom, and so sprinkling the Wet of it toward Heaven, the stirring of Urine or Water with their finger in a Hole in the ground, or boyling of Hogs Bristles in a Pot.'[673]

The throwing of stones as a fertility rite is found in the trial of Jonet Wischert, one of the chief witches at Aberdeen, and is there combined with a nudity rite. 'In hervest last bypast, Mr. William Rayes huikes [saw thee at] the heid of thi awin gudmannis croft, and saw the tak all thi claiss about thi heid, and thow beand naikit from the middill down, tuik ane gryte number of steynis, and thi self gangand baklenis, keist ane pairt behind the our thi heid, and ane wther pairt fordward.'[674]

---

[671] Reg. Scot, Bk. III, p. 60.
[672] Id., Bk. III, p. 60.
[673] More, p. 168.
[674] *Spalding Club Misc.*, i, p. 93.

3. Fertility

Every contemporary writer who gives a general view of the religion and ritual observes the witches' powers over human fertility. Boguet says, 'Ils font encor cacher & retirer les parties viriles, et puis les font ressortir quand il leur plait. Ils empeschent aussi tantost la copulation charnelle de l'homͤ & de la femme, en retirant les nerfs, & ostant la roideur du membre; et tantost la procreation en destournant ou bouchant les conduicts de la semence, pour empescher qu'elle ne descende aux vases de la generation.'[675] Scot, who quotes generally without any acknowledgement and often inaccurately, translates this statement, 'They also affirme that the vertue of generation is impeached by witches, both inwardlie, and outwardlie: for intrinsecallie they represse the courage, and they stop the passage of the mans seed, so as it may not descend to the vessels of generation: also they hurt extrinsecallie, with images, hearbs, &c.'[676] Bodin also remarks that witches, whether male or female, can affect only the generative organs.[677] Madame Bourignon says that the girls, whom she befriended,

'told me, that Persons who were thus engaged to the Devil by a precise Contract, will allow no other God but him, and therefore offer him whatsoever is dearest to them; nay, are constrained to offer him their Children, or else the Devil would Beat them, and contrive that they should never arrive to the State of Marriage, and so should have no Children, by reason that the Devil hath power by his Adherents, to hinder both the one and the other.... So soon as they come to be able to beget Children, the Devil makes them offer the desire which they have of Marrying, to his Honor: And with this all the Fruit that may proceed from their Marriage. This they promise voluntarily, to the end that they may accomplish their Designs: For otherwise the Devil

---

[675] Boguet, p. 211.
[676] R. Scot, p. 77.
[677] Bodin, pp. 125-7.

threatens to hinder them by all manner of means, that they shall not Marry, nor have Children.'[678]

Glanvil, writing on the Scotch trials of 1590, speaks of 'some Effects, Kinds, or Circumstances of Witchcraft, such as the giving and taking away power from sundry men's Genital-members. For which Jannet Clark was accused.'[679] In the official record Jonet Clark was tried and condemned for 'gewing of ane secreit member to Iohnne Coutis; and gewing and taking of power fra sindrie mennis memberis. Item, fylit of taking Iohnne Wattis secreit member fra him.'[680]

Sexual ritual occurs in many religions of the Lower Culture and has always horrified members of the higher religions both in ancient and modern times. In fertility cults it is one of the chief features, not only symbolizing the fertilizing power in the whole animate world, but, in the belief of the actors, actually assisting it and promoting its effects.

Such fertility rites are governed by certain rules, which vary in different countries, particularly as to the age of girls, i.e. whether they are over or under puberty. Among the witches there appears to have been a definite rule that no girl under puberty had sexual intercourse with the Devil. This is even stated as a fact by so great an authority as Bodin: 'Les diables ne font point de paction expresse auec les enfans, qui leurs sont vouëz, s'ils n'ont attaint l'aage de puberté.'[681] The details of the trials show that this statement is accurate. 'Magdalene de la Croix, Abbesse des Moniales de Cordoüe en Espaigne, confessa que Satan n'eust point copulation, ny cognoissance d'elle, qu'elle n'eust douze ans.'[682] Bodin and De Lancre both cite the case of Jeanne Hervillier of Verbery in Compiègne; she was a woman of fifty-two at the time of her trial in 1578. She 'confessa qu'à l'aage de douze ans sa mere la presenta au diable, en forme d'vn grand homme noir, & vestu de noir, botté, esperonné, auec vne espée au costé, et vn cheual noir à la porte, auquel la mere dit: Voicy ma fille que ie vous ay promise: Et

---

[678] Bourignon, *Vie*, pp. 222-3; Hale, pp. 37-8.

[679] Glanvil, pt. ii, p. 301.

[680] Pitcairn, i, pt. ii, p. 206.

[681] Bodin, p. 465.

[682] Id., p. 465. The trial was in 1545, Magdalene being then forty-two. See also *Pleasant Treatise*, p. 6.

à la fille, Voicy vostre amy, qui vous fera bien heureuse, et deslors qu'elle renonça à Dieu, & à la religion, & puis coucha auec elle charnellement, en la mesme sorte & maniere que font les hommes auec les femmes.'[683] De Lancre also emphasizes the age: 'Ieanne Haruillier depose qu'encore sa mere l'eust voüée à Satan dés sa naissance, neantmoins qu'il ne la cognut charnellement qu'elle n'eust attainct l'aage de douze ans.'[684] De Lancre's own experience points in the same direction; he found that the children were not treated in the same way as adults, nor were they permitted to join in all the ceremonies until after they had passed childhood.[685]

The same rule appears to have held good in Scotland, for when little Jonet Howat was presented to the Devil, he said, 'What shall I do with such a little bairn as she?'[686] It is, however, rare to find child-witches in Great Britain, therefore the rules concerning them are difficult to discover.

Another rule appears to have been that there was no sexual connexion with a pregnant woman. In the case of Isobel Elliot, the Devil 'offered to lie with her, but forbore because she was with child; that after she was *kirked* the Devil often met her, and had *carnal copulation* with her'.[687]

Since the days of Reginald Scot it has been the fashion of all those writers who disbelieved in the magical powers of witches to point to the details of the sexual intercourse between the Devil and the witches as proof positive of hysteria and hallucination. This is not the attitude of mind of the recorders who heard the evidence at the trials. 'Les confessions des Sorciers, que i'ay eu en main, me font croire qu'il en est quelque chose: dautant qu'ils out tous recogneu, qu'ils auoient esté couplez auec le Diable, et que la semence qu'il iettoit estoit fort froide; Ce qui est conforme à ce qu'en rapporte Paul Grilland, et les Inquisiteurs de la foy.'[688] 'It pleaseth their new Maister oftentimes to

---

[683] Id., p. 227.

[684] De Lancre, *Tableau*, p. 183.

[685] De Lancre, *Tableau*, pp. 145, 398.

[686] Kinloch, p. 124.

[687] Arnot, p. 360.

[688] Boguet, p. 68.

offer himselfe familiarly vnto them, to dally and lye with them, in token of their more neere coniunction, and as it were marriage vnto him.'[689] '*Witches* confessing, so frequently as they do, that the Devil *lies with them*, and withal complaining of his tedious and offensive *coldness*, it is a shrewd presumption that he doth lie with them *indeed*, and that it is not a meer *Dream*.'[690]

It is this statement of the physical coldness of the Devil which modern writers adduce to prove their contention that the witches suffered from hallucination. I have shown above (pp. 61 seq.) that the Devil was often masked and his whole person covered with a disguise, which accounts for part of the evidence but not for all, and certainly not for the most important item. For in trial after trial, in places far removed from one another and at periods more than a century apart, the same fact is vouched for with just the small variation of detail which shows the actuality of the event. This is that, when the woman admitted having had sexual intercourse with the Devil, in a large proportion of cases she added, 'The Devil was cold and his seed likewise.' These were women of every class and every age, from just above puberty to old women of over seventy, unmarried, married, and widows. It is unscientific to disbelieve everything, as Scot does, and it is equally unscientific to label all the phenomena as the imagination of hysterical women. By the nature of things the whole of this evidence rests only on the word of the women, but I have shown above (pp. 63-5) that there were cases in which the men found the Devil cold, and cases in which the women found other parts of the Devil's person to be cold also. Such a mass of evidence cannot be ignored, and in any other subject would obtain credence at once. But the hallucination-theory, being the easiest, appears to have obsessed the minds of many writers, to the exclusion of any attempt at explanation from an unbiassed point of view.

Students of comparative and primitive religion have explained the custom of sacred marriages as an attempt to influence the course of nature by magic, the people who practise the rite believing that

---

[689] Cooper, p. 92.
[690] More, p. 241.

thereby all crops and herds as well as the women were rendered fertile, and that barrenness was averted. This accounts very well for the occurrence of 'obscene rites' among the witches, but fails when it touches the question of the Devil's coldness. I offer here an explanation which I believe to be the true one, for it accounts for all the facts; those facts which the women confessed voluntarily and without torture or fear of punishment, like Isobel Gowdie, or adhered to as the truth even at the stake amid the flames, like Jane Bosdeau.

In ancient times the Sacred Marriage took place usually once a year; but besides this ceremony there were other sexual rites which were not celebrated at a fixed season, but might be performed in the precincts of the temple of a god or goddess at any time, the males being often the priests or temple officials. These are established facts, and it is not too much to suppose that the witches' ceremonies were similar. But if the women believed that sexual intercourse with the priests would increase fertility, how much more would they believe in the efficacy of such intercourse with the incarnate God of fertility himself. They would insist upon it as their right, and it probably became compulsory at certain seasons, such as the breeding periods of the herds or the sowing and reaping periods of the crops. Yet as the population and therefore the number of worshippers in each 'congregation' increased, it would become increasingly difficult and finally impossible for one man to comply with the requirements of so many women.[691] The problem then was that on the one hand there were a number of women demanding what was in their eyes a thing essential for themselves and their families, and on the other a man physically unable to satisfy all the calls upon him. The obvious solution of the problem is that the intercourse between the Chief and the women was by artificial means, and the evidence in the trials points clearly to this solution.

Artificial phalli are well known in the remains of ancient civilizations. In ancient Egypt it was not uncommon to have statues of which the phallus was of a different material from the figure, and so

---

[691] 'The Deuill your maister, beand in liknes of ane beist, haid carnall [deal] with ilk ane of you.'—*Spalding Club Misc.*, i, p. 149.

made that it could be removed from its place and carried in procession. The earliest of such statues are the colossal limestone figures of the fertility-god Min found at Koptos, dating to the first dynasty, perhaps B.C. 5500.[692] But similar figures are found at every period of Egyptian history, and a legend was current at the time of Plutarch to account for this usage as well as for the festival of the Phallephoria.[693] Unless the phallus itself were the object of adoration there would be no reason to carry it in procession as a religious ceremony, and it is easily understandable that such a cult would commend itself chiefly to women.[694]

The phallus of a divine statue was not always merely for adoration and carrying in procession; the Roman bride sacrificed her virginity to the god Priapus as a sacred rite. This is probably the remains of a still more ancient custom when the god was personated by a man and not by an image. The same custom remained in other parts of the world as the *jus primae noctis*, which was held as an inalienable right by certain kings and other divine personages. As might be expected, this custom obtained also among the witches.

'Le Diable faict des mariages au Sabbat entre les Sorciers & Sorcieres, & leur joignant les mains, il leur dict hautement
Esta es buena paratiEsta parati lo toma.
Mais auant qu'ils couchent ensemble, il s'accouple auec elles, oste la virginité des filles.'—Ieannette d'Abadie, aged sixteen, 's'accusoit elle mesme d'auoir esté depucellee par Satan.'[695]

The occasional descriptions of the Devil's phallus show without question its artificial character:

---

[692] Petrie, pp. 7-9; Capart, p. 223.
[693] Plutarch, *De Iside et Osiride*, xviii, 5.
[694] On the other hand, the female generative organs were also adored, and presumably by men. This suggestion is borne out by the figures of women with the pudenda exposed and often exaggerated in size. Such figures are found in Egypt, where they were called Baubo, and a legend was invented to account for the attitude; and similar figures were actually known in ancient Christian churches (Payne Knight, *Discourse on the Worship of Priapus*).
[695] De Lancre, *Tableau*, pp. 132, 404.

In 1598 in Lorraine 'es sagte die Alexia Dragaea, ihre Bulschafft hätte einen [Glied] so starcken etc. allezeit gehabt, wenn ihm gestanden, und so gross als ein Ofengabel-Stiel, dessgleichen sie zugegen zeigte, denn ohngefehr eine Gabel zugegen war, sagte auch wie sie kein Geleuth weder Hoden noch Beutel daran gemerckt hat'.[696]

'Iaquema Paget adioustoit, qu'elle auoit empoigné plusieurs fois auec la main le membre du Demon, qui la cognoissoit, et que le membre estoit froid comme glace, long d'vn bon doigt, & moindre en grosseur que celuy d'vn homme. Tieuenne Paget et Antoine Tornier adioustoient aussi, que le membre de leurs Demons estoit long et gros, comme l'vn de leurs doigts.'[697] 'Il a au deuant son membre tiré et pendant, & le monstre tousiours long d'vn coudée.—Le membre du Demon est faict à escailles comme vn poisson.—Le membre du Diable s'il estoit estendu est long enuiron d'vne aulne, mais il le tient entortillé et sinueux en forme de serpent.—Le Diable, soit qu'il ayt la forme d'homme, ou qu'il soit en forme de Bouc, a tousiours vn membre de mulet, ayant choisy en imitation celuy de cet animal comme le mieux pourueu. Il l'a long et gros comme le bras.—Le membre du Diable est long enuiron la moitié d'vne aulne, de mediocre grosseur, rouge, obscur, & tortu, fort rude & comme piquant.—Ce mauuais Demon ait son membre myparty, moitié de fer, moitié de chair tout de son long, & de mesme les genitoires. Il tient tousiours son membre dehors.—Le Diable a le membre faict de corne, ou pour le moins il en a l'apparence: c'est pourquoy il faict tant crier les femmes.—Jeannette d'Abadie dit qu'elle n'a iamais senty, qu'il eust aucune semence, sauf quand il la depucella qu'elle la sentit froide, mais que celle des autres hommes qui l'ont cognue, est naturelle.'[698]

Sylvine de la Plaine, 1616, confessed 'qu'il a le membre faict comme vn cheual, en entrant est froid comme glace, iette la semence fort froide, & en sortant la brusle comme si c'estoit du feu'.[699] In 1662

---

[696] Remigius, pt. i, p. 19.
[697] Boguet, pp. 68-9.
[698] De Lancre, *Tableau*, pp. 68, 224-6.
[699] Id., *L'Incredulité*, p. 808.

Isobel Gowdie said, 'His memberis ar exceiding great and long; no man's memberis ar so long & bigg as they ar.'[700]

The artificial phallus will account as nothing else can for the pain suffered by many of the women; and that they suffered voluntarily, and even gladly, can only be understood by realizing that they endured it for motives other than physical satisfaction and pleasure. 'There appeared a great *Black Goat* with a*Candle* between his Horns.... He had carnal knowledge of her which was with great pain.'[701] 'Presque toutes les Sorcieres rapportent que cet accouplement leur est le plus souuent des-agreable, tant pour la laideur & deformité de Satan, que pour ce qu'elles y ont vne extreme douleur.[702] 'Elle fuyoit l'accouplement du Diable, à cause qu'ayant son membre faict en escailles il fait souffrir vne extresme douleur.'[703] At the Sabbath in the Basses-Pyrénées, the Devil took the women behind some sort of screen, and the children 'les oyent crier comme personnes qui souffrent vne grande douleur, et ils les voyent aussi tost reuenir au Sabbat toutes sanglantes'.[704] As regards brides, 'En cet accouplement il leur faict perdre vne infinité de sang, et leur faict souffrir mille douleurs.'[705] Widow Bush of Barton said that the Devil, who came to her as a young black man, 'was colder than man, and heavier, and could not performe nature as man.'[706]

The physical coldness of the Devil is vouched for in all parts of Europe.[707]

---

[700] Pitcairn, iii, p. 610.

[701] F. Hutchinson, *Historical Essays*, p. 42.

[702] Boguet, p. 69.

[703] De Lancre, *Tableau*, p. 132.

[704] De Lancre, *Tableau*, p. 219.

[705] Id. ib., p. 404.

[706] Stearne, p. 29.

[707] The following references are in chronological order, and are only a few out of the many trials in which this coldness of the Devil is noted: 1565, Cannaert, p. 54; 1567, De Lancre, *Tableau*, p. 132; 1578, Bodin, *Fléau*, p. 227; 1590, Pitcairn, i, pt. ii, p. 219; 1598, Boguet, *op. cit.*, pp. 8, 412; 1645, Stearne, p. 29; 1649, Pitcairn, iii, p. 599; 1652, Van Elven, *La Tradition*, 1891, v, p. 215; 1661, Kinloch and Baxter, p. 132; 1662, Pitcairn, iii, pp. 603, 611, 617; 1662, Burns Begg, x, pp. 222, 224, 231-2, 234; 1678, Fountainhall, i, p. 14; 1682, Howell, viii. 1032; 1705, *Trials of Elinor*

'Toutes les Sorcieres s'accordent en cela, que la semence, qu'elles reçoiuent du Diable, est froide comme glace: Spranger & les Inquisiteurs, qui en ont veu vne infinité, l'escriuent ainsi. Remy, qui a fait le procez à plus de deux milles Sorciers, en porte vn tesmoignage irrefragable. Ie puis asseurer au semblable, que celles, qui me sont passées par les mains, en ont confessé tout autant. Que si la semence est ainsi froide, il s'ensuit qu'elle est destituée de ses esprits vitaux, & ainsi qu'elle ne peut estre cause d'aucune generation.'[708]

Isobel Gowdie and Janet Breadheid of Auldearne both said that the Devil was 'a meikle, blak, roch man, werie cold; and I fand his nature als cold within me as spring-well-water'. Isobel continues, 'He is abler for ws that way than any man can be, onlie he ves heavie lyk a malt-sek; a hudg nature, verie cold, as yce.'[709]

Another point which goes to prove that the intercourse was by artificial means was that pregnancy did not follow, except by special consent of the woman. Jeannette d'Abadie, aged sixteen, said, 'Elle fuyoit l'accouplement du Diable, à cause qu'ayant son membre faict en escailles il fait souffrir vne extresme douleur; outre que la semence est extresmement froide, si bien qu'elle n'engrosse iamais, ni celle des autres hommes au sabbat, bien qu'elle soit naturelle.'[710] Boguet remarks, 'Il me souuient, qu'Antoinette Tornier, & Antoinette Gandillon, estans interroguées, si elles craignoient point de deuenir enceintes des œuures du Diable; l'vne respondit qu'elle estoit trop vieille; l'autre que Dieu ne le vouloit pas permettre.'[711] According to Jeanne Hervillier, the Devil 'coucha auec elle charnellement, en la mesme sorte & maniere que font les hommes auec les femmes, horsmis que la semence estoit froide. Cele dit elle continua tous les huict ou quinze iours.... Et vn iour le diable luy demanda, si elle vouloit estre enceinte de luy, ce qu'elle ne voulut pas.'[712] But when the witch was willing to have a child, it is noticeable that there is then no

---

Shaw, p. 6.
[708] Boguet, p. 92.
[709] Pitcairn, iii, pp. 603, 611, 617.
[710] De Lancre, *Tableau*, p. 132.
[711] Boguet, p. 78.
[712] Bodin, p. 227.

complaint of the Devil's coldness. At Maidstone in 1652 'Anne Ashby, Anne Martyn, and one other of their Associates, pleaded that they were with child pregnant, but confessed it was not by any man, but by the Divell.... Anne Ashby and Anne Martyn confessed that the Divell had known them carnally, and that they had no hurt by it.'[713]

The Devil appears to have donned or doffed his disguise in the presence of his worshippers, and this was often the case at the time of the sexual rites, whether public or private:

'Il cognoist les Sorcieres tantost en forme d'homme tout noir, & tantost en forme de beste, comme d'vn chien, d'vn chat, d'vn bouc, d'vn mouton. Il cognoissoit Thieuenne Paget, & Antoine Tornier en forme d'vn homme noir: Et lors qu'il accouploit auec Iaquema Paget, & Antoine Gandillon, il prenoit la figure d'vn mouton noir, portant des cornes. Françoise Secretain a dit que son Demon se mettoit tantost en chien, tantost en chat, et tantost en poule, quand il la vouloit cognoistre charnellement. Or tout cecy me fait de tant mieux asseurer l'accouplement reel du Sorcier, & de la Sorciere auec le Demon.'[714]

In the Basses-Pyrénées Marie d'Aspilcouette 'disoit le mesme, pour ce qui est du membre en escailles, mais elle deposoit, que lors qu'il les vouloit cognoistre, il quitoit la forme de Bouc, & prenoit celle d'homme.'[715] 'Il entra dans sa chambre en forme d'ung chat et se changea en la posture d'un home vestu de rouge.'[716] At an attempt to wreck a ship in a great storm 'the devil was there present with them all, in the shape of a great horse.... They returned all in the same likeness as of before, except that the devil was in the shape of a man.'[717] 'The Deivill apeired vnto her, in the liknes of ane prettie boy in grein clothes.... And at that tyme the Deivil gaive hir his markis; and went away from her in the liknes of ane blak doug.'[718] 'He wold haw carnall dealling with ws in the shap of a deir, or in any vther shap, now and then. Somtym he vold be lyk a stirk, a bull, a deir, a rae, or a

---

[713] *A Prodigious and Tragicall Historie*, pp. 4, 5.
[714] Boguet, p. 70.
[715] De Lancre, *Tableau*, p. 225.
[716] H. G. van Elven, *La Tradition*, 1891, v, p. 215. Place and names not given.
[717] Kinloch, pp. 122, 123.
[718] Pitcairn, iii, p. 601.

dowg, etc., and haw dealling with ws.'[719] 'Yow the said Margaret Hamilton, relict of James Pullwart ... had carnall cowpulatiown with the devil in the lyknes of ane man, bot he removed from yow in the lyknes of ane black dowg.'[720] The most important instance is in Boguet's description of the religious ceremony at the Sabbath: 'Finalement Satan apres auoir prins la figure d'vn Bouc, se consume en feu, & reduit en cendre.'[721]

The witches' habit of speaking of every person of the other sex with whom they had sexual intercourse at the Sabbath as a 'devil' has led to much confusion in the accounts. The confusion has been accentuated by the fact that both male and female witches often used a disguise, or were at least veiled. 'Et pource que les hommes ne cedent guieres aux femmes en lubricité, c'est pourquoy le Demon se met aussi en femme ou Succube.... Ce qu'il fait principalement au Sabbat, selon que l'ont rapporté Pierre Gandillon, & George Gandillon, pere & fils, & les autres, lesquels disent tout vnanimement, qu'en leurs assemblées il y a plusieurs Demons, & que les vns exercent le mestier de l'homme pour les femmes, & les autres le mestier des femmes pour les hommes.'[722] 'The Incubus's in the shapes of proper men satisfy the desires of the Witches, and the Succubus's serve for Whores to the Wizards.'[723] Margaret Johnson said the same: 'Their spirittes vsuallie have knowledge of theire bodies.... Shee also saith, that men Witches usualie have woemen spirittes and woemen witches men spirittes.'[724]The girls under Madame Bourignon's charge 'declared that they had daily carnal Cohabitation with the Devil; that they went to the Sabbaths or Meetings, where they Eat, Drank, Danc'd, and committed other Whoredom and Sensualities. Every one had her

---

[719] Id., iii, pp. 611, 613.

[720] *Scots Magazine*, 1817, p. 201.

[721] Boguet, p. 141.

[722] Id., p. 65.

[723] *Pleasant Treatise of Witches*, p. 6. The remembrance of the numerous male devils at the Sabbath survives in the Samalsain dance in the Basses-Pyrénées, where the male attendants on the King and Queen of the dance are still called Satans. Moret, *Mystères Égyptiens*, p. 247.

[724] Baines, i, pp. 607-8, note.

Devil in form of a Man; and the Men had their Devils in the form of a Woman.... They had not the least design of changing, to quit these abominable Pleasures, as one of them of Twenty-two Years old one day told me. *No*, said she, *I will not be other than I am; I find too much content in my Condition; I am always Caressed.*'[725] One girl of twelve said definitely that she knew the Devil very well, 'that he was a Boy a little bigger than her self; and that he was her Love, and lay with her every Night'; and another girl named Bellot, aged fifteen, 'said her Mother had taken her with her [to the Sabbath] when she was very Young, and that being a little Wench, this Man-Devil was then a little Boy too, and grew up as she did, having been always her Love, and Caressed her Day and Night.'[726] Such connexions sometimes resulted in marriage. Gaule mentions this fact in his general account: 'Oft times he marries them ere they part, either to himselfe, or their Familiar, or to one another; and that by the Book of Common Prayer (as a pretender to witchfinding lately told me in the Audience of many).'[727] This statement is borne out in the trials: 'Agnes Theobalda sagte, sie sey selbst zugegen auff der Hochzeit gewesen, da Cathalina und Engel von Hudlingen, ihren Beelzebub zur Ehe genommen haben.'[728] The Devil of Isobel Ramsay's Coven was clearly her husband,[729] but there is nothing to show whether the marriage took place before she became a witch, as in the case of Janet Breadheid of Auldearne, whose husband 'enticed her into that craft'.[730] I have quoted above (p. 179) the ceremony at the marriage of witches in the Basses-Pyrénées. Rebecca Weste, daughter of a witch, married the Devil by what may be a primitive rite; he came to her 'as shee was going to bed, and told her, he would marry her, and that shee could not deny him; shee said he kissed her, but was as cold as clay, and married her that night, in this manner; he tooke her by the hand and lead her about the chamber, and promised to be her loving husband till

[725] Bourignon, *Parole*, pp. 86, 87; Hale, pp. 26, 27.
[726] Id., *Vie*, p. 211,214; Hale, pp. 29, 31.
[727] Gaule, p. 63.
[728] Remigius, p. 131.
[729] Record of Trial in the Edinburgh Justiciary Court.
[730] Pitcairn, iii, p. 616.

death, and to avenge her of her enemies; and that then shee promised him to be his obedient wife till death, and to deny God, and Christ Jesus.'[731] At Edinburgh in 1658 a young woman called Anderson was tried: 'her confessioun was, that scho did marry the devill.'[732] The Swedish witches in 1670 confessed that at Blockula 'the Devil had Sons and Daughters which he did marry together'.[733] Giraldus Cambrensis gives an account of a 'spirit' in the form of a red-haired young man, called Simon, who 'was begotten upon the wife of a rustic in that parish, by a demon, in the shape of her husband, naming the man, and his father-in-law, then dead, and his mother, still alive; the truth of which the woman upon examination openly avowed'.[734]

[731] Howell, iv, 842.
[732] Nicoll's Diary, p. 212. *Bannatyne Club.*
[733] Horneck, pt. ii, p. 323.
[734] Davies, p. 183. Cp. also the birth of Merlin. Giraldus Cambrensis, *Itinerary*, Bk. I, xii, 91b.

VII. THE ORGANIZATION

The cult was organized in as careful a manner as any other religious community; each district however was independent, and therefore Mather is justified in saying that the witches 'form themselves after the manner of Congregational Churches'.[735]

1. The Officer

The Chief or supreme Head of each district was known to the recorders as the 'Devil'. Below him in each district, one or more officers—according to the size of the district—were appointed by the chief. The officers might be either men or women; their duties were to arrange for meetings, to send out notices, to keep the record of work done, to transact the business of the community, and to present new members. Evidently these persons also noted any likely convert, and either themselves entered into negotiations or reported to the Chief, who then took action as opportunity served. At the Esbats the officer appears to have taken command in the absence of the Grand Master; at the Sabbaths the officers were merely heads of their own Covens, and were known as Devils or Spirits, though recognized as greatly inferior to the Chief. The principal officer acted as clerk at the Sabbath and entered the witches' reports in his book; if he were a priest or ordained minister, he often performed part of the religious service; but the Devil himself always celebrated the mass or sacrament. In the absence of all direct information on the subject, it seems likely that the man who acted as principal officer became Grand Master on the death of the previous Chief. Occasionally the Devil appointed a personal attendant for himself, who waited upon him on all solemn occasions, but does not appear to have held any official position in the community.

Estebene de Cambrue (1567) said that 'elle a veu au Sabbat vn Notaire qu'elle nomme, lequel a accoustumé de leuer les defauts de celles qui ont manqué de se trouuer au Sabbat.'[736] At the North

---

[735] Cotton Mather, p. 160.

[736] De Lancre, *Tableau*, p. 123.

Berwick meetings (1590), there were several officers, of whom Fian was the chief.

'Robert Griersoun being namit, they all ran hirdie-girdie and wer angrie: for it wes promisit he sould be callit "Ro^t the Comptroller, alias Rob the Rowar," for expreming of his name.—Johnne Fiene wes ewer nerrest to the Devill, att his left elbok; Gray Meill kepit the dur.—The accusation of the saide Geillis Duncane aforesaide, who confessed he [Fian] was their Regester, and that there was not one man suffered to come to the Divels readinges but onelie hee.—[Fian's confession] That at the generall meetinges of those witches, he was always present; that he was clarke to all those that were in subiection to the Divels service, bearing the name of witches; that alway hee did take their oathes for their true service to the Divell; and that he wrote for them such matters as the Divell still pleased to commaund him.'[737]

Elizabeth Southerns, otherwise known as old Mother Demdike (1613), 'was generall agent for the Deuill in all these partes'.[738] The 'eminent warlok' Robert Grieve of Lauder (1649) 'was brought to a Confession of his being the *Devils Officer* in that Countrey for warning all Satans Vassals to come to the Meetings, where, and whensoever the Devil required.... The Devil gave him that charge, to be his Officer to warn all to the meetings; (as was said before,) in which charge he continued for the space of eighteen years and more.'[739] The evidence concerning Isobel Shyrie at Forfar (1661) is too long to quote, but it is clear that she acted as the officer.[740] Isobel Gowdie (1662) says definitely, 'Johne Young, in Mebestowne, is Officer to owr Coeven', and remarks in another part of her confession that 'Johne Yownge in Mebestowne, owr Officer, did drywe the plewghe'.[741] The only indication of a change of personnel is given by Janet Breadheid, of the same Coven as Isobel Gowdie.

---

[737] Pitcairn, i, pt. ii, pp. 219, 220, 239, 240.
[738] Potts, B 2.
[739] Sinclair, pp. 46, 47.
[740] Kinloch, pp. 124, 129.
[741] Pitcairn, iii, pp. 603, 605.

'Johne Taylor, my husband, was then Officer, bot Johne Young in Mebestoune, is now Officer to my Coeven. Quhan I cam first ther, the Divell called tham all be thair names, on the book; and my husband, than called thame at the door.... Whan we haid Great Meittingis, Walter Ledy, in Penick, my husband, and Alexander Elder, nixt to the Divell, wer Ruleris; and quhan ther wold be but fewar, I my self, the deceassit Jean Suthirland, Bessie Hay, Bessie Wilsone, and Janet Burnet wold rule thaim.'[742]

In Somerset (1664) Anne Bishop appears to have been the chief personage under the Devil, in other words the Officer.[743] At Paisley (1678) Bessie Weir 'was Officer to their several meetings.—Bessie Weir did intimate to him [John Stewart], that there was a meeting to be at his house the next day: And that the Devil under the shape of a black man, Margaret Jackson, Margery Craige, and the said Bessie Weir, were to be present. And that the said Bessie Weir required the Declarant to be there, which he promised.'[744] In New England (1692) it appears that both Bridget Bishop and Martha Carrier held high rank, and were probably Officers.

One duty seems to have been delegated to a particular individual, who might perhaps hold no other office, or who might, on the other hand, be the chief official; this was the manager, often the leader, of the dance. As pace seems to have been an essential in the dance, the leader was necessarily active and generally young. At North Berwick (1590) 'John Fein mussiled led the ring'.[745] In Aberdeen (1596) Thomas Leyis was the chief person in the dance; 'thow the said Thomas was formest and led the ring, and dang the said Kathren Mitchell, becaus scho spillet your dans, and ran nocht so fast about as the rest.'[746] Isobel Cockie of the same Coven was next in importance; 'in the quhilk danse, thow was the ring leader nixt Thomas Leyis.'[747] Mr. Gideon Penman (1678), who had once been minister at

---

[742] Pitcairn, iii, p. 617.
[743] Glanvil, pt. ii, pp. 139, 147, 148.
[744] Id., pt. ii, pp. 291, 293.
[745] Pitcairn, i, pt. iii, p. 246.
[746] *Spalding Club Misc.*, pp. 97, 98.
[747] Ib., p. 115.

Crighton, went to the Sabbaths, where the Devil spoke of him as 'Mr. Gideon, my chaplain'.[748] The witches said that 'ordinarily Mr. Gideon was in the rear in all their dances, and beat up those that were slow'. This Mr. Gideon seems to be the same person as the 'warlock who formerly had been admitted to the ministrie in the Presbyterian times, and now he turnes a preacher under the devill.—This villan was assisting to Satan in this action' [giving the sacrament] 'and in preaching.'[749]

The personal attendant of the Devil is rare. At Aberdeen (1596) Issobell Richie was accused that 'at that tyme thow ressauit thy honours fra the Dewyll, thy maister, and wer appoynted be him in all tymes thairefter, his speciall domestick servand and furriour'.[750] John McWilliam Sclater (1656) was appointed cloak-bearer to the Devil.[751]

The Devil's piper was also an official appointment in Scotland, but does not occur elsewhere. John Douglas of Tranent (1659) was the Devil's piper,[752] and so also was a man mentioned by Sinclair: 'A reverend Minister told me, that one who was the Devils Piper, a wizzard confest to him, that at a Ball of dancing, the Foul Spirit taught him a Baudy song to sing and play.'[753]

The Queen of the Sabbath may perhaps be considered as an official during the sixteenth and seventeenth centuries, though in early times she was probably the chief personage in the cult, as Pearson has pointed out.[754] It is not unlikely that she was originally the same as the Queen of Elfhame; in Scotland, however, in the seventeenth century, there is a Maiden of the Coven, which was an important position in the Esbat but entirely distinct from the Queen of Faery, while in other places a woman, not the Queen, is often the officer and holds the highest place after the Grand Master.

---

[748] Fountainhall, i, p. 14.

[749] Law, p. 145.

[750] *Spalding Club Misc.*, i, p. 142.

[751] *Spottiswoode Misc.*, ii, p. 67.

[752] Ib., ii, p. 68.

[753] Sinclair, p. 219.

[754] Pearson, ii, p. 26.

Elizabeth Stile of Windsor (1579) said that 'mother Seidre dwelling in the Almeshouse, was the maistres Witche of all the reste'.[755] Marion Grant of Aberdeen (1597) confessed that 'the Devill thy maister causit the dans sindrie tymes with him and with Our Ladye, quha, as thow sayes, was a fine woman, cled in a quhyte walicot'.[756] In France (1609) the custom seems to have been universal, 'en chasque village trouuer vne Royne du Sabbat', who sat at the Devil's left hand during the celebration of the mass and received the offerings of the faithful.[757] The witches called her both the Grande Maîtresse and the Reine du Sabbat.[758] Isobel Gowdie's confession (1662) shows that the Queen of Elthame was not the same as the chief woman of the Coven, for she saw the Queen only on going into the fairy-howe, while the Maiden of the Coven was at each meeting. 'We doe no great mater without owr Maiden.—Quhan we ar at meat, or in any vther place quhateuir, the Maiden of each Coven sittis abow the rest, nixt the Divell.'[759] In New England (1692) Deliverance Hobbs confessed that 'the said G. B. preached to them, and such a woman was their Deacon'.[760]

2. The Covens

The word *coven* is a derivative of 'convene', and is variously spelt *coven*, *coeven*, *covine*, *cuwing*, and even *covey*. The special meaning of the word among the witches is a 'band' or 'company', who were set apart for the practice of the rites of the religion and for the performance of magical ceremonies; in short, a kind of priesthood.

The Coven was composed of men and women, belonging to one district, though not necessarily all from one village, and was ruled by an officer under the command of the Grand Master. The members of the Coven were apparently bound to attend the weekly Esbat; and it

---

[755] *Rehearsall*, par. 26.
[756] *Spalding Club Misc.*, i, p. 171.
[757] De Lancre, *L'Incredulité*, p. 36.
[758] Id., *Tableau*, p. 401.
[759] Pitcairn, iii, pp. 610, 613.
[760] Burr, p. 417.

was they who were instructed in and practised magical arts, and who performed all the rites and ceremonies of the cult. The rest of the villagers attended the Esbats when they could or when they felt so inclined, but did not necessarily work magic, and they attended the Sabbaths as a matter of course. This view of the organization of the religion is borne out by the common belief in modern France:

'Il est de croyance générale qu'il *faut un nombre fixe de sorciers et de sorcières dans chaque canton.* Le nouvel initié reprend les *vieux papiers* de l'ancien.—Les mauvaises gens forment une confrérie qui est dirigée par une sorcière. Celle-ci a la *jarretière* comme marque de sa dignité. Elles se la transmettent successivement par rang d'ancienneté. Il n'existe que cette différence de rang entre les sorciers et les sorcières. Ceux-là se recrutent aussi bien parmi les gens *mariés* que chez les *célibataires.*'[761]

The 'fixed number' among the witches of Great Britain seems to have been thirteen: twelve witches and their officer. The actual numbers can be obtained, as a rule, only when the full record of the trial is available; for when several witches in one district are brought to trial at the same time they will always be found to be members of a Coven, and usually the other members of the Coven are implicated or at least mentioned.

The earliest account of a Coven is in the trial of Bessie Dunlop (1567); when Thom Reid was trying to induce her to join the society, he took her 'to the kill-end, quhair he forbaid her to speik or feir for onye thing sche hard or saw; and quhene thai had gane ane lytle pece fordwerd, sche saw twelf persounes, aucht wemene and four men: The men wer cled in gentilmennis clething, and the wemene had all plaiddis round about thame and wer verrie semelie lyke to se; and Thom was with thame.'[762] Clearly this was a Coven with Thom as the Officer, and he had brought Bessie to see and be seen. The witches tried at St. Osyth in Essex in 1582 were thirteen in number.[763] At the meeting of the North Berwick witches (1590) to consult on the means

---

[761] Lemoine, *La Tradition*, 1892, vi, pp. 108, 109. The italics are in the original.
[762] Pitcairn, i, pt. ii, p. 52.
[763] *Witches taken at St. Oses.*

to compass the king's death, nine witches stood 'in ane cumpany', and the rest 'to the nowmer of threttie persons in ane vthir cumpany'; in other words, there were thirty-nine persons, or three Covens, present.[764] At Aberdeen (1596-7) sixty-four names of witches occur in the trials; of these, seven were merely mentioned as being known to the accused, though not as taking part in the ceremonies, and five were acquitted; thus leaving fifty-two persons, or four Covens. Out of these fifty-two, one was condemned and executed at the assize in 1596 and twelve in 1597, making in all thirteen persons, or one Coven, who were put to death.[765] The great trial of the Lancashire witches in 1613 gives a grand total of fifty-two witches, or four Covens, whose names occur in the record. This includes the three Salmesbury witches mentioned by Grace Sowerbuts, whose evidence was discredited as being the outcome of a 'Popish plot' to destroy the three women as converts to the Reformed Church; but as the record shows that the other accused witches were tried on similar charges and condemned, it may be concluded that other causes occasioned the acquittal. Taking together, however, only those witches who are mentioned, in these trials, as having actually taken part in the ceremonies and practices of witchcraft in the neighbourhood of Pendle, it will be found that there were thirty-nine persons, or three Covens.[766] In Guernsey in 1617 Isabel Becquet confessed that—

'at the Sabbath the Devil used to summon the Wizards and Witches in regular order (she remembered very well having heard him call the old woman *Collette* the first, in these terms: *Madame the Old Woman Becquette*): then the woman *Fallaise*; and afterwards the woman *Hardie*. Item, he also called *Marie,* wife of *Massy,* and daughter of the said *Collette*. Said that after them she herself was called by the Devil: in these terms: *The Little Becquette*: she also heard him call there *Collas Becquet,* son of the said old woman (who [Collas] held her by the hand in dancing, and some one [a woman]

---

[764] Pitcairn, i, pt. ii, p. 245.
[765] *Spalding Club Misc.*, i, pp. 87 seq.
[766] Potts.

whom she did not know, held her by the other hand): there were about six others there she did not know.[767]

At Queensferry in 1644 thirteen women were tried and seven executed for witchcraft.[768]

At Alloa (1658), though thirteen persons, or one Coven, were brought to trial, the word is used to indicate a smaller number: 'Margret Duchall lykewayis declared that ther was sex women mair besyd hir self that was in thair cuwing' [then follow the names of the six].—'Jonet Blak confessed severall meetings with the abowenamed cuwing.—Kathren Renny being asked quhat meetingis scho had with the diwell, and the rest of hir cuwing, scho ansuered scho had severall meitingis with all tham abowenamed.'[769] Little Jonet Howat of Forfar (1661) said, 'Ther was thair present with the divell besyd hirselfe, quhom he callit the prettie dauncer, the said Issobell Syrie, Mairie Rynd, Hellen Alexander, Issobell Dorward, and utheris whoise names shoe did not know, to the number of 13 of all.'[770] The trial of Jonet Kerr and Issobell Ramsay at Edinburgh (1661) gives the names of thirteen persons, or one Coven.[771] At Crook of Devon (1662) there were tried twelve women and one man, i.e. one Coven.[772] Isobel Gowdie of Auldearne (1662) gives the most detail concerning the Covens: 'Jean Mairten is Maiden of owr Coeven. Johne Younge is Officer to owr Coeven.—Ther ar threttein persons in ilk Coeven.' Her evidence shows that there were several Covens in the district: 'The last tyme that owr Coven met, we, and an vther Coven, wer dauncing at the Hill of Earlseat, and befor that we ves beyond the Meikle-burne; and the vther Coven being at the Downie-hillis, we went besyd them.—[She and four others] with the Divell, wer onlie at the making of it [a charm], bot all the multitude of all owr Coevens got notice of it, at the next meitting ... all my owin Coeven gott notice of it werie schortlie.' She also notes that each member of her Coven 'has an Sprit

[767] Goldsmid, p. 13. Translated from the French record.

[768] Fyfe, p. 87.

[769] *Scottish Antiquary*, ix, pp. 50-2.

[770] Kinloch, p. 114.

[771] From the record of the trial in the Edinburgh Justiciary Court.

[772] Burns Begg, pp. 219 seq.

to wait wpon ws, quhan ve pleas to call wpon him'. Janet Breadheid, of the same Coven as Isobel Gowdie, gives the names of thirty-nine persons, or three Covens, who were present in the Kirk of Nairn when she was admitted into the Society.[773] In Somerset (1664) the number of accused was twenty-six persons, or two Covens.[774] At Newcastle-on-Tyne (1673) Ann Armstrong stated that at the meeting at the 'rideing house in the close on the common' she saw ten men and women whom she knew and 'thre more, whose names she knowes not'. At another meeting 'at Rideing Millne bridg-end she see the said Anne Forster, Anne Dryden, and Luce Thompson, and tenne more unknowne to her.—Att the house of John Newton off the Riding, the said Lucy wished that a boyl'd capon with silver scrues might come down to her and the rest, which were five coveys consisting of thirteen person in every covey.' At a large meeting at Allensford, where a great many witches were present, 'every thirteen of them had a divell with them in sundry shapes.' It is also noticeable that Ann Armstrong mentions twenty-six persons by name as having been at various meetings to her knowledge.[775] At Paisley (1692) thirteen persons of high position brought an action for libel against six others for saying that they, the thirteen, had drunk the Devil's health in the house of one of them; the libellers were punished, but the number of persons libelled suggests that the accusation might have been true.[776]

3. Duties

An important part of the organization was the system of reporting to the Grand Master everything which had happened since the previous Great Assembly. The chief work of the Covens was the performance of magical rites, either publicly at the Esbats or privately in the houses of the witches and their neighbours. As these rites, especially when performed privately, were more or less in the nature of experiments, the results were reported and when successful were

[773] Pitcairn, iii, pp. 603-17.
[774] Glanvil, pt. ii, pp. 140 seq.
[775] *Surtees Soc.*, xl, pp. 191, 192; *Denham Tracts*, ii, pp. 300-2, 304.
[776] Hector, i, pp. 51-6.

recorded in writing for future use. The book in which the records were made remained in the hands of the Devil, who in this way had always a store of well-tried magical spells and recipes to kill or cure, from which he could instruct his followers as occasion demanded.

The position of the Devil as the instructor of the witches is to be found in most of the trials in Great Britain. Cooper states this plainly: 'He *deliuers* unto his*Proselite*, and so to the rest, *the Rules of his Art*, instructing them in the manner of *hurting* and *helping*, and acquainting them with such *medicines* and *poysons*as are vsuall herevnto.'[777] Bessie Dunlop (1567) never attempted to cure any disease without first consulting Thom Reid, 'quhen sundrie persounes cam to hir to seik help for thair beist, thair kow or yow, or for ane barne that was tane away with ane evill blast of wind, or elf-grippit, sche gait and sperit at Thom, Quhat mycht help thame?—Sche culd do nathing, quhill sche had first spokin with Thom.'[778] Alison Peirson (1588) learnt her craft from Mr. William Simpson, her mother's brother's son, who lived among the fairy folk; 'the saide Mr Williame tauld hir of ewerie seiknes and quhat herbis scho sould tak to haill thame, and how scho sould vse thame; and gewis hir his directioune att all tymes.'[779] Agnes Sampson, the Wise Wife of Keith (1590), always asked the Devil's advice in serious cases; 'she had a familiar spirit, who upon her call, did appear in a visible form, and resolve her of any doubtful matter, especially concerning the life or death of persons lying sick.'[780] Grissel Gairdner of Newburgh (1610) was executed for consulting with the 'Devill, and seiking of responssis fra him, at all tymes this fourtene or fyftene ʒeir bygane, for effectuating of hir devillisch intentiones'.[781] Elspeth Reoch in Orkney (1616) confessed that the fairy man, whom she met, told her 'he wald lerne her to ken and sie ony thing she wald desyre'.[782] Isobel Haldane of Perth (1623) also obtained all her information as to life and death from

---

[777] Cooper, *Mystery*, pp. 90-2.
[778] Pitcairn, ii, pp. 53, 54.
[779] Id., ii, p. 164.
[780] Id., ii, p. 230.
[781] Id., iii, p. 96.
[782] *County Folklore*, iii, p. 112; *Mait. Cl. Misc.*, ii, p. 188.

the man with the 'grey beird' whom she met among the fairy folk.[783] Jonet Rendall, another Orkney witch (1629), stated that 'the devill apperit to you, Quhom ye called Walliman, claid in quhyt cloathis with ane quhyt head and ane gray beard, And said to you He sould learne yow to win almiss be healling of folk'[784] Sandie Hunter was only moderately successful in curing cattle till he covenanted with the Devil, who 'came to him in the form of a Mediciner, and said, *Sandie, you have too long followed my trade, and never acknowledged me for your Master. You must now take on with me, and be my servant, and I will make you more perfect in your Calling.* Whereupon the man gave up himself to the Devil. After this, he grew very famous throw the Countrey, for his Charming and cureing of diseases in Men and Beasts.'[785] Reginald Scot says that the witches were taught by the Devil to make magical ointments, and that he 'supplied their want of powders and roots to intoxicate withal'.[786] It was the Devil who pointed out which graves were to be opened in order to obtain the material for working magic; and when the bodies had been exhumed and dismembered, he told the witches how to use the fragments.[787] It was the Devil who made[788] or baptized[789] the wax and clay images, and who stuck the first thorn or pin into them.[790] It was the Devil who held the mock plough at Auldearne, and taught the witches of that place all the charms they knew. 'We get all this power from the Divell', says Isobell Gowdie.[791] It was the Devil who instigated and superintended the wrecking of the bridge at Cortaquhie, concerning which Helen Guthrie said, 'shee her selfe, Jonnet Stout, and others of them did thrust ther shoulderis againest the bridge', and

---

[783] Pitcairn, ii, p. 537.
[784] *County Folklore*, iii, p. 103.
[785] Sinclair, p. 122.
[786] Scot, Bk. III, p. 43.
[787] Pitcairn, i, pt. ii, pp. 211, 239, 245-6.
[788] Glanvil, pt. ii, pp. 293-5.
[789] Id., pt. ii, pp. 137-8.
[790] Id., pt. ii, pp. 293-5.
[791] Pitcairn, iii, pp. 603, 605 seq.

Isobel Smyth confessed, 'Wee all rewed that meitting, for wee hurt our selves lifting.'[792]

The book in which the magical recipes were recorded must have been of great value to its owner, and one which he would not willingly allow to pass out of his hands. A volume of this kind was known to be extant till the beginning of the last century; it was called the Red Book of Appin. There are two stories as to how it was taken from the Devil, but both stories agree that it was obtained by a trick. It was in manuscript and contained charms for the cure of cattle, and was consulted when cows were bewitched and refused to give milk. It was also supposed to confer magical powers on the owner, who was said to know what the inquiry would be before the inquirer opened his lips; and it was in itself so magical that the owner had to wear a hoop of iron on his head when turning its leaves.[793] Another Devil's-book was carried away, apparently as a joke, by Mr. Williamson of Cardrona, who took it from the witches as they danced on Minchmoor, but they followed him and he returned it.[794]

The system of reporting everything to the Chief of the community makes it certain that he was supplied with such current information as made his knowledge of public and private affairs appear miraculous to the uninitiated. Even those who supplied that information had firm faith in his supernatural power to kill or cure, and believed with equal ardour in the charms which he taught them to make and use.

In reviewing the evidence it seems clear that the witches of the Covens were bound to exercise their powers in the intervals between the meetings; they were bound to attend those meetings, unless absolutely prevented, in order to learn new methods as well as to make their reports; and they were bound to obey the Grand Master's orders and to treat him with the deference and respect due to his exalted position.

---

[792] Kinloch, pp. 122, 133.

[793] Campbell, pp. 293-4.

[794] *Berwickshire Naturalists Club*, xi, p. 265. Unfortunately the author of the article gives neither her authority for the statement, nor any indication of the date of the occurrence.

4. Discipline

Discipline was maintained by a system of rewards and punishments, enforced or relaxed according to the personal character of the Chief. As a rule only the severer punishments are recorded, but occasionally there are indications of minor chastisements.

The contemporary writers make the system of rewards and punishments very clear:

'Satan calleth them togither into a Diuelish Sinagoge, and that he may also vnderstand of them howe well and diligently they haue fulfilled their office of intoxicating committed vnto them, and whõ they haue slaine.'[795] 'Such as are absent, and have no care to be assoygned, are amerced to this paenalty, so to be beaten on the palms of their feete, to be whipt with iron rods, to be pincht and suckt by their Familiars till their heart blood come, till they repent them of their sloath, and promise more attendance and diligence for the future.'[796] '*Taking account also of the proceedings* of his other Schollers, and so approuing or condemning accordingly.'[797] Sometimes at their solemn assemblies, the Devil commands, that each tell what wickedness he hath committed, and according to the hainousness and detestableness of it, he is honoured and respected with a general applause. Those on the contrary, that have done no evil, are beaten and punished.'[798]

The usual punishment was beating, which was inflicted for various offences, chiefly disrespect or neglect of duty. At Arras in 1460 Jean Tacquet, a rich eschevin, 'had endeavoured to withdraw his allegiance from Satan who had forced him to continue it by beating him cruelly with a bull's pizzle.'[799] In Lorraine (1589) the Grand Master seems to have been peculiarly brutal:

'Jana Gerardina, Catharina Russa, und Francisca Fellaea bezeugten, dass sie mehr als einmal schwerlich mit harten Streichen hätten büssen

---

[795] Danaeus, ch. iv.
[796] Gaule, p. 65.
[797] Cooper, p. 91.
[798] *Pleasant Treatise*, pp. 6-7.
[799] Lea, iii, p. 525.

müssen, wenn sie keinen Schaden oder Unglück angestifft hätten. Und wie Nicolaea Morelia sagt, hat er sie dermassen zerschlagen, dass ihr der Athem davon ausgeblieben, und sie bey nahe gestorben wäre; Uber welches sich dann nicht zu verwundern sey, sintemahl er eiserne Hände habe, mit denen er ihnen so unbarmhertzig die Köpffe zerschlagen, dass sie deren nicht mehr empfinden.'[800]

In the Lyons district (1598) 'les Sorciers rendent conte à Satan de ce qu'ils ont fait dés la derniere assemblée, estans ceux là les mieux venus qui ont commis le plus de meschancetez. Les autres sont sifflez & mocquez de tous; l'on les fait mettre à l'escart, & sont encor le plus souuent battus & maltraitez de leur Maistre'.[801] According to Bodin, 'chacun Sorcier doit rendre compte du mal qu'il a faict sur peine d'estre bien battu.'[802] De Lancre says, 'Les Sorciers le vont adorer trois nuicts durant. Ceux qui par nonchalance, ou autre petit empeschement ne s'y trouuent, sont foüettez & battus à l'outrance.'[803] Alexander Hamilton (1630) stated that 'thair was ane new tryst appointed be him to be keipit wt thame altogidder within xiii days thereftir upon the cauldbit mure Quhilk meitting was nocht keipit be the said Alexr for the quhilk caus and breking of that tryst the said Alexr was maist rigorouslie strukin be the devill wt ane battoun at ane meitting keipit betuix thame schortlie thereftir upone gairnetourne hillis'.[804] In France (1652) two sisters were tried for witchcraft: 'Icelle confesse n'avoir faict mourir qu'un vaulx et d'avoir été battu par le diable, deux fois, parce qu'elle ne vouloit faire mourir aultres personnes et bestiault.' The other sister was 'interrogée sy le diable ne luy avoit conseillé de cracher la Sainte Hostie hors de sa bouche, ou bien ne la point recepvoir, dist que non, mais bien que le diable l'at une fois battue fort parce qu'elle l'avoit receu'.[805] The girls at Lille (1661) informed Madame Bourignon that the witches 'are constrained to offer him their Children, or else the

---

[800] Remigius, pt. i, cap. xiii, p. 59.
[801] Boguet, p. 139.
[802] Bodin, p. 189.
[803] De Lancre, *Tableau*, p. 398.
[804] From the record of the trial in the Edinburgh Justiciary Court.
[805] Van Elven, *La Tradition*, v (1891), p. 215. The names of the witches and the place are not given.

Devil would Beat them'.[806] Isobel Gowdie's account is, as usual, very full:

'Som tymis, among owr felwis, we wold be calling him "Blak Johne", or the lyk, and he wold ken it, and heir ws weill aneughe; and he ewin then com to ws, and say, "I ken weill aneughe what ʒe wer sayeing of me!" And then he vold beat and buffet ws werie sor. We wold be beattin if ve wer absent any tyme, or neglect any thing that wold be appointit to be done. Allexr Elder, in Earlseat, vold be werie often beattin. He is bot soft, and cowld never defend him self in the leist, bot greitt and cry, quhan he vold be scourging him. Bot Margret Wilson, in Auldearne, wold defend hir selfe fynelie, and cast wp hir handis to keip the stroakis off from hir; and Bessie Wilson would speak crustie with hir townge, and wold be belling again to him stowtlie. He wold be beatting and scurgeing ws all wp and downe with cardis [cords] and vther sharp scurges, like naked gwhastis; and we wold still be cryeing, "Pittie! pittie! Mercie! mercie, owr Lord!" Bot he wold haue neither pittie nor mercie. When he vold be angrie at ws, he wold girne at ws lyk a dowge, as iff he wold swallow ws wp.'[807]

The Swedish witches (1669) also had reason to complain of their Grand-Master's cruelty: 'heretofore it was sufficient to carry but one of their Children [to the meeting] or a strangers Child with them, but now he did plague them and whip them if they did not procure him Children.'[808] Among the Northumberland witches (1673):

'All of them who had donne harme gave an account thereof to their protector, who made most of them that did most harme, and beate those who had donne no harme.—At the said meeting their particular divell tooke them that did most evill, and danced with them first, and called every of them to an account, and those that did most evill he maid most of.—The devill, in the forme of a little black man and black cloaths, calld of one Isabell Thompson, of Slealy, widdow, by name, and required of her what service she had done him. She replyd she had gott power of the body of one Margarett Teasdale. And after he had

---

[806] Bourignon, *Vie*, p. 222; Hale, p. 37.
[807] Pitcairn, iii, p. 613.
[808] Horneck, pt. ii, p. 318.

danced with her he dismissed her and call'd of one Thomasine, wife of Edward Watson, of Slealy.'[809]

Punishments for minor offences are rarely recorded. At North Berwick (1590), when the witches returned after sinking a ship, 'seeing that they tarried over long, hee at their comming enjoyned them all to a pennance, which was, that they should kisse his buttockes, in sign of duety to him.'[810] At Aberdeen (1597) Christen Mitchell confessed that when the Devil asked her to join, 'thow ansuerit, I will enter in thy band, bot I will nocht byd thairin; and thairefter that the Devill gawe the a wisk, and thow fell on thy face one the dyk of that yaird.'[811] Beigis Tod, who belonged to one of the North Berwick Covens but was not tried till 1608, was late in arriving at a meeting, 'quhair the Deuill appeirit to thame, and reprovet the said Beigis Tod verrie scherplie, for hir long tayreing; to quhome scho maid this ansuer, "Sir, I could wyn na soner."'[812] At Lille if any witch desired to leave the religion, 'the Devil reproves them then more severely, and obligeth them to new Promises.'[813] Occasionally the witches kept discipline among themselves; this seems to have been the case only when the culprit prevented the proper execution of magical performances. At Aberdeen Thomas Leyis 'led the ring, and dang the said Kathren Mitchell, becaus scho spillit your dans, and ran nocht sa fast about as the rest.'[814] At Auldearne Isobel Gowdie described how the witches used flint arrow-heads: 'I shot at the Laird of Park, as he ves crossing the Burn of Boath; bot, thankis to God now, that he preserwit him. Bessie Hay gaw me a great cuffe, becaus I missed him.'[815] The former minister of Crighton, Mr. Gideon Penman, acted as the Devil's chaplain; 'ordinarily Mr. Gideon was in the rear in all their dances, and beat up all those that were slow.'[816] But a

---

[809] *Surtees Soc.*, xl, pp. 191, 195, 197.
[810] Pitcairn, i, pt. ii, p. 217.
[811] *Spalding Club Misc.*, i, p. 165.
[812] Pitcairn, ii, p. 542.
[813] Bourignon, *Vie*, p. 223; Hale, p. 38.
[814] *Spalding Club Misc.*, i, p. 97.
[815] Pitcairn, iii, p. 615.
[816] Fountainhall, i, p. 14.

reasonable excuse for trifling misdemeanours could be accepted: 'The devill asked at Kathrine Moore quhair hir Husband was that he came not she answered there was a young bairne at home and that they could not both come.'[817]

Capital punishment was reserved for traitors, actual and potential. It must have been brought into use only after the cult had fallen upon evil days, and then only when the Chief himself was in danger. Beating to death, hanging, and poison were the usual means of execution.

The earliest instance occurred in 1450, when the Church had begun to use its power systematically against the witches. 'The Inquisitor of Como, Bartolomeo de Homate, the podestà Lorenzo da Carorezzo, and the notary Giovanni da Fossato, either out of curiosity or because they doubted the witches whom they were trying, went to a place of assembly at Mendrisio and witnessed the scene from a hiding-place. The presiding demon pretended not to know their presence, and in due course dismissed the assembly, but suddenly recalled his followers and set them on the officials, who were so beaten that they died within fifteen days.'[818] Alesoun Peirson (1588) was burnt as a witch, having gained her knowledge from the fairies, who threatened that 'gif scho wald speik and tell of thame and thair doingis, thay sould martir hir'.[819] The Lorraine witches (1589) took an oath of silence, 'welchen Eyd sie so hoch und heilig halten, dass wenn sie Eydbrüchig werden, so darfür halten, also ob sie ewig darumb musten verdampt und gestrafft seyn.'[820] Alice Gooderidge, the Derbyshire witch (1597), was tried for witchcraft, 'she should haue bin executed, but that her spirit killed her in the prison.'[821] Jeannette d'Abadie (1609) was more fortunate than most in that she was not killed, 'elle a esté battue au sabbat reellement & corporellemẽt par deux sorcieres qu'elle nomme,

---

[817] *Highland Papers*, iii, p. 26.
[818] Lea, iii, p. 501.
[819] Pitcairn, i, pt. ii, p. 163.
[820] Remigius, ch. xviii, p. 83.
[821] *Alse Gooderidge*, p. 43.

par ce qu'elle auoit reuelé les mysteres du sabbat.'[822] John Stewart, the 'juglour' of Irvine (1618)—

'for his better preferring to the day of the assys, was put in ane lockfast buith, quhair no maner of persoun might haif access to him quhil the dounsitting of the justice court, and for avoyding of putting violent handis on himself, was verie strictly gairdit and flitherit be the airms, as us is, and upon that same day of the assys, about half ane hour befoir the doun sitting of the justice court, Mr. David Dickson, minister at Irving; and Mr. George Dunbar, minister of Air, having went to him to exhort him to call on his God for mercie for his bygane wicked and evil lyf and that God wold of his infinite mercie, lowis him out of the handis of the devil quhom he had servit thir mony years by gane He acquiescit to their prayer and godlie exhortation, and utterit thir wordis—I am so straitlie gairdit that it lyis not in my hand to tak off my bonnett, nor to gett bread to my mouth. And immediately after the departing of the two ministers from him, the Juglour being sent for at the desyr of my Lord of Eglintoune, to be confrontit with ane woman of the burgh of Air, callit Janet Bous, quha was apprehendit by the Magistrates of the burghe of Air, for witchcraft, to the burghe of Irvine, purposlie for that effer. He was fund be the burrow officers, quha went about him stranglit and hangit be the cruik of the dur, with ane tait of hemp (or a string maid of hemp, supposed to haif been his garten, or string of his bonnet) not above the length of twa span long, his kneyis not being from the grund half ane span, and was brocht out of the hous, his lyf not being so layt expellit: but notwithstanding of quhatsomever meines usit to the contrair for remeid of his lyf, he revievit not, but so endit his lyf miserable by the help of the devill his maister.'[823]

Rebecca West, a young Essex witch (1645), confessed to Matthew Hopkins that 'if shee should discover any thing, they all told the said Rebecca, shee should endure more torments on earth, then could be in hell: and the said Rebecca told this informant that shee promised to keepe all their secrets; and moreover they all told her, that shee must

---

[822] De Lancre, *Tableau*, p. 91.
[823] *Trial of Isobel Inch*, p. 11.

never confesse any thing, although the rope were about her necke, and shee ready to be hanged'.[824] In Fifeshire (1649) 'ane Mistres Hendersone (sister to Fordell Hendersone, in the presbytrey of Dumfermling), sometymes lady of Pittahro, being delated by many to be a witch, was apprehended and caried to Edenbroughe, wher she was keiped fast; and after her remaining in prison for a tyme, being in health att night, vpon the morne was founde dead. It was thought, and spoken by many, that she wronged her selfe, either by strangling or by poyson.'[825] The Swedish children (1670) were not spared: 'if the Children did at any time name the Names of those that had carried them away, they were again carried by force either to Blockula, or to the Cross way, and there miserably beaten, insomuch that some of them died of it.'[826] Whether Deliverance Hobbs (1692) was actually beaten, or whether her statement was made from the knowledge of what might happen to her, cannot be certain without reference to the records of the trial itself, as Mather's bias is apt to distort the evidence: 'She now testifi'd, that this *Bishop* tempted her to Sign the *Book* again, and to deny what she had confess'd. She affirm'd, that it was the Shape of this Prisoner, which whipped her with Iron Rods, to compel her thereunto.'[827] Elizabeth Anderson in Renfrewshire (1696) went with her father to a witch-meeting, 'severals of them being affraid that the Declarant would Confess, and tell of them as she done formerly on her Grand-mother, they threatened to tear her all in pieces if she did so.'[828] John Reid of the same Coven—

'after his Confession had called out of his prison Window, desiring Baily Scott to keep that old body Angus Forrester, who had been his fellow prisoner, closs and secure; whereupon the company asked John when they were leaving him on Friday night the 21th of May, whether he desired company or would be afraid alone, he said he had no fear of anything: So being left till Saturday in the Forenoon, he was found

---

[824] Howell, iv, 842.

[825] Lamont, p. 12. For further particulars of this lady, see Ross, *Aberdour and Inchcolme*, p. 339.

[826] Horneck, pt. ii, p. 319.

[827] Cotton Mather, p. 131.

[828] *Narr. of the Sufferings of a Young Girle*, p. xl.

in this posture, viz. sitting upon a stool which was on the Hearth of the Chimney, with his feet on the floor and his Body straight upward, his shoulders touching the lintel of the Chimney, but his Neck tyed with his own neck-cloath (whereof the knot was behind) to a small stick thrust into a hole above the lintel of the Chimney, upon which the Company, especially John Campbel a Chyrurgeon who was called, thought at first in respect of his being in an ordinary posture of sitting, and the neck-cloath not having any drawn knot (or *run loup*) but an ordinary one which was not very strait, and the sticke not having the strength to bear the weight of his Body or the struggle, that he had not been quite dead; but finding it otherways, and that he was in such a Situation that he could not have been the Actor thereof himself, concluded that some extraordinary Agent had done it, especially considering that the Door of the Room was secured, and that there was a board set over the Window which was not there the night before when they left him.'[829]

A similar fate befell the warlock Playfair in 1597. He was found strangled in his prison at Dalkeith with the 'point' of his breeches tied round his neck.[830]

---

[829] *Narr. of the Sufferings of a Young Girle*, p. xliv; *Sadducismus Debellatus*, pp. 43-4.
[830] Sharpe, p 46.

VIII

FAMILIARS AND TRANSFORMATIONS

The question of familiars is one which has always puzzled the student of witch-trials, and almost more than any other has been the cause of the belief that hysteria and hallucination were the foundation of the witches' confessions. Yet when the accounts are carefully examined, the circumstantial detail given in the evidence shows that here, as elsewhere, a foundation of fact underlies the statements of the accused. These statements are often misunderstood and therefore misrepresented by the recorders, and still more so by the modern commentator, but by comparison of the details a considerable amount of information can be gained.

The familiars can be divided into two types: (1) those by which the witch divined, (2) those who attended on the witch to obey her commands.

1. The Divining Familiar

The essence of this familiar is that it did not belong to the witch but was an animal which appeared accidentally after the performance of certain magical ceremonies. Forbes puts this quite clearly when describing the contract: 'The Devil on his Part articles with such Proselytes, concerning the Shape he is to appear to them in, the Services they are to expect from him, upon the Performance of certain Charms or ceremonious Rites.'[831] From this statement and from the facts revealed in the trials it would seem that the Devil appointed to the witch, on her admission, some kind of animal or animals by which she should divine, and which therefore represented himself for the time being, for he claimed the power, as God, to know and reveal the future. This explanation accounts for the fact that the witches always spoke of such animals as the Devil and believed that they could foretell the future by his means. The actual method of divination is not

---

[831] Forbes, ii, p. 33.

preserved; all that remains of the ceremony are the words and gestures which were used before the appearance of the animal, and these only in few cases. The method was probably such as obtained in other places where auguries by animals and birds were practised, i.e. by the direction and pace of the animal, by its actions, by its voice if it emitted any sound, and so on. The method of making such observations and of translating them when made was part of the instruction given to the witch by the Devil; and was usually employed to discover whether a person were bewitched, the ultimate result of an illness, and the length of life of any given person.

In 1566 John Walsh, of Netherberry in Dorset, who 'knoweth when anye man is bewytched, sayth vpon his oth, that his Familiar would sometyme come vnto hym lyke a gray blackish Culuer, and somtime like a brended Dog, and somtimes lyke a man.'[832] In 1590 Agnes Sampson, the 'wise wife' of Keith, was—

'fylit and convict, that the Dewill apperit to hir in liknes of ane dog, att quhom she socht her haill responsis that quhene sche wes send for to haill the auld Lady Edmestoune, quhene sche lay seik, befoir the said Agnes departit, sche tauld to the gentilwemene, that sche sould tell thame that nycht quhidder the Lady wald haill or nocht; and appointit thame to be in the gardin efter supper, betuix fyve and sax att ewin. Sche passit to the gairdene, to devyise vpoun hir prayer, one quhat tyme sche chargeit the Dewill, calling him "Elva", to cum and speik to hir, quha come in owir the dyke, in liknes of ane dog, and come sa neir to hir, that sche wes effrayit, and chargeit him "on the law that he lewit on", to cum na neirar, bot to ansuer hir; and sche demandit, Quhidder the lady wald leif or nocht. He said, "Hir dayes war gane." Than he demandit, "Gif the gentilwemen hir dochteres, quhair thay wer?" And sche said, that "the gentilwemen said, that thay war to be thair". He ansuerit, "Ane of thame sould be in perrell, and that he sould haif ane of thame." Sche ansuerit, "It sould nocht be sa", and swa departit fra hir zowling. Fra this tyme quhill eftir supper, he remanit in the wall [well]. Quhen the gentilwemen come in, the dog come out of the wall, and apperit to thame; quhairatt thay wer effrayit.

---

[832] *Examination of John Walsh.*

In the mene tyme, ane of the said gentilwemen, the Lady Torsenze, ran to the wall, being forceit and drawin by the Devill, quha wald haif drownit hir, war nocht the said Agnes and the rest of the gentilwemen gatt ane gryp of hir, and with all hir [their?] forceis drew hir abak agane, quhilk maid thame all effrayd. The dog passit away thaireftir with ane zowle.'[833]

Margerat Clarke, like Agnes Sampson a midwife of great reputation, was tried at Aberdeen in 1597 for witchcraft, in that, being sent for to a case

'and ane Androw Mar cuming for the, the Devill thy maister, quhome thow seruis, and quha techis the all this vytchcraft and sorcerie, apperit to the, in the licknes of ane horss, in ane how and den, and spak and conferrit with the a lang speace.—[Being sent for to another case] and the said guidman of Kincragie sendand his awin best horss, with ane boy of his awin, to bring the to his wyiff; and the said boy on horse cuming to the, and thow beand on the horss behind the boy, att thy awin dure, thy maister Satane, the Dewill, apperit in the licknes of ane gray staig, and convoyit the and the boy fra thy awin houss to Kincragie, and keipit cumpanie all the way with you, with quhome thow haid thy secreitt conference.—Vpone Nwris [New-year's] day, thow was att the loche syid besyid Boigloche, and thair thow pudlit be ane lang speace, thy selff alane, in ane deip holl amongis the watter, castand watter, erd and stone oure thi schowlderis, and thair was besyid the thy maister the Deuill, quhome thow seruis, in the licknes of ane hen flichtering, with quhome thow was thane consultand, and quhais directiounis than thow was taikand.'[834]

In Derbyshire in 1597, 'Whereas Alice Gooderige said her familiar was like one William Gregories dog of Stapenhill, there arose a rumor, his dog was her familiar: Wherefore hee with his neighbour maister Coxe went the next day to examin her concerning this report; and she saide, my diuel (I say) was like your dog. Now out vpon thee (saide Gregorie) and departed: she being further examined, saide she had her

---

[833] Pitcairn, i, pt. ii, p. 236.
[834] *Spalding Club Misc.*, i, pp. 157-60.

familiar of her mother.'[835] Alexander Hamilton, tried at Edinburgh in 1630, confessed that—

'haifing ane battoun of fir in his hand the devill than gave the said Alexr command to tak that battoun quhan evir he had ado with him and thairwt to strek thruse upone the ground and to nhairge him to ruse up foule theiff Conforme to the whilk directioun and be streking of the said battone thryse upone the ground the devill was in use sumtymes to appeir to the said Alexr in the liknes of ane corbie at uther tymes in the schape of ane katt and at uther tymes in the schape of ane dog and thereby the said Alexr did ressave reponsis frome him.—The said Alexr Hamiltoun coming to the said Thomas Homes house and seing him visseit with the said seiknes declairit to him that he was bewitchet and promeist to cure him thereof Lykas for this effect the said Alexr schortlie thereftir past to clarkingtoun burne besyde the rottoneraw haifing ane katt under his okister and thair wt his said battoun raisit Sathan his maister quha than appeirit to him in the liknes of ane corbie and thair instructit him be quhat meanis he sould cure the said Thomas of his said seiknes and he haifing ressauit that respons fra the devill the said Alexr thereftir cuist to him the kat quha therewt vanischet away'.[836]

Two of the Somerset witches in 1664 had familiars; to Elizabeth Style the familiar came as a black dog, 'and when she hath a desire to do harm, she calls the Spirit by the name of *Robin*, to whom when he appeareth, she useth these words, *O Sathan give me my purpose*. She then tells him what she would have done. And that he should so appear to her was part of her Contract with him.—Alice Duke saith, that when the Devil doth any thing for her, she calls for him by the name of *Robin*, upon which he appears, and when in the shape of a Man, she can hear him speak'.[837] This shows that the familiar, or Devil as she called him, was not always in the form of a man. The trial of Margaret Nin-Gilbert at Thurso was as late as 1719: 'Being interrogat, If ever the devil appeared afterwards to her? Confessed, That sometimes he

---

[835] *Alse Gooderidge*, p. 27.
[836] From an unpublished trial in the Justiciary Court at Edinburgh.
[837] Glanvil, pt. ii, pp. 136, 137, 152.

appeared in the likeness of a great black horse, and other times riding on a black horse, and that he appeared sometimes in the likeness of a black cloud, and sometimes like a black henn'.[838]

2. The Domestic Familiar

Forbes, the great Scotch lawyer, says that 'to some he [the Devil] gives certain Spirits or Imps to correspond with, and serve them as their Familiars, known to them by some odd Names, to which they answer when called. These Imps are said to be kept in Pots or other Vessels.'[839] Though the domestic familiar is thus mentioned in the law of Scotland, it never occurs in the trials. It is confined so strictly to England that Hutchinson is able to say 'I meet with little mention of *Imps* in any Country but ours, where the Law makes the feeding, suckling, or rewarding of them to be Felony'.[840] It is not found north of Lancashire, and the chief records are in Essex, Suffolk, and the other Eastern counties.

The domestic familiar was always a small animal, was fed in a special manner on bread and milk and blood, and was kept, as Forbes points out, in a box or earthen pot on a bed of wool. It was used for working magic on the persons and property of other people, never for divining. Giffard records the general belief: 'The witches have their spirits, some hath one, some hath more, as two, three, foure, or five, some in one likenesse, and some in another, as like cats, weasils, toades, or mise, whom they nourish with milke or with a chicken, or by letting them suck now and then a drop of bloud.'[841]

In the earlier trials the witches confessed to pricking the hands or face and giving the resulting drop or drops of blood to the familiar. In the later trials this has developed into the sucking of the witch's blood by the familiar; and the supernumerary nipple, which was so marked a feature of the English witches, was popularly supposed to be caused by such sucking. It is more probable, however, that the witch who was

---

[838] Sharpe, p. 191.
[839] Forbes, ii, pp. 33.
[840] F. Hutchinson, *Hist. Essay*, p. 77.
[841] Giffard, p. 18.

possessed of a supernumerary nipple would regard it as something supernatural, and would use it to nourish a supernatural animal.

Elizabeth Francis, tried at Chelmsford in 1556,
'learned this arte of witchcraft of hyr grandmother whose nam mother Eue. Item when shee taughte it her, she counseiled her to renounce God and his worde and to geue of her bloudde to Sathan (as she termed it) whyche she delyuered her in the lykenesse of a whyte spotted Catte, and taughte her to feede the sayde Catte with breade and mylke, and she dyd so, also she taughte her to cal it by the name of Sathan and to kepe it in a basket. Item that euery tyme that he did any thynge for her, she sayde that he required a drop of bloude, which she gaue him by prycking herselfe, sometime in one place and then in an other. When shee had kept this Cat by the space of XV or XVI yeare, and as some saye (though vntruly) beinge wery of it, she came to one mother Waterhouse her neyghbour, she brought her this cat in her apron and taught her as she was instructed by her grandmother Eue, telling her that she must cal him Sathan and geue him of her bloude and breade and milke as before.—Mother Waterhouse receyued this cat of this Frances wife in the order as is before sayde. She (to trye him what he coulde do) wyld him to kyll a hog of her owne, which he dyd, and she gaue him for his labour a chicken, which he fyrste required of her and a drop of her blod. And thys she gaue him at all times when he dyd anythynge for her, by pricking her hand or face and puttinge the bloud to hys mouth whyche he sucked, and forthwith wold lye downe in hys pot againe, wherein she kepte him. Another tym she rewarded hym as before, wyth a chicken and a droppe of her bloud, which chicken he eate vp cleane as he didde al the rest, and she cold fynde remaining neyther bones nor fethers. Also she said that when she wolde wyl him to do any thinge for her, she wolde say her Pater noster in laten. Item, this mother Waterhouse confessed that shee fyrst turned this Cat into a tode by this meanes, she kept the cat a great while in woll in a pot, and at length being moued by pouertie to occupie the woll, she praied in the name of the father and of the sonne, and of the holy ghost that

it wold turne into a tode, and forthwith it was turned into a tode, and so kept it in the pot without woll.'[842]

In 1579 at Windsor—

'one Mother Dutton dwellyng in Cleworthe Parishe keepeth a Spirite or Feende in the likenesse of a Toade, and fedeth the same Feende liyng in a border of greene Hearbes, within her Garden, with blood whiche she causeth to issue from her owne flancke. Mother Deuell, dwellyng nigh the Ponde in Windesore, hath a Spirite in the shape of a Blacke Catte, and calleth it Gille, whereby she is aided in her Witchcrafte, and she daiely feedeth it with Milke, mingled with her owne bloud. Mother Margaret, dwellying in the Almeshouse at Windesore, dooeth feede a Kitlyng or Feende by her named Ginnie, with crummes of bread and her owne blood. The saied Elizabeth Stile, of her self confesseth that she the same Elizabeth kept a Ratte, beeyng in very deede a wicked Spirite, namyng it Philip, and that she fedde the same Ratte with bloode, issuing from her right handwrest, the markes whereof euidently remaine.'[843]

At St. Osyth in Essex in 1582 Thomas Rabbet, aged eight, said that his mother Ursley Kemp 'hath foure seuerall spirites, the one called Tyffin, the other Tittey, the third Pigine, and the fourth Iacke: and being asked of what colours they were, saith, that Tyttey is like a little grey Cat,[844] Tyffin is like a white lambe, Pygine is black like a Toad, and Iacke is blacke like a Cat. And hee saith, hee hath seen his mother at times to giue thē beere to drinke, and of a white Lofe or Cake to eate, and saith that in the night time the said spirites will come to his mother, and sucke blood of her vpon her armes and other places of her body.' Febey Hunt, stepdaughter of Ales Hunt, one of the accused witches, stated that 'shee hath seen her mother to haue two little thinges like horses,[845] the one white, the other blacke, the which shee

---

[842] *Witches at Chelmsford*, pp. 24-32; Philobiblon Soc., viii.

[843] *Rehearsall*, par. 2-5.

[844] Also called Tissey. Compare the name of the magic cat given to Frances More by Goodwife Weed, p. 219.

[845] In Ales Hunt's own confession (q. v.) the animals in question are called *colts*. I would suggest that this is *cotes*, the well-known provincialism for *cats*; but the recorder understood the word as *colts* and further improved it into *horses*.

kept in a little lowe earthen pot with woll, colour white and blacke, and that they stoode in her chamber by her bed side, and saith, that shee hath seene her mother to feede them with milke'. Ales Hunt herself said that 'shee had within VI. dayes before this examination two spirits, like unto little Coltes, the one blacke, and the other white: And saith she called them by the names of *Iacke* and *Robbin*. This Examinate saith that her sister (named Margerie Sammon) hath also two spirites like Toades, the one called *Tom*, and the other *Robbyn*.' Ursley Kemp confessed that 'about a quarter of a yere past, she went vnto mother Bennets house for a messe of milke, the which shee had promised her: But at her comming this examinate saith shee knocked at her dore, and no bodie made her any answere, whereupon shee went to her chamber windowe and looked in therat, saying, ho, ho, mother Bennet are you at home: And casting her eyes aside, shee saw a spirit lift up a clothe, lying ouer a pot, looking much lik a Ferret. And it being asked of this examinate why the spirite did looke vpon her, shee said it was hungrie'. Elizabeth Bennet acknowledged that she had two 'spirits, one called *Suckin*, being blacke like a Dogge, the other called *Lierd*, beeing red like a Lion. Suckin this examinat saith is a hee, and the other a shee. Many tymes they drinke of her milke bowle. And when, and as often as they did drinke of the mylke: This Examynate saith they went into the sayd earthen pot, and lay in the wooll.' Ursley Kemp also gave evidence concerning Ales Hunt's familiars: 'About the foureteene or fifteene day of Januarie last, shee went to the house of William Hunt to see howe his wife did, and shee being from home, shee called at her chamber window and looked in, and then espied a spirite to looke out of a potcharde from vnder a clothe, the nose thereof beeing browne like vnto a Ferret.'[846] In 1588 in Essex an old woman, whose name is not given,

'confessed all: Which was this in effect: that she had three spirits: one like a cat, which she called Lightfoot, another like a toad, which she called Lunch, the third like a Weasill, which she called Makeshift. This Lightfoot, she said, one mother Barlie of W. solde her aboue sixteene yeares agoe, for an ouen cake, and told her the Cat would doe

---

[846] *Witches taken at St. Oses*, A 3, A 5, C 3 and 4, B 2, B 5 and C 1, B 3.

her good seruice, if she woulde, she might send her of her errand: this Cat was with her but a while, but the Weasill and the Toad came and offered their seruice: The Cat would kill kine, the Weasil would kill horses, the Toad would plague men in their bodies.—There was one olde mother W. of great T. which had a spirite like a Weasill: she was offended highlie with one H. M. home she went, and called forth her spirite, which lay in a pot of woll vnder her bed, she willed him to goe plague the man; he required what she would give him. She said she would give him a cocke, which she did.' Another Mother W. 'sayd she had a spirit in the likenesse of a yellow dun cat'.[847]

In Lancashire in 1613 old mother Demdike confessed that 'vpon a Sabbath day in the morning, this Examinate hauing a litle Child vpon her knee, and she being in a slumber, the sayd Spirit appeared vnto her in the likenes of a browne Dogg, forcing himselfe to her knee, to get blood vnder her left Arme: and she being without any apparrell sauing her Smocke, the said Deuill did get blood vnder her left arme'.[848] Of the witches who plagued the Fairfax family at Fewstone in 1621, five had domestic familiars: Margaret Waite's was 'a deformed thing with many feet, black of colour, rough with hair, the bigness of a cat'; her daughter, Margaret Waite, had as 'her spirit, a white cat spotted with black, and named Inges'; Jennet Dibble had 'her spirit in the shape of a great black cat called Gibbe, which hath attended her now above 40 years'; Dibble's daughter, Margaret Thorpe, had a 'familiar in the shape of a bird, yellow of colour, about the bigness of a crow—the name of it is Tewhit'; Elizabeth Dickenson's spirit was 'in the likeness of a white cat, which she calleth Fillie, she hath kept it twenty years'.[849] The witch of Edmonton, Elizabeth Sawyer, in 1621, said: 'It is eight yeares since our first acquaintance, and three times in the weeke, the Diuell would come and see mee; he would come sometimes in the morning, and sometimes in the evening. Always in the shape of a dogge, and of two collars, sometimes of blacke and sometimes of white. I gaue him leaue to sucke of my bloud, the which

---

[847] Giffard, pp. 19, 27, 39.
[848] Potts, B 3.
[849] Fairfax, pp. 32, 33, 34, 79, 82.

hee asked of me. When he came barking to mee he then had done the mischiefe that I did bid him to doe for me. I did call the Diuell by the name of Tom. I did stroake him on the backe, and then he would becke vnto me, and wagge his tayle as being therewith contented.'[850] Margaret Johnson, another Lancashire witch in 1633, 'alsoe saith, yt when her devill did come to sucke her pappe, hee usually came to her in ye liknes of a cat, sometymes of one colour, and sometymes on (*sic*) an other. And yt since this trouble befell her, her spirit hath left her, and shee never sawe him since.'[851]

From 1645 to 1647 are the chief records of the witch trials of Essex and the eastern counties, celebrated as the scene of Matthew Hopkins's work. The Essex trials took place in 1645: John Sterne, Hopkins's assistant, deposed that when watching Elizabeth Clarke,

'the said Elizabeth desired this informant, and the rest that were in the roome with her, to sit downe, and said, shee would shew this informant and the rest some of her impes: and within halfe an houre there appeared a white thing in the likeness of a cat, but not altogether so big: and being asked, if she would not be afraid of her impes, the said Elizabeth answered, "What, do yee think I am afraid of my children?" And that shee called the name of that white impe, Hoult. And this informant further saith, That presently after there appeared another white impe, with red spots, as big as a small dog, which shee then called Jarmara: and that immediately after, there appeared at the threshold of the doore another impe about the bignesse of the first, but did presently vanish away. And then the said Elizabeth being asked, if any more impes would come? she answered, "That Vinegar Tom would come by and by". And forthwith there appeared another in the likenesse of a dumb dogge, somewhat bigger than any of the former. And the said Elizabeth also told this informant, that shee had three impes from her mother, which were of a browne colour, and two from the old beldam Weste; and that there had five [? four] impes appeared, but shee had one more, called Sack and Sugar. And the said Elizabeth further confessed to this informant, that shee had one impe for which

---

[850] *Wonderfull Discouerie of Elisabeth Sawyer.*
[851] Whitaker, p. 216.

she would fight up to the knees in bloud, before shee would lose it; and that her impes did commonly suck on the old beldam Weste, and that the said beldam's impes did suck on her the said Elizabeth likewise.—Anne Leech saith, That she had a grey impe sent to her, and that this examinant, together with the said Elizabeth Clark, and Elizabeth the wife of Edward Gooding, did about a yeer since, send their imps to kill a black cowe and a white cowe of Mr. Edwards, which was done accordingly. And this examinant saith, that she sent her grey impe, Elizabeth Clark a black imp, and Elizabeth Gooding a white imp. And this examinant confesseth, that she and the said Elizabeth Gooding, sent either of them an imp to destroy the childe of the said Mr. Edwards; this examinant's imp being then a white one, and Elizabeth Gooding's a black imp; and that about thirty yeers since, this examinant had the said white imp and two others, a grey and a black imp of one Anne, the wife of Robert Pearce of Stoak in Suffolk, being her brother; and that these imps went commonly from one to another, and did mischief where ever they went; and that when this examinant did not send and imploy them abroad to do mischief, she had not her health, but when they were imployed, she was healthfull and well, and that these imps did usually suck those teats which were found about the privie parts of her body.—Hellen Clark confesseth, that about six weeks since, the Devill appeared to her in her house, in the likenesse of a white dog, and that she calleth that familiar Elimanzer; and that this examinant hath often fed him with milk pottage.—Rebecca West saith, that about a moneth since, the aforesaid Anne Leech, Elizabeth Gooding, Hellen Clark, Anne West, and this examinant, met all together at the house of the aforesaid Elizabeth Clark in Mannyntree, where they spent some time in praying unto their familiars, and every one in order went to prayers; afterwards some of them read in a book, the book being Elizabeth Clarks; and this examinant saith, that forthwith their familiars appeared, and every one of them made their severall propositions to those familiars, what every one of them desired to have effected.—The Information of Matthew Hopkins, Gent. taken upon oath before the said Justices. This informant saith, That being lately at Colchester, he went to the castle, where the said Rebecca Weste, with the other five, are secured until the next gaole delivery: and this informant going to Rebecca Weste, and asking her how shee came first to be a witch, the said Rebecca told this informant, that about a yeare since, or thereabouts, halfe an houre before sun-set, the said Anne Weste (her mother) carried the said Rebecca Weste towards Mannintree (which is about a small mile from the place where the said Anne dwelt) and the said Rebecca told this informant, that as her mother and shee walked together, the said Anne told the said Rebecca, shee must keepe secret whatsoever shee saw, whither they were then going; and the said Rebecca promised so to doe; and the said Rebecca told this informant, that her mother and shee went to the house of the aforesaid Elizabeth Clarke, where at their comming in they found the aforesaid Anne Leech, widow, Elizabeth Gooding, Hellen Clarke, and the house-keeper Elizabeth Clarke, and that forthwith the Devill appeared to them in the shape of a dogge; afterwards in the shape of two kitlyns; then in the shape of two dogges; and that the said familiars did doe homage in the first place to the said Elizabeth Clarke, and skipped up into her lap and kissed her; and then went and kissed all that were in the roome, except the said Rebecca: and the said Rebecca told this informant, that immediately one of the company asked the said Anne her mother, if shee had acquainted her daughter (the said Rebecca) with the businesse. [Rebecca then took an oath of secrecy]; after she had consented to all these things, the Devill came into her lap, and kissed her, and promised to doe for her what she could desire.—The Information of Elizabeth Otley of Wyvenhoe, taken upon oath before the said justices. This informant saith, that Alice Dixon, who now stands committed for a suspected witch, did in the presence of Mary Johnson of the same town, charge and accuse the said Mary Johnson to be the death of this informant's child, saying, that the said Mary Johnson did carry an impe in her pocket to this informant's house, and put the said impe into the house, at an hole in the doore, bidding it go rock the cradle, and do the businesse she sent it about.—The Information of Joseph Long, Minister of Clacton in the County of Essex, taken before the said Justices. This informant saith, that Anne the wife of John Cooper of Clacton aforesaid, being accused for a witch: Confessed unto this informant, that she the said Anne hath had three black impes suckled on the lower parts of her body; called by the names of Wynowe, Jeso, and Panu. And the said Anne further confessed unto this informant, that she the said Anne offered to give unto her daughter Sarah Cooper an impe in the likenes of a gray kite [kit], to suck on the said Sarah; which impes name the said Anne called Tom boy; and told the said Sarah, there was a cat for her.—This informant Henry Cornwall saith, that the said Margaret [Moone] did confesse to him that she had twelve impes, and called them by their names; of which he remembers onely these following: Jesus, Jockey, Sandy, Mrit. Elizabeth, and Collyn.—The information of Francis Milles, taken upon oath before the said Justices. This informant saith, that she asking the said Margaret [Moone] for her impes, which sucked those teats; she said, if she might have some bread and beere, she would call her said impes; which being given unto her, she put the bread into the beere, and set it against an hole in the wall, and made a circle round the pot, and then cried, Come Christ, come Christ, come Mounsier, come Mounsier: And no impe appearing, she cried out and said, she had devilish daughters, which had carried her impes away in a white bagge, and wished they might be searched.—The information of Francis Stock, and John Felgate, taken upon oath before the said Justices. The said Francis and John say, that the said Sarah Barton, told them, that the said Marian [Hocket] had given and delivered unto her the said Sarah three imps, and that the said Marian called them by the names of Littleman, Pretty-man, and Dainty.—This examinant, Elizabeth Harvie saith, that about halfe a yeer since, the said Marian Hocket brought three things to her house, two of them being smaller than mouses, and the other somewhat bigger and longer; and that the said Marian told this examinant they were pretty things, and would do her and this examinant good, if shee this examinant would keep them.—Rose Hallybread saith, that about fifteen or sixteen yeers since, there was an imp brought to her house by one Goodwife Hagtree, which imp this examinant entertained, fed it with oatmeale, and suckled it on her body, for the space of a yeer and a halfe, or thereabouts, and then lost it: And this examinant further saith, that about half a yeer since, one Joyce Boanes (who is now also accused for Witchcraft), brought to this examinants house another imp, in the likenesse of a small grey bird, which this examinant received. And this examinant further saith, that about eight dayes since, Susan Cock, Margaret Landish, and Joyce Boanes, (all which stand now suspected for Witchcraft) brought to this examinants house each of them an imp, (in all three) to which this examinant added one of her own imps; and then the said Joyce Boanes carryed the said four imps to the house of one Robert Turner, to torment his servant.—Joyce Boanes saith, that about thirteen yeers since, shee had two imps which came into the bed to her in the likenesse of mouses, and that they sucked on this examinants body. And this examinant also saith, that she carried one of her said imps, called Rug, to the house of the said Rose Hallybread; and that her said imp Rug, with the three imps of the said Rose Hallybread, Susan Cock, and Margaret Landish, each of them sending one, were carried by this examinant from the house of the said Rose Hallybread, to the house of the said Robert Turner to kill the servant of the said Robert.—Susan Cock saith, that about three or four yeeres since, one Margery Stoakes, this examinants mother, lying upon her death-bed, and this examinant comming to visit her, shee the said Margery desired this examinant privately to give entertainment to two of her imps, and withall told this examinant, they would do this examinant good: And this examinant saith, that the same night her said mother dyed, the said two imps came to her accordingly, and sucked on her body: And this examinant saith, that one of the said imps was like a mouse, and the name of that was Susan; that the other was of a yellow colour, about the bigness of a cat; and that the name of that imp was Besse.—Rebecca Jones saith, that as shee was going to St. Osyth (where this examinant doth now dwell) to sell her said masters butter, a man met with her, being in a ragged sute, and having such great eyes, that this examinant was much afraid of him; who came to this examinant, and gave her three things like to moules, having foure feet a piece, but without tayles, and of a black colour, and bid this examinant nurse the said three things, untill he did desire them againe; And this examinant asked the said man, what she should give them to eate, and he told this examinant milke, and that they would not hurt her, and wished her not to be afraid of them. And the said man told this examinant, that those three things which he gave her, would avenge her on her enemies, and bid her murther some, but not too many, and he would forgive her; and then went away from this examinant. And this examinant saith, that the names of her three imps were Margaret, Amie, and Susan. And that a while after, this examinant and one Joyce Boanes, now in prison, did send each of them an impe to kill one Thomas Bumstead of St. Osyth: And that the impe which the said Joyce Boanes sent was a dund one like unto a mouse.—Johan Cooper saith, That she hath been a witch about twenty yeers, and hath three familiars, two like mouses, and the third like a frog; the names of the two like mouses are Jack, and the other Prickeare, and the name of the third, like a frog, is Frog.—Anne Cate saith, That she hath four familiars, which shee had from her mother, about two and twenty yeeres since, and that the names of the said imps are James, Prickeare, Robyn, and Sparrow: and that three of these imps are like mouses, and the fourth like a sparrow, which she called Sparrow.'[852]

In 1646 the Huntingdonshire witches were tried. Elizabeth Weed of Great Catworth confessed that—
'about one and twenty yeares since she being saying her Prayers in the evening about bedtime, there did appear unto her three Spirits, one in the likeness of a young man or boy, and the other two of two Puppies, the one white and the other black. Being demanded the name of the lesser Spirits, shee saith the name of the white one was Lilly, and the blacke one Priscill; and that the office of Lilly was to hurt man, woman, or childe; and the office of Priscill was to hurt Cattell when she desired.—Francis Moore saith, that about eight yeares since she received a little blacke puppy from one Margaret Simson of great Catworth, which dog the said Margaret had in her bed with her, and took it thence when she gave it to the Examinate: The Examinate further saith, that the said Margaret told her, that she must keep that dogge all her life time; and if she cursed any Cattell, and set the same

---

[852] Howell, iv, 834 et seq.

dog upon them, they should presently dye, and the said Margaret told her that she had named it already, his name was Pretty. And the said Examinate further saith, that about the same time one goodwife Weed gave her a white Cat, telling her, that if she would deny God, and affirme the same by her bloud, then whomsoever she cursed and sent that Cat unto, they should dye shortly after. Whereupon the said Examinate saith that shee did deny God, and in affirmation thereof shee pricked her finger with a thorne, whence issued bloud, which the Cat presently licked, and the said gooodwife (*sic*) Weed named the Cat *Tissy*. And she further saith, that she killed the said Dog and Cat about a yeare since.—Joan Wallis of Keiston said [that the Devil came to her] and shee asked what his name was, and he said his name was Blackeman, and asked her if she were poore, and she said I; then he told her he would send one Grissell and Greedigut to her, that shall do any thing for her. And after Blackman was departed from her, within three or four dayes, Grissell and Greedigut came to her, in the shapes of dogges with great brisles of hogges haire upon their backs.' The accounts given by John Winnick, Ellen Shepheard, and Anne Desborough suggest that they are confused amplifications of the ritual to be observed in taking a familiar, the ritual being clearly given in the confession of Francis Moore when she was presented with the cat Tissy. John Winnick said, 'On a Friday being in the barne [where he lost his purse] there appeared unto him a Spirit, blacke and shaggy, and having pawes like a Beare, but in bulk not fully so big as a Coney. The Spirit asked him what he ailed to be so sorrowfull, this Examinate answered that he had lost a purse and money, and knew not how to come by it againe. The Spirit replied, if you will forsake God and Christ, and fall down and worship me for your God, I will help you to your purse and mony againe: This Examinate said he would, and thereupon fell down upon his knees and held up his hands. Then the Spirit said, tomorrow about this time of the day, you shall find your purse. Whereupon at the time prefixed, this Examinate went unto the place, and found his purse upon the floore and tooke it up, and looking afterwards into it, he found there all the money that was formerly lost: but before he had looked into it, the same Spirit appears unto him, and

said, there is your purse and your money in it: and then this Examinate
fell downe upon his knees and said, my Lord and God I thanke you.
The said Spirit at that time brought with him two other Spirits, for
shape, bignesse, and colour, the one like a white Cat, the other like a
grey Coney: and while this Examinate was upon his knees, the Beare
Spirit spake to him, saying, you must worship these two Spirits as you
worship me, and take them for your Gods also: then this Examinate
directed his bodie towards them, and call'd them his Lords and Gods.
Then the Beare Spirit told him that when he dyed he must have his
soule, whereunto this Examinate yielded. Hee told him then also that
they must suck of his body, to which this Examinate also yielded.—
Ellen Shepheard saith that about five years since, when she was in her
homsted at Molesworth, there appeared unto her a Spirit, somewhat
like a Rat, but not fully so big, of an iron-grey colour, and said you
must goe with me, and she said, I will not, avoid Satan, and thereupon
he went away. Shee saith, that within a short time after, going into the
field, cursing, and fretting, and blaspheming, there appeared three
Spirits more with the former in the fashion of Rats, of an iron-grey,
and said, you must forsake God and Christ, and goe with me, and take
those Spirits for your Gods, and you shall have all happinesse,
whereunto she consented: And moreover they said unto her, that when
she dyed, they must have her body and soule, and said they must have
blood from her, which she granted, and thereupon they sucked her
upon and about her hippes.—Anne Desborough confesseth, that about
thirty yeares since, the first weeke of Cleane Lent, there appeared unto
her a thing some-what bigger than a Mouse, of a brown colour, and of
the likenesse of a mouse. This was while shee lived at Tichmarsh in
the County of Northampton: she being there in bed, and in a dreame,
the said likenesse then gave her a nip, and thereby awakened her out
of her dreame, and then told her (when she was awakened) that it must
have part of her soule; whereupon she was in a great feare, and gave
him no answer, but prayed to God, and thereupon it vanished away
from her. About five dayes after, the same Mouse appeared to her
againe, bringing with it another Mouse, about the bignesse of an
ordinary Mouse, or very little bigger, browne like the former, save

only that the latter had some white about the belly, whereas the former was all browne. Then the Mouse that first appeared, said, we must sucke of your body. She yielded to them, and said, they should; upon her yielding, they went to her and sucked of her bodie, where the markes are found. The bigger mouse she called Tib, and the lesser Jone. Tib told her that she must forsake God and Christ, and take them for her Gods, telling her that when she dyed, they must have her soule, to all which she yielded.'[853]

In Cambridgeshire in 1647 Dorothy Ellis 'saith that about thirtie yeares since shee being much troubled in her minde there appeared unto hir the Devell in the liknes of a great catt and speak unto this ex[t] and demanded of hir hir blood w[ch] she gave hime after which the spirit in the liknes of a catt suck upon the body of this ex[t] and the first thing this ex[t] commanded her spirit to doe was to goe and be witch four of the cattell of Tho. Hitch all which cattell presently died '.[854] John Palmer of St. Albans in 1649, 'upon his compact with the Divel, received a flesh brand, or mark, upon his side, which gave suck to two familiars, the one in the form of a dog, which he called George, and the other in the likeness of a woman, called Jezebell.'[855] Of the Somerset witches in 1664, Alice Duke 'confesseth that her Familiar doth commonly suck her right Breast about seven at night, in the shape of a little Cat of a dunnish colour, which is as smooth as a Want, and when she is suckt, she is in a kind of a Trance.—Christian Green saith, The Devil doth usually suck her left Brest about five of the Clock in the Morning in the likeness of an Hedghog, bending, and did so on Wednesday Morning last. She saith that it is painful to her, and that she is usually in a trance when she is suckt.'[856] In 1665 Abre Grinset of Dunwich in Suffolk 'did confess that the Devil did appear in the form of a Pretty handsom Young Man first; and since Appeareth to her

---

[853] Davenport, pp. 1-12.
[854] Gibbons, p. 113.
[855] Gerish, *The Divel's Delusions*, p. 12.
[856] Glanvil, pt. ii, pp. 151, 157.

in the form of a blackish Gray Cat or Kitling, that it sucketh of a Tett and hath drawn blood.'[857]

The only published account of the animal familiar in France shows a combination of the two classes, for the creature was a toad kept in the house, fed in a particular way, and used for divination.

Silvain Nevillon and Gentien le Clerc were tried at Orleans in 1614. Silvain confessed—

'qu'il y a des Sorciers qui nourrissent des Marionettes, qui sont de petits Diableteaux en forme de Crapaux, & leur font manger de la bouillie composée de laict & de farine, & leur donnent le premier mourceau, & n'oseroient s'absenter de leur maison sans leur demander congé, & luy faut dire combien de temps ils seront absens, comme trois ou quatre iours, & si elles disent que c'est trop, ceux qui les gardent, n'osent faire leur voyage ny outre-passer leur volonté. Et quand ils veulent aller en marchandise ou ioüer, & sçauoir s'il y fera bon, ils regardent si les-dites Marionettes sont ioyeuses, en ce cas ils vont en marchandise, ou ioüer: mais si elles sont maussades & tristes, ils ne bougent de la maison.—Gentil ou Gentiẽ le Clerc dit qu'il y auoit plus d'acquest en sa Marionette qu'en Dieu. Et auoit veu souuent la Marionette dudit Neuillon, qui est comme vn gros crapaut tout noir, comme d'vne fourrure noire, & estoit dans vne boëtte caché soubs vn carreau, qui sautoit & leuoit quand on vouloit donner à manger audit crapaut. Qu'il l'a veu encore puis six sepmaines en la ruelle du lict dudict Neuillon, & qu'il a veu qu'il l'apportoit vne autre fois dans son manteau, qu'il luy a dit vne douzaine de fois, que s'il vouloit il luy en feroit auoir vne. Qu'il y auoit plus profit en icelle qu'en Dieu, & qu'il gagneroit rien à regarder Dieu: mais que sa Marionette luy apportoit tousiours quelque chose.'[858] With this may be compared the account of a Lapp familiar in 1653: 'Dans chaque maison il y a un gros chat noir, duquel ils font grand estime, parlant à luy comme s'il avoit de la raison, ne font rien qu'il ne luy communique, croyans qu'il leur aide en leurs entreprises, ne manquans tous les soirs de sortir de leurs cabannes pour le consulter, & les suit par tout où ils vont, tant à la

---

[857] Petto, p. 18.
[858] De Lancre, L'Incredulité, pp. 801, 803.

pesche qu'à la chasse. Quoy que cet animal ait la figure d'un chat par son regard, qui est épouvantable, j'ay creu & croy encore que c'est un Diable familier.'

3. Methods of obtaining Familiars

There seem to have been four methods of obtaining familiars: 1, by gift from the Devil; 2, by gift from a fellow-witch; 3, by inheritance; 4, by magical ceremonies. Of these, Nos. 2 and 3 appear to be confined to the domestic familiar, consequently they are found chiefly in the eastern counties of England.

1. The gift of the Devil was sometimes a divining familiar, sometimes a domestic familiar, commonly presented at the admission ceremony. As the divining familiar it represented the Devil himself, and the 'responses' received to questions were believed to come from him. As the essential point of this class of familiar was that it should be a species of animals and not one special animal, the devil merely appointed to the witch what species she should observe in divining. The domestic familiar, being a small animal, could be actually given into the hands of the witch, with instructions for its feeding and for the method of using it. It was sometimes, but not always, identified with the devil, and was usually[859]called an 'imp',[860] perhaps with the idea of a small or miniature Devil, like the Marionette of Silvain Nevillon. It acted as the Devil's substitute when he himself was not present, and was endowed with some, though not all, of his power; for this reason the witch often had more than one familiar, each to serve a single purpose. In 1645 at Ipswich Mother Lakeland confessed that after she had signed the covenant with the Devil, 'he furnished her with three Imps, two little Dogs and a Mole.'[861] In the same year, Rebecca Jones, an Essex witch,

'saith, that as shee was going to St Osyth to sell her masters butter, a man met with her, being in a ragged sute, and having such great eyes,

---

[859] La Martinière, pp. 42-3 (ed. 1671).

[860] Imp = A slip, sapling, scion; hence applied to persons with the meaning child, lad, boy.

[861] *Lawes against Witches*, p 7.

that this examinant was much afraid of him; who came to this examinant and gave her three things like to moules, having foure feet a piece, but without tayles, and of a black colour, and bid this examinant nurse the said three things, untill he did desire them againe; And the said man told this examinant, that those three things which he gave her, would avenge her on her enemies, and bid her murther some, but not too many, and he would forgive her; and then went away from this examinant.'[862]

In 1646 the Huntingdonshire witch, Joane Wallis, said that Blackman 'told her he would send one Grissell and Greedigut to her, that shall do any thing for her. And after Blackman was departed from her, within three or four dayes, Grissell and Greedigut came to her, in the shapes of dogges.'[863] Another witch of the same Coven, Elizabeth Weed, confessed that 'there did appeare unto her three Spirits, one in the likenesse of a young man or boy, and the other two of two Puppies, the one white and the other black.'[864]

2. The gift from a fellow-witch was always a domestic familiar, as to the Devil alone belonged the power of appointing a divining familiar; therefore this method of obtaining a familiar is found only in the eastern counties and other places where the domestic or sucking familiar is recorded. In 1556 Elizabeth Francis, whose evidence was corroborated by Mother Waterhouse, said that 'she came to one mother Waterhouse her neighbour, she brought her this cat in her apron and taught her as she was instructed by her grandmother Eue, telling her that she must cal him Sathan and geue him of her bloude and bread and milke as before.—Mother Waterhouse said, she receyued this cat of this Frances wife in the order as is before sayde.'[865] In 1566 John Walsh, the Dorset witch, 'being demaunded whether he had euer any Familiar or no: he sayth that he had one of his sayde mayster. He being demaunded howe long he had the vse of the Familiar: He sayd one

---

[862] Howell, iv, 855.
[863] Davenport, p. 12.
[864] Id., p. 1.
[865] *Witches at Chelmsford*, pp. 20, 29.

yeare by his sayd maister's life, and iiii yeres after his death.'[866] An Essex witch in 1588 had three familiars, 'one like a cat, which she called Lightfoot. This Lightfoote, she said, one mother Barlie, of W., solde her aboue sixteene yeares ago, for an ouen cake, and told her the Cat would do her good seruice, if she woulde, she might send her of her errand.'[867] At Orleans in 1614 Gentil le Clerc said that he had seen Nevillon's familiar, and that Nevillon 'luy a dit vne douzaine de fois, que s'il vouloit il luy en feroit auoir vne'.[868] Elizabeth Clarke in Essex in 1645 said she 'had three impes from her mother, which were of a broune colour, and two from old beldam Weste. The said Anne Weste seemed much to pitie this examinant for her lamenesse (having but one leg) and her poverty; And said to this examinant, That there was wayes and meanes for her to live much better then now shee did: And said, that shee would send to this examinant a thing like a little kitlyn, which would fetch home some victualls for this examinant; and that it should doe her no hurt.'[869] The Huntingdonshire witch, Francis Moore, in 1646, 'saith that about eight yeares since she received a little blacke puppy from one Margaret Simson of great Catworth. The Examinate further saith, that the said Margaret told her, that she must keep that dogge all her life time; and if she cursed any Cattell, and set the same dog upon them, they should presently dye. And the said Examinate further saith, that about the same time one goodwife Weed gave her a white Cat, telling her, that if she would deny God, and affirme the same by her bloud, then whomsoever she cursed and sent that Cat unto, they should dye shortly after.'[870]

3. The profession of the witch-religion being hereditary, it is not uncommon to find that the familiar descended from mother to daughter. This, like the familiar given by one witch to another, was the domestic familiar. It was sometimes presented during the mother's lifetime or was left as a legacy at her death. Elizabeth Francis in 1556

---

[866] *Examination of John Walsh.* His master was Sir Robert Draiton.

[867] Giffard, p. C., see *Percy Soc.*, viii.

[868] De Lancre, *L'Incredulité*, p. 803.

[869] Howell, iv, 834, 836.

[870] Davenport, p. 5.

stated that 'she learned this arte of witchcraft at the age of xii yeres of hyr grandmother whose nam mother Eue of Hatfyelde Peuerell, disseased. Item when shee taughte it her, she counseiled her to renounce GOD and his worde and to geue of her bloudde to Sathan (as she termed it) whyche she delyuered her in the lykenesse of a whyte spotted Catte.'[871] In 1582 Ales Hunt of St. Osyth confessed to having two spirits, and 'saith, that her sister (named Margerie Sammon) hath also two spirites like Toades, the one called Tom, and the other Robbyn: And saith further, her sayde Syster and shee had the sayd spyrites of their Mother, Mother Barnes.'[872] In 1597 the Derbyshire witch, Alse Gooderidge, stated that 'the Diuell appeared to me in lykenesse of a little partie-colored dog red and white, and I called him Minny. She saide she had her familiar of her mother.'[873] The Essex witches, tried in 1645, also inherited familiars from their mothers. Anne Cooper confessed 'that she the said Anne offered to give unto her daughter Sarah Cooper an impe in the likenes of a gray kite (i.e. kit, or cat), to suck on the said Sarah.—Susan Cock saith, that about three or four yeeres since, one Margery Stoakes, this examinants mother, lying upon her death-bed, and this examinant comming to visit her, shee the said Margery desired this examinant privately to give entertainment to two of her imps, and withall told this examinant, they would do this examinant good; And this examinant saith, that the same night her said mother dyed, the said two imps came to her accordingly, and sucked on her body.—Anne Cate saith, That she hath four familiars, which shee had from her mother, about two and twenty yeeres since.'[874] In 1667 at Liverpool, 'Margaret Loy, being arraigned for a witch, confessed she was one; and when she was asked how long she had so been, replied, Since the death of her mother, who died thirty years ago; and at her decease she had nothing to leave her, and this widow Bridge, that were sisters, but her two spirits; and named them, the eldest spirit to this widow, and the other spirit to her

[871] *Witches at Chelmsford*, p. 24. Philobiblon Soc., viii.
[872] *Witches taken at St. Oses*, p. C 4.
[873] *Alse Gooderidge*, pp. 26, 27.
[874] Howell, iv, 845, 853, 856.

the said Margaret Loy.'[875] This inheritance of a familiar may be compared with the Lapp custom: 'The Laplanders bequeath their Demons as part of their inheritance, which is the reason that one family excels another in this magical art.'[876]

4. The method of obtaining a familiar by means of magical words or actions is clearly described in two modern examples:

'Sometime in the beginning of the last century, two old dames attended the morning service at Llanddewi Brefi Church, and partook of the Holy Communion; but instead of eating the sacred bread like other communicants, they kept it in their mouths and went out. Then they walked round the Church outside nine times, and at the ninth time the Evil One came out from the Church wall in the form of a frog, to whom they gave the bread from their mouths, and by doing this wicked thing they were supposed to be selling themselves to Satan and become witches.—There was an old man in North Pembrokeshire, who used to say that he obtained the power of bewitching in the following manner: The bread of his first Communion he pocketed. He made pretence at eating it first of all, and then put it in his pocket. When he went out from the service there was a dog meeting him by the gate, to which he gave the bread, thus selling his soul to the Devil. Ever after, he possessed the power to bewitch.'[877]

On the analogy of these two examples, I suggest that in the accounts of familiars offering themselves to the witch, there was, previous to such appearance, some formula of words or some magical action which are not recorded. The animal, which first appeared after such words or actions, would be considered as the Devil, as in the two cases quoted above. Such an explanation accounts for the statements of some of the witches that on the appearance of the animal they at once renounced the Christian religion and vowed obedience to the new God. It is noticeable that in many cases the accused acknowledged

[875] *Moore Rental*, Chetham Society, xii, p. 59.
[876] Scheffer, quoting Tornaeus.
[877] Davies, p. 231. For a similar practice in modern England, see *Transactions of the Devonshire Association*, vi (1874), p. 201.

that, before the appearance of the animal, they had been 'banning and cursing', in other words, calling on the Devil; the appearance of the animal, after such summons, produced neither surprise nor alarm, and in fact seems to have been regarded as the effect of their words.

In 1556 Joan Waterhouse, the eighteen-year-old daughter of the witch Mother Waterhouse, of Hatfield Peveril, being angry with another girl, 'shee goinge home dydde as she had seene her mother doe, callynge Sathan, whiche came to her (as she sayd) in the lykenes of a great dogge'.[878] At Aberdeen in 1597 Agnes Wobster said that the Devil appeared 'in the liknes of a lamb, quhom thow callis thy God, and bletit on the, and thaireftir spak to the'.[879] James Device, one of the chief of the Lancashire witches in 1613, confessed 'that vpon Sheare Thursday was two yeares, his Grand-Mother Elizabeth Sothernes, alias Dembdike, did bid him this Examinate goe to the Church to receiue the Communion (the next day after being Good Friday) and then not to eate the Bread the Minister gaue him, but to bring it and deliuer it to such a thing as should meet him in his way homewards: Notwithstanding her perswasions, this Examinate did eate the Bread; and so in his comming homeward some fortie roodes off the said Church, there met him a thing in the shape of a Hare, who spoke vnto this Examinate, and asked him whether hee had brought the Bread.'[880] In 1621 Elizabeth Sawyer, the witch of Edmonton, said that 'the first time that the Diuell came vnto me was, when I was cursing, swearing, and blaspheming'.[881] The evidence of the Huntingdonshire witches, John Winnick and Ellen Shepheard, in 1646 (see above, p. 219), and of Dorothy Ellis of Cambridgeshire in 1647, also show that the animal which appeared to the witch after an access of emotion was at once acknowledged as God and accepted as the familiar. Mary Osgood of Andover in 1692 'confesses that about 11 years ago, when she was in a melancholy state and condition, she used to walk abroad in her orchard; and upon a certain time, she saw the

---

[878] *Witches at Chelmsford*, p. 34. Philobiblon Soc., viii.
[879] *Spalding Club Misc.*, i, p. 129.
[880] Potts, H 3.
[881] Goodcole, *Wonderfull Discoverie*, p. C.

appearance of a cat, at the end of the house, which yet she thought was a real cat. However, at that time, it diverted her from praying to God, and instead thereof she prayed to the devil.[882]

The familiars in human form were human beings usually of the sex opposite to that of the witch. As these familiars were generally called 'Devils' it is sometimes difficult to distinguish them from the Grand-master;[883] but the evidence, taken as a whole, suggests that at certain parts of the ritual every individual of the company was known as a Devil. This suggestion is borne out in the modern survival of an ancient dance in the Basses-Pyrénées, where the dancers to this day are called Satans.[884]

Lady Alice Kyteler, in 1324, was accused that the Devil came to her 'quandoque in specie cujusdam aethiopis cum duobus sociis'.[885] In 1598 the Lyons witches, Thievenne Paget and Antoine Tornier, speak of 'leurs Demons' as distinct from the great Devil, and the evidence of all the other witches shows that 'il y a encor des Demons, qui assistent à ces danses'.[886] De Lancre says that there was more than one Devil: the great one, who was called Maître Leonard, and a little one called Maître Jean Mullin. It was this smaller Devil who held the meetings in the absence of the Chief:

'en la place du Grãd maistre, il n'y auoit qu'vn petit Diable ou Demon qui n'auoit point de cornes, lequel ne contentoit pas la compagnie comme son maistre. Qu'elles n'auoient tant de confiance en toute la trouppe des mauuais Anges qu'en celuy seul qu'ils auoient accoustumé d'adorer & seruir.—À table on se sied selon sa qualité, ayant chacun son Demon assis auprés, & parfois vis à vis. Et quand ils ont mangé, chaque Demon prèd sa disciple par la main, & danse auec elle.'[887]

In 1618 Joan Willimott of Leicester confessed 'that shee hath a Spirit which shee calleth Pretty, which was giuen vnto her by William

---

[882] J. Hutchinson, ii, p. 31; Howell, vi, 659.
[883] 'Nos sorciers tiennent la plus-part de ces Demons pour leurs Dieux,' De Lancre, *Tableau*, p. 23.
[884] Moret, pp. 247 seq.
[885] Camden Soc., *Dame Alice Kyteler*, p. 3
[886] Boguet, pp. 69, 132.
[887] De Lancre, *Tableau*, pp. 67, 197.

Berry, whom she serued three yeares; the Spirit stood vpon the ground in the shape and forme of a Woman, which Spirit did aske of her her Soule, which shee then promised vnto it, being willed thereunto by her Master'.[888] In 1633, Margaret Johnson, the Lancashire witch, stated that 'besides theire particular familiars or spirits, there was one greate or grand devill, or spirit, more eminent than the rest. Shee allsoe saith, yt if a witch have but one marke, shee hath but one spirit; if two, then two spirits; if three, yet but two spirits. Shee alsoe saith, that men witches usually have women spirits, and women witches men spirits.'[889] In 1649 at St. Albans a man witch had 'two familiars, the one in the form of a dog, which he called George, and the other in the likeness of a woman, called Jezebell'.[890]In 1662 at Auldearne Issobell Gowdie confessed

'ther is threttein persones in ilk Coeven; and ilk on of vs has an Sprit to wait wpon ws, quhan ve pleas to call wpon him. I remember not all the Spritis names; bot thair is on called Swein, quhilk waitis wpon the said Margret Wilson in Aulderne; he is still [always] clothed in grass-grein. The nixt Sprit is called Rorie, who waitis wpon Bessie Wilsone, in Aulderne; he is still clothed in yallow. The third Sprit is called The Roring Lyon, who waitis wpon Issobell Nicoll, in Lochlow, and he is still clothed in sea-grein. The fowrth Spirit is called Mak Hector, qwho waitis wpon Jean Martein, dawghter to the said Margret Wilson; he is a yowng-lyk Devill, clothed still in grass-grein.... The nam of the fyft Sprit is Robert the Rule, and he still clothed in sadd-dun, and seimis to be a Comander of the rest of the Spritis; and he waittis wpon Margret Brodie, in Aulderne. The name of the saxt Sprit is called Thieff of Hell, Wait wpon Hir Selfe; and he waitis also on the said Bessie Wilson. The name of the sevinth Sprit is called The Read Reiver; and he is my owin Spirit, that waittis on my selfe, and is still clothed in blak. The aucht Spirit is called Robert the Jackis, still clothed in dune, and seimes to be aiged. He is ane glaiked gowked Spirit. The nynth Spirit is called Laing. The tenth Spirit is named

---

[888] *Wonderfull Discoverie of Margaret and Phillip Flower*, E 3.
[889] Whitaker, p. 216.
[890] Gerish, *The Divel's Delusions*, p. 12.

Thomas a Fearie, &c.[891] Ther wilbe many vther Divellis, waiting wpon our Maister Divell; bot he is bigger and mor awfull than the rest of the Divellis, and they all reverence him. I will ken them all, on by on, from vtheris, quhan they appeir lyk a man.'

In a later confession Issobell gave the names more fully. 'The names of owr Divellis that waited wpon ws, ar thes. First, Robert, the Jakis; Sanderis, the Read Reaver; Thomas, the Fearie; Swein, the roaring Lion; Thieffe of Hell, wait wpon hir self; Makhectour; Robert, the Rule; Hendrie Laing; and Rorie.'[892] In Connecticut in 1662 'Robert Sterne testifieth as followeth: I saw this woman goodwife Seager in ye woods wth three more women and with them I saw two black creatures like two Indians but taller. I saw the women dance round these black creatures and whiles I looked upon them one of the women G. Greensmith said looke who is yonder and then they ran away up the hill. I stood still and ye black things came towards mee and then I turned to come away.'[893]

4. Transformations into Animals

The belief that human beings can change themselves, or be changed, into animals carries with it the corollary that wounds received by a person when in the semblance of an animal will remain on the body after the return to human shape. This belief seems to be connected with the worship of animal-gods or sacred animals, the worshipper being changed into an animal by being invested with the skin of the creature, by the utterance of magical words, by the making of magical gestures, the wearing of a magical object, or the performance of magical ceremonies. The witches of the sixteenth and seventeenth centuries appear to have carried on the tradition of the pre-Christian cults; and the stories of their transformations, when viewed in the light of the ancient examples, are capable of the same explanation. Much confusion, however, has been caused by the

---

[891] Pitcairn notes: 'Issobell, as usual, appears to have been stopped short here by her interrogators, when she touched on such matters', i.e. the fairies.

[892] Pitcairn, iii, pp. 606, 614.

[893] Taylor, p. 81.

religious and so-called scientific explanations of the contemporary commentators, as well as by the unfortunate belief of modern writers in the capacity of women for hysteria. At both periods pseudo-science has prevented the unbiassed examination of the material.

There are no records extant of the animals held sacred by the early inhabitants of Great Britain, but it is remarkable that the range of the witches' transformations was very limited; cats and hares were the usual animals, occasionally but rarely dogs, mice, crows, rooks, and bees. In France, where the solemn sacrifice of a goat at the Sabbath points to that animal being sacred, it is not surprising to find both men and women witches appearing as goats and sheep. Unless there were some definite meaning underlying the change of shape, there would be no reason to prevent the witches from transforming themselves into animals of any species. It would seem then that the witches, like the adorers of animal gods in earlier times, attempted to become one with their god or sacred animal by taking on his form; the change being induced by the same means and being as real to the witch as to Sigmund the Volsung[894] or the worshipper of Lycaean Zeus.[895]

In the earlier cults the worshipper, on becoming an animal, changed his outward shape to the eye of faith alone, though his actions and probably his voice proclaimed the transformation. The nearest approach to an outward change was by covering the body with the skin of the animal, or by wearing a part of the skin or a mask. The witches themselves admitted that they were masked and veiled, and the evidence of other witnesses goes to prove the same. Boguet suggests that the disguise was used to hide their identity, which was possibly the case at times, but it seems more probable, judging by the evidence, that the masking and veiling were for ritual purposes.

In Lorraine in 1589 a male witness stated that 'indem wird er eine Höle, welche sie nennen die Morelianische Klippe, gewahr, darinnen

---

[894] *Volsunga Saga*, Bks. I, II; Wm. Morris, *Collected Works*, xii, pp. 32. 77.
[895] Pausanias, viii, 2, 3, 6, ed. Frazer. Cp. also the animal names applied to priests and priestesses, e.g. the King-bees of Ephesus; the Bee-priestesses of Demeter, of Delphi, of Proserpine, and of the Great Mother; the Doves of Dodona; the Bears in the sacred dance of Artemis; the Bulls at the feast of Poseidon at Ephesus; the Wolves at the Lupercalia, &c.

sechs Weiber mit Larven umb ein Tisch voll guldernen und silbernen Geschieren herumb tanzten'.—Bernhardt's Nicolaea said that she had seen in an open field 'mitten am hellen Tage, einen Tantz von Männern und Weibern, und weil dieselben auff eine besondere Weise und hinterrücks tantzten, kam es ihr frembd für, stunde derhalben still, und sahe mit allem Fleiss zu da ward sie gewahr, das etliche in dem Reyhen waren so Geiss und Kuhfuss hatten'.[896] At North Berwick in 1590 seven score witches 'danced endlong the Kirk yard. John Fian, missellit [muffled, masked] led the ring.'[897] The witches whom Boguet examined in 1598 confessed to using masks: 'Les Sorciers dansent doz côtre doz, pour ne pas estre recogneus; pour la mesme raison ils se masquent encor' auiourd'huy pour la plus part.—Ils se masquent pour le iour d'huy, selon que Clauda Paget l'a confessé, & auec elle plusieurs autres.—Estienne Poicheux rapportoit que partie des femmes, qu'elle auoit veuës au Sabbat, estaient voilées. Et pour cela aussi les Lombards par leurs loix les appellent *Mascas*.'[898] In 1609 de Lancre points out that in the Basses-Pyrénées there were two grades of witches: 'Il y en a de deux sortes. Aucũs sont voilez pour doñer opinion aux pauures que ce sont des Princes & grãds seigneurs. Les autres sont decouuerts & tout ouuertemêt dãcent, & ceux cy ne sont si prés du maistre, si fauoris ne si employez.'[899] In 1613 Barbe, the wife of Jean-Remy Colin de Moyemont, said that 'elle a veu dancer les assistans en nombre de sept à huict personnes, partie desquelles elle ne cognoissoit ad cause des masques hideux qu'elles auoient de noire.'[900]

Josine Deblicq in Hainault (1616) was asked, 'Que savez vous de la troisième danse? R. Elle eut lieu au Rond-Chêneau, sur le chemin de Nivelles, près d'une fontaine. Il y avait bien 21 ou 22 femmes, toutes masquées, chacune avec son amoureux accoutré d'un déguisement bleu, jaune ou noir.'[901] In 1652 a French witch 'dist qu'elles dansoient

---

[896] Remigius, pt. i, pp. 65, 67.
[897] Pitcairn, i, pt. ii, pp. 245-6.
[898] Boguet, pp. 120, 132-3.
[899] De Lancre, *Tableau*, p. 129.
[900] Fournier, p. 16.
[901] Monoyer, p. 30.

les dots l'une à l'autre et qu'au milieux il y auoit vne feme masquée tenant vne chandelle'.[902]

It will be seen from the above that the witches were often disguised at the dance, a fact strongly suggesting that the masking was entirely ritual. As the witch trials in Great Britain seldom mention, much less describe, the dance, it follows that the greater number of the cases of masks are found in France, though a few occur in Scotland, still fewer in England.

The transformation by means of an animal's skin or head is mentioned in the *Liber Poenitentialis* of Theodore in 668 (see p. 21). It continued among the witches, and in 1598 in the Lyons district 'il y a encor des Demons, qui assistent à ces danses en forme de boucs, ou de moutons. Antoine Tornier dit, que lors qu'elle dansoit, vn mouton noir la tenoit par la main auec ses pieds bien haireux, c'est à dire rudes & reuesches'.[903]

In many cases it is very certain that the transformation was ritual and not actual; that is to say the witches did not attempt to change their actual forms but called themselves cats, hares, or other animals. In the Aberdeen trials of 1596-7 the accused are stated to have 'come to the Fish Cross of this burgh, under the conduct of Sathan, ye all danced about the Fish Cross and about the Meal market a long space'. Here there is no suggestion of any change of form, yet in the accusation against Bessie Thom, who was tried for the same offence, the dittay states that 'there, accompanied with thy devilish companions and faction, transformed in other likeness, some in hares, some in cats, and some in other similitudes, ye all danced about the Fish Cross'.[904] In 1617 in Guernsey Marie Becquet said that 'every time that she went to the Sabbath, the Devil came to her, and it seemed as though he transformed her into a female dog'.[905] Again at Alloa in 1658, Margret Duchall, describing the murder of Cowdan's bairns, said 'after they

---

[902] Van Elven, v, p. 215.

[903] Boguet, p. 132.

[904] *Spalding Club Misc.*, i, pp. 97, 114-15, 165; Bessie Thom, p. 167. Spelling modernized.

[905] Goldsmid, p. 10.

war turned all in the liknes of cattis, they went in ouer Jean Lindsayis zaird Dyk and went to Coudans hous, whair scho declared, that the Dewill being with tham went up the stair first with margret tailzeor Besse Paton and elspit blak'. On the other hand, Jonet Blak and Kathren Renny, who were also present and described the same scene, said nothing about the cat-form, though they particularize the clothes of the other witches. Jonet Blak said, 'the diwell, margret tailzeor with ane long rok, and kathren renny with the short rok and the bony las with the blak pok all went up the stair togidder'; while Kathren Renny said that 'ther was ane bony las with ane blak pok, who went befor ower Jean Lindsayis zaird dyk and Margret tailzeor with hir'.[906] The evidence of Marie Lamont (1662) suggests the same idea of a ritual, though not an actual, change; 'shee confessed, that shee, Kettie Scot, and Margrat Holm, cam to Allan Orr's house in the likenesse of kats, and followed his wif into the chalmer'; and on another occasion 'the devil turned them in likeness of kats, by shaking his hands above their heads'.[907] In Northumberland (1673) the same fact appears to underlie the evidence. Ann Armstrong declared that at a witch meeting Ann Baites 'hath been severall times in the shape of a catt and a hare, and in the shape of a greyhound and a bee, letting the divell see how many shapes she could turn herself into.—They [the witches] stood all upon a bare spott of ground, and bid this informer sing whilst they danced in severall shapes, first of a haire, then in their owne, and then in a catt, sometimes in a mouse, and in severall other shapes.—She see all the said persons beforemencioned danceing, some in the likenesse of haires, some in the likenesse of catts, others in the likenesse of bees, and some in their owne likenesse.'[908]

The method of making the ritual change by means of magical words is recorded in the Auldearne trials, where Isobel Gowdie, whose evidence was purely voluntary, gives the actual words both for the change into an animal and for the reversion into human form. To become a hare:

---

[906] *Scottish Antiquary*, ix, pp. 50-2.
[907] Sharpe, pp. 132, 134.
[908] *Surtees Soc.*, xl, pp. 191, 193, 194.

'I sall goe intill ane haire,With sorrow, and sych, and meikle
caire,And I sall goe in the Divellis nam,Ay whill I com hom againe.'
To become a cat or a crow the same verse was used with an alteration
of the second line so as to force a rhyme; instead of 'meikle caire', the
words were 'a blak shot' for a cat, and 'a blak thraw' for a crow or craw.
To revert again to the human form the words were:
'Hare, hare, God send thee care.I am in an hare's likeness just
now,But I shall be in a woman's likeness even now',
with the same variation of 'a black shot' or 'a black thraw' for a cat or
a crow. The Auldearne witches were also able to turn one another into
animals:

'If we, in the shape of an cat, an crow, an hare, or any other likeness,
&c., go to any of our neighbours houses, being Witches, we will say,
I (or we) conjure thee Go with us (or me). And presently they become
as we are, either cats, hares, crows, &c., and go with us whither we
would. When one of us or more are in the shape of cats, and meet with
any others our neighbours, we will say, Devil speed thee, Go thou with
me. And immediately they will turn in the shape of a cat, and go with
us.'[909]

The very simplicity of the method shows that the transformation
was ritual; the witch announced to her fellow that she herself was an
animal, a fact which the second witch would not have known
otherwise; the second witch at once became a similar animal and went
with the first to perform the ritual acts which were to follow. The
witches were in their own estimation and in the belief of all their
comrades, to whom they communicated the fact, actually animals,
though to the uninitiated eye their natural forms remained unchanged.
This is probably the explanation of Marie d'Aspilcouette's evidence,
which de Lancre records in 1609:

'Elle a veu aussi les sorcieres insignes se changer en plusieurs sortes
de bestes, pour faire peur à ceux qu'elles rencontroient: Mais celles
qui se transformoyent ainsi, disoyent qu'elles n'estoyent veritablement
transformees, mais seulement qu'elles sembloyent l'estre &

---

[909] Pitcairn, iii, pp. 607, 608, 611. Spelling modernized.

neantmoins pendant qu'elles sont ainsi en apparences bestes, elles ne parlent du tout point'.[910]

The best example of transformation by means of a magical object placed on the person is from Northumberland (1673), where Ann Armstrong stated that 'Anne Forster come with a bridle, and bridled her and ridd upon her crosse-leggd, till they come to [the] rest of her companions. And when she light of her back, pulld the bridle of this informer's head, now in the likenesse of a horse; but, when the bridle was taken of, she stood up in her owne shape.... This informant was ridden upon by an inchanted bridle by Michael Aynsly and Margaret his wife, Which inchanted bridle, when they tooke it of from her head, she stood upp in her owne proper person.... Jane Baites of Corbridge come in the forme of a gray catt with a bridle hanging on her foote, and bridled her, and rid upon her in the name of the devill.'[911] This is again a clear account of the witch herself and her companions believing in the change of form caused by the magical object in exactly the same way that the shamans believe in their own transformation by similar means.

The Devil had naturally the same power as the witches, but in a greater degree. The evidence of Marie Lamont quoted above shows that he transformed them into animals by a gesture only. It seems possible that this was also the case with Isobel Shyrie at Forfar (1661), who was called 'Horse' and 'the Devil's horse'. The name seems to have given rise to the idea that 'she was shod like a mare or a horse'; she was in fact the officer or messenger who brought her companions to the meetings. She was never seen in the form of a horse, her transformation being probably effected by the Devil, in order that she might 'carry' the witches to and from the meetings; Agnes Spark said that Isobel 'carried her away to Littlemiln, [and] carried her back again to her own house'.[912]

There is also another method of transformation, which is the simplest. The witches themselves, like their contemporaries, often

---

[910] De Lancre, *Tableau*, p. 128.
[911] *Surtees Soc.*, xl, pp. 192, 194, 197.
[912] Kinloch, p. 129. Spelling modernized.

believed that the actual animals, which they saw, were human beings in animal form. Jeannette de Belloc, aged twenty-four, in the Basses-Pyrénées (1609), described the Sabbath as 'vne foire celebre de toutes sortes de choses, en laquelle aucuns se promenẽt en leur propre forme, & d'autres sont transformez ne scayt pourquoy, en animaux. Elle n'a iamais veu aucune d'elles se trãsformer en beste en sa presence, mais seulement certaines bestes courir par le sabbat.'[913] Helen Guthrie of Forfar (1661) states the case with even greater simplicity: 'The last summer except one, shee did sie John Tailzeour somtymes in the shape of a todde, and somtymes in the shape of a swyn, and that the said Johne Tailzeour in these shapes went wp and doune among William Millne, miller at Hetherstakes, his cornes for the destructioune of the same, because the said William hade taken the mylne ouer his head; and that the diuell cam to her and pointed out Johne Tailzeour in the forsaid shapes unto her, and told her that that wes Johne Tailzeour.'[914]

---

[913] De Lancre, *Tableau*, pp. 129, 130.
[914] Kinloch, p. 123.

APPENDIX I

FAIRIES AND WITCHES

The dwarf race which at one time inhabited Europe has left few concrete remains, but it has survived in innumerable stories of fairies and elves. Nothing, however, is known of the religious beliefs and cults of these early peoples, except the fact that every seven years they made a human sacrifice to their god—'And aye at every seven years they pay the teind to hell'—and that like the Khonds they stole children from the neighbouring races and brought them up to be the victims.

That there was a strong connexion between witches and fairies has been known to all students of fairy lore. I suggest that the cult of the fairy or primitive race survived until less than three hundred years ago, and that the people who practised it were known as witches. I have already pointed out that many of the witch-beliefs and practices coincide with those of an existing dwarf race, viz. the Lapps. The Devil and the witches entered freely into the fairy mounds, the Devil is often spoken of as a fairy man, and he consorts with the Queen of Elfhame; fairy gold which turns to rubbish is commonly given by the Devil to the witches; and the name Robin is almost a generic name for the Devil, either as a man or as his substitute the familiar. The other name for the fairy Robin Goodfellow is Puck, which derives through the Gaelic Bouca from the Slavic Bog, which means God.

The evidence given below shows the close connexion between the fairies and the witches, and shows also the witches' belief in the superiority of the fairies to themselves in the matter of magic and healing powers.

1431. Joan of Arc. Not far from Domremy there is a certain tree that is called the Ladies' Tree [Arbor Dominarum], others call it the Fairies' Tree [Arbor Fatalium, gallice *des Faées*], beside which is a spring [which cured fevers]. It is a great tree, a beech [fagus], from which comes the may [unde venit mayum, gallice *le beau may*]. It belongs to Seigneur Pierre de Bourlemont. Old people, not of her lineage, said that fairy-ladies haunted there [conversabantur]. Had heard her godmother Jeanne, wife of the Mayor, say she had seen fairy-women there. She herself had never seen fairies at the tree that she knew of. She made garlands at the tree, with other girls, for the image of the Blessed Mary of Domremy. Sometimes with the other children she hung garlands on the tree, sometimes they left them, sometimes they took them away. She had danced there with the other children, but not since she was grown up. She had sung there more than she had danced. She had heard that it was said 'Jeanne received her mission at the tree of the fairy-ladies'.[915] The saints [Katharine and Margaret] came and spoke to her at the spring beside the Fairies' tree, but she would not say if they came to the tree itself.[916]

Denied having a mandrake, but knew there was one near the Fairies' tree.[917]

My godmother, who saw the fairy-ladies, was held as a good woman, not a diviner or a witch.[918]

Refused to say if she believed fairies to be evil spirits.[919]

She did not put chaplets on the Fairies' tree in honour of SS. Katharine and Margaret.[920]

Had never done anything with, or knew anything of, those who came in the air with the fairies [gallice *en l'erre avec les faées*]. Had heard they came on Thursdays, but considered it witchcraft.[921]

4th Article of Accusation. Jeanne was not instructed in her youth in the belief and primitive faith, but was imbued by certain old women in the use of witchcraft, divination, and other superstitious works or magic arts; many inhabitants of those villages have been noted from antiquity for the aforesaid misdeeds. Jeanne herself has said that she had heard from her godmother, and from many people, of visions and apparitions of Fairies, or Fairy spirits [gallice*faées*]; by others also she has been taught and imbued with wicked and pernicious errors of such

---

[915] Quicherat, i, p. 67; Murray, pp. 25 6.
[916] Id., i, p. 87; M., p. 42.
[917] Id., i, pp. 88-9; M., p. 43.
[918] Id., i, p. 177; M., p. 80.
[919] Id., i, p. 178; M., 80.
[920] Id., i, p. 186; M., p. 84.
[921] Id., i, p. 187; M., p. 84.

spirits, insomuch that in the trial before you she confessed that up to this time she did not know that Fairies were evil spirits. Answer: As to the Fairy-ladies, she did not know what it was. As to instruction she learnt to believe and was well and duly taught to do what a good child should. As to her godmother she referred to what she had said before.[922]

5th Article. Near the village of Domremy is a certain great, big, and ancient tree called vulgarly The Charmed Fairy-tree of Bourlemont[923] [l'arbre charmine faée de Bourlemont]; beside the tree is a spring; round these gather, it is said, evil spirits called fairies, with whom those who use witchcraft are accustomed to dance at night, going round the tree and spring. Answer: as to the tree and spring, referred to her previous answers; denied the rest.[924]

6th Article. Jeanne frequented the said tree and spring alone, chiefly at night, sometimes in the day most often at the hour that divine service was celebrated in church, in order to be alone; and dancing went round the spring and tree; afterwards hung many garlands of various herbs and flowers on the branches of the tree, made with her own hands, saying and singing before and after, certain incantations and songs with certain invocations, witchcrafts and other misdeeds; which [garlands] the following morning, were not found. Answer: Referred for part to previous answers, denied the rest.[925]

23rd Article. Her letters showed that she had consulted evil spirits. Denied ever having done anything by inspiration of evil spirits.[926]

1566. John Walsh, of Netherberry, Dorset. He being demaunded how he knoweth when anye man is bewytched: He sayth that he knew it partlye by the Feries, and saith that ther be .iii. kindes of Feries, white, greene, and black. Which when he is disposed to vse, hee speaketh with them vpon hyls, where as there is great heapes of earth, as namely in Dorsetshire. And betwene the houres of .xii. and one at

---

[922] Id., i, p. 209; M., p. 91.

[923] Bour-le-mont, cp. Bour-jo, 'a word of unknown derivation'. See Walter Scott, *Witchcraft and Demonology*.

[924] Q., i, p. 210; M., p. 91.

[925] Q., i, pp. 211-12; M., pp. 91-2.

[926] Id., i, p. 242; M., pp. 96-7.

noone, or at midnight he vseth them. Whereof (he sayth) the blacke Feries be the woorst.[927]

1576. Bessie Dunlop of Lyne, Ayrshire. Thom Reid apperit in hir awin hous to hir, about the xij hour of the day, quhair thair was sittand thre tailzeouris, and hir awin gudeman; and he tuke hir apperoun and led hir to the dure with him, and sche followit, and zeid [went] vp with him to the kill end, quhair he forbaid hir to speik or feir for onye thing sche hard or saw; and quhene thai had gane ane lytle pece fordwerd, sche saw twelf persounes, aucht wemene and four men: The men wer cled in gentilmennis clething, and the wemene had all plaiddis round about thame, and wer verrie semelie lyke to se; and Thome was with thame: And demandit, Gif sche knew ony of thame? Ansuerit, Nane, except Thom. Demandit, What thai said to hir? Ansuerit, Thai baid hir sit down, and said, 'Welcum, Bessie, will thow go with ws?' Bot sche ansuerit nocht; becaus Thom had forbidden hir. And forder declarit, That sche knew nocht quhat purpois thai had amangis thaime, onlie sche saw thair lippis move; and within a schort space thai pairtit all away; and ane hiddeous vglie sowche of wind followit thame: and sche lay seik quhill Thom came agane bak fra thame. [In the margin, 'Confessit and fylit.'] Item, Sche being demandit, Gif sche sperit at Thom quhat persounes thai war? Ansuerit, That thai war the gude wychtis that wynnit in the Court of Elfame; quha come thair to desyre hir to go with thame: And forder, Thom desyrit hir to do the sam; quha ansuerit, 'Sche saw na proffeit to gang thai kynd of gaittis, vnles sche kend quhairfor'. Thom said, 'Seis thow nocht me, baith meit-worth, claith-worth, and gude aneuch lyke in persoun, and [he] suld make hir far better nor euer sche was?' Sche ansuerit, 'That sche duelt with hir awin husband and bairnis, and culd nocht leif thame.' And swa Thom began to be verrie crabit [angry] with hir, and said, 'Gif swa sche thocht, sche wald get lytill gude of him.' ... Interrogat, Gif sche neuir askit the questioun at him, Quhairfoir he com to hir mair [than] ane vthir bodye? Ansuerit, Remembring hir, quhen sche was lyand in chyld-bed-lair, with ane of hir laiddis, that ane stout woman com in to hir, and sat doun on the forme besyde hir, and askit ane drink at hir,

---

[927] *Examination of John Walsh.*

and sche gaif hir; quha alsua tauld hir, that that barne wald de, and that hir husband suld mend of his seiknes. The said Bessie ansuerit, that sche remembrit wele thairof; and Thom said, That was the Quene of Elfame his maistres, quha had commandit him to wait vpoun hir, and to do hir gude. Confessit and fylit.[928]

1588. Alesoun Peirsoun of Byrehill, Fifeshire. Was conuict for hanting and repairing with the gude nichtbouris and Quene of Elfame, thir diuers ȝeiris bypast, as scho had confesst be hir depositiounis, declaring that scho could nocht say reddelie how lang scho wes with thame; and that scho had friendis in that court quhilk wes of hir awin blude, quha had gude acquentance of the Quene of Elphane.... And that scho saw nocht the Quene thir sewin ȝeir: And that scho had mony guid friendis in that court, bot wer all away now: And that scho wes sewin ȝeir ewill handlit in the Court of Elfane and had kynd freindis thair, bot had na will to visseit thame eftir the end.... In Grange-mure thair come ane man to hir, cled in grene clothis, quha said to hir, Gif scho wald be faithfull, he wald do hir guid. He gaid away thane, and apperit to hir att ane vthir tyme, ane lustie mane, with mony mene and wemen with him: And that scho sanit hir and prayit, and past with thame forder nor scho could tell; and saw with thame pypeing and mirrynes and good scheir.[929]

1589. Beatrix Baonensis, in Lorraine. Etliche geben Späher, etliche Vögel oder sonst nicht viel besonders, als da sein möchte gemüntzt Geld aus Rindern Ledder, und wenn sie dergleichen nichts haben, so verschafft es ihnen ihr Geist, auf dass sie staffirt seyn.[930]

1593. Another of my neighbours had his wife much troubled, and he went to her [the white witch], and she told him his wife was haunted with a fairie.[931]

1593. She had three or foure impes, some call them puckrels, one like a grey cat, another like a weasel, another like a mouse.[932]

---

[928] Pitcairn, i, pt. ii, pp. 52-3, 56-7.
[929] Id., i, pt. ii, pp. 162-3.
[930] Remigius, pt. i, p. 55.
[931] Giffard, p. 10; *Percy Soc.* viii.
[932] Id. ib., p. 9.

1597. Christian Livingston of Leith. Scho affermit that hir dochter was tane away with the Farie-folk, and declarit to Gothrayis wyff, than being with barne, that it was a man chyld scho was with; as it provit in deid: And that all the knawlege scho had was be hir dochter, wha met with the Fairie.[933]

1597. Isobell Strathaquhin and her daughter, of Aberdeen. Theye depone that hir self confessis that quhat skill so ever scho hes, scho hed it of hir mother; and hir mother learnit at ane elf man quha lay with hir.[934]

1597. Andro Man of Aberdeen. Thriescoir yeris sensyne or thairby, the Devill, thy maister, com to thy motheris hous, in the liknes and scheap of a woman, quhom thow callis the Quene of Elphen, and was delyverit of a barne, as apperit to the their.... Thow confessis that be the space of threttie twa yeris sensyn or thairby, thow begud to have carnall deall with that devilische spreit, the Quene of Elphen, on quhom thow begat dyveris bairnis, quhom thow hes sene sensyn.... Vpon the Ruidday in harvest, in this present yeir, quhilk fell on ane Wedinsday, thow confessis and affermis, thow saw Christsonday cum owt of the snaw in liknes of a staig, and that the Quene of Elphen was their, and vtheris with hir, rydand vpon quhyt haiknayes, and that thay com to the Binhill, and Binlocht, quhair thay vse commonlie to convene, and that thay quha convenis with thame kissis Christsonday and the Quene of Elphenis airss, as thow did thy selff. Item, thow affermis that the elphis hes schapes and claythis lyk men, and that thay will have fair coverit taiblis, and that thay ar bot schaddowis, bot ar starker nor men, and that thay have playing and dansing quhen thay pleas; and als that the quene is verray plesand, and wilbe auld and young quhen scho pleissis; scho mackis any kyng quhom scho pleisis, and lyis with any scho lykis.... The said Andro confessis that Chrystsonday rydis all the tyme that he is in thair cumpanie, and hes carnall deall with thame; also, that the men that cumis with thame, hes do with the Quene of Elfane.[935] ... Thou confesses that the devil thy

---

[933] Pitcairn, ii, p. 25.
[934] *Spalding Club Misc.*, i, p. 177.
[935] *Spalding Club Misc.*, i, pp, 119, 121, 125.

master, whom thou terms Christsunday, and supposes to be an angel and God's godson—albeit he has a thraw by God, and sways to the Quene of Elphin—is raised by the speaking of the word *Benedicite*. Suchlike thou affirms that the Queen of Elphin has a grip of all the craft, but Christsunday is the goodman, and has all power under God.[936]

1608. Lyons district. Ils dansent deux à deux, & par fois l'vn çà & l'autre là; estans telles danses semblables à celles des Fées, vrais Diables incorporez, qui regnoient il n'y a pas long temps.[937]

1615. Jonet Drever of Orkney. To be convict and giltie of the fostering of ane bairne in the hill of Westray to the fary folk callit of hir our guid nichtbouris. And in haveing carnall deall with hir. And haveing conversation with the fary xxvj ʒeiris bygane. In respect of her awne confessioun.[938]

1616. Katherine Caray of Orkney. At the doun going of the sun are great number of fairie men mett her together with a maister man.[939]

1616. Elspeth Reoch of Orkney. Sho confest that quhen shoe wes ane young las of twelf yeiris of age or therby and haid wandereit out of Caithnes quher sho wes borne to Lochquhaber ye cam to Allane McKeldowies wyfe quha wes your ant That she upon ane day being out of the loch in the contrey and returning and being at the Loch syd awaiting quhen the boit sould fetch hir in. That thair cam tua men to her ane cled in blak and the uther with ane grein tartane plaid about him And that the man with the plaid said to her she was ane prettie And he wald lerne her to ken and sie ony thing she wald desyre.... And thairefter within tua yeir she bure her first bairne And being delyverit in hir sisteris hous the blak man cam to her that first came to hir in Lochquhaber And callit him selff ane farie man.... On yule day she confest the devell quhilk she callis the farie man lay with her At quhilk tyme he bade hir leave Orkney.[940]

---

[936] Burton, i, p. 253.
[937] Boguet, p. 132.
[938] *Maitland Club Misc.*, ii, p. 167.
[939] Dalyell, p. 536.
[940] *County Folklore*, iii, Orkney, pp. 112-14; *Maitland Club Misc.*, ii, pp. 188-9.

1618. Joan Willimot of Leicester. This Examinate saith, That shee hath a spirit which shee calleth Pretty, which was giuen vnto her by William Berry of Langholme in Rutlandshire, whom she serued three yeares; and that her Master when hee gaue it vnto her, willed her to open her mouth, and hee would blow into her a Fairy which should doe her good; and that shee opened her mouth, and he did blow into her mouth; and that presently after his blowing, there came out of her mouth a Spirit, which stood vpon the ground in the shape and forme of a Woman, which Spirit did aske of her her Soule, which shee then promised vnto it.[941]

1633. Isobel Sinclair of Orkney. Sex times at the reathes of the year, shoe hath bein controlled with the Phairie.[942]

1653. 'Yorkshire. There was (he saith) as I have heard the story credibly reported in this Country a Man apprehended for suspicion of Witchcraft, he was of that sort we call white Witches, which are such as do cures beyond the ordinary reasons and deductions of our usual practitioners, and are supposed (and most part of them truly) to do the same by ministration of spirits (from whence under their noble favours, most Sciences at first grow) and therefore are by good reason provided against by our Civil Laws, as being ways full of danger and deceit, and scarce ever otherwise obtained than by a devillish compact of the exchange of ones Soul to that assistant spirit, for the honour of its Mountebankery. What this man did was with a white powder which, he said, he received from the Fairies, and that going to a Hill he knocked three times, and the Hill opened, and he had access to, and conversed with a visible people; and offered, that if any Gentleman present would either go himself in person, or send his servant, he would conduct them thither, or shew them the place and persons from whom he had his skill.' [Hotham's account ends here; Webster continues first in his own words and then in inverted commas as if quoting, but gives no authority.] To this I shall only add thus much, that the man was accused for invoking and calling upon evil spirits, and was a very simple and illiterate person to any mans judgment, and

---

[941] *Wonderfull Discoverie of Margaret and Phillip Flower*, E 3.
[942] Dalyell, p. 470.

had been formerly very poor, but had gotten some pretty little meanes
to maintain himself, his Wife and diverse small children, by his cures
done with this white powder, of which there were sufficient proofs,
and the Judge asking him how he came by the powder, he told a story
to this effect. 'That one night before day was gone, as he was going
home from his labour, being very sad and full of heavy thoughts, not
knowing how to get meat and drink for his Wife and Children, he met
a fair Woman in fine cloaths, who asked him why he was so sad, and
he told her it was by reason of his poverty, to which she said, that if
he would follow her counsel she would help him to that which would
serve to get him a good living: to which he said he would consent with
all his heart, so it were not by unlawful ways: she told him it should
not be by any such ways, but by doing of good and curing of sick
people; and so warning him strictly to meet her there the next night at
the same time, she departed from him, and he went home. And the
next night at the time appointed he duly waited, and she (according to
promise) came and told him that it was well he came so duly,
otherwise he had missed of that benefit, that she intended to do unto
him, and so bade him follow her and not be afraid. Thereupon she led
him to a little Hill and she knocked three times, and the Hill opened,
and they went in, and came to a fair hall, wherein was a Queen sitting
in great state, and many people about her, and the Gentlewoman that
brought him, presented him to the Queen, and she said he was welcom,
and bid the Gentlewoman give him some of the white powder, and
teach him how to use it, which she did, and gave him a little wood box
full of the white powder, and bad him give 2 or 3 grains of it to any
that were sick, and it would heal them, and so she brought him forth
of the Hill, and so they parted. And being asked by the Judge whether
the place within the Hill, which he called a Hall, were light or dark,
he said indifferent, as it is with us in the twilight; and being asked how
he got more powder, he said when he wanted he went to that Hill, and
knocked three times, and said every time I am coming, I am coming,
whereupon it opened, and he going in was conducted by the aforesaid
Woman to the Queen, and so had more powder given him. This was
the plain and simple story (however it may be judged of) that he told

before the Judge, the whole Court, and the Jury, and there being no proof, but what cures he had done to very many, the Jury did acquit him.[943]

1655. It might be here very seasonable to enquire into the nature of those large *dark Rings* in the grass, which they call *Fairy Circles*, whether they be the*Rendezvouz* of Witches, or the dancing place of those little Puppet Spirits which they call *Elves* or *Fairies*.[944]

1661. Jonet Watson Of Dalkeith. She confessed that three months before the Devill apeired vnto her, in the liknes of ane prettie boy, in grein clothes. As also about the tyme of the last Baille-fyre night, shoe was at a Meitting in Newtoun-dein with the Deavill, who had grein cloathes vpone him, and ane blak hatt vpone his head; wher schoe denyd Christ, and took her self to be the servant of the Deivill.[945]

1662. Isobel Gowdie of Auldearne. I was in the Downie-hillis, and got meat ther from the Qwein of Fearrie, mor than I could eat. The Qwein of Fearrie is brawlie clothed in whyt linens, and in whyt and browne cloathes, &c.; and the King of Fearrie is a braw man, weill favoured, and broad faced, &c. Ther wes elf-bullis rowtting and skoylling wp and downe thair and affrighted me.... As for Elf-arrow-heidis, the Devill shapes them with his awin hand, and syne deliueris thame to Elf-boyes, who whyttis and dightis them with a sharp thing lyk a paking needle.... We went in to the Downie hillis; the hill opened, and we cam to an fair and large braw rowme in the day tym. Thair ar great bullis rowtting and skoylling ther, at the entrie, quhilk feared me.... The Devill wold giw ws the brawest lyk money that ewer wes coyned; within fowr and twantie houris it vold be horse-muke.[946]

1662. Janet Breadheid of Auldearne. He gaw me ane piece of money, lyk a testain ... and gaw me an vthir piece of money, lyk the first, bot they both turned read, and I got nothing for thaim.[947]

---

[943] Webster, pp. 300-2.
[944] More, p. 232.
[945] Pitcairn, iii, p. 601.
[946] Pitcairn, iii, pp. 604, 607, 611, 613.
[947] Id., iii, p. 617.

1662. Bute. [The devil] 'gave her ane elf errow stone to shott him [a child of seven] which she did ten dayes therafter that the child dyed imediately therafter. Jonet Morisoune declares the devill told her it was the fayries that took John Glas child's lyfe. Mcfersone in Keretoule his dochter lay sick of a very unnaturall disease. The disease quhilk ailed her was blasting with the faryes and that she healed her with herbes. Item being questioned about her heileing of Alester Bannatyne who was sick of the lyk disease answred that he was blasted with the fairyes also and that she heiled him thereof with herbs and being questioned anent hir heileing of Patrick Glas dochter Barbara Glas answred that she was blasted with the faryes also. Being inquired quhat difference was betwix shooting and blasting sayes that quhen they are shott ther is no recoverie for it and if the shott be in the heart they died presently bot if it be not at the heart they will die in a while with it yet will at last die with it and that blasting is a whirlwinde that the fayries raises about that persone quhich they intend to wrong quhich may be healed two wayes ether by herbs or by charming.'[948]

1664. Alice Duke of Wincanton, Somerset. When the Devil doth anything for her, she calls for him by the name of *Robin*, upon which he appears.[949]

1664. Elizabeth Style of Wincanton, Somerset. When she hath a desire to do harm, she calls the Spirit by the name of *Robin*.[950]

1670. Jean Weir of Edinburgh. When she keeped a school at Dalkeith, and teached childering, ane tall woman came to the declarant's hous when the childering were there; she had, as appeared to her, ane chyld upon her back, and on or two at her foot; and the said woman desyred that the declarant should imploy her to spick for her to the Queen of Farie, and strik and battle in her behalf with the said Queen (which was her own words).[951]

1677. Inveraray. Donald McIlmichall was tried 'for that horrid cryme of corresponding with the devill'; the whole evidence being that

---

[948] *Highland Papers*, iii, pp. 19, 23, 27.
[949] Glanvil, pt. ii, p. 152.
[950] Id., ii, p. 137.
[951] Law, p. 27 note.

he entered a fairy hill where he met many men and women 'and he playd on trumps to them quhen they danced'.[952]

1697. Margaret Fulton in Renfrewshire. She was reputed a Witch, has the Mark of it, and acknowledged that her Husband had brought her back from the *Faries*.[953]

1697. James Lindsay, alias Curat, in Renfrewshire. He was called the Gleid, or Squint-Ey'd Elff.[954]

Nineteenth century. It was the common rumour that Elphin Irving came not into the world like the other sinful creatures of the earth, but was one of the Kane-bairns of the fairies, whilk they had to pay to the enemy of man's salvation every seventh year. The poor lady-fairy,—a mother's aye a mother, be she Elve's flesh or Eve's flesh,—hid her Elf son beside the christened flesh in Marion Irving's cradle, and the auld enemy lost his prey for a time.... And touching this lad, ye all ken his mother was a hawk of an uncannie nest, a second cousin of Kate Kimmer, of Barfloshan, as rank a witch as ever rode on ragwort.[955]

---

[952] *Highland Papers*, iii, pp. 36-8.
[953] *Sadducismus Debellatus*, p. 50.
[954] Id., p. 25.
[955] Cunningham, pp. 246, 251

APPENDIX II

TRIAL OF SILVAIN NEVILLON AND GENTIEN LE CLERC AT ORLEANS, 1614-15

[This trial is included here as a specimen of purely ritual witchcraft, without spell-casting.]

Arrest & procedure faicte par le Lieutenant Criminel d Orleans, contre Siluain Neuillon, Gentien le Clerc dit Niuelle, & Mathurin Ferrand du village de Nouan en Sologne, conuaincus de sortilege le 20 Juin 1614.

Le Vendredy 20 Iuin 1614 ledit Lieutenant procedant à l'audition dudit Neuillon couureur & Masson, aagé de 77 ans.

Ledit Lieutenant Criminel luy ayant dit qu'il luy vouloit faire raire ou razer le poil & changer d'habits: afin qu'il dict verité. L'accusé s'escria en ces mots, Comment me veut-on faire mourir, Messieurs, si ie vous confesse la verité, vous ne me ferez pas razer.

A confessé auoir esté au Sabbat prez Nouan, en vn lieu nommé Oliuet.

Dit que le Sabbat se tenoit dans vne maison, où il vit à la cheminée coṁe ledit Sabbat se faisoit, vn homme noir duquel on ne voyoit point la teste, & deux cheures ou boucs en la mesme maison ayant grand poil noir. Il y auoit 200. personnes tous masquez, excepté vn nommé Ferrand. Qu'allant à l'offrande aucuns baillent de l'argent comme à l'Eglise.

Vit aussi vn grand homme noir à l'opposite de celuy de la cheminée, qui regardoit dans vn liure, dont les feuillets estoient noirs & bleuds, & marmotoit entre ses dents sans entendre ce qu'il disoit, leuoit vne hostie noire, puis vn calice de meschant estain tout crasseux. Vit que tous les assistans dançoient en bransles dos à dos, & deux boucs ou cheures auec eux. Il y auoit des viandes si fades qu'il n'en peut aualler, & croit que c'estoit de la chair de cheual, & que ledit hoṁe noir parloit comme si la voix fut sortie d'vn poinson: Et vit enuiron douze enfans portez par des femmes, & que le Diable batit vne femme auec vn baston, de ce qu'elle n'auoit pas apporté son enfant comme elle auoit promis, bailloit ledit homme noir des gasteaux auxdits petits enfans.

Dit que ceux qui ne vont au Sabbat, payent huict sols, qu'il y a des processions où il a veu par fois six cens personnes, que les deux Diables qui estoient au Sabbat, l'vn s'appelloit l'Orthon, & l'autre Traisnesac, & qu'ils se baissoient enuers ceux qui leur emmenoient leurs enfans comme pour les remercier, & baisoient leursdits enfans au cul.

Dit qu'il a veu le Diable en plusieurs façons, tantost comme vn bouc, ayant vn visage deuant & vn autre derriere, ores comme vn gros mouton.

Qu'on baptise des enfans au Sabbat auec du Cresme, que des femmes apportent, & frottent la verge de quelque homme, & en font sortir de la semence qu'elles amassent, & la meslent auec le Cresme, puis mettent cela sur la teste de l'enfant en prononçant quelques paroles en Latin.

Dit aussi auoir veu des Sorciers & Sorcieres qui apportoient des Hosties au Sabbat, lesquelles elles auoient gardé lors qu'on leur auoit baillé à communier à l'Eglise, & que le Diable faisoit des gestes comme en depitant sur icelles Hosties, desquelles on faisoit de la poudre, & quelque fois on les mettoit dans l'eau, & que le Diable estoit fort ayse quand on luy apportoit lesdites Hosties.

Dit auoir ouy dire à Guilleaume le Clerc dit Nitelle, que pour auoir faict mourir vn homme le Diable donnoit de recompence huict sols, & pour vne femme cinq sols.

Dit que le Diable les bat au Sabbat, quand ils ne sçauent rendre compte d'auoir fait quelque mal, & qu'il leur dit en se separant vengez vous, autrement vous mourrez.

Dit que le iour qu'on a esté à la Messe, on ne peut estre ensorcellé, ou qu'on a vn *Agnus Dei* sur soy, que bien souuent ils appellent l'Hostie Iean le blanc, que les femmes chantent des châsons en l'honneur du Diable, & qu'à l'entree & sortie de table au Sabbat, on dit au Diable nous vous recognoissons pour nostre maistre, nostre Dieu, nostre Createur.

Que le Diable dit le Sermõ au Sabbat, mais qu'on n'entend ce qu'il dit, parce qu'il parle cõme en grõdant, & qu'il iette de la poudre par toute l'assemblée, cõme on fait de l'eau beniste.

Vit qu'on frappoit dans l'eau d'vne baguette, & aussi tost vit comme il luy sembloit que c'estoit de la gresle.

Dit estre allé souuent au Sabbat de son pied tout esueillé, & ne se grassoit point, d'autant que c'estoit folie de se graisser quand on ne va pas loing.

Dit que le Diable monstre une forme de membre viril au Sabbat, ong comme vne chandelle, & qu'il vit vne femme qui le baisa par là.

Dit que les Sorciers ne peuuent faire mal le Vendredy, à cause que Dieu y auoit souffert la mort, & estoit venu au monde ledit iour.

Dit qu'il y a des Sorciers qui nourrissent des Marionettes, qui sont de petits Diableteaux en forme de Crapaux, & leur font manger de la bouillie composée de laict & de farine, & leur donnent le premier mourceau, & n'oseroient s'absenter de leur maison sans leur demander congé, & luy faut dire combien de temps ils seront absens, comme trois ou quatre iours, & si elles disent que c'est trop, ceux qui les gardent, n'osent faire leur voyage ny outre-passer leur volonté.

Et quand ils veulent aller en marchandise ou ioüer, & sçauoir s'il y fera bon, ils regardent si lesdites Marionettes sont ioyeuses, en ce cas ils vont en marchandise, ou ioüer: mais si elles sont maussades & tristes, ils ne bougent de la maison, & le plus souuent lesdites Marionettes vsent enuers eux de grandes menaces.

Interrogé ledit Neuillon par ledit Lieutenant Criminel, si à son aduis vn Iuge pourroit faire prendre lesdites Marionettes, veu que ce sont Demons familliers.

Respond qu'vn bon Iuge pourroit bien faire emporter lesdites Marionettes, d'autant qu'elles craignent fort les bons Iuges: mais qu'vn Iuge qui ne feroit pas bien la Iustice, ny gagneroit rien, & que les Sorciers peuuent ensorceller vn meschant Iuge, parce que Dieu l'a abandonné.

Dit qu'il a veu bailler au Sabbat du pain benist, & de l'encens, mais il ne sentoit bon comme celuy de l'Eglise, & que c'estoit vn des Diables nommé Orthon qui le donnoit, lorsque Tramesabot disoit la

Messe, & qu'auant la commencer il iettoit de l'eau beniste qui estoit faicte de pissat, & faisoit la reverence de l'espaule, & disoit, *Asperges Diaboli*.

Ledit Neuillon estoit conuaincu par le procez, d'auoir empoisonné & faict mourir plusieurs personnes & bestiaux, & d'auoir faict d'autres maux.

Gentil ou Gentiẽ le Clerc dit, que sa mère le presenta (dit-on) en l'aage de trois ans au Sabbat, à vn bouc, qu'on appelloit l'Aspic. Dit qu'il fut baptisé au Sabbat, au Carroir d'Oliuet, auec quatorze ou quinze autres, & que Ieanne Geraut porta du Chresme qui estoit jaune dans vn pot, & que ledit Neuillon ietta de la semence dans ledit pot, & vn nommé Semelle, & broüilloient cela auec vne petite cuilliere de bois, & puis leur en mirent à tous sur la teste.

Il vit marquer plusieurs personnes, mais les femmes principalement entre les tetins.

Qu'on baille à baiser la paix comme à l'Eglise, & que cela semble vne tuille, & qu'on y baille vn denier ou vn double allant à l'offrande, l'eau beniste est iaune comme du pissat d'asne, & qu'apres qu'on la iettée on dit la Messe, & que c'est le Diable qui la dit, qu'il a vne Chasuble qui a vne croix: mais qu'elle n'a que trois barres: & tourne le dos à l'Autel quand il veut leuer l'Hostie & le Calice, qui sont noirs, & marmote dans vn liure, duquel la couuerture est toute veluë comme d'vne peau de loup, auec des feuillets blancs & rouges, d'autres noirs.

Et quand ledit homme noir a ietté, ou iette de l'eau beniste, chacun des assistans, se iette en terre comme on faict à l'Eglise sur la fosse des trespassez, auec vn morceau de hou qui a trois feuilles au bout. Après la Messe on dance, puis on couche ensemble, hommes auec hommes, & auec des femmes. Puis on se met à table, où il n'a iamais veu de sel. Et n'y a autre viande que grenouille & anguilles, & point de vin ains de l'eau.

Dit qu'il a cognu des hommes & s'est accouplé auec eux; qu'il auoit vne couppe ou gondolle par le moyen de laquelle toutes les femmes le suiuoient pour y boire.

Qu'au Sabbat on y blasphemoit souuent, disant chardieu, c'est vne belle chose qu'ils font blanchir pour qu'on la voye de plus loing, &

puis la mangent, & quand ils l'ont mangé il n'y en a plus, que les Prestres font cela pour amuser le monde, & que c'est vn beau Ianicot, qu'il y auoit plus d'acquest en sa Marionette qu'en Dieu. Et auoit veu souuent la Marionette dudit Neuillon, qui est comme vn gros crapaut tout noir, comme d'vne fourrure noire, & estoit dans vne boëtte caché soubs vn carreau, qui sautoit & leuoit quand on vouloit donner à manger audit crapaut. Qu'il l'a veu encore puis six sepmaines en la ruelle du lict dudict Neuillon, & qu'il a veu qu'il l'apportoit vne autre fois dans son manteau, qu'il luy a dit vne douzaine de fois, que s'il vouloit il luy en feroit auoir vne. Qu'il y auoit plus profit en icelle qu'en Dieu, & qu'il ne gagnoit rien à regarder Dieu: mais que sa Marionette luy apportoit tousiours quelque chose.

Confesse auoir faict mourir plusieurs personnes, & qu'il sçait faire dancer les bœufs dans vn cercle qu'il fait, & qu'vne vieille luy apprins.

Ils furent condamnez, par sentence à estre pendus & bruslez. Appel en la Cour, ou au rapport de Monsieur Berulle, Conseiller en la seconde Chambre des Enquestes, deux Sorciers moururent. Cependant Gentien le Clerc seul, fut condamné par Arrest du 4 Feurier 1615.

APPENDIX III

A. NAMES OF WITCHES IN COVENS

1
1440. Machecoul

[Three were executed; of four equally guilty two fled, and two had died previously.]

- 1. Antonio Prelati
- 2. Bertrand Poulein
- 3. Etienne Corrillaut [executed]
- 4. Etiennette Blanchu
- 5. Eustache Blanchet
- 6. Gilles de Rais [executed]
- 7. Gilles de Sillé [fled]
- 8. Henri Griart [executed]
- 9. Jean Rossignol [dead]
- 10. Lenano Ceva
- 11. Perrine Martin
- 12. Robin Romulart [dead]
- 13. Roger de Bricqueville [fled]

2
1582. Essex. St. Osyth

- 1. Ales Hunt
- 2. Ales Manfield
- 3. Ales Newman
- 4. Annis Glascocke
- 5. Annys Heade
- 6. Cysley Celles
- 7. Elizabeth Bennet
- 8. Elizabeth Ewstace
- 9. Joan Pechey
- 10. Joan Robinson
- 11. Margaret Grevell

- 12. Margery Sammon
- 13. Ursley Kemp

3
1590. North Berwick

[Those marked with a star are the nine who took part in the great attempt on James VI's life. Of these four were tried and executed. Of the rest of the Covens, Christian Tod, Donald Robson, and Robert Grierson were executed as witches in 1594, and Beigis Tod in 1608. The others appear to have escaped altogether.]

- *1, 2. Agnes Sampson and her daughter
- 3. Agnes Stratton
- 4. Alexander Quhytelaw
- 5. Annie Richardson
- *6. Barbara Napier
- 7. Beigis Tod
- 8. Bessie Broune
- 9. Bessie Gwlene [Cowan]
- 10. Bessie Robson
- 11. Bessie Thomson
- 12. Bessie Wright
- 13. Catherine Campbell
- 14. Catherine Duncan
- 15. Catherene McGill
- 16. Christian Carrington
- 17. Christian Tod
- *18. Donald Robson
- 19. Duncan Buchanan
- *20. Euphemia McCalyan
- 21. Geillis Duncan
- 22. Gilbert McGill
- 23. Helen Lauder
- 24. Helen Quhyte
- 25. Issobell Gylour [Gylloun]
- 26. Issobell Lauder

- 27. Jannet Blandilands
- 28. Jonnet Campbell
- 29. Jonet Gaw [Gall]
- 30. Jonet Logan
- 31. Jonet Nicholson
- *32. Jonet Stratton
- 33. John Couper
- *34. John Fian [officer]
- 35. John Gordon [Gray-meill]
- 36. John McGill
- 37. Kaet Gray
- 38. Kait Wallace
- 39. Malie Geddie
- 40. Margrett Aitchison
- 41. Meg Begton
- 42. Meg Dunn
- 43. Meg Stillcart
- *44. Margret Thomsoun
- 45. Marion Bailzie
- 46. Marion Congilton
- 47, 48. Marion Linkup and her sister
- 49. Marion Nicholson
- 50. Marion Paterson
- 51. Marion Scheill [Shaw]
- 52. Marion ... [Irish Marion]
- 53. Masie Aitchison
- 54. Michael Clark
- 55. Richard Graham
- *56. Robert Grierson
- 57, 58. Thomas Burnhill and his wife
- 59, 60. ... Stobbeis [2 women]
- 61. Archie Henillis' wife
- *62. George Mott's wife
- 63. John Ramsay's wife
- 64. Nicoll Murray's wife

4
1597. Aberdeen
1

[The following were executed.]

- 1. Andro Man
- 2. Christen Reid
- 3. Issobell Oige
- 4. Issobell Richie
- 5. Helen Rogie
- 6. Jonet Grant
- 7. Jonet Spaldarg
- 8. Jonet Wishert
- 9. Katherine Gerard
- 10. Margrat Bean
- 11. Margrat Og
- 12. Marion Grant
- 13. Thomas Leyis [officer]

2

[The following took a leading part in the ceremonies and were tried; seven were banished; no record as to the fate of the rest.]

- 1. Agnes Wobster
- 2. Beatrice Robbie [banished]
- 3. Bessie Thom
- 4. Christen Mitchell
- 5. Ellen Gray
- 6. Elspet Leyis [banished]
- 7. Issobell Coky
- 8. Helen Fraser
- 9. John Leyis [banished]
- 10. Jonet Davidson [banished]
- 11. Jonet Leyis [banished]
- 12. Jonet Lucas [banished]
- 13. Violet Leyis [banished]

5
1613. Lancashire

[Ten were executed; Elizabeth Demdike died in prison; Jennet Preston was acquitted, but was executed later. I suggest Jennet Hargreaves as the thirteenth, for she was the only one who was first at Malking Tower and afterwards in prison.]

- 1. Alice Nutter
- 2. Alizon Device
- 3. Anne Redferne
- 4. Anne Whittle
- 5. Elizabeth Demdike [officer]
- 6. Elizabeth Device
- 7. Isobel Robey
- 8. James Device
- 9. Jane Bulcock
- 10. Jennet Hargreaves
- 11. Jennet Preston
- 12. John Bulcock
- 13. Katherine Hewit

6
1617. Guernsey

- 1. Collas Becquet
- 2. Collette du Mont [officer]
- 3. Isabel Becquet
- 4. Marie Becquet
- 5. The woman Fallaise
- 6. The woman Hardie
- 7. A woman she did not know
- 8-13. Six others there she did not know

7
1644. Queensferry
[Seven were executed.]

- 1. Catherine Logie
- 2. Catherine Thomson
- 3. Elspet Cant
- 4. Helen Hill
- 5. Helen Thomson
- 6. Isobel Young
- 7. Janet Lowrie
- 8. Janet Mowbray
- 9. Margaret Brown
- 10. Margaret Dauline
- 11. Marion Dauline
- 12. Marion Little
- 13. Marion Stein

8
1649. Herts. St. Albans

- 1. Anne Smith
- 2. John Lamen S^r.
- 3. John Lamen J^r.
- 4. John [? Joan] Lamen
- 5. John Palmer
- 6. John Salmon, S^r
- 7. Joseph Salmon
- 8. Judeth Salmon
- 9. Mary Bychance
- 10. Mary Lamen, S^r
- 11. Mary Lamen, J^r
- 12. Sarah Smith
- 13. Widow Palmer

9
1658. Alloa

- 1. Barbara Erskin
- 2. Bessie Paton
- 3. Elspet Black

- 4. James Hudston
- 5. James Kirk
- 6. Jonet Millar
- 7. Jonet Paterson
- 8. Jonet Reid
- 9. Kathren Black
- 10. Kathren Renny
- 11. Margret Demperstoun
- 12. Margret Duchall
- 13. Margret Tailzeour

10
1661. Forfar

[The two Covens were led, one by Helen Guthrie, the other by Helen Cothills. I have put in the first Coven the names which occur most frequently together.]
- 1. Agnes Sparke
- 2. Andrew Watson
- 3. Elspet Alexander
- 4. Elspet Bruce
- 5. Helen Alexander
- 6. Helen Guthrie [officer]
- 7. Isobel Dorward
- 8. Isobel Shyrie
- 9. John Tailzeour
- 10. Jonet Howit
- 11. Jonet Stout
- 12. Katherene Portour
- 13. Mary Rynd

2

- 1. Bessie Croket
- 2. Christen Whyte
- 3. George Ellies
- 4. Helen Cothills [officer]

- 5. Isobel Smith
- 6. Jonet Barrie
- 7. Katharene Wallace
- 8. Margaret Nicholl
- 9. Marjorie Ritchie
- 10. ... Finlason
- 11. ... Hebrone
- 12, 13. Two unnamed women mentioned by Katharene Portour.

11
1662. Auldearne

- 1. Barbara Ronald
- 2. Bessie Hay
- 3. Bessie Wilson
- 4. Elspet Nishie
- 5. Issobell Gowdie
- 6. Issobell Nicoll
- 7. Janet Breadheid
- 8. Janet Burnet
- 9. John Taylor
- 10. John Young [officer]
- 11. Jean Marten [the Maiden]
- 12. Margret Brodie
- 13. Margret Wilson

12
1662. Kinross-shire. Crook of Devon

- 1. Agnes Brugh
- 2. Agnes Murie
- 3. Agnes Pittendreich
- 4. Bessie Henderson
- 5. Bessie Neil
- 6. Christian Grieve
- 7. Isabel Rutherford

- 8. Janet Brugh
- 9. Janet Paton (of Crook)
- 10. Janet Paton (of Kilduff)
- 11. Margaret Huggon
- 12. Margaret Litster
- 13. Robert Wilson

13
1662. Hartford, Conn.

[Though the published records are incomplete, the number of names surviving suggests that a Coven existed here.]

- 1. Andrew Sanford
- 2. Elizabeth Seager
- 3. James Walkley
- 4. Judith Varlet
- 5. Mary Sanford
- 6. Nathaniel Greensmith
- 7. Rebecca Greensmith
- 8. William Ayres
- 9. Goodwife Ayres
- 10. Goodwife Grant
- 11. Goodwife Palmer
- 12. Goodwife Sanford

14
1662. Bute

- 1. Agnes ... in Gortenis
- 2. Annie Heyman [the Maiden]
- 3. Cirstine Ballantyne [the Maiden]
- 4. Donald McCartour
- 5. Elspet Galie
- 6. Elspeth Gray
- 7. Elspet NcWilliam
- 8. Elspeth Spence
- 9. Issobell More McKaw

- 10. Issobell NcNeill
- 11. Issobell NcNicoll
- 12. Jonet McConachie
- 13. Jonet McNeill
- 14. Jonet McNickell
- 15. Jonet Isack
- 16. Jonet Morison
- 17. Jonet Nicoll
- 18. John Galy
- 19. Kathrine Cristell
- 20. Kathrine Frissell
- 21. Kathrine McWilliam
- 22. Kathrine Moore
- 23. Kathrine Stewart
- 24. Margaret McNeill
- 25. Margaret McNickell
- 26. Margaret Ncilduy
- 27. Margaret NcLevin
- 28. Margaret NcWilliam
- 29. Margaret Smith
- 30. Marie McKaw
- 31. Marie More NcCuill
- 32. Marie Stewart
- 33. Patrick McKaw

[Besides eleven other incomplete names, of which five can be identified as being already mentioned above, leaving six to add to that number, i.e. thirty-nine in all.]

15

1664. Somerset

[In the first Coven I have put the names which occur most frequently together in the evidence.]

1

- 1. Alice Duke
- 2. Alice Green

- 3. Anne Bishop [officer]
- 4. Catharine Green
- 5. Christian Green
- 6. Dinah Warberton
- 7. Dorothy Warberton
- 8. Elizabeth Stile
- 9. Henry Walter
- 10. Jone Syms
- 11. Mary Green
- 12. Mary Penny
- 13. Mary Warberton

2

- 1. Christopher Ellen
- 2. James Bush
- 3. John Combes
- 4. John Vining
- 5. Julian Cox
- 6. Margaret Agar [officer?]
- 7. Margaret Clarke
- 8. Rachel King
- 9. Richard Dickes
- 10. Richard Lannen
- 11. Thomas Bolster
- 12. Thomas Dunning
- 13. ... Durnford

16
1673. Northumberland

- 1. Anne Driden
- 2. Anne Foster
- 3. Anne Usher
- 4. Elizabeth Pickering
- 5. John Crauforth
- 6. Lucy Thompson

- 7. Margaret Aynsley
- 8. Margarett (whose surname she knowes not)
- 9. Michael Aynsley
- 10. William Wright
- 11-13. And three more, whose names she knowes not

17
1657. Renfrewshire. Bargarran

- 1. Agnes Naismith
- 2. Alexander Anderson
- 3. James Lindsay
- 4. Janet Rodgers
- 5. Janet Wagh
- 6. Jean Fulton [officer]
- 7. John Lindsay
- 8. John Reid
- 9. Katherine Campbel
- 10. Margaret Fulton
- 11. Margaret Laing
- 12. Margaret Rodgers
- 13. Martha Semple

B. NAMES OF WITCHES

[Guernsey being a law unto itself in the matter of names, the following remarks refer only to England and Scotland.]

The lists of witch-names bring to light several facts as regards the women. One of these is the entire absence of Saxon names, such as Gertrude, Edith, Hilda; Old Testament names are so few in number as to be negligible; Scandinavian names are not found; the essentially Puritan names, such as Temperance, hardly occur; but the great mass of the names fall under eight heads with their dialectical differences: 1, Ann (Annis, Agnes, Annabel); 2, Alice (Alison); 3, Christian (Christen, Cirstine); 4, Elizabeth (Elspet, Isobel, Bessie); 5, Ellen (Elinor, Helen); 6, Joan (Jane, Janet, Jonet); 7, Margaret (Marget, Meg, Marjorie); 8, Marion (Mary).

At first sight the list suggests New Testament and Greek influence; and though I am not prepared to dispute this, I would point out (1) that there was a British goddess called Anna, which may account not only for all the forms of Ann but also for the terminations in Alison and Marion; (2) that the name*Christian* clearly indicates the presence of another religion; (3) that there is at present nothing to prove that Isobel is a variant of Elizabeth—it is quite possible that Isobel was the original name and that the missionaries 'Christianized' it as Elizabeth; (4) that Helen was a pre-Christian name in Great Britain; (5) that Margaret may have been originally Marget, the spelling and pronunciation being influenced by the Greek form; and as g and y are dialectically interchangeable, Marget would be the same as, or closely allied to, the Finnish Marjatta.

If Christianity had obtained the hold on the people which the ecclesiastical writers would have us believe, the name Mary should surely have been the most common, but it hardly occurs in Great Britain before 1645, while Marion is hardly used after that date. This looks as though Marion were the earlier form, and Mary may therefore be merely the contraction of the longer name.

As regards the name Joan I can offer no explanations or suggestions. I can only call attention to its overwhelming preponderance in comparison with the others.

In the lists the names are arranged without regard to local differences of spelling. The surnames are in alphabetical order.

Abre Ginset	Dunwich	1663
Agnes Allene	Crook of Devon	1662
Agnes Beveridge	Crook of Devon	1662
Agnes Brodie	Auldearne	1662
Agnes Browne	Northampton	1612
Agnes Brugh	Crook of Devon	1662
Agnes Finnie	Edinburgh	1644
Agnes Forbes	Aberdeen	1597
Agnes Frame	Aberdeen	1597
Agnes Grant	Auldearne	1662

Agnes Murie	Crook of Devon	1662
Agnes Naismith	Bargarran	1697
Agnes Pittendreich	Crook of Devon	1662
Agnes Rawsterne	Lancs	1613
Agnes Sampson	North Berwick	1590
Agnes Sharp	Crook of Devon	1662
Agnes Sparke	Forfar	1661
Agnes Stratton	North Berwick	1590
Agnes Torrie	Auldearne	1662
Agnes Williamson	Samuelston	1662
Agnes Wobster	Aberdeen	1597
Agnes ... in Gortenis	Bute	1662
Alester McNiven	Bute	1642
Alexander Bell	Auldearne	1662
Alexander Elder	Auldearne	1662
Alexander Hamilton	Edinburgh	1630
Alexander Hunter	East Lothian	1649
Alexander Ledy	Auldearne	1662
Alexander Quhytelaw	N. Berwick	1590
Alexander Shepheard	Auldearne	1662
Alexander Sussums	Suffolk	1646
Alice Dixon	Essex	1645
Alice Dixon	Northumberland	1673
Alice Duke	Somerset	1664
Alice Gooderidge	Burton-on-Trent	1597
Alice Gray	Lancs	1613
Alice Green	Somerset	1664

Ales Hunt	St. Osyth	1582
Alice Huson	Burton Agnes	1664
Alice Kyteler	Ireland	1324
Ales Mansfield	St. Osyth	1582
Ales Newman	St. Osyth	1582
Alice Nutter	Lancs	1613
Alice Priestley	Lancs	1613
Alse Young	Connecticut	1647
Alizon Device	Lancs	1613
Alison Dick	Kirkcaldy	1636
Alesoun Peirsoun	Fifeshire	1588
Allan McKeldowie	Orkney	1616
Amy Duny	Essex	1645
Amie Hyndman, Snr.	Bute	1662
Amie Hyndman, Jnr.	Bute	1662
Andro Man	Aberdeen	1597
Andrew Sanford	Conn.	1662
Andrew Watson	Forfar	1661
Anne Ashby	Maidstone	1652
Ann Baites	Northumberland	1673
Anne Baker	Leicester	1619
Anne Bishop	Somerset	1664
Anne Blampied	Guernsey	1629
Anne Bodenham	Salisbury	1633
Anne Cate	Much Holland, Essex	1645

Anne Cooper	Clacton, Essex	1645
Annas Craigie	Crook of Devon	1662
Anne Crunkshey	Lancs	1613
Anne Desborough	Hunts	1646
Anne Driden	Northumberland	1673
Anne Foster	Northumberland	1673
Ann Foster	Northampton	1674
Annis Glascocke	St. Osyth	1582
Anne Grut	Guernsey	1614
Annis Heade	St. Osyth	1582
Annie Heyman	Bute	1662
Anne Hunnam	Scarborough	1651
Anne Leach	Misley, Essex	1645
Anne Martyn	Maidstone	1652
Anne Massq	Guernsey	1617
Anne Parker	Suffolk	1645
Anne Parteis	Northumberland	1673
Anne Pearce	Suffolk	1645
Anne Redferne	Lancs	1613
Annie Richardson	N. Berwick	1590
Anne Smith	St. Albans	1649
Annabil Stuart	Paisley	1678
Anie Tailzeour	Orkney	1633
Annaple Thomson	Borrowstowness	1679
Anne Usher	Northumberland	1673
Anne West	Lawford, Essex	1645
Anne Whitfield	Northumberland	1673
Anne Whittle	Lancs	1613
Anthony Hunter	Northumberland	1673
Archibald Man	Auldearne	1662

Arthur Bill	Northampton	1612
Barbara Erskeine	Alloa	1658
Barbara Friece	Auldearne	1662
Barbara Napier	N. Berwick	1590
Barbara Ronald	Auldearne	1662
Beak Taiss	Aberdeen	1597
Beigis Tod	N. Berwick	1598
Beatrice Laing	Pittenweem	1704
Beatrice Robbie	Aberdeen	1597
Cirstine Ballantyne	Bute	1662
Christian Carington	N. Berwick	1597
Christian Carrington	N. Berwick	1590
Christian Graham	Glasgow	1622
Christian Green	Somerset	1664
Christian Grieve	Crook of Devon	1662
Christine Harnon	Guernsey	1617
Christiane Lewingstone	Leith	1597
Christen Miller	Aberdeen	1597
Christen Mitchell	Aberdeen	1597
Christen Reid	Aberdeen	1597
Christian Saidler	Edinburgh	1597
Christian Tod	N. Berwick	1590
Christen Whyte	Forfar	1661
Christiane Wilson	Dalkeith	1661
Christian Young	Crook of Devon	1662

Christopher Dixon	Northumberland	1673
Christopher Ellen	Somerset	1664
Christopher Hargreaves	Lancs	1613
Christopher Howgate	Lancs	1613
Cysley Celles	St. Osyth	1582
Cecile Vaultier	Guernsey	1610
Collas Becquet	Guernsey	1617
Collette Becquet	Guernsey	1617
Collette de l'Estal	Guernsey	1622
Collette Dumont	Guernsey	1617
Collette Gascoing	Guernsey	1563
Collette la Gelée	Guernsey	1624
Collette Robin	Guernsey	1622
Collette Salmon	Guernsey	1563
Collette Sauvage	Guernsey	1639
Collette Tourtel	Guernsey	1576
Deliverance Hobbs	Salem	1692
Dinah Warberton	Somerset	1664
Donald McCartour	Bute	1662
Donald Robesoune	N. Berwick	1590
Doll Bilby	Burton Agnes	1664
Dorothy Green	Northumberland	1673
Dorothy Warberton	Somerset	1664

Duncan Buchquhannane	N. Berwick	1590
Bessie Aiken	Edinburgh	1597
Elspet Alexander	Forfar	1661
Elizabeth Astley	Lancs	1613
Elizabeth Atchinson	Northumberland	1673
Bessie Bathgate	Eymouth	1634
Elizabeth Bennet	St. Osyth	1582
Elspet Blak	Alloa	1658
Bessie Browne	N. Berwick	1590
Elspet Bruce	Forfar	1661
Elspet Cant	Queensferry	1644
Elizabeth Chandler	Hunts	1646
Elspet Chisholme	Auldearne	1662
Elizabeth Clark	Manningtree	1645
Elizabeth Clawson	Conn.	1692
Bessie Croket	Forfar	1661
Elizabeth Demdike	Lancs	1613
Elizabeth Dempster	Crook of Devon	1662
Elizabeth Device	Lancs	1613
Elizabeth Dickenson	Knaresborough	1621
Bessie Dunlop	Ayrshire	1576
Elizabeth Duquenin	Guernsey	1610
Elizabeth Ewstace	St. Osyth	1582
Elspet Falconer	Auldearne	1662
Elspet Findlay	Aberdeen	1597
Elizabeth Fletcher	Knaresborough	1621
Elspett Forbes	Aberdeen	1597
Elizabeth Francis	Chelmsford	1556

Bessie Friece	Auldearne	1662
Elspet Galie	Bute	1662
Elizabeth Garlick	Conn.	1657
Elizabeth Gauvein	Guernsey	1639
Elspet Gilbert	Auldearne	1662
Elizabeth Godman	Conn.	1653
Elizabeth Gooding	Manningtree	1645
Bessie Graham	Kilwinning	1649
Elspet Graham	Dalkeith	1661
Elspet Gray	Bute	1662
Bessie Gulene	N. Berwick	1590
Elizabeth Hare	Essex	1645
Elizabeth Hargraves	Lancs	1613
Elizabeth Harvy	Ramsey, Essex	1645
Bessie Hay	Auldearne	1662
Bessie Henderson	Crook of Devon	1662
Elizabeth Howgate	Lancs	1613
Bessie Hucheons	Auldearne	1662
Elizabeth Knap	Groton	1671
Elspet Laird	Auldearne	1662
Elizabeth le Hardy	Guernsey	1631
Elspet Leyis	Aberdeen	1597
Elspet Macbeith	Auldearne	1662
Elspet Makhomie	Auldearne	1662
Bessie Moffat	Dalkeith	1661
Elspet Moinness	Aberdeen	1597
Elspet NcWilliam	Bute	1662
Bessie Neil	Crook of Devon	1662
Elspet Nishie	Auldearne	1662
Bessie Paton	Alloa	1658
Bessie Paul	Aberdeen	1597
Bessie Peterkin	Auldearne	1662

Elizabeth Pickering	Northumberland	1673
Elspeth Reoch	Orkney	1616
Bessie Robson	N. Berwick	1590
Elizabeth Sawyer	Edmonton	1621
Elizabeth Seager	Conn.	1662
Elspet Smyth	Aberdeen	1597
Elspeth Spence	Bute	1662
Elizabeth Stile	Somerset	1664
Elizabeth Stile	Windsor	1579
Elspet Strathaquhin	Aberdeen	1597
Bessie Thom	Aberdeen	1597
Bessie Thomson	N. Berwick	1590
Bessie Vickar	Borrowstowness	1679
Elizabeth Weed	Hunts	1646
Bessie Weir	Paisley	1678
Bessie Wilson	Auldearne	1662
Bessie Wright	N. Berwick	1590
Elizabeth Wright	Burton-on-Trent	1597
Bessie Young	Auldearne	1662
Ellen Bierley	Lancs	1613
Ellen Gray	Aberdeen	1597
Ellen Green	Leicester	1619
Elinor Shaw	Northampton	1705
Euphemia McCalyan	N. Berwick	1590
Frances Dicconson	Lancs	1613
Frances Moore	Hunts	1646
George Ellies	Forfar	1661

Gideon Penman	Crighton	1678
Gilbert Fidlar	Aberdeen	1597
Gilbert McGill	N. Berwick	1590
Giles Fenderlin	Leaven Heath	1652
Geillis Duncan	N. Berwick	1590
Gilles Hutton	Crook of Devon	1662
Girette le Parmentier	Guernsey	1620
Gracyenne Gousset	Guernsey	1563
Grace Hay	Lancs	1613
Grissell Gairdner	Newburgh	1610
Grissall Sinklar	Auldearne	1662
Guillemine la Bousse	Guernsey	1622
Guillemine Vaultier	Guernsey	1610
Hellen Alexander	Forfar	1661
Hellen Clark	Manningtree	1645
Helen Cothills	Forfar	1661
Helen Fraser	Aberdeen	1597
Helen Guthrie	Forfar	1661
Helen Hill	Queensferry	1644
Helen Inglis	Auldearne	1661
Hellen Jenkinson	Northampton	1612
Helen Lauder	N. Berwick	1590

Helène le Brun	Guernsey	1609
Helen Makkie	Aberdeen	1597
Hellen Pennie	Aberdeen	1597
Helen Rogie	Aberdeen	1597
Helen Thomson	Queensferry	1644
Helen White	N. Berwick	1590
Henry Graver	Knaresborough	1621
Henry Walter	Somerset	1665
Hugh Crosia	Conn.	1693
Isobel Adams	Pittenweem	1704
Issabel Andrews	Northumberland	1673
Isobel Bairdie	Edinburgh	1649
Issobell Barroun	Aberdeen	1597
Isabel Becquet	Guernsey	1617
Isobel Black	Crook of Devon	1662
Issobell Burnett	Aberdeen	1597
Issobell Coky	Aberdeen	1597
Isabel Condie	Crook of Devon	1662
Isobell Crawford	Irvine	1618
Isobel Dorward	Forfar	1661
Issobell Forbes	Aberdeen	1597
Isobel Friece	Auldearne	1662
Isobel Gairdner	Edinburgh	1649
Isabel Gibson	Crook of Devon	1662
Issobell Gowdie	Auldearne	1662
Issobell Griersoune	Edinburgh	1607
Isobell Gylour	N. Berwick	1590
Isobel Haldane	Perth	1607
Isobel Inch	Irvine	1618

Issabell Johnson	Northumberland	1673
Isobell Lauder	N. Berwick	1590
Issobell Menteithe	Aberdeen	1597
Isobel More NcKaw	Bute	1662
Isobel More	Auldearne	1662
Issobell NcNeill	Bute	1662
Issobell NcNicoll	Bute	1662
Issobell Nicoll	Auldearne	1662
Issobell Oige	Aberdeen	1597
Isobel Ramsay	Edinburgh	1661
Issobell Richie	Aberdeen	1597
Issobell Robbie	Aberdeen	1597
Isobel Robey	Lancs	1613
Isabel Rutherford	Crook of Devon	1662
Issobell Shyrie	Forfar	1661
Isabel Sidegraves	Lancs	1613
Issobell Smith	Forfar	1661
Issobell Strathaquhin	Aberdeen	1597
Issabell Thompson	Northumberland	1673
Isobel Young	Queensferry	1644
James Bush	Somerset	1664
James Device	Lancs	1613
James Hudston	Alloa	1658
James Kirk	Alloa	1658
James Og	Aberdeen	1597
James Walkley	Conn.	1662
Jonet Anderson	Edinburgh	1657
Jane Baites	Northumberland	1673
Jonet Barrie	Forfar	1661

Jeanne Bichot	Guernsey	1619
Jennet Bierley	Lancs	1613
Jannet Blandilands	Edinburgh	1590
Janet Breadheid	Auldearne	1662
Janet Brown	Edinburgh	1649
Janet Brugh	Crook of Devon	1662
Jane Bulcock	Lancs	1613
Janet Burnet	Auldearne	1662
Jonet Campbell	Edinburgh	1590
Jonet Campbell	N. Berwick	1590
Joan Cariden	Faversham	1645
Joan Carrington	Conn.	1651
Jonett Clark	Edinburgh	1590
Jonet Cleracht	Aberdeen	1597
Jennot Cooke	Dalkeith	1661
Johan Cooper	Much Holland, Essex	1645
Jonet Corset	Pittenweem	1704
Jennet Cronkshaw	Lancs	1613
Janet Cunningham	Edinburgh	1590
Jonet Davidson	Aberdeen	1597
Jeanne de Bertran	Guernsey	1626
Jenette de Garis	Guernsey	1631
Jonet Degeddes	Aberdeen	1597
Jennet Device	Lancs	1613
Jennit Dibble	Knaresborough	1621
Jonet Drever	Orkney	1615
Jeannette Dumaresq	Guernsey	1570
Janet Finlay	Auldearne	1662
Jean Fulton	Bargarran	1697
Jonet Gaw (Gall)	N. Berwick	1590
Jonet Grant	Aberdeen	1597

Jonett Grant	Edinburgh	1590
Jeanne Guignon	Guernsey	1570
Jonet Guissett	Aberdeen	1597
Jennet Hargraves	Lancs	1613
Jonet Hird	Crook of Devon	1662
Jonet Hood	Crook of Devon	1662
Jane Hopper	Northumberland	1673
Jane Hott	Faversham	1645
Jonet Howit	Forfar	1661
Jonet Hunter	Ayrshire	1605
Jonet Isack	Bute	1662
Jonat Kaw	Perth	1607
Jean King	Innerkip	1662
Jeanne le Cornu	Guernsey	1620
Jeannette le Gallées	Guernsey	1570
Jonet Leisk	Aberdeen	1597
Jonet Leyis	Aberdeen	1597
Jonet Logan	N. Berwick	1590
Janet Lowry	Queensferry	1644
Jonet Lucas	Aberdeen	1597
Joane Lucus	Northampton	1612
Jane Makepiece	Northumberland	1673
Janet Man	Auldearne	1662
Janet Mathie	Paisley	1678
Jonet McConachie	Bute	1662
Jonet Mcilmertine	Bute	1642
Jonet McNeill	Bute	1662
Jonet McNickell	Bute	1662
Jonet Mctyre	Bute	1642
Jenot Meiklejohn	Dalkeith	1661
Jonet Millar	Alloa	1658
Jonet Morison	Bute	1662

Janet Mowbray	Queensferry	1644
Jonet Nctyre	Bute	1642
Jonet Nicholson	N. Berwick	1590
Jonet Nicoll	Bute	1662
Jonet Paiston	Dalkeith	1661
Jonet Paterson	Alloa	1658
Janet Paton	Crook of Devon	1662
Janet Paton	Kilduff	1662
Joan Pechey	St. Osyth	1582
Joan Peterson	Wapping	1652
Jennet Preston	Lancs	1613
Jonet Reid	Alloa	1658
Jonet Reid	Orkney	1633
Jonet Rendall	Orkney	1629
Joan Robinson	St. Osyth	1582
Janet Rodgers	Bargarran	1697
Janet Scot	Innerkip	1662
Janet Smith	Auldearne	1662
Jonet Smyth	Aberdeen	1597
Jane Southworth	Lancs	1613
Jonet Spaldarg	Aberdeen	1597
Jonet Stewart	Edinburgh	1597
Jonet Stout	Forfar	1661
Jonet Stratton	N. Berwick	1590
Jean Sutherland	Auldearne	1662
Jone Syms	Somerset	1664
Janet Thomson	Edinburgh	1649
Jeanne Tourgis	Guernsey	1622
Joane Vaughan	Northampton	1612
Janet Wagh	Bargarran	1697
Joan Walliford	Faversham	1645
Joane Wallis	Hunts	1646

Joan Waterhouse	Chelmsford	1556
Jonet Watson	Dalkeith	1661
Jean Weir	Edinburgh	1670
Jennet Wilkinson	Lancs	1613
Joane Willimot	Leicester	1619
Jonet Wishert	Aberdeen	1597
John Brugh	Edinburgh	1643
John Bulcock	Lancs	1613
John Carington	Conn.	1651
John Clarke	Hunts	1646
John Combes	Somerset	1664
John Couper	N. Berwick	1590
John Crauforth	Northumberland	1673
Johnne Damiet	Edinburgh	1597
John Douglas	Tranent	1659
John Fian	N. Berwick	1590
John Galie	Bute	1662
John Gordon (Gray-meill)	N. Berwick	1590
John Lamen, Snr.	St. Albans	1649
John Lamen, Jnr.	St. Albans	1649
John Leyis	Aberdeen	1597
John Lindsay	Bargarran	1697
John McGill	N. Berwick	1590
John Palmer	St. Albans	1649
John Ramsden	Lancs	1613
John Reid	Bargarran	1697
John Robertson	Auldearne	1662
John Salmon	St. Albans	1649
John McWilliam Sclater	Edinburgh	1656

John Stewart	Irving	1618
John Stuart	Paisley	1678
John Tailzeour	Forfar	1661
John Taylor	Auldearne	1662
John Vining	Somerset	1664
John Whitfield	Northumberland	1673
John Winnick	Hunts	1646
John Young	Auldearne	1662
Joseph Salmon	St. Albans	1649
Josine Deblicq	Hainault	1616
Joyce Boanes	St. Osyth	1645
Judith Moone	Thorp, Essex	1645
Judeth Salmon	St. Albans	1649
Judith Varlet	Conn.	1662
Julian Cox	Somerset	1665
Katherine Blair	Glasgow	1622
Kathren Blak	Alloa	1658
Katherine Campbell	N. Berwick	1590
Katherine Campbell	Bargarran	1697
Katherine Carruthers	N. Berwick	1590
Katherine Craige	Orkney	1633
Katherine Cristell	Bute	1662
Katherine Duncan	N. Berwick	1590
Katherine Earle	Yorks	1654
Catherine Ellot	Northumberland	1673

Katherine Eustache	Guernsey	1581
Katherine Fernsche	Aberdeen	1597
Katherine Ferris	Aberdeen	1597
Katherine Frissell	Bute	1662
Katherine Gerard	Aberdeen	1597
Kait Gray	N. Berwick	1590
Catherine Green	Somerset	1665
Catherine Halloudis	Guernsey	1622
Katherine Harrison	Conn.	1662
Katherine Heirst	Lancs	1613
Catherine Logie	Queensferry	1644
Katherine McGill	N. Berwick	1590
Katherine McTeir	Ayrshire	1605
Katherine McWilliam	Bute	1662
Katherine Miller	Orkney	1633
Kathren Mitchell	Aberdeen	1597
Kathrin Moore	Bute	1662
Katherine Oswald	Edinburgh	1629
Katharene Portour	Forfar	1661
Catherine Prays	Guernsey	1563
Kathren Renny	Alloa	1658
Catherine Robert	Guernsey	1639
Katherine Scott	Innerkip	1662
Kathren Sowter	Auldearne	1662
Katherine Stewart	Bute	1662
Catherine Thomson	Queensferry	1644
Kait Wallace	N. Berwick	1590
Katharene Wallace	Forfar	1661
Lawrence Hay	Lancs	1613
Laurenche Jehan	Guernsey	1570

Laurence l'Eustache	Guernsey	1617
Lilias Adie	Torryburn	1704
Lillie Wallace	Pittenweem	1704
Lucy Thompson	Northumberland	1673
Lydia Gilbert	Conn.	1654
Malie Geddie	N. Berwick	1590
Manie Haliburton	Dirlton	1649
Marable Cooper	Orkney	1633
Margaret Agar	Somerset	1664
Margaret Aitchison	N. Berwick	1590
Margaret Aynsley	Northumberland	1673
Margaret Barclay	Irvine	1618
Margret Bean	Aberdeen	1597
Meg Begtoun	N. Berwick	1590
Marget Beveridge	Crook of Devon	1662
Margret Brodie	Auldearne	1662
Margaret Brown	Queensferry	1644
Margaret Clarke	Somerset	1664
Margrat Cleraucht	Aberdeen	1597
Margaret Craige	Paisley	1678
Margaret Dauline	Queensferry	1644
Margret Demperstoun	Alloa	1658
Margret Duchall	Alloa	1658

Margaret Duncane	Ayrshire	1605
Margaret Duncane	Crook of Devon	1662
Margaret Dwn	N. Berwick	1590
Margaret Fulton	Bargarran	1697
Margaret Grevell	St. Osyth	1582
Margaret Hamilton (Mitchell)	Borrowstowness	1679
Margaret Hamilton (Pullwart)	Borrowstowness	1679
Margrat Holm	Innerkip	1662
Margret Hucheons	Auldearne	1662
Margaret Huggon	Crook of Devon	1662
Marget Hutton	Crook of Devon	1662
Margrat Innes	Aberdeen	1597
Margaret Jackson	Paisley	1678
Margaret Jennings	Conn.	1661
Margaret Johnson	Lancs	1633
Margaret Keltie	Crook of Devon	1662
Margaret Kyllie	Auldearne	1662
Margaret Laing	Bargarran	1697
Margaret Landish	St. Osyth	1645
Margaret Litster	Crook of Devon	1662
Margaret Loy	Liverpool	1667
Margaret McGuffok	Ayrshire	1605
Margret McKenzie	Innerkip	1662
Margaret McNeill	Bute	1662
Margaret McNickell	Bute	1662
Margaret McNish	Crook of Devon	1662
Margaret McWilliam	Bute	1662
Margaret Moone	Thorp, Essex	1645
Margaret Morton	Yorks	1650

Margaret Ncilduy	Bute	1662
Margaret NcLevin	Bute	1662
Margaret Nicoll	Forfar	1661
Margaret Nin-Gilbert	Thurso	1719
Margret Og	Aberdeen	1597
Margaret Pearson	Lancs	1613
Marguerite Picot	Guernsey	1629
Margaret Pringle	Borrowstowness	1679
Margrat Reauch	Aberdeen	1597
Margaret Rodgers	Bargarran	1697
Margrat Scherar	Aberdeen	1597
Margaret Simson	Hunts	1646
Margaret Smith	Bute	1662
Margrat Smyth	Aberdeen	1597
Meg Stillcart	N. Berwick	1590
Margret Tailzeour	Alloa	1658
Marguerite Tardif	Guernsey	1624
Margaret Thomson	N. Berwick	1590
Margaret Waite, Snr.	Knaresborough	1621
Margaret Waite, Jnr.	Knaresborough	1621
Margaret Wallace	Glasgow	1622
Margret Wilson	Auldearne	1662
Margaret Young	Crook of Devon	1662
Margarett (surname unknown)	Northumberland	1673
Marion Bailzie	N. Berwick	1590
Marion Congilton	N. Berwick	1590
Marion Dauline	Queensferry	1644
Marion Frissell	Bute	1642

Marrion Fyfe	Crook of Devon	1662
Marion Grant	Aberdeen	1597
Marion Hocket	Ramsey, Essex	1645
Marion Linkup	Leith	1590
Marion Little	Queensferry	1644
Marion Nicholson	N. Berwick	1590
Marion Paterson	N. Berwick	1590
Marion Richart	Orkney	1633
Marion Scheill (Shaw)	N. Berwick	1590
Marion Stein	Queensferry	1644
Marrion Thomson	Crook of Devon	1662
Marion Wod	Aberdeen	1597
Marion (Irish Marion)	N. Berwick	1590
Marjorie Dunbar	Auldearne	1662
Marjorie Man	Auldearne	1662
Marjorie Mutch	Aberdeen	1597
Marjorie Ritchie	Forfar	1661
Margery Sammon	St. Osyth	1582
Margery Stoakes	St. Osyth	1645
Marjorie Taylor	Auldearne	1662
Martha Semple	Bargarran	1697
Martin Tulouff	Guernsey	1563
Mary Barber	Northampton	1612
Mary Barnes	Conn.	1662
Marie Becquet	Guernsey	1617
Mary Bychance	St. Albans	1649

Marie Clouet	Guernsey	1631
Marie de Calais	Guernsey	1617
Marie de Calais	Guernsey	1631
Marie du Mont	Guernsey	1617
Marie Gauvein	Guernsey	1570
Mary Green	Somerset	1664
Mary Greenleife	Alresford, Essex	1645
Marie Guilbert	Guernsey	1639
Marie Guillemotte	Guernsey	1634
Mary Hunter	Northumberland	1673
Mary Johnson	Wyvenhoe, Essex	1645
Mary Johnson	Conn.	1647
Mary Lamen, Snr.	St. Albans	1649
Mary Lamen, Jnr.	St. Albans	1649
Marie Lamont	Innerkip	1662
Marie Mabille	Guernsey	1631
Marie Martin	Guernsey	1588
Marie McKaw	Bute	1662
Mary McNiven	Bute	1662
Marie Mortimer	Guernsey	1631
Marie More NcCuill	Bute	1662
Marie Paterson	N. Berwick	1590
Mary Penny	Somerset	1664
Mary Phillips	Northampton	1705
Mary Read	Lenham	1652
Marie Roland	Guernsey	1601
Marie Roland	Guernsey	1634
Mary Rynd	Forfar	1661
Mary Sanford	Conn.	1662
Marie Shuttleworth	Lancs	1613
Mary Sikes	Yorks	1649

Marie Sohier	Guernsey	1626
Marie Spencer	Lancs	1613
Marie Stewart	Bute	1662
Mary Trembles	Bideford	1682
Mary Warberton	Somerset	1665
Masie Aitchison	N. Berwick	1590
Mercy Disborough	Conn.	1692
Meslie Hirdall	Auldearne	1662
Michael Aynsley	Northumberland	1673
Michael Clark	N. Berwick	1590
Mildred Wright	Maidstone	1652
Nathaniel Greensmith	Conn.	1662
Nicholas Jennings	Conn.	1661
Patrick Lowrie	Ayrshire	1605
Patrick McKaw	Bute	1662
Patrik Watson	Dirlton	1649
Perine Marest	Guernsey	1622
Philipine le Parmentier	Guernsey	1617
Rachel King	Somerset	1665

Rebecca Greensmith	Conn.	1662
Rebecca Jones	St. Osyth	1645
Rebecca Weste	Lawford, Essex	1645
Richard Dickes	Somerset	1665
Richard Graham	Edinburgh	1590
Richard Lannen	Somerset	1665
Robert Griersoun	N. Berwick	1590
Robert Grieve	Lauder	1649
Robert Wilkinson	Lancs	1613
Robert Wilson	Crook of Devon	1662
Rose Cullender	Bury	1664
Rose Hallybread	St. Osyth	1645
Sarah Barton	Harwich	1645
Sarah Cooper	Essex	1645
Sarah Hating	Ramsey, Essex	1645
Sarah Smith	St. Albans	1649
Susan Cock	St. Osyth	1645
Susanna Edwards	Bideford	1682
Susanne Prudhomme	Guernsey	1629
Susanne Rouanne	Guernsey	1631
Temperance Lloyd	Bideford	1682
Thomas Bolster	Somerset	1665

Thomas Burnhill	N. Berwick	1590
Thomas Durning	Somerset	1665
Thomas Leyis	Aberdeen	1597
Thomas Weir	Edinburgh	1670
Thomasse de Calais	Guernsey	1617
Thomazine Ratcliffe	Suffolk	1645
Thomasse Salmon	Guernsey	1570
Thomasine Watson	Northumberland	1673
Ursley Kemp	St. Osyth	1582
Vyolett Leyis	Aberdeen	1597
Walter Ledy	Auldearne	1662
William Ayres	Conn.	1662
William Barton	Queensferry	1655
William Berry	Rutland	1619
William Coke	Kirkcaldy	1636
William Craw	Borrowstowness	1679
William Wright	Northumberland	1673

APPENDIX IV

JOAN OF ARC AND GILLES DE RAIS

These two personages—so closely connected in life and dying similar deaths, yet as the poles asunder in character—have been minutely studied from the historical and medical points of view, and in the case of Joan from the religious standpoint also. But hitherto the anthropological aspect has been disregarded. This is largely due to the fact that these intensive studies have been made of each person separately, whereas to obtain the true perspective the two should be taken together. This individual treatment is probably owing to the wide divergence of the two characters; the simplicity and purity of the one is in marked contrast with the repulsive attributes of the other. Yet anthropologically speaking the tie between the two is as strongly marked as the contrast of character.

The case of Joan is easily studied, as the documents are accessible.[956] Anatole France has realized that behind Joan there lay some unseen power, which Charles VII feared and from which he unwillingly accepted help. M. France sees in this power a party in the Church, and in his eyes the Church was a house divided against itself. Though agreeing with the view that Joan was the rallying-point of a great and powerful organization, I see in that organization the underlying religion which permeated the lower orders of the people in France as in England; that religion which I have set forth in the foregoing chapters. The men-at-arms, drawn from the lower orders, followed without hesitation one whom they believed to have been sent by their God, while the whole army was commanded by Marshal Gilles de Rais, who apparently tried to belong to both religions at once.

---

[956] It is advisable to read the trial in the original Latin and French, as the translations have often a Christian bias, e.g. 'the King of Heaven' being rendered as 'our Lord', and 'my Lord' as 'our Saviour'. This is not merely inaccurate but actually misleading.

1. Joan of Arc

The questions asked by the judges at Joan's trial show that they were well aware of an underlying organization of which they stood in some dread. The judges were ecclesiastics, and the accusation against the prisoner was on points of Christian faith and doctrine and ecclesiastical observance. It was the first great trial of strength between the old and the new religions, and the political conditions gave the victory to the new, which was triumphant accordingly. 'We have caught her now', said the Bishop of Beauvais, and she was burned without even the formality of handing her over to the secular authorities. After the execution, the judges and counsellors who had sat in judgement on Joan received letters of indemnity from the Great Council; the Chancellor of England sent letters to the Emperor, to the kings and princes of Christendom, to all the nobles and towns of France, explaining that King Henry and his Counsellors had put Joan to death through zeal for the Christian Faith; and the University of Paris sent similar letters to the Pope, the Emperor, and the College of Cardinals. Such action can hardly be explained had Joan been an ordinary heretic or an ordinary political prisoner. But if she were in the eyes of the great mass of the population not merely a religious leader but actually the incarnate God, then it was only natural for the authorities, who had compassed her death, to shelter themselves behind the bulwark of their zeal for the Christian religion, and to explain to the heads of that religion their reasons for the execution. On the other hand, the belief that Joan was God Incarnate will account, as nothing else can, for the extraordinary supineness of the French, who never lifted a finger to ransom or rescue Joan from the hands of either the Burgundians or the English. As God himself or his voluntary substitute she was doomed to suffer as the sacrifice for the people, and no one of those people could attempt to save her.

In comparing the facts elicited at the trial with the Dianic Cult as set out in the previous chapters, the coincidences are too numerous to be merely accidental. I do not propose to enter into a detailed discussion of the trial, I only wish to draw attention to a few points in this connexion.

The questions put to Joan on the subject of fairies appear to the modern reader to be entirely irrelevant, though much importance was evidently attached to her answers by the Court. She could not disprove, though she denied, the popular rumour that 'Joan received her mission at the tree of the Fairy-ladies' (Iohanna ceperat factum suum apud arborem Dominarum Fatalium), and she was finally forced to admit that she had first met the 'Voices' near that spot. Connexion with the fairies was as damning in the eyes of the Bishop of Beauvais and his colleagues as it was later in the eyes of the judges who tried John Walsh and Aleson Peirson.

The names of Christian saints, given to the persons whom Joan called her 'Voices', have misled modern writers; but the questions showered upon her show that the judges had shrewd suspicions as to the identity of these persons. That the 'Voices' were human beings is very clear from Joan's own testimony: 'Those of my party know well that the Voice had been sent to me from God, they have seen and known this Voice. My king and many others have also heard and seen the Voices which came to me ... I saw him [St. Michael] with my bodily eyes as well as I see you.' She refused to describe 'St. Michael'; and bearing in mind some of the descriptions of the Devil in later trials, it is interesting to find that when the judges put the direct question to her as to whether 'St. Michael' came to her naked, she did not give a direct answer. Later the following dialogue took place: 'If the devil were to put himself in the form or likeness of an angel, how would you know if it were a good or an evil angel?' asked the judges. Again Joan's reply was not direct: 'I should know quite well if it were St. Michael or a counterfeit.' She then stated that she had seen him many times before she knew him to be St. Michael; when a child she had seen him and had been afraid at first. Pressed for a description, she said he came 'in the form of a true honest man' [tres vray preudomme, forma unius verissimi probi hominis].[957] The accounts of the trial prove that Joan continually received advice from the 'saints'. The person whom she called 'St. Katherine' was obviously in the castle

---

[957] Compare Bessie Dunlop's more homely description of Thom Reid: 'An honest wele elderlie man.'

and able to communicate with the prisoner: this was not difficult, for the evidence shows that there was a concealed opening between Joan's room and the next. It was in the adjoining room, close to the opening, that the notaries sat to take down Joan's words when the spy Loyseleur engaged her in conversation; and it was evidently through this opening that 'St. Katherine' spoke when she awoke Joan 'without touching her', and again when Joan could not hear distinctly what she said 'on account of the noise in the castle'. A remark of Joan's that 'she often saw them [the Voices] among the Christians, they themselves unseen', is noteworthy for the use of the word *Christian*, suggesting that the 'Voices' were of a different religion. The remark should also be compared with the account given by Bessie Dunlop as to her recognizing Thom Reid when those about him did not know him; and with the statement by Danaeus that 'among a great company of men, the Sorcerer only knoweth Satan, that is present, when other doo not know him, although they see another man, but who or what he is they know not'.

The points of mortal sin, of which Joan finally stood accused, were the following: 1, The attack on Paris on a feast day; 2, taking the horse of the Bishop of Senlis; 3, leaping from the tower of Beaurevoir; 4, wearing male costume; 5, consenting to the death of Franquet d'Arras at Lagny.

Of these the most surprising to modern ideas is the one referring to costume, yet it was on this that the judges laid most stress. Even the severest of sumptuary laws has never made the wearing of male dress by a woman a capital crime; yet, though Joan had recanted and been received into the Church, the moment that she put on male attire she was doomed on that account only. Whether she donned it by accident, by treachery, by force, or out of bravado, the extraordinary fact remains that the mere resuming of male garments was the signal for her death without further trial. On the Sunday she wore the dress, on the Monday she was condemned, on the Tuesday the sentence was communicated to her, on the Wednesday she was burned, as an 'idolator, apostate, heretic, relapsed'. If, as I suppose, she were a member of the Dianic Cult, the wearing of male attire must have been, for her, an outward sign of that faith, and the resuming of it indicated the relapse; the inscription on the high cap, which she wore at her execution, shows that the judges at least held this opinion. Throughout the trial questions were poured upon her as to her reasons for wearing the dress, and she acknowledged that she wore it, not by the advice of a human man [per consilium hominis mundi] ... 'Totum quod feci est per praeceptum Domini, et si aliam praeciperet assumere ego assumerem, postquam hoc esset per praeceptum Dei.' Asked if she thought she would have been committing mortal sin by wearing women's clothes, she answered that she did better in obeying and serving her supreme Lord, who is God. She refused to wear women's dress except by command of God: 'I would rather die than revoke what God has made me do.'

On her letters were placed sometimes the words Jhesus Maria or a cross. 'Sometimes I put a cross as a sign for those of my party to whom I wrote so that they should not do as the letters said.' Though the mark was merely a code-signal to the recipient of the letter, it seems hardly probable that a Christian of that date would have used the symbol of the Faith for such a purpose. She also consistently refused to take an oath on the Gospels, and was with difficulty persuaded to do so on the Missal. When she was asked whether she had ever blasphemed [blasphemaverit] God, she replied that she had never cursed the Saints [maledixit Sanctum vel Sanctam]. When pressed whether she had not denied [denegaverit] God, she again refused a direct answer, saying that she had not denied the Saints [denegaverit Sanctum nec Sanctam].

The general feeling towards her among the Christian priesthood is shown by the action of Brother Richard. When he first entered her presence 'he made the sign of the cross and sprinkled holy water, and I said to him, Approach boldly, I shall not fly away.'

Another point to be noted is her answer that she learned the Paternoster, Ave Maria, and Credo from her mother, thus proving that she was not of a witch-family. According to Reginald Scot it was sufficient evidence to condemn a woman to death as a witch if her mother had been a witch before her. At the same time, however, Joan refused to say the Paternoster except in confession, when the priest's lips would have been sealed if she had proved herself not to be a Christian. She was very urgent to confess to the Bishop of Beauvais, but he was too wary to be caught.

She first heard the 'Voices' at the age of thirteen, the usual time for the Devil and the witch to make 'paction'. One of her followers, Pierronne, was burnt as a witch, avowing to the last that she had spoken with God as friend with friend, and describing the costume of her Deity with a detail which shows the reality of the occurrence. If also there is any weight to be attached to certain names—as seems likely after studying the lists given above—then we have in this history four of the chief witch-names; Joan, the daughter of Isabel, and the two saints Katherine and Margaret. These coincidences may be small, but there are too many of them to be ignored.

There is evidence from Joan's own words that she felt herself divine and also that she knew her time was limited, but she never realized till the last that the end meant death; this, however, the 'Voices' knew and it was for this that they were preparing her. At the beginning of the trial, 'she said she had come from God, and had nothing to do here, asking to be sent back to God from whom she came [dixit quod venit ex parte Dei, et non habet quid negotiari quidquam, petens ut remitteretur ad Deum a quo venerat]. 'Many times she said to him [the King], I shall live a year, barely longer. During that year let as much as possible be done.' The 'Voices' told her she would be taken before the feast of St. John, and that thus it must be, and that she must not be troubled but accept willingly and God would help her. They also said it was necessary for her to be captured: 'Receive all willingly, care not for thy martyrdom, thou shalt come at last to the kingdom of paradise.' On the fatal Tuesday when she learned her doom, flesh and spirit quailed at the prospect of the agony to come, and she cried out that her 'Voices' had deceived her, for she had thought that in her imprisonment she had already suffered the promised martyrdom. Yet within twenty-four hours she went to the stake with courage unquenched, acknowledging that her 'Voices' were from God. Like John Fian nearly two centuries later, her spirit had sunk at first, and again like Fian she endured to the end, dying a martyr to the God who had exploited her confidence and simplicity and whom she had served so well. To her de Lancre's words might well apply, 'The witches are so devoted to his service that neither torture nor death can affright[276] them, and they go to martyrdom and to death for love of him as gaily as to a festival of pleasure and public rejoicing.'

The ashes were collected and thrown into running water; a common rite, in religions of the Lower Culture, after the sacrifice of the Incarnate God. It is also worth noting that Rouen was one of the French cities in which there was still a living tradition of human sacrifice.

2. Gilles de Rais

Like Joan of Arc, Gilles de Rais was tried and executed as a witch; and in the same way, much that is mysterious in this trial can also be explained by the Dianic Cult.

On the mother's side he descended from Tiphaine de Champtocé, and on the father's from Tiphaine de Husson; this latter was the niece of Bertrand du Guesclin, and called after du Guesclin's wife, who was a fairy woman.

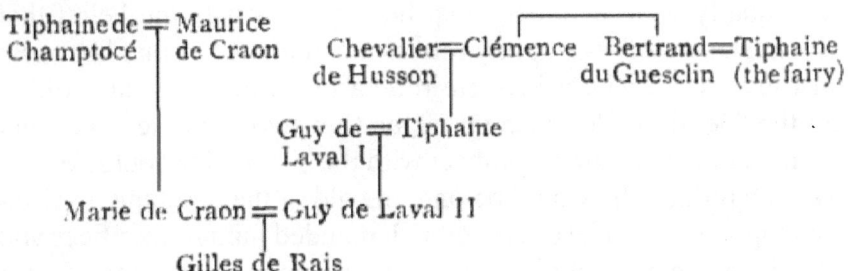

The name Tiphaine appears to come from the same root as Fein, Finn, and Fian, all of which meant 'fairy' in Great Britain, and probably in Brittany as well. There is therefore a strong suggestion of a strain of fairy blood, and with that blood there may also have descended to Gilles many of the beliefs and customs of the dwarf race.

The bond between Gilles and Joan was a very close one. She obtained permission from the King to choose whom she would for her escort; her choice at once fell on Gilles, for she would naturally prefer those of her own faith. He held already a high command in the relieving force, and added the protection of Joan as a special part of his duties. Later on, even after he had reached the high position of Marshal of France, he still continued those duties, remaining with her all day when she was wounded at the assault on Paris. It is an interesting point also that Charles VII granted permission to both these great leaders to bear the royal arms on their escutcheons. It seems incredible that a soldier of Gilles's character and standing should have made no move to rescue Joan by ransom or by force, when she was captured. She was not only a comrade, she was especially under his protection, and it is natural for us to think that his honour was involved. But if he regarded her as the destined victim, chosen and set apart for death, as required by the religion to which both he and she belonged, he could do nothing but remain inactive and let her fate be consummated. If this is so, then the 'Mystery of Orleans', of which he was the author, would be a religious play of the same class as the mystery-plays of the Christians.

The extraordinary prodigality and extravagance of Gilles may have been due, as is usually suggested, to profligacy or to madness, but it may equally well have been that he took seriously the belief that as the Incarnate God—or at any rate as a candidate for that honour—he must give to all who asked. He rode a black horse, as also did Joan and the 'Devils' of later centuries; and on two separate occasions he attempted to enter into a compact with the 'Devil'. He could not decide to which religion he would belong, the old or the new, and his life was one long struggle. The old religion demanded human sacrifices and he gave them, the new religion regarded murder as mortal sin and he tried to offer expiation; openly he had Christian masses and prayers celebrated with the utmost pomp, secretly he followed the ancient cult; when he was about to remove the bodies of the human victims from the castle of Champtocé, he swore his accomplices to secrecy by the binding oaths of both religions; on the other hand members of the old faith, whom he consulted when in trouble, warned him that as long as he professed Christianity and practised its rites they could do nothing for him.

An infringement of the rights of the Church brought him under the ecclesiastical law, and the Church was not slow to take advantage of the position. Had he chosen to resist, his exalted position would have protected him, but he preferred to yield, and like Joan he stood his trial on the charge of heresy. The trial did not take long; he was arrested on September 14, and executed on October 26. With him were arrested eight others, of whom two were executed with him. Seeing that thirteen was always the number of witches in a Coven, it is surely more than an accidental coincidence that nine men and women, including Gilles, were arrested, two saved themselves by flight, and two more who had played a large part in the celebration of the rites of the old religion were already dead. Thus even as early as the middle of the fifteenth century the Coven of thirteen was in existence.

Gilles was charged with heresy before a Court composed of ecclesiastics only, and like Joan he was willing to be tried for his faith. He announced that he had always been a Christian, which may be taken to mean that there was some doubt as to whether he was not a heathen. He suddenly gave way to a curious outburst against the authority of the Court, saying that he would rather be hanged by the neck with a lace than submit to them as judges. This can only be understood by comparing his reference to 'hanging with a lace' with the method by which Playfair in 1597 (p. 204), John Stewart in 1618 (p. 202), and John Reid in 1697 (p. 203), met their deaths.

The sudden change of front in this haughty noble may be accounted for by the excommunication which was decreed against him, but this explains neither his passionate haste to confess all, and more than all, of which he was accused, nor his earnest and eager desire to die. How much of his confession was true cannot be determined now, but it is very evident that he was resolved to make his own death certain. His action in this may be compared with that of Major Weir in 1670, who also was executed on his own voluntary confession of witchcraft and crime. Gilles's last words, though couched in Christian phraseology, show that he had not realized the enormity of the crimes which he confessed: 'We have sinned, all three of us', he said to his two companions, 'but as soon as our souls have left our bodies we shall all see God in His glory in Paradise.' He was hanged on a gibbet above a pyre, but when the fire burned through the rope the body was snatched from the flames by several ladies of his family, who prepared it for burial with their own hands, and it was then interred in the Carmelite church close by. His two associates were also hanged, their bodies being burned and the ashes scattered.

On the spot where Gilles was executed his daughter erected a monument, to which came all nursing mothers to pray for an abundance of milk. Here again is a strong suggestion that he was regarded as the Incarnate God of fertility. Another suggestive fact is the length of time—nine years—which elapsed between the death of Joan and the death of Gilles. This is a usual interval when the Incarnate God is given a time-limit.

It required twenty-five years before an action of rehabilitation could be taken for Joan. In the case of Gilles, two years after the execution the King granted letters of rehabilitation for that 'the said Gilles, unduly and without cause, was condemned and put to death'.

An intensive study of this period might reveal the witch organization at the royal Court and possibly even the Grand-master to whom Joan owed allegiance, the 'God' who sent her. Giac, the King's favourite, was executed as a witch, and Joan's *beau duc*, the Duke d'Alençon, was also of the fraternity.

APPENDIX V

FLYING OINTMENTS

The three formulae for the 'flying' ointment used by witches are as follows:

1. Du persil, de l'eau de l'Aconite, des feuilles de Peuple, et de la suye.

2. De la Berle, de l'Acorum vulgaire, de la Quintefeuille, du sang de chauuesouris, de la Morelle endormante, et de l'huyle.

3. De graisse d'enfant, de suc d'Ache, d'Aconite, de Quintefeuille, de Morelle, et de suye.

These formulae may be translated as follows:

1. Parsley, water of aconite, poplar leaves, and soot.

2. Water parsnip, sweet flag, cinquefoil, bat's blood, deadly nightshade, and oil.

3. Baby's fat, juice of water parsnip, aconite, cinquefoil, deadly nightshade, and soot.

These prescriptions show that the society of witches had a very creditable knowledge of the art of poisoning: aconite and deadly nightshade or belladonna are two of the three most poisonous plants growing freely in Europe, the third is hemlock, and in all probability 'persil' refers to hemlock and not to the harmless parsley, which it resembles closely.

The other ingredients have no marked toxic action, unless 'berle' and 'ache' refer not to the harmless water parsnip but to the poisonous water hemlock or cowbane. The baby's fat and bat's blood would of course have no action.

Aconite was one of the best-known poisons in ancient times; indeed it was so extensively used by professional poisoners in Rome during the Empire that a law was passed making its cultivation a capital offence. Aconite root contains about 0.4 per cent. of alkaloid and one-fifteenth of a grain of the alkaloid is a lethal dose. The drug has little effect upon the consciousness, but produces slowing, irregularity, and finally arrest of the heart.

The use of belladonna as a poison was also known in classical times; fourteen of the berries have been known to produce death; a moderate dose will produce wild excitement and delirium.

Hemlock is also a well-known and ancient poison; the fruit may contain as much as 0.9 per cent. of alkaloid, and ¼ grain of the alkaloid may produce death. The action of hemlock usually is to produce a gradual motor paralysis, consciousness being unimpaired, and death being caused by paralysis of respiration, but sometimes hemlock may produce delirium and excitement.

There is no doubt, therefore, about the efficacy of these prescriptions and their ability to produce physiological effects. They were administered by being rubbed into the skin, which is not an efficient way of introducing most drugs into the body, indeed some have denied that alkaloids can be absorbed from the unbroken skin; but there is no doubt that alkaloids can be absorbed when rubbed into scratches or into the quick of the nails, and it must be remembered that an unbroken skin is only possessed by those who are free from vermin and who wash regularly, and neither of these conditions would be likely to apply to a mediaeval witch. Cases of poisoning associated with delirium have actually been recorded following the application of belladonna plasters to the skin.

Of the three prescriptions the first is a watery solution and would not be very efficacious when rubbed into the skin, but the second and third are ointments, and if they were rubbed into the skin in sufficient quantities definite physiological results would be produced.

The first preparation, which contains hemlock and aconite, would produce mental confusion, impaired movement, irregular action of the heart, dizziness and shortness of breath.

The belladonna in the second ointment would produce excitement which might pass into delirium.

The third ointment, containing both aconite and belladonna, would produce excitement and irregular action of the heart.

I cannot say whether any of these drugs would produce the impression of flying, but I consider the use of aconite interesting in this respect. Irregular action of the heart in a person falling asleep produces the well-known sensation of suddenly falling through space, and it seems quite possible that the combination of a delirifacient like belladonna with a drug producing irregular action of the heart like aconite might produce the sensation of flying.

A. J. CLARK.

BIBLIOGRAPHY

- *Abbotsford Club Miscellany*, vol. i. Edinburgh, 1837.
- Ady, Thomas. *A Candle in the Dark.* London, 1656.
- *Alse Gooderige, The most wonderfull and true Storie of.* London, 1597.
- Arnot, Hugo. *Criminal Trials.* Edinburgh, 1785.
-
- Baines, Edward. *History of the County Palatine and Duchy of Lancaster.* London, 1836.
- Bannatyne Club. *Memoirs of Sir James Melville.* Edinburgh, 1827.
- —— *Historie and Life of King James the Sext.* Edinburgh, 1825.
- —— *Diary of John Nicoll.* Edinburgh, 1836.
- —— *Spottiswode's History of the Church of Scotland.* Edinburgh, 1847-50.
- Baxter, Richard. *Certainty of Worlds of Spirits.* London, 1691.
- Beaumont, John. *Historical Treatise of Spirits.* London, 1705.
- Bede, Venerable. *Ecclesiastical History* (ed. Giles). London, 1843.
- Bernard, Richard. *Guide to Grand-Iury men.* London, 1627.
- *Berwickshire Naturalists' Club*, vol. xi. Alnwick, 1887.
- Black, G. F. *Scottish Antiquary*, vol. ix. Edinburgh, 1895.
- *Blackwood's Edinburgh Magazine*, vol. i. Edinburgh, 1817.
- Bodin, Jean. *De la Démonomanie des Sorciers.* Rouen, 1604.
- —— *Le Fléau des Demons et Sorciers.* Nyort, 1616.
- Boguet, Henri. *Discours des Sorciers.* Lyons, 1608.
- Bourignon, Antoinette. *La Parole de Dieu.* Amsterdam, 1683.
- —— *La vie exterieur.* Amsterdam, 1683.
- Bournon, Jacques. *Chroniques de la Lorraine.* Nancy, 1838.
- Bovett, Richard. *Pandaemonium.* London, 1684.
- Bower, Edmund. *Dr. Lamb revived.* London, 1653.
- Bromhall, Thomas. *Treatise of Spectres.* London, 1658.
- Burns Begg. *Proceedings of the Society of Antiquaries of Scotland.* New Series, vol. x. Edinburgh.
- Burr, George Lincoln. *Narratives of the Witchcraft Cases.* New York, 1914.
- Burton, John Hill. *Criminal Trials.* London, 1852.

- —— *History of Scotland.* Edinburgh, 1873.
-
- Calef, Robert. *More Wonders of the Invisible World.* Salem, 1861.
- Calendar of State Papers. Domestic, 1584. London, 1865.
- Cambrensis, Giraldus. *Itinerary* (Bohn's edition). London, 1847.
- Camden Society. *Lady Alice Kyteler.* London, 1843.
- Campbell, John Gregorson. *Superstitions of the Highlands.* Glasgow, 1902.
- Cannaert, J. B. *Olim procès des Sorcières en Belgique.* Gand, 1847.
- Chambers, Robert. *Domestic Annals of Scotland.* Edinburgh, 1861.
- Chartier, Jean. *Chronique de Charles VII* (ed. Vallet de Viriville). Paris, 1858.
- Chetham Society. *Moore Rental.* Manchester, 1847.
- —— *Potts, Discoverie of Witchcraft.* Manchester, 1858.
- *Chronicon de Lanercost* (ed. Stevenson). Maitland Club. Glasgow, 1839.
- *Collection of rare and curious Tracts relating to Witchcraft.* London, 1838.
- Cooper, Thomas. *Mystery of Witchcraft.* London, 1617.
- —— *Pleasant Treatise of Witches.* London, 1673.
- Cotta, John. *Infallible, true and assured Witch.* London, 1625.
- —— *Trial of Witchcraft.* London, 1616.
- County Folklore, iii. *Orkney.* London, 1901.
- Cunningham, Allan. *Traditional Tales of the English and Scottish Peasantry.* London, 1874.
-
- Dalyell, John Grahame. *Darker Superstitions of Scotland.* Edinburgh, 1834.
- Danaeus, Lambert. *Dialogue of Witches.* [London?], 1575.
- Davenport, John. *Witches of Huntingdon.* London, 1646.
- Davies, J. Ceredig. *Welsh Folklore.* Aberystwith, 1911.
- De la Martinière. *Voyage des Pais Septentrionaux.* Paris, 1682.
- De Lancre, Pierre. *L'Incredulité et Mescreance du Sortilege.* Paris, 1622.
- —— *Tableau de l'Inconstance des mauvais Anges.* Paris, 1613.

- *Denham Tracts.* London, 1895.
- *Detection of damnable Drifts.* 1579.
-
- Elven, Henry van. *La Tradition*, vol. v. Paris, 1891.
- *Examination of certain Witches at Chelmsford.* Philobiblon Society, viii. London, 1863-4.
- *Examination of A. Baker, Joane Willimot, and Ellen Greene.* London, 1619.
- *Examination of Joane Williford, Joan Cariden, and Jane Hott.* (See *Collection of rare and curious Tracts.*) London, 1645.
- *Examination of John Walsh.* London, 1566.
-
- Fairfax, Edward. *Demonologia* (ed. W. Grainge). Harrogate, 1882.
- *Flower, The Wonderful Discoverie of the Witchcrafts of Margaret and Philip.* London, 1619.
- Forbes, William. *Institutes of the Law of Scotland.* Edinburgh, 1722-30.
- *Foster, Tryall of Ann.* Northampton, 1881.
- Fountainhall, Lord. *Decisions.* Edinburgh, 1759.
- Fournier, Alban. *Epidémie de Sorcellerie en Lorraine.* Nancy, 1891.
- *French Intelligencer*, No. 21. Thomason Tracts. London, 1652.
- *Full Tryals of Notorious Witches at Worcester.* London, n. d.
-
- Gaule, John. *Select Cases of Conscience.* London, 1646.
- Gerish, William Blyth. *Relation of Mary Hall of Gadsden.* 1912.
- —— *The Divel's Delusions.* Bishops Stortford, 1914.
- —— *The Severall Practices of Johane Harrison.* 1909.
- Gibbons, A. *Ely Episcopal Records.* Lincoln, 1891.
- Giffard, George. *Discourse of the subtill Practises of Devilles.* London, 1587.
- —— *Dialogue concerning Witches. Percy Society, VIII.* London, 1843.
- Gilbert, William. *Witchcraft in Essex.* London, 1909.
- Giraldus Cambrensis. *Itinerary* (Bohn's edition). London, 1847.
- Glanvil, Joseph. *Sadducismus Triumphatus.* London, 1681.

- Goldsmid, E. *Confessions of Witches under Torture.* Edinburgh, 1886.
- Goodcole, Henry. *Wonderfull Discoverie of Elizabeth Sawyer.* London, 1621.
- *Gooderige, The most wonderfull and true storie, of a certaine Witch named Alse.* London, 1597.
- Green, Samuel Abbott. *Groton in the Witchcraft Times.* Cambridge, Mass., 1883.
-
- Hale, John. *A modest Enquiry* (ed. Burr). New York, 1914.
- Hale, Sir Matthew. *Collection of Modern Relations.* London, 1693.
- Harou, Alfred. *La Tradition*, vol. vi. Paris, 1892.
- Hector, William. *Judicial Records of Renfrewshire.* Paisley, 1876.
- Hibbert, Samuel. *Description of the Shetland Isles.* Edinburgh, 1822.
- Highland Papers, vol. iii. *Witchcraft in Bute.* Edinburgh, 1920.
- Holinshed, Raphael. *Chronicles.* London, 1587.
- Hopkins, Matthew. *The Discovery of Witches.* London, 1647.
- Horneck, Anthony. Appendix to Glanvil's *Sadducismus Triumphatus.* London, 1681.
- Howell, Thomas Bayly. *State Trials.* London, 1816.
- Humborg, Ludwig. *Die Hexenprozesse in der Stadt Münster.* [Münster?] 1882.
- Hunt, William. *History of the English Church.* London, 1901.
- Hutchinson, Bishop Francis. *Historical Essay.* London, 1718.
- Hutchinson, John. *History of the Province of Massachuset's Bay.* 1828.
-
- *Inch, Trial of Isabel.* Ardrossan (1855?).
-
- James I. *Demonologie.* Edinburgh, 1597.
- *James the Sext, Historie and Life of.* Bannatyne Club. Edinburgh, 1825.
- *Journal of Anatomy*, vols. xiii and xxv. London, 1879, 1891.
- *Journal d'un bourgeois de Paris.* Panthéon Littéraire. Paris, 1838.

- *Justiciary Court, Edinburgh, Records of the Proceedings of.* Edinburgh, 1905.

-

- Kinloch, George Ritchie. *Reliquiae Antiquae Scoticae.* Edinburgh, 1848.

-

- Lamont, John. *Diary.* Maitland Club. Edinburgh, 1830.
- Law, Robert. *Memorialls* (ed. Sharpe). Edinburgh, 1818.
- *Lawes against Witches and Conivration.* Published by Authority. London, 1645.
- Lea, Henry Charles. *History of the Inquisition.* London, 1888.
- Lemoine, Jules. *La Tradition*, vol. vi. Paris, 1892.

-

- Mackenzie, Sir George. *Laws and Customs of Scotland.* Edinburgh. 1699.
- Maitland Club. *Chronicon de Lanercost.* Glasgow, 1839.
- —— *Lamont's Diary.* Glasgow, 1830.
- *Maitland Club Miscellany*, vol. ii. Glasgow, 1840.
- *Manchester Oriental Society's Journal.* Manchester, 1916-17.
- Mather, Cotton. *Wonders of the Invisible World.* London, 1862.
- —— Increase. *Remarkable Providences.* London, 1890.
- Melville, Sir James. *Memoirs.* Bannatyne Club. Edinburgh.
- Michaelis, Sebastian. *Admirable Historie of the Possession and Conversion of a Penitent Woman.* London, 1613.
- —— *A Discourse of Spirits.* London, 1613.
- Monoyer, Jules. *La Sorcellerie en Hainault.* Essais d'histoire et d'archéologie. Mons, 1886.
- Monseur, Eugène. *Le Folklore Wallon.* Bruxelles (1892).
- *Moore Rental.* Chetham Society, vol. xii. Manchester, 1847.
- More, Henry. *Antidote against Atheism.* London, 1655.
- Moret, A. *Mystères Égyptiens.* Paris, 1913.
- Murray, T. Douglas. *Jeanne d'Arc.* London, 1902.

-

- *Narrative of the Sufferings of a young Girle.* Edinburgh, 1698.
- Nicoll, John. *Diary.* Bannatyne Club. Edinburgh, 1836.

- Notestein, Wallace. *History of Witchcraft in England.* Washington, 1911.

-

- Pearson, Karl. *Chances of Death.* London, 1897.
- Percy Society. *Giffard's Dialogue of Witches.* London, 1843.
- Perkins, William. *Discourse of the damned Art of Witchcraft.* Cambridge, 1608.
- *Peterson, Tryall of Mrs. Joan.* Thomason Tracts. London, 1652.
- Petto, Samuel. *A faithful Narrative.* London, 1693.
- Philobiblon Society. *Examination of certain Witches.* London, 1863-4.
- Pinkerton, John. *Voyages.* London, 1808-14.
- Pitcairn, Robert. *Criminal Trials.* Edinburgh, 1833.
- *Pittenweem, A true and full Relation of the Witches of.* Edinburgh, 1704.
- *Pleasant Treatise of Witches.* London, 1673.
- Potts, Thomas. *Discoverie of Witches.* Chetham Society. Manchester, 1845.
- *Prodigious and Tragicall History.* See *Collection of rare and curious Tracts.* London, 1652.

-

- Quibell, James Edward. *Hierakonpolis*, ii. London, 1902.
- Quicherat, Jules Étienne Joseph. *Procès de condemnation et de réhabilitation de Jeanne d'Arc.* Paris, 1841.

-

- Ravaisson, François. *Archives de la Bastille.* Paris, 1873.
- *Records of the Justiciary Court of Edinburgh.* Edinburgh, 1905.
- *Registrum Magni Sigilli Regum Scotorum.* Edinburgh, 1886.
- *Rehearsall both straung and true.* London, 1579.
- Remigius, Nicholas. *Daemonolatria.* Hamburg, 1693.
- Roberts, Alexander. *Treatise of Witchcraft.* London, 1616.
- Ross, William. *Aberdour and Inchcolme.* Edinburgh, 1885.
- Rymer, Thomas. *Foedera.* London, 1704.

-

- *Sadducismus Debellatus.* London, 1698.

- *St. Osees, A true and iust Recorde of all the Witches taken at.* London, 1582.
- Sandys, George. *Relation of a Journey.* London, 1632.
- *Sawyer, Wonderfull Discouerie of Elisabeth.* 1621.
- Scot, Reginald. *Discoverie of Witchcraft.* London, 1584.
- *Scots Magazine.* Edinburgh, 1772 and 1814.
- Scott, Sir Walter. *Demonology and Witchcraft.* Morley's Universal Library. London, 1883.
- *Scottish Antiquary*, vol. ix. Edinburgh, 1891.
- *Scottish History Society*, vol. xxv. Edinburgh, 1896.
- Sharpe, Charles Kirkpatrick. *Historical Account of Witchcraft in Scotland.* London, 1884.
- *Shaw, Elinor, and Mary Phillips.* Northampton, 1866.
- Sinclair, George. *The Hydrostaticks.* Edinburgh, 1672.
- —— *Satan's Invisible World Discovered.* Edinburgh, 1871.
- Sinclair, John. *Statistical Account of Scotland*, vol. xviii. Edinburgh, 1796.
- Sinistrari de Ameno, Ludovico Maria. *Demoniality.* Paris, 1879.
- *Society of Antiquaries of Scotland.* New Series, x. Edinburgh.
- *Spalding Club Miscellany.* Aberdeen, 1841.
- Spottiswode, John. *History of the Church of Scotland.* Edinburgh, 1847-50.
- *Spottiswoode Miscellany.* Edinburgh, 1844-5.
- Stearne, John. *Confirmation and Discovery of Witchcraft.* London, 1648.
- Stevenson, J. *Chronicon de Lanercost.* Maitland Club. Glasgow, 1839.
- Stewart, William Grant. *Popular Superstitions of the Highlanders.* Edinburgh, 1823.
- *Surtees Society*, vol. xl. Durham, 1861.
-
- Taylor, John. *Tracts relating to Northamptonshire.* Northampton, 1866.
- Taylor, John. *The Witchcraft Delusion in Colonial Connecticut.* New York, n. d.

- Thomson, H. A., and Miles, A. *Manual of Surgery.* Oxford, 1913.
- Thorpe, Benjamin. *Monumenta Ecclesiastica.* [London] 1840.
- *Tradition, La,* vol. v. van Elven's *Les Procès de Sorcellerie au Moyen Age.* Paris, 1891.
- —— vol. vi. Harou's *Sorciers et Sorcières.* Paris, 1892.
- —— vol. vi. Lemoine's *Sorcellerie contemporaine.* Paris, 1892.
- *True and exact Relation of the severall Informations, Examinations and Confessions of the late Witches executed in the County of Essex.* London, 1645.
- *True and iust Recorde of all the Witches taken at St. Oses.* By W. W. London, 1582.
- *Tryalls of Four Notorious Witches at Worcester.* London, n. d.
-
- Wagstaffe, John. *Question of Witchcraft.* London, 1671.
- *Walsh, Examination of John.* London, 1566.
- Webster, John. *Displaying of Supposed Witchcraft.* London, 1677.
- Wellhausen, Julius. *Reste arabischen Heidenthums.* Berlin, 1897.
- Whitaker, T. D. *History of Whalley.* London, 1818.
- Wilson, Daniel. *Memorials of Edinburgh in the Olden Time.* Edinburgh, 1891.
- *Witch of Wapping, The.* Thomason Tracts. London, 1652.
- *Witchcraft, Collection of rare and curious tracts on.* Edinburgh, 1820.
- *Witches of Northamptonshire.* London, 1612.
- *Wonderfull Discouerie of Elizabeth Sawyer.* London, 1621.
- *Wonderful Discoverie of Margaret and Philip Flower.* London, 1619.

ADDENDUM

1324 Kilkenny, Ireland.

[This is the earliest record to give the names of all those who took part in the ceremonies. Two of the poorer women were burned; Dame Alice Kyteler returned to England; William Outlaw, her son, was imprisoned for a time. Nothing is known of the fate of the rest.]

- 1. Alice Kyteler
- 2. Alice, wife of Henry the Smith
- 3. Annota Lange
- 4. Eva de Brounstoun
- 5. Helena Galrussyn
- 6. John Galrussyn
- 7. Petronilla de Meath